Arab Political Demography
VOLUME ONE

Forthcoming

Arab Political Demography
Volume Two
Country Case Studies

Volume 2 of *Arab Political Demography* features an examination of the major demographic developments and policies as well as detailed socio-developmental statistics on Egypt, Syria, Jordan, the Israeli-Arabs, Saudi Arabia, Kuwait, Qatar, Oman and Bahrain.

Arab Political Demography, volumes 1 and 2, is part of the series: Sussex Studies in Demographic Developments and Socioeconomic Policies in the Middle East and North Africa

Full details of the series are presented on the Press website
sussex-academic.co.uk

Arab Political Demography

VOLUME ONE
POPULATION GROWTH AND NATALIST POLICIES

Onn Winckler

sussex
ACADEMIC
PRESS

BRIGHTON • PORTLAND

2 4 6 8 10 9 7 5 3 1

First published in 2005 in Great Britain by
SUSSEX ACADEMIC PRESS
P.O. Box 2950
Brighton BN2 5SP

and in the United States of America by
SUSSEX ACADEMIC PRESS
920 NE 58th Ave.   Suite 300
Portland, Oregon 97213-3786

British Library Cataloguing in Publication Data
A CIP catalogue record for this book is available from the British Library.

Library of Congress Cataloging-in-Publication Data
Winckler, Onn.
    Arab political demography / Onn Winckler.
       v. cm.
    Includes bibliographical references and index.
    Contents: v. 1. Population growth and natalist policies.
    ISBN 1-902210-70-0 (v. 1 : hardcover : alk. paper) —
    ISBN 1-902210-71-9 (v. 1 : pbk. : alk. paper)
    1. Arab countries—Population. 2. Demography—Research—
Arab countries. 3. Arab countries—Economic conditions.
4. Fertility, Human—Arab countries. 5. Arab countries—
Population policy.
    I. Title.
    HB3660.A3W56 2005
    304.6'0917'5927—dc22

                                                        2004026128
                                                        CIP

Typeset and designed by G&G Editorial, Brighton.
Printed by MPG Books, Bodmin, Cornwall.
This book is printed on acid-free paper.

Contents

List of Tables, Figures and Charts

Tables

Figures

List of Charts

To
Iris, Hadar and Yael

Preface & Acknowledgments

During the last three decades, but particularly since the end of the "oil decade" (1973–1982), the "demographic problem" has become the most acute socioeconomic problem for an increasing number of Arab countries, with a wide variety of implications. This book examines the connection between demography and politics in the Arab countries from three major perspectives: internal political dimensions; inter-Arab politics; and the nature of relationships between Arab and Western countries. A better understanding of this connection, I believe, will serve to broaden our understanding of the Arab political system. Specifically, the book aims to describe and analyze four major areas. The first consists of the various demographic sources on the Arab countries in the twentieth century, their limitations, and the reasons for these limitations. The second focus is on the process of rapid population growth among the Arab countries in the twentieth century, particularly during the second half of the century. The third focus is on the fundamental socioeconomic consequence of this rapid population growth, namely, the emergence of the structural unemployment problem and its various implications for the short and the long terms. The fourth and most important focus of the book is on the natalist policies of the Arab countries since the mid-twentieth century.

Many people helped me during the process of writing this book. First and foremost, I am deeply indebted to Professor Gad G. Gilbar from the Department of Middle Eastern History at the University of Haifa, not only for his instruction in both my M.A. and Ph.D. theses and his ongoing support and guidance, but also for his useful comments on the manuscript of this book. I am also sincerely thankful to my teacher and colleague, Dr. Uri M. Kupferschmidt from the Department of Middle Eastern History at the University of Haifa for his time and effort devoted to reading the manuscript and for his important comments; to Professor Israel Gershoni from the Department of Middle Eastern and African History at Tel Aviv University, not only for his remarks on the manuscript, but also for "forcing" me to precisely define the meaning of "*political demography*." Parts of Chapter 3 are based on my article, "The Demographic Dilemma of the Arab World: The Employment Aspect," *Journal of Contemporary History*, Vol. 37, No. 4 (October 2002), pp. 617–36. Parts of Chapter 4 are based on two articles written with Professor Gad G. Gilbar, "Nasser's Family Planning in Perspective," in Elie Podeh and Onn Winckler (eds.), *Rethinking Nasserism: Revolution and Historical Memory in Modern Egypt* (Gainesville: University Press of Florida, 2004), pp. 284-304; and "From Encouragement to Fertility Limitation: Fifty Years of Family Planning in the Arab Countries, 1953–2003,"

Hamizrah Hehadash (forthcoming, Hebrew). The sections dealing with Syria's and Jordan's fertility policies during the 1970s and 1980s are based on my two previous books, published by Sussex Academic Press: *Population Growth and Migration in Jordan, 1950–1994* (1997); and *Demographic Developments and Population Policies in Ba'thist Syria* (1999).

Regarding the transliteration of the Arabic names, I followed the most common rules employed by *Middle Eastern Studies* and other leading Middle Eastern journals. However, for personal names, I followed the most common usage rather than the transliteration rules, such as 'Abd al-Nasser instead of 'Abd al-Nasir.

This book was financially supported by the Research Authority, by the Faculty of Humanities and by the Jewish–Arab Center at the University of Haifa. I would like to extend a special thanks to Dr. Faisal Azaiza for his generous support and encouragement for publishing this book. I have been fortunate in receiving help in the process of collecting the sources for this book from the librarians in the Middle East Documentation Unit at Durham University, UK; the Arab World Documentation Unit in the University of Exeter, UK; the Cairo Demographic Center; the Newspaper Archive of the Moshe Dayan Center for Middle Eastern and African Studies at Tel-Aviv University; and the University of Haifa Library. Last, but not least, I would like to thank Ms. Sharon Woodrow for editing the manuscript; Mr. Shai Spiler for preparing the figures and the cartoons; and Mr. Eran Segal for his useful help in collecting the sources for the research.

Finally, and most importantly, special thanks to my family, my wife Iris and my two daughters Hadar and Yael, to whom this book is dedicated.

Abbreviations

ALO	Arab Labor Organization
b/d	Barrel per day (oil production)
CAPMAS	Central Agency for Public Mobilisation and Statistics
CBS	Central Bureau of Statistics
ECWA	UN Economic Commission for Western Asia
EIU	Economic Intelligence Unit
ESCWA	UN Economic and Social Commission for Western Asia
ECA	UN Economic Commission for Africa
EU	European Union
FAO	UN Food and Agricultural Organization
FDI	Foreign Direct Investment
GCC	Gulf Cooperation Council
GCHS	Gulf Child Health Survey
GDP	Gross Domestic Product
GFHS	Gulf Family Health Survey
GNP	Gross National Product
IBRD	International Bank for Reconstruction and Development
IJMES	International Journal of Middle East Studies
ILO	International Labour Office
IMF	International Monetary Fund
IPPF	International Planned Parenthood Federation
MECS	Middle East Contemporary Survey
MEED	Middle East Economic Digest
MEES	Middle East Economic Survey
MENA	Middle East and North Africa
NGO	Non-Governmental Organization
NRR	Net Reproductive Rate
PNA	Palestinian National Authority
OECD	Organization for Economic Cooperation and Development
OPEC	Organization of Petroleum Exporting Countries
PCBS	Palestinian Central Bureau of Statistics
PLO	Palestinian Liberation Organization
PPP	Purchasing Power Parity
SR	Saudi Riyal
UNDP	United Nations Development Programme

UNFPA	United Nations Fund for Population Activities
UNICEF	United Nations Children's Fund
UNRWA	United Nations Relief and Works Agency
UNESCO	United Nations Educational, Scientific, and Cultural Organization
USAID	United States Agency for International Aid
WB	The World Bank
WHO	UN World Health Organization

Introduction: The Methodological Framework

1 The Emergence of "Poor and Rich" Arab States

If someone looks for proof that "there is no justice in the world," the Arab region is the ultimate example, with very poor and very rich countries co-existing side by side within a short distance. As one can see in Appendices 1 and 2, Yemen is one of the poorest countries worldwide, with a per capita GNI (Gross National Income) of less than $500 in 2002, while the United Arab Emirates (UAE), which is just a short distance away, has a per capita GNI of more than $20,000. It should be emphasized, however, that this huge economic gap between the Arab countries is a relatively new phenomenon. Even in the late 1960s, the socioeconomic gap between the Arab countries was quite small, with the exception of Kuwait and Libya.[1] In 1968, the per capita GNP (Gross National Product) was $130 in Sudan, $190 in Egypt, $240 in Tunisia, $250 in Oman, $290 in Syria, $300 in Algeria, and $500 in Saudi Arabia.[2] Thus, with the exception of Kuwait and Libya, the economic gap between the various Arab countries was no more than three-fold. However, this relatively small gap has widened dramatically since the early 1970s due mainly to the following five factors:

(a) Oil export revenues Although oil exports constituted the major factor impacting on the economies of the Arabian/Persian Gulf[3] countries since the 1950s, the dramatic increase in oil prices following the October 16, 1973 "oil boom" transformed the major Arab oil exporters into not only the wealthiest Arab countries but also among the wealthiest countries worldwide within a very short period of only several years. Thus, whereas in 1972, the last year prior to the "oil boom," the oil exports of the ten Middle Eastern OPEC members (including Iran) amounted to $10 billion, in 1980, at the peak of oil prices, they reached $217 billion (in current prices), representing an increase of almost twenty-two fold in only eight years.[4] Thus, by 1981, Kuwait's per capita GNP amounted to $20,900 and that of the UAE to $24,660, as compared with $10,210 in Japan and $12,820 in the United States (US). Although the non-oil Arab countries were also enjoying the highest economic growth rates in their history during the 1973–1982 "oil decade" (see Chapter 3), the per capita GNP in 1981 remained quite low at $650 in Egypt, $860 in Morocco, $1,420 in Tunisia, $1,570 in Syria, and $1,620

in Jordan.[5] Since that time, the paramount factor determining the economic situation in each of the Arab countries has been the value of per capita oil exports, despite the rapid and frequent changes in oil prices in the international markets.

(b) Internal political stability   The second major factor distinguishing the level of socioeconomic development between the various Arab countries was and still is the degree of political stability. The most important factor accounting for the poor socioeconomic conditions in Yemen and Sudan is the political instability hampering the implementation of socioeconomic development plans, not to mention foreign investments in these two countries. Thus, despite the substantial natural resources that these two countries are enjoying – Yemen from oil and Sudan from the Nile water – they remain the poorest Arab countries (see Appendixes 1 and 2).

(c) Involvement in the Arab–Israeli conflict   The third important factor affecting the economic gap between the various Arab countries was the degree of direct involvement in the Arab–Israeli conflict. Generally speaking, the degree of involvement in the Arab–Israeli conflict had five major impacts on the economies of the countries that were directly involved in the conflict itself: 1) amount of defense allocations; 2) both direct and indirect damage from the wars and the continuation of the conflict; 3) decline in potential foreign investments; 4) rise in the public pro-natalist environment; and 5) above all, attention directed by the leadership to the conflict rather than to socioeconomic development (see **Chapter 4**). Naturally, the more intense was the direct involvement in the conflict, the more devastating was the economic damage, both direct and indirect. It must be emphasized, however, that the huge military expenditures of the Arab countries were not allocated for the sole purpose of dealing with the Arab–Israeli conflict. The mere existence of the current Arab regimes depends on the loyalty of their armies, which are often called upon to protect the regime, as was the case, for example, in the 1970 Black September incidents in Jordan and the February 1982 clashes between the Ba'thi-'Alawi regime and the "Muslim brothers" in Syria. Moreover, the army and the other civilian security forces have served as a major source for alleviating the pressures of the skyrocketing unemployment among youth during the past three decades.

Until the June 1967 War, the economic implications of the conflict on the Arab countries directly involved in it were quite marginal. However, the June 1967 War constituted a turning point not only from political and geo-strategic viewpoints, but even more so from a purely economic one as the economic price of the war became too high. Jordan was the hardest hit of all the countries involved in the June 1967 War. First and foremost, Jordan lost the West Bank, with almost 40% of the Kingdom's population, valuable agricultural land, and the vast majority of the country's tourism sites.[6] Egypt lost the oil fields of Sinai. In addition, due to the instability along the Suez Canal, Egypt could not develop the oil fields on the west bank of the Canal. This alone damaged the Egyptian revenues by billions of dollars annually. Furthermore, between June 1967 and June 1975, the Suez Canal was closed, meaning that during these seven years Egypt lost its most important source for hard currency. To this direct damage should be added the indirect damage, primarily the small number of tourists and the small scale of foreign investments relative to the potential in these areas.[7]

As a result, during the period 1966–1973, Egypt's GDP grew by less than 1% on annual average,[8] representing a decline of almost 2% on annual average in per capita terms. In the case of Syria, the economy was also considerably damaged from the June 1967 and the October 1973 Wars, albeit substantially less than both Egypt and Jordan. The main damage of the conflict with Israel resulted from the huge defense burden, amounting to more than half of the governmental budget during the early 1980s,[9] and the high priority accorded to the conflict in the leadership agenda at the expense of socioeconomic development. The Arab oil states on the other hand, benefited from the huge increase in oil prices brought about by the October 1973 War without having to shoulder any economic burden, as they were not directly involved in the War.

The withdrawal from the conflict through the peace agreements by Israel with Egypt in March 1979 and with Jordan in October 1994, however, reaped tremendous economic dividends, both direct and indirect. For Egypt these dividends included a huge increase in tourism revenues; the return of the oil fields in Sinai; the reopening of the Suez Canal; massive US financial aid; and an influx of foreign investments.[10] In the case of Jordan, the economic bonuses of peace included the abolishment of a large part of the external debt; a sharp increase in tourism revenues; a rise in financial foreign aid; increased foreign investments; and privileged access to the US market through the Qualifying Industrial Zones (QIZs), which resulted in a tremendous increase in Jordan's exports to the US.[11] There is no doubt, however, that the most important economic dividend of the peace treaty with Israel for both Egypt and Jordan is the US obligation to the economic survival of both regimes. Thus, the true value of the free trade agreement signed between Jordan and the US lies in "securing the political allegiance of Amman and preserving the cold peace between Jordan and Israel."[12] In a very similar way, following the US-led invasion of Iraq, the US and the World Bank provided Egypt with $3.3 billion in assistance so as to ensure that Egypt's balance of payments deficit would "remain at a manageable level . . . "[13]

(d) Adoption of macroeconomic reforms   In retrospect, in almost all of the developing countries worldwide, the economic crisis associated with socialist policies and authoritarian regimes has constituted the major lever for economic liberalization. Since the ability of the regime to secure finances from *rental* sources – in the case of the Arab countries, the exports of oil and gas as well as the contribution of foreign aid – is diminished, the regime is forced to collect more taxes or to narrow the socioeconomic benefits given to the population in exchange for more political participation.[14] This represents a withdrawal from the Gunnar Myrdal "Soft State,"[15] at least in part, and a move toward the Western-democratic formula of "no taxation without representation." Regarding this process in the Middle East, Iliya Harik claimed that:

> The main drive for change came from the fact that regimes were losing credibility and legitimacy among the general public in proportion to their inability to deliver. Having total control over the national economy deprived political leaders of sharing the burden and the responsibility for failure with others . . . Thus, the state moved toward economic liberalization both in order to partition the blame and responsibility and in the hope that an injection of fresh economic actors and capital would help a declining economy to regain its fortunes.[16]

Many of the Arab countries witnessed a gradual shift from *étatism* to more economic liberalization, starting in Tunisia in 1970 and then in Egypt following the October 1973 War, with Anwar al-Sadat's "open door" policy (*al-Infitah al-Iqtisadi*), and continuing during the 1980s and 1990s in many other Arab countries. This economic liberalization consisted mainly of trade and financial liberalization, exchange rate reforms, as well as increasing privatization in the industrial and service sectors. This change in economic approach was due mainly to the deepening economic pressure resulting from the basic imbalance between economic and population growth. The economic history of the Arab countries in the past three decades indicates that the more extensive the economic reforms, the greater the foreign investments and the higher the economic growth rates. Tunisia, it should be emphasized, was the first country outside Europe to sign a partnership agreement with the European Union (EU), paving the way not only to increasing trade with the EU, but also to attracting larger EU investments in the country.[17]

While the majority of the Arab countries have adopted substantial economic reforms during the past two decades, a group of six Arab countries, namely, Syria, Iraq, Yemen, Sudan, Algeria, and Libya, have implemented only minor reforms toward economic liberalization. Clement Henry and Robert Springborg dubbed these countries as "bunker states." They claimed that in these countries, with the exception of Algeria, the regimes are based on tribal or religious minorities and are thus "typically ones despised by much of the remainder of the population . . .In these circumstances, coercion is necessarily the primary and in some cases, such as that of Iraq or in much of Sudan, virtually the only means by which government can ensure the public's compliance."[18]

(e) Implementation of efficient anti-natalist measures   The final factor determining the degree of socioeconomic gap between the Arab countries during the past generation was their demographic policies, particularly their natalist policies. In the 1960s the fertility levels in the various Arab countries were quite similar, with only insignificant variations between them, whereas by the end of the twentieth century the fertility gaps between the Arab countries were considerable (see table 2.5). The history of the non-oil Arab countries in the last quarter of the twentieth century reveals that the lower fertility rate, the better the overall macroeconomic performance.

These five factors together explain, to a large extent, the socioeconomic variability of the Arab countries at the dawn of the twenty-first century. The oil states hold the position at the top of the Arab economic pyramid, in line with their per capita oil revenues. Bahrain stands out as the only one of these oil countries that has succeeded in developing various economic sectors other than the oil industry during the past two decades. Thus, although the per capita oil revenue of Saudi Arabia exceed that of Bahrain, Bahrain's per capita GDP in 2002 was considerably higher than that of Saudi Arabia due to its more diverse economy (see Appendix 1). At the bottom of the economic pyramid, far behind the other Arab countries, are Yemen and Sudan with their typically Sub-Saharan socioeconomic patterns: high infant and child mortality rates; low life expectancy; high illiteracy rates; and an overall low standard of living.

The rest of the Arab countries are located in the middle of the pyramid. Tunisia leads this middle group with a per capita GDP in 2002 of $6,760 in terms of PPP (Purchasing Power Parity),[19] followed by Lebanon with $4,360, Jordan with $4,200, and Syria, Egypt and Morocco with approximately $3,800 (see Appendix 1). Thus, although Tunisia does not enjoy considerable natural resources, in PPP terms its GDP per capita at the dawn of the twenty-first century was almost double that of the other non-oil Arab countries. This is a combined result of its having the lowest fertility rates among all of the Arab countries; its implementation of macroeconomic reforms since the early 1970s, prior to the other Arab countries; its avoidance of direct involvement in the Arab–Israeli conflict; and its political stability since its independence in 1956.

At the bottom of the middle group is Syria, with a per capita GDP of little more than $1,100 in 2002 (nominal terms),[20] as compared with almost $1,700 in the early 1980s (current prices).[21] This decline was due mainly to Hafiz al-Asad's failure to implement both macroeconomic reforms and decisive anti-natalist measures, as well as the continuing, albeit indirect, involvement of Syria in the Arab–Israeli conflict (through Lebanon). Egypt, on the other hand, started to adopt effective anti-natalist steps in the mid-1980s and substantial macroeconomic reforms even earlier. Thus, despite the fact that at the peak of the "oil boom" in the early 1980s, Syria's per capita GDP was almost three-fold that of Egypt, by the dawn of the twenty-first century Syria was lagging behind Egypt in almost every socioeconomic indicator. Even with substantial oil exports and considerable water and agricultural land resources, Syria's economic performance has not kept pace with the progress made through Egypt's "good governance" in the political economy arena, combined with the economic dividends of its peace treaty with Israel.

2   The Concept of Arab Political Demography

Among the above-mentioned five factors, the focus of this book is on the fifth factor – the demographic aspect – as seen through the prism of *political demography*. The term "population" or "demography" raises a variety of images. To some, "population" is a set of numbers and tables. To others, it is a target group for companies, businesses, and other commercial organizations attempting to sell products and services. Both views approach "population" as a static entity. To the demographer, on the other hand, "population" also has a dynamic aspect, since the "population" never remains the same and is always changing in many aspects. First and foremost is the number of people that is always changing through fertility, mortality, and migration. Other dynamic aspects are the spatial distribution and the various socioeconomic characteristics of the population that affect each of the demographic parameters of any given society.[22] These dynamics constitute the core of the demographic research.

2.1   The Various Aspects of Political Demography

The term *political demography* represents a specific branch of the socio-demographic research and concentrates on the various connections between *demography*, on the one hand, and *politics* on the other. Although the term "political demography" is used quite commonly in the demographic literature, its definition is not universal and it represents different things to different researchers. Here the term will be defined according to the three major categories that seem to represent the most important connections between "politics" and "demography" for the modern demographic research of the Arab countries.

The first category is the **ethno-religious composition of the society**. The ethno-religious composition of the Lebanese population has constituted the most important single factor in its political history since the nineteenth century, rendering its entire modern political history "a demographic history." In the case of the other Arab countries, although the ethno-religious composition has not been so crucial as in Lebanon, it was and, in many cases, still is of immense political consequences, as illustrated in Chapter 1. The political "fingerprints" on the demographic records in each of the Arab countries can be seen even in the early stages of data collection, namely, in the decision-making about what to include and what to exclude in the censuses and the Civil Registration System in terms of ethno-religious composition. Almost each of the Arab countries is "hiding" something, either the religious or the ethnic composition, for a wide range of political reasons that vary from one country to another. Thus far, the only Middle Eastern country that publishes official data on a regular basis regarding both the ethnic and the religious composition of the population is Israel (see Chapter 1).

The second category of the Middle Eastern "political demography" is that of national political struggle based on **the ethno-religious quantity factor**. The most representative case of this category in the Middle East is the Arab–Israeli conflict, particularly the Palestinian–Israeli conflict. The demographic quantity factor has played a major role in the conflict since its onset more than a century ago, insofar as each side is trying to increase the number of members in its community at the expense of the other side. This effort is based on the fundamental assumption that the demographic advantage will prove to be one of the most, if not the most, important factors determining the outcome of the struggle, whether through a peace treaty or through another cycle of war. Thus, the two sides, the Palestinians and the Zionists, adopted a pro-natalist concept from the very beginning of the conflict.[23] With their constant emphasis on the "demographic factor," the authorities on both sides have indeed succeeded in creating a "pro-natalist environment" among the populations themselves. Thus, according to a survey conducted by the Israeli NGO *Mishpaha Hadasha* [New Family] in early 2004 among Israeli married couples regarding their "fertility intentions," 25% of the Jewish couples said that the aim of keeping a Jewish majority in Israel is one of the considerations regarding their desired number of children.[24]

The third category of the Arab political demography deals with the **political influence on the demographic policy per se**, in most cases on the natalist policy. This category refers to all of the various political factors influencing the governmental demographic policy, including the regime's ideology; the political structure of the society; the religious impact on the political structure; and the influence of the relationship between the regime and the opposition, in other words the role of the "balance of power," in determining the demographic policy itself as well as its implementation. It is worth noting in this respect that the influence of economic policy on the demographic trends and policies of the Arab countries was marginal at best (see Chapter 4).

Despite the different natalist and migration policies adopted by each of the Arab countries during the second half of the twentieth century, the political influence on both areas was and still is immense. Thus, one cannot deal with the modern political history of the Arab countries without taking the demographic factor into consideration. At the same time, it is impossible to deal with the modern Arab demographic history without examining the various political aspects. Accordingly, it is the goal of this book to address the mutual influence of demography and politics.

★ ☆ ★ ☆

In the mid-1970s, André Burguière wrote that: "Historical demography is a young science, barely thirty years old, and yet it already suffers from the ailments of old age: recent work has become repetitive, and seems always to come up against the same contradictions."[25] I hope that this book will not fall into that category.

In light of the aims described in the Preface, the book contains four chapters. The aim of **Chapter 1** is twofold. First, it examines the quantity and quality of the demographic records of the Arab countries during the twentieth century. The major barrier to conducting demographic research in the Arab countries is limited resources and, in many cases, also low reliability of the official demographic records. The second aim of the chapter is to analyze the political influence on the demographic records of the Arab countries, specifically in terms of which demographic records are missing and why.

Chapter 2 deals with the causes of the rapid population growth in the Arab countries during the twentieth century, particularly in the second half of the century. The first part of the chapter compares the Arab countries with other developing and developed countries worldwide in order to "locate" the Arab countries in the global demographic picture. It addresses the factors accounting for the high fertility rates in the Arab countries; the factors accounting for the decline in fertility rates in the vast majority of the Arab countries since the mid-1980s; and the factors accounting for the immense fertility gaps between urban and rural areas, as well as the gaps differentiated by mother's educational level. The second part of the chapter consists of the history of mortality trends in the Arab countries during the second half of the twentieth century. The final part of the chapter examines the major differences between the "Western demographic transition" pattern and the pattern of developing countries.

Chapter 3 analyzes the most acute socioeconomic consequence of the high natural increase rates among the Arab countries during the second half of the twentieth century for both the short and the long term, namely, the emergence of the immense employment pressure that has characterized the non-oil and the oil-based Arab countries alike. The first part of the chapter deals with the short- and long-term consequences of the wide-based age pyramid, concentrating on the labor force participation rates, particularly among women, and on the "demographic momentum" and its influence on future population and labor force growth rates. The second part of the chapter uses a historical perspective to examine the emergence of the unemployment, both open and disguised, during the past four decades. The final part of the chapter examines the major differences between the unemployment patterns of the Arab countries and the prevailing unemployment characteristics of the Western developed countries.

Chapter 4 analyzes the natalist policies of the Arab countries. The first part of the chapter examines the various academic and philosophical attitudes toward rapid population growth since this phenomenon first emerged in Western European countries in the late eighteenth century as a direct result of the Industrial Revolution. The second part of the chapter examines and analyzes the various natalist policies implemented by the Arab countries since the 1950s, focusing on the differences between the various countries and the changing perceptions and policies within the countries themselves throughout the past two generations. The final part of the chapter examines the crucial and fundamental question of why some Arab countries have succeeded more than others in the implementation of family planning programs.

The **Conclusions and Prospects** evaluates first the balance of achievements and failures of the natalist policies among the various Arab countries and relates the macroeconomic reforms to the changing natalist approaches adopted by the Arab countries during the past two decades. The final part examines the effect of the ongoing rise in unemployment on the political stability of the Arab countries at the dawn of the twenty-first century.

1 | Sources for Demographic Research of the Arab States

The extent and quality of statistical data are paramount indicators of the degree of the central authority's control over the population and the territory in a given country. Generally, the more extensive and accurate the statistical data, the higher the degree of the regime's control. Thus, the improvement in the overall socioeconomic and demographic data of the Arab countries during the past four decades has occurred in parallel to the increase in control of the central authorities over their populations and territories. However, in many cases, governments are trying to "hide" sensitive demographic facts and thus do not collect and publish particular data, usually related to the ethno-religious composition of the population. In other cases, due to the basic ideological approach of the regime, the data are simply not recorded, even if available, such as the religious distribution of the US population, or Syria and Iraq in the case of the Arab countries.

I   The Demographic Records History of the Arab States

Overall, population censuses and registration of births, deaths, marriages, and divorces, as well as changes in place of residence – all of which constitute the most important sources for comprehensive demographic research – have had a very short history in most of the Arab countries. Only two Arab countries conducted population censuses prior to the end of World War II – in 1882 in Egypt and 1886 in Algeria. Due to this absence of demographic data, it is impossible to conduct comprehensive demographic research on the Arab region for the period preceding the end of the 1950s and the early 1960s.

In place of recorded census data, these countries have general population estimates, which were based on the partial censuses or general enumerations that were conducted in most of the Arab countries during the first half of the twentieth century. Most of these partial censuses were conducted under the Mandatory rule of either Britain or France. However, these censuses have their share of limitations and inaccuracies as well. For example, nomadic and semi-nomadic populations may be markedly under-reported. Other segments of the population, such as young children, and especially young girls, may also be underreported. Together with age misreporting, this produces noticeable distortions in the apparent age-sex distributions of the population of many Arab countries prior to the 1960s.[1]

1.1   Sources for Demographic Research of the Arab Areas under Ottoman Rule (1517–1917)

Until the mid-nineteenth century, the flimsy rule of the Ottoman Empire over the Arab provinces was not conducive to comprehensive population registration. Given that the Ottoman regime provided almost no social services to its subjects, there was likewise no need to accurately determine their demographic characteristics. Moreover, since the tax collection system was based on *Iltizam*,[2] the central as well as the province authorities did not need a specific record of the rural populations, which constituted the main target of the tax collections. As a result, we have only very limited demographic data of the areas that were ruled by the Ottomans. Stanford Shaw noted in this regard that: "No problem has perplexed students of modern Ottoman history more than that of determining the state of the empire's population during its last century."[3] The only sources regarding the scope of the population in many regions of the Ottoman Empire during the early nineteenth century are the sporadic estimates of European travelers, such as Volney, Seetzen, Burckhardt, and others.[4] However, these estimates are general and cannot serve as a primary source for comprehensive demographic research.

Since the mid-nineteenth century, as part of the reform movement (*Tanzimat*) that took place in the Ottoman Empire, the demographic data were also improved. A census was undertaken during the period 1831–1838 by Sultan Mahmud II (1808–1839) as part of his efforts to create a new army and bureaucracy following the destruction of the *Janissart* Corps in 1826. Only men were included in the census because only they served in the army and paid taxes. Although Christians and Jews did not serve in the Ottoman army at that time, they were also recorded in the census data, as they were subject to head tax. Females, however, were not recorded in this census at all.[5]

Knowledge of the size and changes in the spatial distribution of the population throughout the Empire became much more important during the latter part of the nineteenth century. This was due mainly to administrative reasons, as roads, railways, and a variety of professional schools were planned in accordance with the spatial distribution of the population in the Empire's various provinces.[6] As the Ottoman control over the provinces improved during the last quarter of the nineteenth century, the population registrations improved accordingly. The Ottoman authorities kept the population registrations in the provincial capitals of the Empire, where they were published in the *Salname* (provincial yearbook), as well as in the *Defter Nüfus* in the capital of the Empire, Istanbul.[7]

1.2   The Official Demographic Records in the Arab States since the Mandatory Period

Since the beginning of the Mandatory period, following the end of World War I, there has been a steady improvement in the statistical database, including the demographic data, in all of the Arab countries except for Lebanon. The first and only census conducted to date in Lebanon was in 1932 under the French Mandate. Considering the large-scale migration from Lebanon, particularly following the onset of the second Civil War in 1975, combined with the substantial fertility gaps between the various religious groups in the country, we can only roughly estimate the ethnic composition of the Lebanese population.[8] But Lebanon, it should be emphasized, is a unique case in this respect among the Arab countries.

In all of the other Arab countries, the socioeconomic data, including demographic data, were further improved following independence. The large-scale socioeconomic development plans, as well as the changing economic policy from capitalism to some form of socialism-étatism, required accurate socio-demographic data for the total population, particularly in regard to sex, educational level, and spatial distribution. This information on the age pyramid was needed because the socialism-étatism system provided, *inter alia*, a wide variety of public services, first and foremost, health care and education, which were either totally free of charge or highly subsidized by the government. Thus, as one can see in table 1.1, almost all of the Arab countries conducted population censuses during the 1950s and the early 1960s.

A further improvement in the socioeconomic and demographic data in the vast majority of the Arab countries occurred in the 1960s and 1970s, resulting from both the implementation of the massive socioeconomic development plans and the steady rise in awareness of many Arab governments regarding the "demographic issue." This heralded the beginning of the implementation of direct and indirect anti-natalist measures, which required accurate and updated demographic data. Thus, the population censuses conducted during that period also included information on fertility patterns that had largely been missing from the previous censuses of the 1940s and 1950s. Nevertheless, these population censuses also suffered from some basic shortcomings, first and foremost, the under-enumeration of nomads, young girls, and the like. Nevertheless, these censuses constituted the basic sources for the earlier demographic research on the Arab countries. In addition to the censuses, some of the Arab countries, as we will see below, started to conducted specific fertility surveys during the 1970s.

During the early 1980s, but more so in the 1990s, acceleration of the devastating results of rapid population growth and the high natural increase rates led many Arab governments to adopt national family planning programs, as will be examined in Chapter 4. The precondition for implementing these programs was accurate and detailed data on fertility patterns, mainly on women's age, educational level and employment status, average and median age of first marriage, average family income, and fertility differences between rural and urban dwellers. Some of this information was obtained through international fertility surveys conducted in the late 1970s and early 1980s, such as the *World Fertility Survey*, which included Egypt, Tunisia, Morocco, Jordan, Syria, and the Republic of Yemen. Other data were obtained within the framework of the Arab League, such as through the *Pan-Arab Child Health Survey* initiated during the late 1980s, or within the GCC organization[9] framework, such as through the *Family Health Survey* conducted in the mid-1990s in each of the GCC countries (see below).

Table 1.1 Demographic Censuses in the Arab Countries, 1945–2000

Country	Before 1950	1950–1959	Period 1960–1969	1970–1979	1980–1989	1990–2000
Algeria	31.10.1948	31.10.1954	15.9.1960 4.4.1966	1.12.1977	20.4.1987	25.6.1998
Egypt	26.3.1947	—	20.9.1960 30.5.1966(a)	22/23.11.1976	17/18.11.1986	18/19.11.1996
Libya	—	31.7.1954	31.7.1964	31.7.1973	31.7.1984	2.8.1995
Morocco	—	—	18.6.1960	20.7.1971	—	9.4.1994
Sudan	—	1.7.1955 2.9.1956	—	3.4.1973	1.2.1983	15.4.1993
Tunisia	1.11.1946	1.2.1956	3.5.1966	8.5.1975	—	20.4.1994
Bahrain	—	3.3.1950 5.2.1959	13.2.1965	4.3.1971	5.4.1981	16.11.1991
Iraq	19.10.1947	12.10.1957	14.10.1965	17.10.1977	17.10.1987	16.10.1997
Jordan	—	8.9.1952	18.11.1961	10/11.11.1979	—	15.12.1994
Kuwait	—	28.2.1957	20.5.1961 25.4.1965	19.4.1970 21.4.1975	20/21.4.1985	20.4.1995
Lebanon	1932	—	—	15.11.1970(a)	—	—
Oman	—	—	—	—	—	1.12.1993
Qatar	—	—	—	4.5.1970	16.3.1986	1.3.1997
Saudi Arabia	—	—	—	9/14.9.1974	—	27.9.1992
Syria	—	—	20.9.1960	23.9.1970	3.9.1981	3.9.1994
UAE	—	—	13.3/16.4.1968	30/31.12.1975	15.12.1980 16/23.12.1985	17.12.1995
Yemen (United)	—	—	—	—	—	16/17.12.1994(b)

(a) Sample Census.
(b) North and South Yemen united to one country in May 1990.

Source: The U.S. Department of Commerce, U.S. Census Bureau [http://www.census.gov].

2 Case Studies in Demographic Records History

Despite the considerable improvement in the overall demographic data of the vast majority of the Arab countries since the 1970s, a variety of basic demographic data are still conspicuously absent from the demographic records, in most cases due to purely political calculations. However, due to limited space, this section examines the demographic records history only in several Arab states, namely, Syria, Jordan, and five of the GCC countries, for all of whom the demographic academic literature is quite scant as compared with countries that have long and reliable demographic data, first and foremost, Egypt[10] and Tunisia.[11]

2.1 Jordan

The 1952 census of housing is considered as the first enumeration of the Jordanian population following independence (1946). However, since it was a housing rather than a population census, it only ascertained the total number of males and females. Thus, its usefulness for comprehensive demographic research is very limited. The first population census in Jordan, which is considered as the first comprehensive enumeration of the population in line with the modern type of censuses, was implemented in November 1961. The coverage of the census is considered to be reasonably complete. The reported annual natural increase rate of approximately 3% is also reasonable and is consistent with the demographic data of other sources, official and unofficial alike.[12]

The second population census in Jordan was conducted in November 1979 in order to establish a comprehensive demographic database for purposes of formulating the socioeconomic development plans. It was also the first population census following the June 1967 War in which Jordan lost the West Bank and East/Arab Jerusalem and absorbed approximately 310,000 Palestinian refugees in the East Bank following their displacement from the West Bank and the Gaza Strip.

The latest census in the Kingdom was carried out in December 1994. There was some debate regarding the aim of this census, and there were arguments in the press that the decision to implement it was politically motivated, aiming to divide the population between "Jordanians" and "Palestinians." This issue was a sensitive one, following the return of about 350,000 Jordanian citizens to the Kingdom after their deportation in 1990 and 1991 from Kuwait and Saudi Arabia due to the refusal of King Husayn to support the US-led anti-Iraqi coalition (see Chapter 3). The executive Director of the census, 'Abd al-'Aziz Zoubi, claimed that the aim of the census was "to establish an accurate demographic picture of the Kingdom."[13] The higher steering committee of the General Population and Housing Census is currently discussing preparations for the Kingdom's fifth census, scheduled for October 1, 2004.[14]

In addition to the population censuses, various demographic and health surveys constitute another important source for demographic research on Jordan. The *1972 National Fertility Survey in Jordan* was the first demographic survey in the Kingdom, and its results were published by the Department of Statistics in 1976. The second survey was the *Jordan Fertility Survey* conducted in 1976, with its results published in 1983. The third survey was the *Jordan Demographic Survey*, which was carried out in 1981 and had its results published two years later, in 1983. The fourth survey was the *1983 Jordan Fertility and Family Health Survey*, and its results were published in 1985.

The fifth survey was the *1985 Jordan Husbands' Fertility Survey*, conducted with the aim of investigating the attitude of husbands regarding fertility patterns. The sixth survey was the *1990 Jordan Population and Family Health Survey*, aimed at collecting data on fertility patterns, knowledge and use of contraceptives, and infant and child mortality rates. The survey's results were published in 1992. The latest survey was the *1997 Jordan Population and Family Health Survey*, which had similar aims as the 1990 survey. Its results were published a year later, in 1998.

2.2 Syria

The first census in Syria following the collapse of the Ottoman Empire was conducted by the French Mandatory regime in 1921–22.[15] However, there were many defects in the census. As Robert Widmer commented: "The census of 1921–22 . . . can scarcely be considered as even an approximation."[16] Even during the decade and a half after independence (1946), Syrian demographic statistics remained unreliable, preventing the conduct of any comprehensive socio-demographic research on the country regarding any period prior to 1960. As Bent Hansen wrote in the late 1960s: "Syrian population statistics are poor. The first modern census was made in 1960 and the population registration statistics are not very reliable."[17] Since that time, both the quality and the quantity of Syrian socio-demographic and economic data have substantially improved. This improvement has found expression mainly in three sources:

(a) Population censuses Since its independence until the present, Syria has carried out five population censuses. The first was conducted in 1947, but with the aim of establishing an election list to the parliament. In any case, the results of the census, other than those regarding the distribution of the population by sex and religion, have never been published.[18] The need for reliable socio-demographic data was underscored in the late 1950s with the preparation of the First Five-Year Development Plan (1960–65). Hence, the 1960 census, which was conducted under the United Arab Republic (UAR)[19] regime, headed by Gamal 'Abd al-Nasser, constituted the first comprehensive demographic investigation to be scientifically undertaken in covering the entire Syrian region. However, there were apparently some serious defects in the census data, including a marked under-enumeration of nomads and semi-nomads.[20] The third census was conducted in September 1970. The questionnaires, as well as the methods used for the organization of the census, were probably similar to those used in the previous census. It was also flawed by under-enumeration, which was estimated at about 2% among the urban population and 11% in the rural areas. Nevertheless, it was believed that the 1970 census data were more accurate than those of the former censuses and that more information was obtained about various demographic characteristics.[21] Moreover, the 1970 census was the first in which the data were computer-tabulated.[22] In 1976, the Syrian authorities conducted a sample census in order to draw a numerical picture of the structural composition of the Syrian population, to trace the socioeconomic factors affecting it, and to obtain indicators comparable to the data collected in the 1960 and 1970 censuses.[23] The fourth Syrian census was conducted in September 1981, while the latest census was implemented in September 1994.[24]

(b) Demographic and health surveys The second important source for Syrian demo-

graphic research are the demographic surveys that were carried out in the country by the Central Bureau of Statistics (CBS), the most important of which were: the *1973–Infant and Child Mortality Survey in Damascus*; the *1976–1979 Follow-Up Demographic Survey*; the *1978–Syrian Fertility Survey* and the *1993–Syrian Maternal and Child Health Survey* (SMCHS).

(c) The Civil Registration System The Syrian Civil Registration System, although established as early as 1923, continued to suffer from high underreporting rates, even after independence, particularly in the area of death registration, for several reasons. First, it was apparently impossible to register a birth unless both parents were on the population register. Second, it was a costly operation to the public, especially in those cases when the registration office was located at a long distance. Finally, and most importantly, there was no incentive for the population to register deaths – on the contrary, the Syrian pro-natalist regime created an incentive *not* to register deaths of family members, particularly children (see **Chapter 4**).[25]

The GCC Countries

While there are numerous demographic data for the past three decades on many Arab countries, regarding their total populations, natural increase rates, total fertility rates, age composition, sex composition, etc., this is not the case regarding the GCC countries. Indeed, until today, with the exception of Oman since 1993, they do not publish official data even regarding certain basic demographic characteristics, namely, crude birth and death rates, total fertility rates, and infant and child mortality rates. In the case of Qatar, the official demographic data do not even include a breakdown of the country's population according to nationals and foreigners. In contrast to the past, however, the reason for this lack of basic demographic data published by the GCC authorities is political, that is, to disguise the huge number and percentage of foreigners.

Another major problem in regard to the data published by international organizations on the GCC natural increase rates is that in many cases they include both the national and the foreign populations together. This method twists the real demographic picture of the indigenous populations insofar as both the fertility and the mortality rates of the foreigners are very small. This is not surprising in light of the fact that males make up the majority and that foreign workers tend not to bear offspring in the host countries. Thus, for example, in the World Bank's *World Development Report–1992*, Kuwait's crude birth rate in 1990 was estimated at 25 per 1,000, while that of the UAE was estimated as low as 22 per 1,000.[26] In reality, however, while the crude birth rates of the nationals in 1990 were above 40 per 1,000 in both countries (see **table 2.5**), this rate was, naturally, extremely low among the foreign population. In the same way, the data on total fertility rates were twisted as well. For example, the World Bank indicated Kuwait's total fertility rate in 1994 as 3.0 and that of the UAE as 4.1.[27] In fact, the total fertility rate in that year for Kuwait was estimated at 6.52 children per woman for the indigenous population and as low as 2.0 for the non-national population.[28] In the case of the UAE, the estimates were 5.3 for the indigenous population and only 3.0 for the foreign population.[29]

Until recently, another major obstacle to researching the socioeconomic trends in the GCC countries was the absence of undated and accurate employment data. The lack of available GCC socioeconomic data prompted 'Abd al-Rahman al-Rashid to write an article in *al-Sharq al-Awsat* in late 1999 entitled "Saudi Arabia without Data."[30] During the past few years, however, the demographic data published on the GCC countries, particularly in Saudi Arabia and Oman, have been largely improved and extended, covering new fields and providing more specific information in regard to many socio-demographic aspects. The improvement in the GCC socio-demographic data reflects, *inter alia*, the authorities' understanding that a complete and updated socio-demographic and economic database constitutes a precondition for any socioeconomic planning. As the *Arab Human Development Report–2002* noted in this regard: "Any program is only as good as the information on which it is based."[31] Nevertheless, with the exception of Oman, none of the other GCC countries publishes official data on a regular basis regarding the fertility and mortality rates of their indigenous populations. Such data can be obtained from only one source, the UNESCWA publications.[32]

2.3   Saudi Arabia

The first population census in Saudi Arabia was carried out in 1962–1963 and was considered to be incomplete even by the Saudi authorities themselves. In any case, only part of its results, those pertaining to certain cities, were later published by the Saudi Department of Statistics.[33] The major reason for the fact that the census results were never published officially is that the total number of the population, 3.3 million, looked "too low" to the Saudi authorities.[34]

The second population census, conducted in September 1974, was considered by the Saudi authorities to be the first complete national enumeration of the population, including both the Saudi nationals and the foreign population. However, some serious problems in the accuracy and reliability of the data are apparent, first and foremost regarding the reported age-sex composition of the national population.[35] Moreover, it is generally believed that the official census results are not reliable, as the figure for Saudi citizens, 5,935,361 seems to be much too high. True indigenous population estimates in 1974–1975 were varied, running from as low as 3.3 million to 5.6 million.[36] Regarding the accuracy of the official Saudi demographic data, Peter Wilson and Douglas Graham claimed that: "Staffers at both the Ministry of Planning and the Ministry of Finance and National Economy told the authors that they regularly used padded figures on the orders of their superiors."[37]

Three major reasons can account for the Saudi manipulation in the number of Saudi nationals. First, the Saudi authorities desired to show that the Kingdom is not only rich in oil, but also has a large population – a major factor in the balance of power in the three major circles, namely, the Gulf, the Arab countries, and OPEC. Second, the absolute number of the population was an important factor in determining OPEC quotas for oil production. This was particularly important during the period when oil prices were low and each member of OPEC was attempting to increase its quota at the expense of the other members.[38] The third factor was the wish of the Saudi Wahhabi-Hanbali royal family to minimize the percentage of the Shi'a minority concentrated in al-Hasa province within the total Saudi indigenous population.[39]

Since the publication of the official results of the 1974 census, the Saudi authorities are "sticking" to the published figure as the official number of Saudi citizens. The findings of the third census, held in 1976, were never published.[40] The latest census in Saudi

Arabia was conducted in September 1992. As in the 1974 census, while the unofficial estimate of the number of Saudi citizens in 1992 was 8–9 million,[41] the number according to the census results was as high as 12,304,835 (see Chart 1.1).

Chart 1.1   Saudi Arabian Demographic Data Prior to 1999

Population and Housing:

Preliminary results of the population and housing census taken on 1/4/1413 AH (27/9/1992 AD) show the following:

Total Population is	16,929,294
Number of Saudis is	12,304,835 representing 72.7 % of total population
Number of Saudi males is	6,211,213 representing 50.5% of Saudi population
Number of Saudi females is	6,093,622 representing 49.5% of total population
Number of non-Saudis is	4,624,459 representing 27.3% of total population
Number of non-Saudi males is	3,255,328 representing 70.4% of non-Saudi population
Number of non-Saudi females is	1,369,131 representing 29.6% of non-Saudi population

Number of houses is 2,791,044, some of which are occupied by a larger number of inhabitants.

Source: The Kingdom of Saudi Arabia, Ministry of Planning, Central Department of Statistics, *Statistical Yearbook – 1995* (Riyadh, 1996), p. 16.

Since the late 1990s, the demographic data published by the Saudi authorities on both the indigenous and the foreign populations have been expanded to include age structure, spatial distribution, and educational level. The most prominent indicator in this regard is that since 1999, the Saudi authorities started to publish demographic and employment data on a regular basis in their official publications, including the annual *Statistical Yearbook* of the Ministry of Planning. This stands in contrast to their previous official publications, which were limited to the total number and the sex composition of the indigenous and the foreign populations in accordance with the 1974 and 1992 population censuses (see Charts 1.1 and 1.2). However, the demographic data published by the Saudi authorities in the national *Statistical Yearbook*, it should be emphasized, are based on the 1992 census results, thereby casting a heavy shadow on their accuracy and reliability.

Following the demographic censuses, the second most important source for fertility patterns in the Kingdom consists of the two fertility and health surveys. The first was the *1987 Saudi Arabia Child Health Survey* and the second was the *1996 Saudi Arabia Health Survey*, which were conducted within the framework of the *Gulf Family Health Survey (GFHS)*.[42] The *1996 Saudi Arabia Health Survey* is extremely important in that it is the first survey covering the area of contraceptive prevalence rates, which was not included in the *Saudi Arabia Child Health Survey*.[43]

Chart 1.2   Saudi Arabian Demographic Data Since 1999

Population by Age Groups, Sex and Nationality

Age group	Total			Non Saudi			Saudi		
	T.	F.	M.	T.	F.	M.	T.	F.	M.
Less than one year	560570	276637	283933	89886	43663	46223	470684	232974	237710
1–4	2562058	1263328	1298730	393498	199629	193869	2168560	1063699	1104861
5–9	2726244	1346584	1379660	439496	223397	216099	2286748	1123187	1163561
10–14	2260602	1119110	1141492	310658	157233	153425	1949944	961877	988067
15–19	1817888	917084	900804	192881	100330	92551	1625007	816754	808253
20–24	1663633	808931	854702	379184	122859	256325	1284449	686072	598377
25–29	1850351	736490	1113861	777260	184437	592823	1073091	552053	521038
30–34	1763449	714918	1048531	890852	272740	618112	872597	442178	430419
35–39	1403071	540684	862387	668587	171424	497163	734484	369260	365224
40–44	988804	376937	611867	409760	86659	323101	579044	290278	288766
45–49	653176	263352	389824	218917	43996	174921	434259	219356	214903
50–54	462696	201348	261348	123836	27677	96159	338860	173671	165189
55–59	325126	154347	170779	55142	12400	42742	269984	141947	128037
60–64	248410	124218	124192	34648	11440	23208	213762	112778	100984
65–69	238555	99554	139001	19462	7978	11484	219093	91576	127517
70–74	151184	58805	92379	8542	3791	4751	142642	55014	87628
75–79	93675	35687	57988	5061	2727	2334	88614	32960	55654
80–84	63672	27728	35944	2405	866	1539	61267	26862	34405
85 and more	62068	24364	37704	2353	1406	947	59715	22958	36757
Total	**19895232**	**9090106**	**10805126**	**5022448**	**1674652**	**3347776**	**14872804**	**7415454**	**7457350**

Source: The Kingdom of Saudi Arabia, Ministry of Planning, Central Department of Statistics, *Statistical Yearbook – 1999* (Riyadh, 2000), p. 502, table 12–2.

2.4   Bahrain

Among the GCC oil states, Bahrain has the longest history of population censuses, dating back to as early as 1941 and continuing until the latest, which was conducted in 2001. In addition to the population censuses, another important demographic source is the Civil Registration System, which has attained almost a complete record of births and deaths of the indigenous population since the early 1980s.[44] The third important source, as in the other GCC countries, is the fertility and health surveys, the first of which was the *1989 Bahrain Child Health Survey* conducted within the framework of the *Gulf Child Health Survey Program* (*GCHS*) of the Council of Health Ministers.[45] The second was the *1995 Bahrain Family Health Survey*.

2.5   Kuwait

Among the GCC countries, second only to Bahrain, Kuwait has the longest history of population censuses. The first was conducted in 1957 and was followed by seven others, the most recent of which was conducted in April 1995. These censuses were conducted at more or less regular five-year intervals. The 1990 census was not carried out due to the Iraqi invasion in August of that year. As in Bahrain, also in Kuwait, the population censuses represent the basic and most important source for demographic research in this country.

Registration of births and deaths has been required in Kuwait since 1952. In 1960, the first law requiring the compulsory registration of births and deaths was issued. Although six health bureaus were subsequently established, this arrangement did not initially result in accurate registration because of the many births that did not take place in public hospitals, especially among desert dwellers.[46] By 1970, however, it seems that birth registration had become virtually universal and death registration almost complete as well.[47] In 1977, an automated information center was established in the Civil Service Department in order to modernize public administration through a personal information system. By 1982, a civil data system was set up, containing a complete registry of both nationals and foreigners residing in the country and other data on the entire population.[48]

The major source for fertility patterns among the indigenous Kuwaiti population during the 1980s is the *1987 Kuwait Child Health Survey* (KCHS), which was conducted as part of the *GCHS*. The survey provides data on the levels, trends, and differentials of child mortality in Kuwait. It also identifies the major diversities in bio-demographic patterns, preferences, and behaviors and examines the way in which social and economic modernization in Kuwait has influenced and shaped these patterns. In 1996, Kuwait, like the other GCC countries, conducted a *Family Health Survey* that provides data on a wide variety of demographic issues, including fertility patterns, marriage patterns, and contraceptive prevalence rates among indigenous Kuwaiti married women.

2.6   Oman

Oman has the shortest history of population censuses and demographic surveys, not only among the GCC countries, but among the entire Arab countries as well. As a result of the severe limitations on the entrance of foreigners into the country, combined with the absence of accurate and updated statistical data or any other official demographic publications, very little was known about Oman's socioeconomic situation until the 1970s. As Dale Eickelman noted: "Oman was almost as isolated as Tibet until a British-supported palace coup in 1970 replaced the Sultan with his son, the present ruler, Qabus bin Sa'id."[49] The only source regarding the Omani population during the 1970s is the 1975 socio-demographic survey of housing units and households, which was conducted in five towns in Oman and later extended to another six towns. The topics covered by this survey included name, sex, current age, place of birth, age at first marriage, number of children, educational level, relationship with the head of household, nationality, and economic characteristics.[50]

From the late 1970s onward, however, the demographic data on Oman steadily improved. The most important source for demographic research in Oman during the last decade is the *General Census of Population, Housing and Establishments*, which was conducted in December 1993. In addition to the census, the two other significant demographic sources on Oman are the two demographic surveys, which provide data on fertility patterns and contraceptive prevalence rates, and the five-year development plans. The demographic surveys are the *1988-1989 Oman Child Health Survey* (OCHS), which was conducted as part of the *GCHS*, and the *1995 Oman Family Health Survey*. The *Five-Year Socio-Economic Development Plans* extend from the first, which covered the period from 1976–1980, until the latest, which covers the years 2000–2004, include data and official estimates regarding labor force structure, both national and foreign, as well as some demographic data on the indigenous population. In addition, all of the development plans contain detailed data regarding educational services, including the number of students and their distribution according to age and sex. Such information is extremely important for demographic research in any country, but particularly in a country like Oman, which lacked many of the basic demographic statistics until the first census was conducted.

Following the 1993 population census, the Omani demographic data became the most diverse and accurate among the entire GCC countries. Thus, Oman is the only GCC country publishing data on an annual basis regarding the crude birth and death rates, the total fertility rate and the infant mortality rates of the Omani indigenous population,[51] as well as the number of foreign workers and their national composition, both in the public and the private sectors.[52]

2.7 Qatar

Qatar is one of the least experienced countries among the GCC countries in the acquisition and provision of demographic data. A 1980 ECWA report on Qatar's demography noted that: "Qatar does not maintain a system of vital registration, and though there is some recording on births in the capita Doha, there is virtually no information on a national scale of births, deaths, migration, marriage and divorce."[53] Since 1982, the Qatari nationals are required to inform the authorities of births, deaths, marriages, and changes in place of residence. However, despite the improvement in the demographic records, the Qatari authorities still do not publish these data in their annual *Statistical Yearbook*.[54] Overall, there is no doubt that Qatar is the country publishing the least official demographic data on its indigenous population among all of the GCC countries.

The first national population census in Qatar was conducted in April-May 1970. According to the report of the Middle East Development Division of the British

Embassy in Beirut, the general under-enumeration of the census was approximately 6%. Other serious shortcomings of the census were age misreporting, high under-enumeration of females, and misreporting of nationality by older immigrants.[55] The second population census was conducted in Qatar in March 1986. However, only a small number of tabulations were published. Moreover, the results that were published suffered from fundamental defects and inaccuracies.[56] The third population census in Qatar was conducted in March 1997 (see table 1.1). Other important sources for demo-graphic research in Qatar are the two health surveys: the *1987 Qatar Child Health Survey*, which was conducted as part of the *GCHS*, and the *1998 Qatar Family Health Survey*. Both of these surveys provide information on fertility patterns and contra-ceptive prevalence rates among the indigenous as well as the foreign populations.

The paramount barrier for conducting comprehensive demographic research on Qatar is that the authorities do not publish any data on a regular basis regarding the composition of the population according to nationals and foreigners, but rather consider them as one entity. This is apparently done with the aim of disguising the huge majority of the foreign population within the total population, estimated at 73.8% in the year 2000 (see table 2.4).[57] As a result, the demographic characteristics published in the *Annual Statistical Abstract* do not appear to be "normal." Thus, for example, it is reported that males comprise far greater than 50% of the population, as the vast majority of the foreign workers in Qatar are males. According to the March 1997 census results, there were 522,023 people in Qatar, of whom 342,459 were males (65.6%).[58] However, it is unknown as to how many of these males are nationals.[59]

In the same way, the authorities are publishing birth and death records, but only in nominal figures, and they are not specifying whether these data are related only to nationals or to the total population, including foreigners.[60] This missing information is preventing an accurate calculation of the crude birth and total fertility rates of the indigenous Qatari population. Due to such a lack of official data, demographic research on Qatar has to draw primarily on semi-official data (such as the publications of the various UN bodies) and on unofficial estimates of independent research.

3   The "Missing" Ethno-Religious Composition of the Arab States

Similar to many other countries worldwide, in the Middle Eastern countries as well there is no correlation between ethnicity and political borders. The major reason for this lack of correlation is the fact that many of the current Middle Eastern states were established following World War I through a series of agreements between the Superpowers, namely, the UK and France, according to their own interests rather than the interests of the local populations. However, due to the political sensitivity of the ethno-religious composition, none of the other Middle Eastern countries, with the exception of Israel,[61] are publishing official data regarding the ethno-religious makeup of its citizens. Why is the issue of ethno-religious composition of the Arab countries so politically sensitive? The answer to this question changes from one country to another, as will be examined in the following section.

3.1. Lebanon

The most famous case in this regard among the Middle Eastern countries is Lebanon. According to the 1932 census, Christians constituted a slight majority (51.7%) of the total Lebanese population.[62] The political structure of Lebanon, as outlined in the 1943 National Pact, was based on this small Christian majority, mandating that the head of the state, namely, the President, would be a Maronite Christian. Furthermore, every six of 11 sits in the Parliament were designated for Christians and five for Muslims, including Sunnis, Shi'is, and Druzes, thus ensuring Christian domination of Lebanese political life.[63] However, the large-scale emigration of Christians from Lebanon, particularly following the onset of the second Civil War, combined with their much lower fertility rate than that of the Muslims, particularly the Shi'a population in the south, markedly changed the Lebanese religious composition during the past three decades.

According to Colbert Held, by 1990, 33% of the Lebanese population were Shi'is, 20% Sunni-Muslims, 20% Maronite, 8% Greek Orthodox, 6% Greek Catholic, 4% Armenian Christians, and 8% Druzes.[64] Thus, by 1990, according to this estimate, the percentage of the Christians within the total Lebanese population had declined to less than 40%. Taking into consideration the almost 392,000 Palestinian refugees that are living in Lebanon,[65] of whom the vast majority – more than 90%, as in other Palestinian communities – are Sunni-Muslims, then the percentage of the Christians within the total Lebanese population at the dawn of the twenty-first century did not exceed 30%–34%, while that of the Muslims, both Sunnis and Shi'is, was approximately 70%.[66] This being the case, it is understandable why the Lebanese Christian authorities have refrained from conducting a population census.

3.2. Syria

The first and only census that enumerated the Syrian population according to their ethno-religious composition was conducted in 1960 during the rule of the UAR. However, since the rise to power of the Ba'th party on March 1963, the official Syrian statistics divided the population into three categories in line with the secular party's ideology of *al-Qawmiyya al-'Arabiyya* (Arab nationalism): Syrian citizens, Palestinian refugees, and foreigners. At the same time, some major developments were occurring in Syria that substantially affected its ethno-religious composition. First and foremost was the large-scale migration of Sunni-Muslims in the early 1960s, which involved hundreds of thousands of businessmen and professionals who resented the Arab Socialism policy [*al-Ishtiraqiyya al-'Arabiyya*] taken by the new Ba'thi regime.[67] This migration, combined with the substantial fertility differences between the various regions of the country affected Syria's religious composition through the following three dynamics:

First, the majority of the Syrian 'Alawites are still rural dwellers and, as in the other Arab countries, fertility rates in the Syrian rural areas are much higher than in the urban centers. Therefore, it is reasonable to conclude that the average fertility rate of the 'Alawites since the implementation of the 1960 census was higher than the Syrian average, leading to a steady increase in the percentage of the 'Alawites within the total Syrian population. Moreover, the 'Alawites became the rulers of the country and, in contrast to the past, started to enjoy the economic benefits of belonging to the "ruling class." They were not harmed by the "socialist measures" taking place in the new Ba'thi regime, as they were almost totally absent from the urban middle class prior to the mid-1960s. Thus, it is also reasonable to assume that the scale of emigration from Syria among them was very minor in comparison to both the Christian and the Sunni-Muslim urban middle class.

Second, quite similar processes were occurring among the Syrian Kurds and the Druzes, leading to a steady increase in their percentages of the total Syrian population at the expense of both the Christians and the Sunni-Muslims, who made up the vast majority of the urban dwellers.

Third, the fertility rates of the Syrian Christians were, and probably still are, considerably lower than the Syrian average, *inter alia*, since almost all of them live in urban centers in which fertility rates, on average, are much lower than those prevailing in the countryside. It is therefore likely that during the past four decades, their percentage within the total Syrian population has steadily decreased. Moreover, it seems that the large-scale emigration from Syria of the urban middle class and professionals during the 1960s and early 1970s involved many Christians that were represented in considerable numbers in these two groups.

Thus, taking into consideration the probably higher than average fertility rates among the 'Alawites, the Kurds, and the Druzes, on the one hand, and the probably lower than average fertility rates among the Christians and the Sunni-Muslim urban dwellers, on the other hand, combined with the large-scale emigration from Syria, the end result is that Syria's religious composition at the dawn of the twenty-first century is considerable different from the structure presented by the 1960 census results. How much different? According to the EIU estimate, in the late 1990s, some 70% of the Syrian population were Sunni-Muslims, while the rest of the population consisted of 'Alawite (12%), Christians of the Maronites, Greek, Armenian and Syrian Orthodox churches, as well as Protestant and Roman Catholic sects of Christianity (9%), Druzes (3.5%), and the rest were Isma'ilis, Shi'is, and a very small number of Jews. The largest ethnic minority in Syria is that of the Kurds, located in the north of the country near the Syrian–Turkish border and representing approximately 6.6% of the total population. While the vast majority of the Kurds in Syria are Sunnis, a small number are Yazidis.[68] The second ethnic minority is that of the Armenians, all of whom are Christians. There are also a small number of Turkman and Circassian minorities.[69] To what extent are these estimates accurate? Unfortunately, this question, for the meantime, remains open.

3.3 Jordan

In sharp contrast to Syria, from a religious point of view Jordan is one of the most homogenous among the Arab countries, with the Arab Sunni-Muslims constituting approximately 93% of the total population. The largest minority group is that of the Christians, which, according to the CIA (Central Intelligence Agency) estimates, constituted 6% of the total Jordanian population in 2001.[70] There are two major ethnic minorities in Jordan. First is that of the Circassians, who were deliberately planted in the area of current Jordan by the Ottoman rulers during the late nineteenth century and early twentieth century. Indeed, modern Amman itself owes its revival to the Circassians.[71] Currently, their number is estimated at 35,000. The second important ethnic minority in the Kingdom is that of the Shishanis, totaling approximately 4,000 at the beginning of the twenty-first century.[72]

In Jordan, the "demographic sensitivity" is the division between "Jordanians" and "Palestinians." The fear of the Hashemite regime in this respect is that if the regime officially admits that the majority of Jordanian citizens are Palestinians, then its legitimacy would disappear among the Jordanian population itself. Thus, the only two official demographic figures published about Jordan are: first, the division of the population according to religion – given that this is not a sensitive political issue due to the homogeneity of the Kingdom's population in this respect – and second, the number of Palestinians living in the refugee camps and the total number of Palestinian refugees, both of which are published regularly by United Nations Relief and Works Agency (UNRWA).[73]

The only methodological option, it seems, to estimate the percentage of the "Jordanians," that is, those who were living in the East Bank before 1948 and their offspring, is to add the natural increase rates to the number of the East Bank population before 1948, assuming zero migration balance. The rest are Palestinians. The only figure on the East Bank population prior to the 1948 War is the British data – 433,659 people in 1946.[74] Considering a 3% annual average natural increase rate since 1948 until the year 2000, it seems that the number of "Jordanians" in the East Bank of Jordan by the year 2000 was no more than 2.1 million of the 5.039 million Jordanians.[75] The meaning of these calculations is clear: By the year 2000, the Palestinian origin population in Jordan constituted at least 58% of the total Kingdom's population.

3.4 Egypt

From an ethnic point of view, Egypt is the most homogeneous among the Arab countries, as almost 100% of its population are Arabs. From a religious point of view as well, Egypt is a homogeneous country. According to the 1986 census, 94.1% of the population were Muslims, almost all of them Sunnis, while the Christian Copts constituted 4.9% of the total population. In addition, approximately 50,000 Egyptians belong to other Christian sects.[76] According to one estimate from the mid-1980s, the Christians represented approximately 6.3% of the total Egyptian population.[77] The CIA estimates the percentage of the Copts within the total Egyptian population in the early 2000s at 6%.[78] Although the exact percentage of the Copts is still debatable, it is generally accepted that the share of the Copts within the Egyptian population is considerably higher than the official figures, estimated at roughly 8%–10%.[79]

3.5 Saudi Arabia

From ethno-religious points of view, almost 100% of the Saudi indigenous population are Arabs and Muslims. The dominant and the official Saudi religious sect is that of Wahhabi-Hanbali (Sunnis),[80] representing approximately 25% of the total indigenous Saudi population and concentrated in the Najd region. The vast majority of the Hejaz's population are Sunnis-Shafi'i, some of whom originated from South Arabia. In the southern areas, there are also Isma'ilis and Zaydis,[81] originally from Yemen. The only official religious minority in Saudi Arabia is that of the Shi'is, with most of them concentrated in al-Hasa (the Eastern) province of the Kingdom, mainly in the city of Qatif and around the city of Madina. The number of the Shi'is in Saudi Arabia is unknown; although officially estimated at approximately 1 million,[82] unofficial sources estimate the number at 1.5 to 2 million.[83]

3.6 Bahrain

Although 65%–70% of the indigenous Bahraini population are Shiʻis, and the rest of the indigenous population, including the royal family, al-Khalifa, are Sunnis,[84] the Bahraini authorities have long insisted that the Shiʻi community in the country comprises only approximately 35% of the total indigenous population. The issue of Sunni-Shiʻi relations rose to the forefront during the mid-1990s when Shiʻi activists staged violent confrontations with the security forces, mostly due to domestic developments.[85]

4   The Lacuna of Accurate Official Employment Data

The employment issue poses another prominent challenge for any socio-demographic and economic research on the Arab countries. This is because official unemployment data are either almost totally absent, as in the cases of Syria, Iraq and Yemen, regarding most of the period examined in this book, or are reported as being much lower than they are in reality, as in the case of most of the Arab countries, particularly the GCC countries, Jordan and Egypt.

Regarding the overall quality of the employment and unemployment data of the Middle Eastern countries, Richards and Waterbury noted in the mid-1990s that: "All data must be treated with considerable caution."[86] In the poorer non-oil Arab countries, there is no system of unemployment insurance and therefore no reason to register as unemployed. Thus, as Rodney Wilson rightly claimed in the mid-1990s: "Any unemployment statistics which are published in the region are meaningless, even those reported to the ILO."[87] The 2003 ESCWA socioeconomic report noted that: "official figures may well underestimate the unemployment situation . . ."[88] *The Middle East* monthly also noted in regard to the problematic employment data that: "Accurate figures are impossible to obtain since many states in the Middle East do not collect detailed labor statistics."[89] Specifically, on Syria's official unemployment data, Eliyahu Kanovsky claimed that: "the unemployment figures are not very meaningful."[90]

Generally speaking, the misreporting of employment data in the Arab countries has three major dimensions. The first dimension is the under-counting and under-estimation of women's participation in the labor force. This is because in most cases females are working in agriculture within the rural household framework and thus are not taken into consideration in calculating the overall female labor force participation rate. This rate is calculated only on the basis of those who are receiving salaries, mainly in the urban formal sectors. Since the rural population continues to constitute a significant percentage of the economy in the non-oil Arab countries, in both employment and national income, it is quite clear that the actual female labor force participation rates in the poorer Arab countries are considerably higher than the national official figures as well as the various semi-official estimates, first and foremost those of the UN and the ILO (International Labour Office). In the 2004 ESCWA socioeconomic report, it was written in this regard that: "Because of measurement problems in estimating rural employment or the urban informal sector especially in the diversified regional economies, it is difficult to pin a number on the rates of women's labor force participation."[91] Specifically regarding Oman's female labor force participation, Dawn Chatty wrote that:

> Women from pastoral households are not included in official statistics on the economically active labor force in Oman. And in spite of their very active role in animal husbandry, which often provides their families with the income required for subsistence food purchases, these women are categorized in the first Oman General Population Census [1993] as "housewives," and hence are excluded from enumeration.[92]

The second dimension of the inaccurate employment data is the rural migrants and lower urban dwellers who are unable to find employment in the formal economy, neither the public nor the private sector, occupy such jobs as servants, porters, watchmen, and newspaper and cigarette vendors. In these varied capacities, they constitute another considerable segment of the urban informal employment, though they are often included on the waiting list for public sector employment.

The third dimension is a deliberate under-reporting of actual unemployment rates by the authorities in an effort to hide, or at least minimize, the steady increase of unemployment among the indigenous labor forces during the past decade. This phenomenon is particularly prevalent in the GCC oil states. This is because acknowledgement by the GCC royal families of the high unemployment rates among nationals, taken together with the overall decline in the standard of living during the past two decades, would be tantamount to an admission of failure in their basic role as "providers" as well as of the ineffectiveness of the *"rentier"* political system. For example, in an interview to the weekly economic publication *MEED* in September 2002, the Secretary General of the Supreme Economic Council of Saudi Arabia and former Saudi representative to the IMF, 'Abd al-Rahman 'Abd al-'Aziz al-Tuwayjri, said as follows:

> Lots of figures are thrown about for unemployment. But there are new statistics from the Central Department of Statistics. I checked with them and found that the unemployment rate in Saudi Arabia is not more than 8% for Saudis . . .I think this is a new and important figure to dispel all this nonsense about 20%–30% unemployment.[93]

In another *MEED* interview with al-Tuwayjri published in late June 2003, he repeated his claim that "some people talk about an unemployment rate of 20%–30% – are simply incorrect."[94] However, in the September 2002 interview with *MEED*, al-Tuwayjri stated that: "One of the major challenges we face is providing jobs for the new generation."[95] Likewise, the discussion on employment policy in the current Saudi Seventh Development Plan for the years 2000–2004 also begins by stating that: "Labor force development issues present some of the most important challenges for the Seventh Development Plan . . ."[96] Indeed, during the past decade, all of the socioeconomic development plans and economic reports of the GCC countries, almost without exception, have emphasized the issue of providing employment opportunities to the young generation as the main or at least one of their major aims. Indeed, the 2001–2002 ESCWA socioeconomic report noted: "a high-level Saudi Arabian official stated that the estimated unemployment in the country to be 20% in 2001."[97] If the unemployment rate among Saudi nationals is in fact only 8%, which is the figure quoted by al-Tuwayjri as well as the official unemployment figure,[98] then the Saudi economy is sure to have much more severe socioeconomic challenges.

A very similar phenomenon is also found in Bahrain, where the unemployment problem presents not only a socioeconomic challenge but a political one as well, insofar as the vast majority of the unemployed are Shi'is. In 1998, according to unofficial estimates, while the unemployment rate among the nationals in Bahrain averaged 15%, it was as high as 30% among the Shi'a rural population.[99] Taking into consideration that the number of Shi'is in Bahrain is twice that of the Sunnis, these data reveal that the unemployment rate among the Shi'is was several times higher than among the Sunnis. According to an unofficial estimate, the unemployment rate in Bahrain in 2000 was 17%, while the official Bahraini figure was only 3%[100] – lower than in all of the OECD countries. If the unemployment rate in Bahrain was indeed as low as 3%, then it is puzzling as to why the Bahraini Minister of Finance and National Economy, 'Abdallah Sayf, said at the same time that: "The most important challenge facing the Bahraini economy is job creation."[101] An economy with an unemployment rate of only 3% does not actually have an "unemployment problem" at all and could not possibly consider it to be its "most important challenge." Eventually, in early 2003, the Bahraini Crown Prince, Salman bin Hamed al-Khalifa, openly acknowledged that the actual unemployment rate in the country is 15%.[102] The reality could no longer be avoided in light of the increasing visibility of the unemployment problem and in the wake of the demonstrations in which many of the unemployed participated, the vast majority of whom were Shi'is.[103]

Among the poorer non-oil Arab countries, the same phenomenon of official unemployment rates being considerably lower than the actual or the accurate rate prevails as well. For example, while the official Jordanian unemployment rate for 1998 was 15.2%, unofficial sources estimated that the real rate is far higher the official one.[104] In the case of Egypt, while the official unemployment rate for the year 2000 was 8%,[105] according to unofficial estimates the actual rate was more than double, approximately 15% to 25%.[106] Two years later, in 2002, the official number of the unemployed in Egypt was 1.9 million, while unofficial sources argued that this number was "far lower than reality."[107] In the case of Yemen, while official data indicated an unemployment rate of 11.5% in 2000, unofficial sources claimed that the rate "exceeded 23%"[108] – more than double the official rate.

The unemployment data published by international official bodies were often based on the official figures and thus in many cases were not very useful. For example, in a recently published article in the IMF *Finance and Development* journal, Edward Gardner used official unemployment data for the year 2000, with 7.9% for Egypt and 13.7% for Jordan.[109] Likewise, the ILO publishes the official unemployment rates as they appear in the *2001 World Employment Report*, with the rate of 8.2% for Egypt.[110]

In the 1970s and 1980s, at the peak of labor emigration from the poorer non-oil Arab countries to the Arab oil-states (see **Chapter 3**), a major obstacle to monitoring the labor markets of both the Arab labor-exporting and the labor-importing countries was the inconsistency in the number of migrant workers, particularly in the case of Egypt, Jordan, and North Yemen (Yemen Arab Republic). For example, according to an official Egyptian report for 1981, the number of Egyptian workers in other Arab countries was 1.149 million, while according to unofficial estimates the number was considerably higher – running between 1.5–2.5 million.[111] In the mid-1980s, according to the vast majority of sources, official and unofficial alike, the number of Egyptian workers abroad was 3.0–3.4 million,[112] while according to the *MEED* reporter in Cairo, their real number was "about half" of the prevailing estimates.[113] Indeed, according to a survey conducted by the National Population Council [*al-Majlis al-Qawmi lil-*

Sukan], the number of Egyptians working abroad in 1985 was 1.4 million.[114] The HRD Base published quite a similar figure of 1.430 million Egyptian workers in other Arab countries in 1985.[115] In regard to the number of Egyptian workers abroad in mid-1984, the EIU noted as follows:

> How many expatriates are there? . . . In the late 1970s the consensus was that the number was somewhere around 1 million. The 1976 census derived a figure of 1.6 million for Egyptian residents abroad, though this clearly included both workers and non workers, as well as temporary and permanent migrants – the latter being less likely to be making remittances . . . Last year [in 1983] the minister responsible for migration produced figures showing 3.3 million Egyptians living abroad . . . Some people claimed that the numbers were even higher, the total for Egyptians in Iraq, for example, being nearer 2 million than the 1.25 million given by the minister. The counterclaim is that even 1.25 million is too high . . .[116]

Thus, if the actual number of Egyptian workers abroad in the mid-1980s was not over 3 million, but only 1.5 to 1.8 million, then the real unemployment rate in Egypt in the mid-1980s was much higher than the prevailing unemployment estimates at that time – as much as 7%–10% higher, considering that Egypt's total labor force at that time was approximately 11 million. Regarding the other major Arab labor-exporting countries, mainly Jordan and North Yemen, one can find a quite similar problem of considerable gaps between the various estimates of the number of workers in the Arab oil-states.

Overall, there are two major reasons for the inconsistent data on the number of Arab foreign workers in the GCC countries. One is that some of the labor-exporting countries tend to inflate the number of migrants, while the labor-importing countries tend to underestimate their number,[117] mainly in the smaller GCC oil-states in which the foreigners represent a vast majority not only in the workforce, but in the total population as well (see Chapter 2). The second factor is the huge number of illegal foreign workers, mainly in Saudi Arabia, where any Muslim is entitled to enter the Kingdom in order to fulfill the *Hajj* duty. Instead of returning to their home countries after fulfilling the *Hajj* duty, many of the pilgrims remain in the Kingdom as illegal workers. In Kuwait the number of illegal foreign workers in 1979 was estimated at more than 100,000.[118] In the other major labor-importing countries, one finds a similar phenomenon of large-scale illegal foreign workers.

In regard to conducting demographic research on the GCC countries, Michael Bonine noted that: "It is particularly difficult because of the great number of foreigners within each country, some of whom may be working illegally."[119] Roger Owen and Şevket Pamuk raised a very similar argument, claiming that: "so many workers entered the Gulf states illegally . . ."[120] Thus, due to the large unrecorded number of migrant workers who came from the poorer Arab countries to the Arab oil countries following the October 1973 "oil boom" and until the early 1990s, the employment data of both the Arab labor-exporting and the labor-importing countries are only partial.

5 The "Informal (Hidden) Economy"

Another major obstacle to conducting socioeconomic and demographic research on the poorer Arab countries is the vast extent of the "informal economy," sometimes called a "cash economy," "underground economy," or "hidden economy." Although the definitions for the term "informal economy" are quite varied, it basically refers to an economy in which a significant percentage of its direct or indirect financial transaction and employment activities are not reported and thus do not appear in the official national accounts.[121] Delwin Roy wrote that: "The main components of the hidden economy represent economic activity – capital flows, imports, production, factor payments, rents, etc. – that is mostly unreported and unrecorded, legal [barters, home and small scale industrial production], illegal [smuggling, tax evasion, and corruptions] or quasi-legal but have nevertheless the effects of which are not entirely invisible."[122] The ILO defined the urban informal sector in the developing countries as "a survival sector for many, including former members of the middle class."[123]

In the poorer non-oil Arab countries, in addition to the informal employment of both males and females, there are three main dimensions of the widespread urban informal economy:

(a) Low salaries paid in the public sector, in most cases amounting to less than $100 per month, are not sufficient for supporting a family. Consequently, many public sector employees are working in another workplace after, or even within, the formal working hours as taxi drivers, tourist guides, waiters, and the like or they are taking bribes, known as *baqshish.* All of these financial activities naturally go unreported and thus are not included in the official national accounts.

(b) Workers' remittances in the major Arab labor-exporting countries constituted the largest foreign exchange earner during the 1970s and 1980s, as well as a considerable percentage of the total GDP. In the case of Jordan, workers' remittances in the early 1980s constituted one-fourth to one-third of the total GDP, thus representing the largest non-governmental contributor to the national income.[124] Likewise, in Egypt, Yemen, Syria, and Sudan, the amount of the official workers' remittances during the 1970s and 1980s far exceeded that obtained through the export of goods and services.[125] However, a considerable percentage of the workers' remittances was not included in the official national accounts of the labor-exporting countries, due to the huge gap between the formal and the informal ("black market") exchange rates.[126] Rather, they were transferred through unofficial channels, mainly in cash by the workers themselves or by relatives and friends traveling home. In some cases, special agents dealt with these money transfers.

Thus, the real scale of the workers' remittances during the 1970s and 1980s cannot be calculated due to the absence of both the actual number of migrant workers and the real wages of the migrant workers in the host countries. Consequently, the unofficial estimates of the workers' remittances were varied. Nazli Choucri noted in this regard that: "Formally recorded remittances are only the tip of the iceberg. The size of that which remains submerged is not known."[127] She claims that in the mid-1980s, Egyptian workers' real remittances did not amount only to the $3 billion recorded in the official statistics, but were actually closer to $20 billion.[128] Egyptian economists and officials of the Ministry of Economy and the Egyptian Central Bank estimated that in addition to the official remittances of $2.2–$3.1 billion reported in the late 1980s,[129] there was approximately $3–$4 billion of unofficial remittances.[130] However, if the real number of Egyptians working abroad at that time was actually less than 2 million, as we saw earlier, then Choucri's estimate that the real remittances of the Egyptian workers abroad was five or even close to six times higher than the official figures, must be greatly exaggerated. In any case, a difference of billions of dollars in workers' remittances dramatically changed the whole picture of Egypt's economic condition, including the employment situation, at that time.

In the other major Arab labor-exporting countries, one finds a similar phenomenon of large-scale unofficial workers' remittances. In the case of Syria, while the official workers' remittances in 1979 amounted to $901 million, one year later, in 1980, this amount was sharply reduced to only $774 million and continued to decline to $436 million in 1981.[131] However, according to the various sources and estimates, the number of Syrian migrant workers in the oil-rich Arab states and in Jordan during those years was more or less the same, and maybe even slightly increased. Moreover, there is no information indicating a sharp reduction in the wages of the migrant workers in the GCC countries or in Libya at that time. Hence, it seems that the only logical explanation for these sharp oscillations in the scale of the official workers' remittances is the large-scale transfer through unofficial channels.[132] In the case of Jordan one can find a similar phenomenon. In 1983, for example, while the official workers' remittances of the Jordanian workers abroad amounted $1.1 billion,[133] it was estimated that undocumented remittances was as much as one-third this amount.[134]

However, since the mid-1980s and particularly during the 1990s, almost all of the former "socialist-étatist" Arab countries conducted exchange rate reforms, narrowing, or even abolishing almost totally, such as in the case of Egypt, the gap between the "black market" exchange rate and the official one. Consequently, there was a sharp decline in the amount of unofficial workers' remittances, as evidenced by the substantial increase in the scale of official workers' remittances, despite the sharp decrease in both the number of Arab foreign workers in the GCC countries and their wages. In the case of Egypt, for example, the scale of the official workers' remittances in 1994 was $5.1 billion,[135] constituting a higher amount than ever before, while the number of Egyptian workers in the rich-oil Arab states was considerable lower than a decade earlier. According to the 1996 census, the number of temporary Egyptian migrants was 2.18 million, including both workers and family members.[136] This means that the number of Egyptian workers abroad by the mid-1990s was only two-thirds their number in the mid-1980s.

(c) *Tourism receipts* constitute another significant part of the urban informal economy in the poorer Arab countries. In these countries, where there is a considerable gap between the formal and the informal exchange rates, many tourists are inclined to change their foreign currency in the "black market" rather than in the banks, similar to the situation with workers' remittances. These financial activities are not reported and thus are not included in the official national statistics. Another unreported aspect of the informal economy in the tourism area is that of the services provided to tourists around the hotels and the tourism sites, in many cases by public sector employees, such as informal tour guides. Even children participates in these activities, such as by carrying the tourists' suitcases (see Chapter 4). Not only do these activities go unreported, but it is impossible to calculate or even estimate their scale, changing from one instance to another.

Thus, the major question is: What is the share of the informal economy within the national economy and in employment? Richards and Waterbury estimated the share of informal urban employment in the Middle East as "at least one-third to one-half of the labor force."[137] According to a recently published World Bank report, the overall percentage of informal employment in Egypt amounted to 48% of the total employment, and as high as 65% to 70% of the private sector employment.[138] Regarding the share of the informal economy in the overall Egyptian economy, it was written in the EIU as follows:

> The 1988 US report points out that estimates of GDP, for which the government is the only source, are unreliable because of the growing "unofficial" economy in Egypt on which there are no statistics; actual activity could be as much as 25–50 percent higher than reported.[139]

According to research conducted by the National Bank of Egypt on the Egyptian underground economy and its influence on the national statistics, it appears that by the year 1990, while the official Egyptian national income was £E (Egyptian Pound) 117.7 billion, in reality the national income was much higher, estimated at almost twice the official figures and running between £E 196 and £E 222 billion. This means that:

> Egypt's underground economy may be at least equal to the published figure of the country's national income . . . Even if an estimate can be made to the size of the legal activities . . . it is almost impossible to know with some degree of reliability the extent of the illegal transactions.[140]

In many other Arab countries as well, one can find a similar structure with a widespread informal economy that hampers socioeconomic and demographic research. The widespread phenomenon of the hidden economy leads to a situation in which the magnitude of the economic activities conducted in the Arab countries are largely unknown, substantially distorting macroeconomic analysis.

6   Conclusions

Despite all of the limitations and obstacles examined in this chapter regarding the ability to conduct socio-demographic research on the Arab states, it should be emphasized that in contrast to prior periods, including the Ottoman and the Mandatory periods, it is possible to describe and analyze the major socio-demographic developments of the Arab countries during the second half of the twentieth century, albeit within the framework of these limitations.

<table>
<tr><td>

2

</td><td>

Beyond the Expectations:
Arab Population Growth in the Twentieth Century

</td></tr>
</table>

"The total number of Egyptians is 22 million . . . In 50 years [i.e., in 2003] the population of Egypt will reach 44 million . . ."

Gamal 'Abd al-Nasser, November 1953.[1]

I   Worldwide Population Growth in Retrospect

During most of human history, only a few million people were living on earth, due to the limited ability of the hunting and gathering way of life to support larger numbers of people.[2] However, with the development of agriculture approximately 12,000 years ago, the earth's "carrying capacity" has grown substantially. Since then, the world's population has steadily increased, although at very low rates, as one can see in table 2.1. Until modern times, during periods of epidemics and prolonged droughts, the world's population decreased, sometimes even substantially, such as in the Black Death from 1347 to 1350.[3] Thus, according to the prevailing estimates, the world's population numbered about 250 million at the beginning of the Christian Era and 245–275 million around the year 1000,[4] and then climbed to 545 million by 1650 and 728 million by 1750, on the eve of the Industrial Revolution. This means that during 1750 years, the world's population increased by less than three-fold and that there was almost zero population growth during the period 1 AD until the year 1000.

The Industrial Revolution first started in Britain in the mid-eighteenth century and later spread to other European countries in the nineteenth century, leading to accelerated population growth in Western Europe. By the year 1900, the total world population numbered 1.6 billion. This means that during the nineteenth century alone, global population increased by 77.5%, representing a net increase of 702 million. During the twentieth century, worldwide population grew more rapidly than ever before, particularly in the second half. By 1950, the world's population numbered 2.576 billion, representing an increase of 60.2% within only half a century, as compared with 37.3% during the second half of the nineteenth century. During the second half of the twentieth century, world population growth rates accelerated, peaking at more

Table 2.1 Estimation of World Population Growth (millions)

Year	Estimated World Population (millions)	Nominal Population Increase (millions)
AD 1	250	—
1650	545	295
1750	728	183
1800	906	178
1850	1,171	265
1900	1,608	437
1950	2,576	968
1960	3,040	464
1970	3,708	668
1980	4,454	746
1981	4,530	76
1982	4,611	81
1983	4,691	80
1984	4,770	79
1985	4,850	80
1986	4,932	82
1987	5,017	85
1988	5,103	86
1989	5,189	86
1990	5,275	86
1991	5,359	84
1992	5,443	84
1993	5,524	81
1994	5,605	81
1995	5,685	80
1996	5,764	79
1997	5,844	80
1998	5,923	79
1999	6,001	78
2000	6,079	78
2001	6,154	75
2002	6,228	74

Sources: Michael P. Todaro, *Economic Development*, seventh edition (Reading, Mass.: Addison-Wesley, 1999), p. 212, table 6.1; WB, *World Development Report – 2002*, p. 233, table 1; The U.S., Department of Commerce, U.S. Census Bureau, *International Data Base* [http:/www.census.gov].

than 2% on annual average during the first half of the 1960s.[5] Thus, the total world population numbered more than 4 billion by 1975 and reached 6.2 billion by the end of the twentieth century. The net population increase during the twentieth century amounted to 4.471 billion and 3.5 billion in the second half of the century alone (see table 2.1).

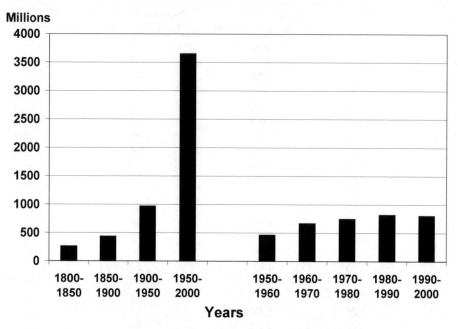

Millions

Years

Figure 2.1   Nominal World Population Growth, 1950–2000 (millions)

2   Demographic Transition Theory and the Arab Countries

Since birth and death rates determine population growth rates, the connection between them, or the mutual influence of one on the other, was and still is a major research topic. The most famous theory on the relationship between crude birth and death rates used to explain the mechanism of population growth rates is the *Demographic Transition Theory*,[6] first published in 1945 by Frank W. Notestein.[7] Some glimmer of the theory had appeared 16 years earlier, in mid-1929, in an article written by Warren S. Thompson.[8]

The basic assumption of the Demographic Transition Theory is that the number of births in any given society in any given period is based on a rational decision of the parents. Thus, in pre-industrial agrarian societies, a large number of births was an inescapable necessity in order to maintain population growth, due to the high death rates, particularly among infants and children. Moreover, due to lack of machinery, a large number of children was essential to cultivating the fields. The Industrial Revolution brought with it rapid machinery development, thus reducing the need for child labor. Improvements were made in nutrition, health care facilities, and both private and public sanitation. Furthermore, the development of the steam engine in boats and trains enabled the transfer of food supplies from one place to another. A rapid urbanization process took place, accompanied by the spread of education from the elite to the middle class and later to the lower stratums. These developments all led to a steady decline in death rates, which, combined with economic progress, was followed by a decline in birth rates as well. This phenomenon was first evident in the major urban centers and subsequently in the countryside.

Thus, according to the Demographic Transition Theory, "modernization," namely, the transfer from an autarky pre-industrial economy[9] to the modern pattern of an industrial market economy, was the sole factor responsible for fertility decline in the Western European developed countries.[10] As Notestein argued: "There are abundant evidence that the [fertility] decline came about primarily through rational control . . ."[11] On the question of why death rates started to decline earlier than fertility rates in response to the modernization process, Notestein claimed that: "The reduction of mortality is a universally acceptable goal and faced no substantial social obstacles. But the reduction of fertility requires a shift in social goals from those directed toward the survival of the group to those directed toward the welfare and development of the individual."[12]

In line with this basic assumption, the demographic history of the Western European developed/industrialized countries can be divided into the following three main stages, with the crossing from one stage to another explained as an outcome of a macroeconomic and social developments.

(a) *The first stage* of the Demographic Transition was characterized by high crude birth and crude death rates, leading to low, or even negative, natural increase rates. This stage ruled most of human history until the onset of the Industrial Revolution. During that time, the average life expectancy was approximately 40 years and the total fertility rate was between five to eight children per woman. Although population censuses or demographic surveys for that period do not exist, it seems that until the mid-eighteenth century, the natural increase rate of the world's population was marginal, averaging as low as 0.1% annually.[13]

(b) *The second stage* of the Demographic Transition was characterized by a steady decrease in crude death rates. However, crude birth rates did not decline substantially in the first stages of the Industrial Revolution because it took several decades until the population became convinced that the decline in death rates, particularly among infants and children, was more than just a temporary phenomenon. Only then did the population change its reproductive patterns to lower fertility. Thus, during the period 1750–1800, the world's natural increase rate was estimated at 0.4% on an annual average[14] – four times the rates that prevailed prior to the onset of the Industrial Revolution, but still very low in comparison to later periods. During the nineteenth century, with the widespread expansion of the Industrial Revolution, the trend of declining death rates was strengthened by a sharp decrease in infant and child mortality rates in parallel to a considerable increase in life expectancy. However, since crude birth rates continued to be high, the natural increase rates in the Western European developed countries substantially accelerated, reaching slightly above 1% on annual average by the end of the period, mainly during the first decade of the twentieth century.[15]

(c) *The third stage* of the demographic transition started following World War I and was characterized by a marked and steady fertility decline combined with a continued decline in the crude death rates and together leading to an overall steady decline in the natural increase rates in the developed countries.[16]

Since the 1970s, the fertility rates in Western European countries, as well as in other worldwide industrialized countries, have been very low, in many cases even lower than the replacement-level fertility, that is, less than 2.1 children per woman on average.[17] During the past decade, the natural increase rates in most of the European Union (EU) countries have been very low, even approaching zero. These low natural increase rates are the combined result of below-replacement-level fertility, on the one hand, and increasing crude death rates due to the very old age structure in these countries, on the other hand. By 1998, the natural increase rate of the developed countries worldwide averaged 0.3%, down from 0.7% in 1970 (see table 2.2).

This new phenomenon, called "the Second Demographic Transition," or "the fourth stage of the Demographic Transition,"[18] has immense socioeconomic and political implications for these countries, in both the short and the long run, as will be examined in Chapter 3. These implications are illustrated by the description of one 33-year-old Swedish woman regarding her attitude toward children:

> There are times when I think perhaps I will be missing something important if I don't have a child. But today women finally have so many chances to have the life they want. To travel and work and learn. It's exciting and demanding. I just find it hard to see where the children would fit in.[19]

The *New York Times* reporter who interviewed her characterized her as part of "a cadre in one of the fundamental social revolutions of the [twentieth] century."[20] Such a turn of events raises the question of why the fertility rates in developed countries have declined so rapidly during the second half of the twentieth century, particularly during the last quarter of the century. Was it a natural process or an outcome of governmental policy? What interests do these low fertility rates serve? Who benefits from these new demographic patterns and who does not? The rapid fertility decline in developed countries, it should be emphasized, took place *despite* the governmental pro-natalist approach. The changing role of women from "mother" to "provider," with their increasing economic autonomy and higher career aspirations, on the one hand, occurred in parallel to the extremely high cost of living, particularly in the urban centers,[21] and the rising consumer aspirations that called for dual salaries among the predominant group of urban middle class in the developed countries, on the other hand.

2.1 The Western European Demographic Transition

The Western European "Demographic Transition" is well illustrated by taking the example of Finland. During the period 1785–1790, Finland's crude birth rate averaged 38 per 1,000, while the crude death rate averaged 32 per 1,000, leading to an average natural increase rate of 0.6%. This was the end of the first stage of the Demographic Transition. During the years 1825–1830, Finland's crude birth rate remained at the same level of 38 per 1,000, while the crude death rate declined to 24 per 1,000 on average, meaning a natural increase rate of 1.4% – more than twice that of the previous period. The third stage of Finland's Demographic Transition began in the early twen-

Table 2.2 Natural Increase Rates in Different Parts of the World, 1970, 1998

Region	Year						Average Annual Growth, 1970–1990 (%)	Average Annual Growth, 1990–1998 (%)
	1970			1998				
	CBR	CDR	NI (%)	CBR	CDR	NI (%)		
Sub-Saharan Africa	48	21	2.7	41	16	2.5	2.8	2.6
Middle East and North Africa	45	17	2.8	28	7	2.1	2.9	2.3
South Asia	41	18	2.3	27	9	1.8	2.2	1.9
East Asia and Pacific	35	10	2.5	18	7	1.1	1.7	1.2
Latin America and Caribbean	37	10	2.7	23	6	1.7	2.2	1.7
East Europe and Baltic states	20	9	1.1	14	11	0.3	0.9	0.3
Developed countries	17	10	0.7	12	9	0.3	0.7	0.6
Developing countries	38	14	2.4	25	9	1.6	2.1	1.7
Least developing countries	48	22	2.6	38	15	2.3	2.5	2.5
World total	33	12	2.1	22	9	1.3	1.7	1.4

Source: UNICEF, *The State of the World's Children – 2000* (Published for UNICEF by Oxford University Press, 2000), p. 103, table 5.
CBR = crude birth rate per 1,000 people.
CDR = crude death rate per 1,000 people.
NI = natural increase (%).

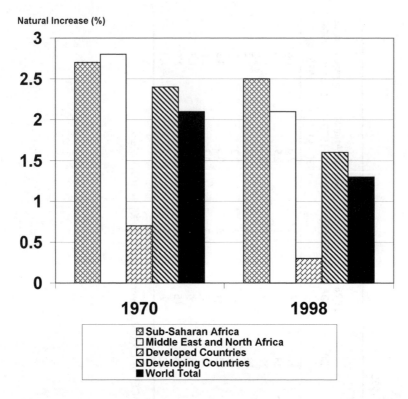

Figure 2.2   Natural Increase Rates in Different Parts of the World, 1970, 1998 (%)

tieth century. During the period 1910–1915, Finland's crude birth rate averaged 29 per 1,000, while the crude death rate averaged 17 per 1,000, leading to an annual increase rate of 1.2% – a decline of 15% as compared with the natural increase rate during the period 1825–1830.[22]

Following World War I, the downward trend in both the crude birth and crude death rates in Finland continued, although the birth rates declined more rapidly than the death rates, leading to a steady shrinking of natural increase rates. In 1960, the crude birth rate was 19 per 1,000 and the crude death rate was 9, meaning a natural increase rate of 1.0%[23] – a decline of 20% as compared with the natural increase rate that had prevailed in the early twentieth century. Two decades later, in 1980, Finland's crude birth and crude death rates were 14 and 9 per 1,000, respectively, namely, a natural increase rate of 0.5%, or half the rate of 1960.[24] Since then, due to a combination of the declining fertility rates and the increasing death rates attribut-able to the older age-pyramid – a direct result of the low fertility rates and the sharp increase in life expectancy – Finland's natural increase rates have continued to decline. In 1990, the natural increase rate amounted to only 0.3% (13 per 1,000 of the crude birth rate and 10 per 1,000 for the crude death rate)[25] – representing a decline of 40% within one decade only. By the year 2000, Finland's natural increase rate was marginal at 0.1%,[26] representing a reduction of 90% in the natural increase rate since 1960. Considering that Finland's total fertility rate is currently lower than 2 children per woman, one may expect the natural increase rates to be negative within a few years, with crude death rates exceeding the crude birth rates. Thus, if Finland's net migration balance is not turned to the positive side, then its population will soon begin to decline.

These demographic trends in Western Europe were strengthened at the beginning of the twenty-first century. By the year 2002, the natural increase rate was already negative in some EU countries. For example, in Germany, the number of live births was 725,000, while the number of deaths amounted to 845,000, leading to a net decline in population of 120,000. In Greece and Italy, one can find the same phenomenon of higher crude death rates than crude birth rates.[27] Overall, by 2002, the average total fertility rate in the EU countries was 1.47 births per woman, declining from 1.82 births in 1980.[28] It must be emphasized that this represents a new worldwide demographic phenomenon in which declining population is due to low fertility rates, rather than epidemics, diseases, or emigration. Thus, since the onset of the Industrial Revolution, Western European demography has undergone three transitions: from low natural increase rates to high natural increase rates during the nineteenth century and the early twentieth century; then to low natural increase rates in the second half of the twentieth century, particularly since the 1960s, due to low fertility rates; and to negative natural increase rates in the early twenty-first century as the result of prolonged below-replacement-level fertility in the past four decades.

2.2 The Application of the Demographic Transition Theory

From a historical perspective, the application of the Demographic Transition Theory to the Arab countries' demographic history during the twentieth century raises three major reservations:

(a) Even if the basic assumption of the Demographic Transition Theory on the relationship between "modernization" and fertility behavior is correct in the case of the developing countries as well, it is quite clear that the *patterns* of both socioeconomic and political developments during the second half of the twentieth century in the developing countries, including both the oil-based and the non-oil Arab countries, were almost totally different from those occurring in the Western developed countries. Such was the case in a wide variety of aspects, including economic policy and structure, women's role in economic and political life, level of industrialization, governmental income sources, average per capita income, and political structure. All of these aspects, as will be examined in **Chapter 4**, have an immense influence on demographic behavior in general and on fertility patterns in particular.

(b) In the Western developed countries, overall socioeconomic development – in all its aspects, but particularly in the rise in the standard of living – was the major factor offered by the "Demographic Transition Theory" as an explanation for the sharp decline in both the crude death rates and later the crude birth rates. In contrast, in many developing countries worldwide, the decline in death rates has been caused by external factors, first and foremost by the import of modern health facilities, *and not by their internal socioeconomic development*. Among the Arab countries, one can find some examples for this pattern, such as that of Yemen. While Yemen remains one of the poorest countries in the world (see Appendix 1), its crude death rate sharply declined from 29 per 1,000 people in 1960[29] to 11 per 1,000 in the year 2000.[30] Moreover, in the GCC countries, where the overall standard of living has sharply improved during the past four decades, particularly following the October 1973 "oil boom" (see Chapter 3), the fertility rates not only did not decline, but rather they increased, peaking at more than 7 children per woman in the mid-1980s. Also in the case of Egypt, the demographic trends from the mid-1960s until the mid-1980s were opposite to what they should be according to the Demographic Transition theory. During the decade between the mid-1960s and until the October 1973 War, Egypt's fertility rates sharply declined despite the overall deterioration in the economic conditions as a result of the June 1967 War and the War of Attrition (1969–1970). During the decade between the mid-1970s and the mid-1980s, although Egypt's economy sharply improved, with a doubling of the per capita income and a continuing rapid decline in infant and child mortality rates, fertility rates substantially increased (see Chapter 4). A similar trend can also be found among the Israeli-Arabs during the 1950s and 1960s.[31]

(c) The Demographic Transition theory did not take into consideration three factors that have a substantial influence on fertility behavior, the first of which is the influence of migration. When the population of Europe considerably increased during the nineteenth and the early twentieth centuries, Europe found a way to relieve its demographic pressure through emigration to "The New World," that is, to North America and to the European colonies worldwide. This option was not relevant to the developing countries during the second half of the twentieth century. The second factor is the influence of governmental fertility policy on fertility levels (see Chapter 4). The third is the cultural-religious factor, which was subject to change not only from one society to another, but also within the same society between parents and their children.[32]

However, despite all the criticism of the Demographic Transition theory, it still remains a useful framework for analyzing demographic changes and trends from a historical perspective. The applicability of the Demographic Transition theory to the demographic developments of the developing countries is not a mere academic debate, but has immense practical importance for favorable demographic policy. If socioeconomic development is the sole, or at least the paramount, factor accounting for fertility decline, then governmental policy aimed at reducing fertility should concentrate on socioeconomic development itself without devoting scarce resources to expensive family planning programs. However, if in fact there are many other factors, including religious-cultural ones, impacting on fertility patterns, then developing countries would do well to allocate some of their limited financial resources to family planning programs.[33] Thus, those following Notestein's basic assumption contend that family planning programs, by themselves, would not be much help in bringing about fertility decline,[34] while the other approach argues that well-designed family planning programs can effectively reduce unwanted childbearing, which, in turn, can contribute significantly to reducing fertility in developing countries.[35]

The worldwide natural increase rate, which had averaged 1.7% during the decade of 1950–1960, skyrocketed to more than 2% in the second half of the 1960s. The meaning of an annual 2% growth rate is so great that "if the human race had begun with a single couple at the time of Christ and had grown steadily at 2% per year since then, there would now be 20 million people for every person alive on the earth today."[36] Since the early 1970s, however, the decline in worldwide fertility rates has been higher than the decline in death rates, leading to a consistent decline in worldwide natural increase rates. During the 1970s, the worldwide natural increase rate dropped back down to an average of 1.7%, further declined to 1.4% during the period 1990–1998,[37] and reached 1.3% (a crude birth rate of 22 per 1,000 and a crude death rate of 9 per 1,000) between mid-2002 and mid-2003, representing the lowest rate ever since World War II. In nominal figures, the 1.3% natural increase rate of the early 2000s meant a net increase of 74 million people to the worldwide population[38] – a decline of 7 million people as compared with a net increase of 81 million on annual average during the 1990s.[39]

Overall, at the dawn of the twenty-first century, the vast majority of countries worldwide were still at the beginning of the third stage of the Demographic Transition, namely, their death rates were quite low, but their fertility rates, albeit considerably lower as compared with those prevailing three decades ago, were still far above the replacement-level fertility. As a result, their natural increase rates were higher than 1.5% annually. According to UNICEF data, by the year 1998, of the 189 member countries in the organization, the total fertility rate was below the replacement-level fertility only among 30 countries, while the total fertility rate was above 3 among 53 countries and above 4 among 41 countries.[40]

3   Population Growth in the Arab Countries

Although demographic statistics on the Middle East prior to the nineteenth century are completely lacking, "it is possible, wrote Charles Issawi, to hazard educated guesses about magnitudes and trends."[41] Accordingly, one can say that in the second century AD, the population of the Middle East region amounted to 40 to 45 million – a fifth of the total global population at that time. Subsequently, the region's population fluctuated without a clear trend until the nineteenth century, when a steady rise in number became evident. During the period 1840–1914, the Middle Eastern population doubled at an average annual growth rate of just under 1%.[42]

By 1914, on the eve of World War I, the Middle Eastern population (including Iran and Turkey) was estimated at 68 million. By the year 2000, it reached 374 million (including Iran, Turkey, and Israel, as well as the Palestinians living in the Occupied Territories of the West Bank and the Gaza Strip).[43] Thus, within less than nine decades, despite the huge emigration from the region, the Middle Eastern population increased by almost six-fold as a result of the accelerating natural increase rates. Similar to other developing regions worldwide, the Middle Eastern population grew by particularly increasing rates during the two decades between the mid-1960s and the mid-1980s. The following two tables present the population growth rates during the second half of the twentieth century in some non-oil and oil Arab countries.

Table 2.3   Population Growth in Some non-Oil Arab Countries, 1950–2002 ('000)

Country	Year						
	1950	1960	1970	1980	1990	2000	2002
Egypt	21,437 (a)	26,085	33,053	42,126	55,543	70,492	73,313
Jordan*	600	781	1,668	2,218	3,453	5,178	5,307
Syria	3,252	4,656	6,305	8,704	12,116	16,320	17,156
Tunisia	3,517	4,149	5,099	6,443	8,207	9,590	9,816
Morocco	9,343	12,423	15,909	19,487	24,685	30,122	31,168

* East Bank only.
(a) Data related to 1952.

Sources: Arab Republic of Egypt, CAPMAS (Central Agency for Public Mobilisation and Statistics). *Statistical Yearbook*, 1984–2002, various issues (Cairo); The Hashemite Kingdom of Jordan, Department of Statistics, *Statistical Abstract*, various issues (Amman); Syrian Arab Republic, Office of the Prime Minister, Central Bureau of Statistics, *Statistical Abstract*, various issues (Damascus); ECWA/ESCWA, *Demographic and Related Socio-Economic Data Sheets for Countries of the Economic and Social Commission for Western Asia*, various issues (Baghdad, Amman, New York, and Beirut); The U.S., Department of Commerce, U.S. Census Bureau, *International Data Base* [http:/www.census.gov].

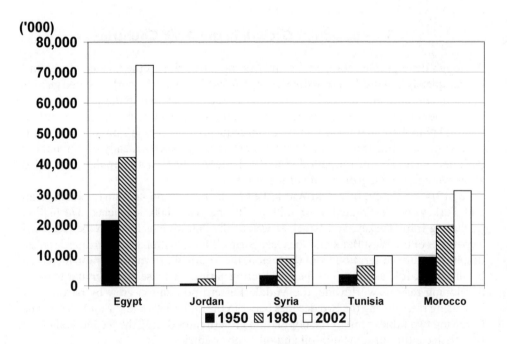

Figure 2.3   Population Growth in Some non-Oil Arab Countries, 1950–2002 ('000)

Table 2.4   GCC National and non-National Populations, 1975–2000 ('000)

Country	Nationals	Foreigners	Total	% Foreigners
		1975		
Saudi Arabia	4,593	1,565	6,158	25.4
Kuwait	472	522	994	52.5
Bahrain	214	56	270	20.7
Oman	550	132	682	19.4
Qatar	60	97	157	61.8
UAE	170	388	556	69.8
Total	6,059	2,760	8,819	31.3
		1980		
Saudi Arabia	7,079	2,150	9,229	23.3
Kuwait	565	792	1,357	58.4
Bahrain (a)	239	112	351	31.9
Oman	805	179	984	18.2
Qatar	65	178	243	73.3
UAE	237	746	983	75.9
Total	8,990	4,157	13,147	31.6
		1985		
Saudi Arabia (b)	7,849	4,505	12,354	36.5
Kuwait	470	1,016	1,486	68.4
Bahrain	263	122	385	31.7
Oman	857	391	1,248	31.3
Qatar (b)	102	267	369	72.4
UAE	434	1,239	1,362	76.2
Total	9,975	7,540	17,515	43.1
		1990		
Saudi Arabia (c)	8,847	5,939	14,786	40.2
Kuwait	572	1,563	2,135	73.2
Bahrain	336	167	503	33.2
Oman	1,024	371	1,395	26.6
Qatar	100	350	450	77.8
UAE (c)	531	1,014	1,545	65.6
Total	11,410	9,404	20,814	45.2
		1994		
Saudi Arabia	13,053	5,127	18,180	28.2
Kuwait	671	949	1,620	58.6
Bahrain	346	205	551	37.2
Oman	1,511	538	2,049	26.3
Qatar	129	403	532	75.8
UAE	629	1,522	2,151	70.8
Total	16,339	8,744	25,083	34.9
		2000		
Saudi Arabia	16,210	5,800	22,010	26.4
Kuwait	832	1,358	2,190	62.0
Bahrain	391	261	652	40.0
Oman	1,778	624	2,402	26.0
Qatar	152	428	580	73.8
UAE	703	2,187	2,890	75.7
Total	20,066	10,658	30,724	34.7

(a) Data related to 1981.
(b) Data related to 1986.
(c) Data related to 1988.

Sources: The State of Kuwait, Ministry of Planning, Central Statistical Office, *Annual Statistical Abstract*, various issues (Kuwait); The State of Bahrain, Central Statistical Organization, Directorate of Statistics, *Statistical Abstract – 1992* (Manama); Dawlat al-Bahrayn, al-Jihaz al-Markazi lil-Ihsa, *al-Ta'dad al-'Amm lil-Sukan wal-Masakin wal-Mabani wal-Munsha'at – 1991* (Manama, 1992); Sultanate of Oman, *Statistical Year-Book*, various issues (Muscat); idem, Ministry of Development, *The Fifth Five-Year Development Plan, 1996–2000* (Muscat, July 1997); J. S. Birks and C. A. Sinclair, *International Migration and Development in the Arab Region* (Geneva: ILO, 1980); ILO, *International Migration for Employment: Manpower and Population Evolution in the GCC and Libyan Arab Jamahiriya*, World Employment Programme Research, Working Paper, by J. S. Birks and C. A. Sinclair (Geneva, October 1989); ESCWA, *Demographic and Related Socio-Economic Data Sheets for Countries of the Economic and Social Commission for Western Asia, 1978–2001*, various issues (Beirut, Baghdad, and Amman); idem, *Population Situation in the ESCWA Region, 1990* (Amman, May 1992); EIU, *Country Profile, Bahrain, Qatar, Oman, Saudi Arabia, and the United Arab Emirates*, various issues; Birks, Sinclair & Associates Ltd. *GCC Market Report*, 1990 and 1992 (Durham: Mountjoy Research Centre); Onn Winckler, "The Immigration Policy of the Gulf Cooperation Council (GCC) States," *Middle Eastern Studies*, Vol. 33, No. 3 (July 1997); Andrzej Kapiszewski, *National and Expatriates: Population and Labour Dilemmas of the Gulf Cooperation Council States* (Reading, MA: Ithaca Press, 2001); "al-Simat al-Asasiyya li-Sukan al-Kuwayt wa-Kuwwat al-'Amal fi Nihayat 1994," *al-Iqtisadi al-Kuwayti*, No. 324 (May 1995).

('000)

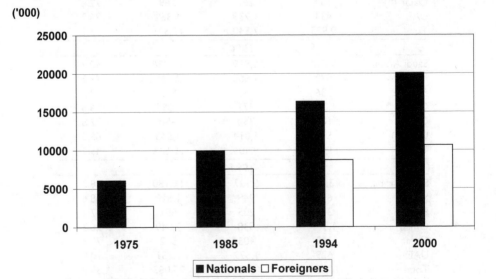

Figure 2.4   GCC National and non-National Populations, 1975–2000

3.1   The Causes for High Fertility Rates of the Arab Countries

Despite the lack of population censuses and accurate demographic records regarding many of the Arab countries until the 1960s, from those available it appears that during the first half of the twentieth century, similar to other developing regions worldwide, the fertility rates in the Arab region were very high. For example, according to the 1907 census results, Egypt's crude birth rate was 45.9 per 1,000 and remained at that high level throughout the following three decades.[44] In the other Arab countries, one can find quite similar fertility patterns as well. From the 1950s until the mid-1980s, the fertility rates in the Arab countries continued to be very high, and in Kuwait even increased by 10% (see **table 2.5**).

This phenomenon raises the question as to why the fertility rates in all of the Arab countries, with the exception of Tunisia, have remained so high until very recently despite the overall improvement in the standard of living, including a sharp decline in infant and child mortality rates (see below). In other words, why were the fertility trends in the Arab countries not in line with the Western fertility patterns or even in line with the prevailing fertility patterns of many other developing countries in the rest of the world? It seems that there are ten major factors accounting for the delay in the fertility decline in the Arab countries, as follows:

(a) Children as a cheap labor force   In pre-industrial agrarian societies, children constituted an important workforce from a very early age, sometimes even from the age of four or five. Until the present day in the cotton fields in Egypt, it is very common to see small children working in the family fields. It should be remembered that until the 1970s, all of the Arab countries, with the exception of Lebanon and the oil-rich GCC countries, were still agrarian societies in which more than half of the population resided in rural areas and made their living in agriculture. By 1970, the rural population constituted 58% of the total population in Egypt, 56% in Syria, and 65% in Morocco. Even during the second half of the 1980s, the percentage of the rural population within the total population of the non-oil Arab countries remained high by international comparison, amounting in 1990 to 53% in Egypt, 50% in Syria, 52% in Morocco, and 48% in Algeria (see **table 2.6**). Consequently, the high percentage of the rural population within the total population had an overall impact on the national average fertility rates in these countries, with high fertility rates viewed as an economic necessity.

(b) Children as "social security" for the elder generation   In most developing societies until very recently, and in many countries even today, a national social security system in the format of the Western style of a "welfare state" either does not exist or is inadequate. This refers to the government's responsibility for providing a "minimum living standard" to its citizens through elder allowances, children's allowances, allowances to poor people, disabled allowances, and the like. Such provisions are generally not available in the Arab countries, with the exception of the rich-oil countries. Moreover, in such poor agrarian societies, the average income is not enough to save for a pension, as is very common in the developed countries, in addition to the national social security system. Thus, the major, and sometimes the only, economic security of the elder population is provided by their male children.[45] As a result, parents attempt to reach the desirable number of adult boys in order to secure their own future. Three to four

Table 2.5 Natural Increase Rates and Total Fertility Rates in Some Arab Countries, non-Arab Developing Countries, and Developed Countries, 1960–2000

Country	1960				1970				1980				1990				2000			
	CBR	CDR	NI	TFR	CBR	CDR	NI	TFR	CBR	CDR	NI	TFR	CBR	CDR	NI	TFR	CBR	CDR	NI	TFR
Arab Countries																				
Egypt	43	17	2.6	6.1	35	15	2.0	5.2	38	10	2.8	5.2	33	8	2.5	4.3	26	7	1.9	3.3
Jordan	48	20	2.8	6.8	48	16	3.2	7.1	47	11	3.6	7.3	39	6	3.3	5.8	29	5	2.4	3.8
Syria	48	18	3.0	7.3	48	16	3.2	7.6	46	8	3.8	7.3	44	6	3.8	6.5	28	4	2.4	3.8
Lebanon	43	14	2.9	6.3	35	11	2.4	5.5	30	8	2.2	4.1	27b	5b	2.2b	3.4b	21	7	1.4	2.4
Tunisia	49	21	2.8	7.1	41	15	2.6	6.5	35	10	2.5	5.3	29	7	2.2	3.7	20	7	1.3	2.5
Morocco	52	23	2.9	7.2	47	17	3.0	7.1	44	12	3.2	6.9	34	9	2.5	4.5	25	6	1.9	3.1
Sudan	47	25	2.2	6.7	47	22	2.5	6.7	47	19	2.8	6.7	44	15	2.9	6.3	39	10	2.9	5.5
Saudi Arabia*	49	23	2.6	7.2	48	18	3.0	7.3	46	14	3.2	7.3	42	7	3.5	7.1	29	4	2.5	4.4
Kuwait*	44	10	3.4	7.3	48	6	4.2	7.2	48	6	4.2	7.2	42b	3b	3.9b	6.2 b	37	3	3.4	4.9
Oman*	51	28	2.3	7.2	50	19	3.1	7.2	50	13	3.7	7.2	45	8	3.7	—	39	4	3.5	6.2
Bahrain*	46	15	3.1	7.1	43a	8a	3.5a	6.7	—	—	—	—	40b	5b	3.5	5.8b	28	4	2.4	3.5
Non-Arab Developing Countries																				
Turkey	45	18	2.7	6.3	37	12	2.5	5.6	32	10	2.2	4.4	28	8	2.0	3.5	19	6	1.3	2.2
South Korea	43	14	2.9	5.6	30	10	2.0	4.2	24	7	1.7	3.0	16	6	1.0	1.7	13	6	0.7	1.5
Brazil	43	13	3.0	6.2	35	10	2.5	5.0	30	9	2.1	4.1	27	8	1.9	3.3	19	6	1.3	2.1
Mexico	46	12	3.4	6.8	45	10	3.5	6.6	37	7	3.0	5.1	28	6	2.2	3.3	23	5	1.8	2.7
Pakistan	49	24	2.5	7.5	48	19	2.9	7.1	47	24	2.3	6.1	44	12	3.2	6.2	32	10	2.2	4.6
Developed Countries																				
Belgium	17	12	0.5	2.2	15	12	0.3	2.2	13	12	0.1	1.8	13	11	0.2	1.6	11	10	0.1	1.6
Norway	18	9	0.9	2.5	18	10	0.8	2.5	13	10	0.3	1.9	13	10	0.3	1.8	13	10	0.3	1.8
France	18	12	0.6	2.5	17	11	0.6	2.5	14	11	0.3	1.9	13	10	0.3	1.8	13	9	0.4	1.9
United States	24	9	1.5	2.5	17	9	0.8	2.5	16	9	0.7	1.9	17	9	0.8	1.9	14	9	0.5	2.1
UK	17	12	0.5	2.3	16	12	0.4	2.4	14	12	0.2	1.8	13	11	0.2	1.8	11	10	0.1	1.7

CBR = crude birth rate per 1,000 people.
CDR = crude death rate per 1,000 people.
NI = natural increase (%).
* Nationals only.

TFR = total fertility rate.
— No data available.
a. Data related to 1971.

b. Data related to 1988.

Sources: Arab Republic of Egypt, CAPMAS, *Statistical Yearbook*, 1984–2002, various issues (Cairo); The Hashemite Kingdom of Jordan, Department of Statistics, *Statistical Yearbook*, 1970–2002, various issues (Amman); Syrian Arab Republic, Office of the Prime Minister, Central Bureau of Statistics, *Statistical Abstract*, 1960–2002, various issues (Damascus); WB, *World Tables*, 1984–1995, various issues (Published for the WB by Johns Hopkins University Press); idem, *World Development Report*, 1978–2002, various issues (Published for the WB by Oxford University Press); UN, *Demographic Yearbook*, 1970–1999, various issues (New York: UN Publications); ECWA/ESCWA, *Demographic and Related Socio-Economic Data Sheets for Countries of the Economic and Social Commission for Western Asia*, 1978–2001, various issues (Beirut, Baghdad, and Amman); idem, *Statistical Abstract of the ECWA/ESCWA Region*, 1970–2000, various issues (New York, Baghdad, and Amman); UNICEF, *The State of the World's Children*, 1984–2001, various issues (Published for UNICEF by Oxford University Press); The U.S., Department of Commerce, U.S. Census Bureau, *International Data Base* [http:/www.census.gov].

Figure 2.5 Natural Increase Rates in Some Arab Countries, non-Arab Developing Countries, and Developed Countries, 1960–2000

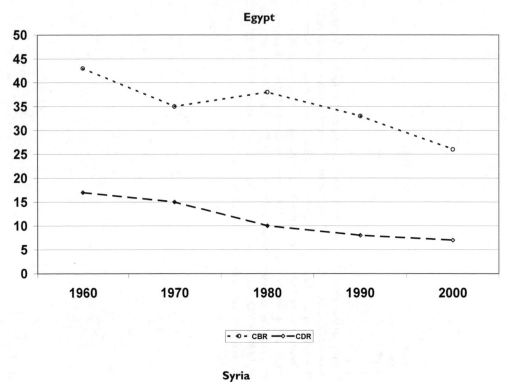

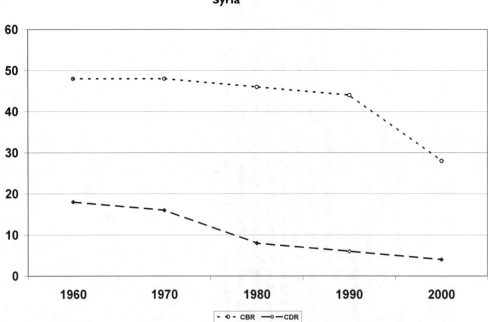

Saudi Arabia

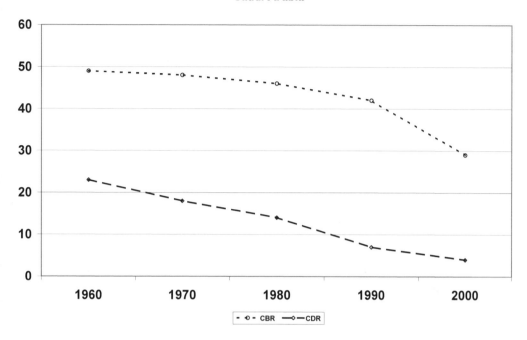

Tunisia

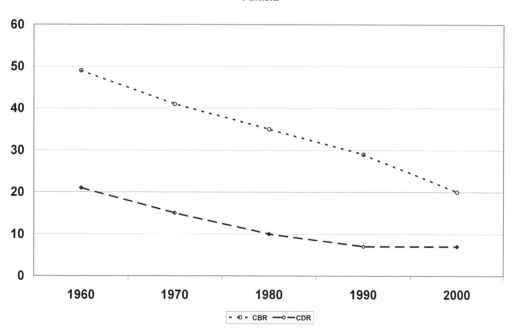

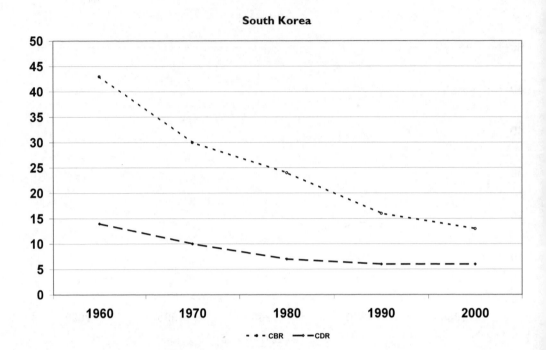

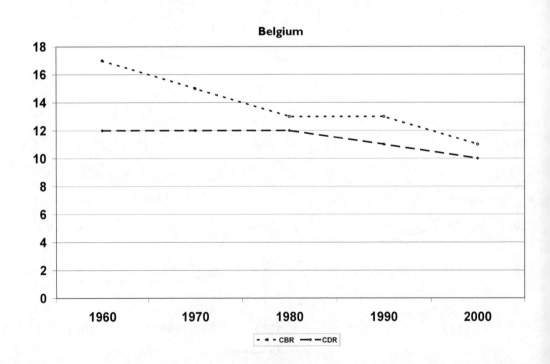

male adult children are generally considered as a minimum, meaning that parents in poor agrarian societies would need to have six to eight adult children.

Table 2.6 The Percentage of the Urban Population within the Total Population in Some Arab Countries, 1950–2000 (%)

Country	Year					
	1950	1960	1970	1980	1990	2000
Egypt	30 (b)	38	42	45	47	43
Syria	32 (b)	37	44	50	50	51
Jordan	38 (d)	43	51	56	61	79
Tunisia	30 (a)	32	44	52	54	66
Morocco	18 (d)	30	35	41	48	56
Algeria	24 (c)	31	40	44	52	57
Saudi Arabia	—	12	49	67	77	86
Kuwait	—	69	72	88	96	96

— No available data.
(a) Data related to 1946.
(b) Data related to 1947.
(c) Data related to 1948.
(d) Data related to 1952.

Sources: WB, *World Development Report*, various years (Published for the WB by Oxford University Press); UN, *Demographic Yearbook*, various issues (New York); UNDP, *Human Development Report*, various years (Published for the UNDP by Oxford University Press); "L'Explosion Démographique en Syrie," *Syrie & Monde Arabe*, Vol. 12, No. 253 (Fevrier 1975).

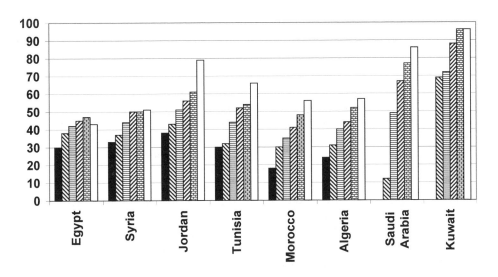

Figure 2.6 The Percentage of the Urban Population within the Total Population in Some Arab Countries, 1950–2000 (%)

(c) Women's status The status of women in any given society has a critical impact on fertility rates.[46] Generally speaking, one can say that as the status of women rises, fertility rates tend to be lower. As long as the woman's role is to raise children and as long as her status in the extended family is a function of the number of her children, mainly males, then *it is in the basic interests of the woman herself* to bear as many children as possible.[47] The main argument of the modern feminist academic literature regarding the issue of family planning is that: "Women must be the subjects, rather than the objects, of population policy – or population policy simply won't work."[48] As examined in Chapter 4, the Arab countries are no different in this respect insofar as when women's status is better, fertility rates are lower. For instance, one of the prominent explanations for the huge fertility difference between Tunisia and Saudi Arabia focuses on the differences in women's status.

(d) The religious–cultural factor Consequent to suffering throughout their history from high infant and child mortality rates, many pre-industrial societies worldwide have adopted social and religious concepts that encourage high fertility, including a ban on contraceptive use of any kind. In many cultures, early marriage of females is a deeply rooted cultural norm. As John Weeks described regarding the Islamic societies: "Once married, there is immediate pressure to bear a child, in order especially to prove the wife's fecundity to her husband's family . . . Youthful marriage is thus part and parcel of the traditional family system, reinforced by (but not necessarily caused by) Islam."[49] Naturally, the vast majority of people conform to the prevailing manners and norms of their own society, including in the area of marriage and fertility. In this respect of "cultural fertility," it should be emphasized, there is no apparent difference between urban and rural societies. This is demonstrated by the fact that even in the GCC societies, which underwent a rapid urbanization process following the discovery of oil, the fertility rates did not decline in accordance with the Demographic Transition theory, despite tremendous socioeconomic development. One major reason for this, it seems, is that these societies have maintained their extended family arrangements and even tribal systems in the cities as well.

Another factor accounting for high fertility rates in traditional societies is the absence of openness regarding sex, including the proper use of contraceptives for married women. Thus, a large number of unwanted pregnancies occur even among married couples in worldwide traditional societies. It can be said in general that the more traditional the society, the lower the willingness to use contraceptives and, consequently, the higher the fertility rates. A related religious-cultural factor reinforcing high fertility is the fatalistic belief that everything is "a decree from Heaven," or *al-Qadar* in Arabic, and that "Allah will provide." As such, it is not seen as necessary or even desirable to attempt to control one's own fertility.

(e) Early age at first marriage Within the overall framework of traditional societies, another important factor contributing to the high fertility rates in the Arab countries was and still is the early marriage of women, which is clearly evident from the population censuses and the demographic surveys conducted in the Arab countries since the 1960s. For example, according to the 1960 Syrian population census, the average age at first marriage for females was 19.51 years. According to the *Syrian Fertility Survey–1978* (*SFS–1978*), 52.5% of the females aged 45–49 who participated in the survey were married before the age of 20.[50]

However, the median and average age at first marriage for women in almost all of the Arab countries has increased considerably during the past two and a half decades, with the exception of Yemen where early age at first marriage continues to be very common.[51] For example, whereas in 1956 only 43% of the women aged 15–24 in Tunisia were unmarried, this percentage dramatically increased to 75% in 1980.[52] By 1995, only 3% of the Tunisian women less than 20 years old were married.[53] One finds a similar phenomenon of increasing age at first marriage among females in Syria. According to the *SMCHS–1993*, the median age at first marriage increased from 18 for women aged 35–39 to 20 for women aged 25–29.[54] Also in Bahrain, the country with the lowest fertility rates among the GCC countries, the median age at first marriage rose from 15 for women currently aged 45–49 to 21 for women currently aged 30–34 and to 23 for women currently aged 25–29.[55]

Nevertheless, it should be remembered that despite the increase in the average age of women at first marriage in most of the Arab countries, early marriages among women are still quite common. For example, according to the *SMCHS–1993*, 2.4% of women aged 20–24 were married between the ages of 10 to 14 years.[56] In the rural areas of Egypt, one can find a similar phenomenon of early marriages among women (see **Chapter 4**).[57] However, in parallel to the trend of increasing age at first marriage, the reproductive period has also increased considerably due to the sharp increase in life expectancy (see below). The length of the reproductive period within the framework of marriage is crucial in Arab-Islamic societies, as births outside the marriage system are very rare. Thus, while in most Arab-Islamic societies the reproductive period within the framework of marriage did not decline despite the increase in the average age of women at first marriage, in Western developed societies, in contrast, the reproductive period within the framework of marriage considerably declined as the average age of women at first marriage has increased by more than 10 years.

(f) High marriage stability Another prominent characteristic of Arab-Islamic societies that has implications for fertility rates is the high stability of marriage, that is, low divorce rates. For example, according to the *SFS–1978*, 92.9% of the women who participated in the survey reported that they were still married to their first husbands. Among the remaining 7.1%, 3.7% were widows and only 3.1% were divorced. It appears from the *SMCHS–1993* data that 95% of the women who participated in the survey were still married to their first husbands.[58] The *Saudi Arabia Child Health Survey*, conducted in 1987, indicated that almost all of the women participating in the survey were still married to their first husbands.[59] One can find the same trend of high marriage stability in other Arab-Islamic societies as well, unlike developed societies in which a considerable percentage of the women at reproductive age are either single or divorced.

(g) Shortage of contraceptive methods and poor knowledge of their proper use According to many studies conducted in developing societies worldwide, including Arab countries, one major reason for high fertility rates is the "unmet need" for both contraceptives themselves and knowledge about their proper use. This argument is enhanced by research conducted among elites, whose fertility rates traditionally were and still are considerably lower than those found among the lower stratums. As noted by Valentine Moghadam: "As women from elite families are generally those with the most access to education and employment, fertility is also variable by class."[60] The

question is whether the lower number of children among elites is a function of their higher accessibility to both the contraceptives themselves and knowledge about their proper use, or whether it should be attributed to other factors, such as lower infant and child mortality rates or absence of the need for a large number of children from a purely economic point of view. Although this question remains open, it would appear that higher accessibility to contraceptives and family planning education would likely reduce fertility rates, given the considerable number of unwanted pregnancies in developing societies (see **Chapter 4**).

(h) Wars and political instability In times of war and intensive international political conflicts, governing authorities tend to be more focused on managing the situation at hand rather than on operating in line with long-term socioeconomic calculations. Moreover, in many cases, it appears that the basic instinct of both the authorities and the public itself is to treat a large population as a security–political asset and not as a socioeconomic burden. The Arab–Israeli conflict, particularly the Palestinian–Israeli conflict, constitutes a good example in which each side has been attempting to increase its population as a political–security asset. Since many of the Arab countries were involved, either directly or indirectly, in the Arab–Israeli conflict or in other regional conflicts (such as the Iraq–Iran War between 1980–1988), the issue of family planning has been widely neglected until very recently (see **Chapter 4**). Higher fertility levels are also desired in cases of local tribal conflicts or in rural areas where the presence of a central authority is lacking or ineffective in enforcing law and order, thereby creating the need for as many fighters as possible.[61] This phenomenon was not limited to the Arab states alone, and similar situations existed during the 1960s and 1970s in Southeast Asia as well as in South America. Thus, for example, in 1977, Shin Hyon Hwack, South Korea's Minister of Health and Social Affairs, and later the Prime Minister, was worried that the success of South Korea's family planning policy would leave the country at a disadvantage in the conflict with North Korea, despite the fact that South Korea's population outnumbered North Korea's by 20 million! Likewise, the Thai leaders were worried that the larger population of the neighboring Vietnam would give them the advantage in times of conflict between the two countries. A similar phenomenon prevailed among South American leaders as well.[62]

(i) The socioeconomic policy A prominent contributor to high fertility rates in many developing countries, including Arab countries, has been the pro-natalist socioeconomic policies that prevailed until the mid-1980s and even into the 1990s in some countries. The policy of socialism adopted during the 1950s and 1960s in many Arab countries, including Egypt, Iraq, Syria, and Tunisia, in effect promoted higher fertility, although not officially. The high subsidies provided for basic foodstuffs, healthcare facilities, educational services at all levels, transportation, electricity, gasoline, housing and the like created a situation in which governments, rather than parents, were responsible for providing the basic needs of children. Moreover, in many rural areas, the new economic policy made it cheaper for parents to raise a child than to pay an employee on their farm. It should be mentioned that even in the Arab countries which did not adopt socialism, mainly the GCC oil-states and Jordan, many of its components were adopted, particularly in the area of massive governmental subsidies and public sector employment. In addition, the GCC oil-states adopted pro-natalist

measures following the October 1973 "oil boom," albeit not officially with the exception of Kuwait (see Chapter 4).

(j) The absence of national family planning programs   The Arab countries, with the exception of Tunisia, were among the last global developing countries to implement effective national family planning programs. In retrospect, it appears that avoiding the adoption of comprehensive national family planning programs contributed to the continuing high fertility rates in many of the Arab countries during the 1970s and 1980s. A major factor accounting for this avoidance was the effects of the "oil boom" in both the oil-rich and the non-oil Arab countries. The overall feeling among many leaders, but also among some researchers, as will be illustrated in Chapter 4, was that the "oil boom" obviated the need to reduce fertility rates and made it possible to substantially improve the standard of living despite the prevailing high fertility.

3.2. Arab Fertility Decline since the Mid-1980s

In the mid-1980s, fertility rates in all of the Arab countries, even in Yemen and Sudan, started to decline. By 1990, the total fertility rate for the region was lower than it had been in 1980, even in the pro-natalist GCC oil-states. This trend was further enhanced throughout the 1990s. By the year 2000, the crude birth rate in Egypt was 26 per 1,000, as compared with 33 per 1,000 in 1990 and 38 in 1980. In Tunisia, the crude birth rate declined from 41 per 1,000 in 1970 to 35 in 1980 and reached the lowest level among its Arab neighbors in 2000, at only 20 per 1,000. A similar trend was also evident in Syria, Jordan, Morocco, and Algeria. Moreover, even in the GCC countries, fertility rates have declined during the past decade (see table 2.5).

What factors are responsible for this general fertility decline among the Arab countries since the mid-1980s? Why has this process taken place almost simultaneously during the second half of the 1980s in almost all the Arab countries, both the pro-natalist oil states and the poorer anti-natalist countries alike? It seems that the following seven factors can provide an explanation to these questions.

(a) Sharp drop in infant and child mortality rates   Since the 1950s, the infant and child mortality rates in all of the Arab countries declined substantially (see below). Due to the declining infant and child mortality rates, the "desired number of children" started to be achieved by a much lower number of births than that of the previous period, with the amount of time depending on how long it took for the survival chances of children to substantially increase in any given society. This period time in effect constituted the second stage of the Demographic Transition, later culminating in a fertility decline – that is, the third Demographic Transition stage.[63] In the Arab countries, it should be noted, the pace and rate of the decline in infant and child mortality rates during the 1970s and 1980s were faster than in most other developing countries worldwide [64] – a direct result of the "oil boom" that led to a sharp improvement both in the standard of living and in health care facilities.

(b) "Economic births."   As noted earlier, in pre-industrial agrarian societies, children constituted an important labor force asset to their families. This situation, however, has rapidly changed with the improvement in salaries, the introduction of the "welfare state" and, most importantly, the enactment of child labor laws and compulsory

education. Whereas children in traditional societies provided economic services to their families, in modern urban societies they represent an increasing economic burden in line with the advance of modernization.[65] In other words, in modern society, in contrast to traditional society, the parents exchanged "quantity" for "quality" in their fertility behavior.

(c) Rapid urbanization   All of the population censuses and demographic surveys conducted in developing societies, including the Arab countries, point to the fact that the fertility rates in the urban centers were and still are much lower than in the rural areas. In the Arab countries, this phenomenon prevails in both the oil-based economies and the poorer non-oil countries alike. For example, according to the *Oman Child Health Survey*, while the fertility rate in the urban centers averaged 5.3 children per woman, it was as high as 9.1 children per woman in the rural areas.[66] A similar fertility trend was found in the *Oman Family Health Survey–1995*, according to which the total fertility rate in the urban centers averaged 6.6 children per woman, as compared with 8.0 children in the rural areas (see table 2.10). One can find a similar fertility gap in the non-oil Arab countries. For example, according to the *SMCHS–1993* data, while the average total fertility rate in the urban centers was 3.57 children per woman, this number increased to 5.06 in the countryside.[67] By 1999, the average urban fertility rate in Syria was 2.99, as compared with 4.41 in the rural areas.[68] Likewise, in Morocco, according to the *National Survey on Population and Health–1992*, the urban total fertility rate was 2.5 children per woman – less than half of the 5.5 children per woman in the rural areas.[69] A similar trend appeared in the demographic survey conducted in the country in 1995.[70]

The reasons for the considerably lower fertility rates in the cities than in the countryside are fourfold. First, due to the fact that children no longer constitute an economic asset to their parents in the cities, the economic motivation to have a large number of children naturally declines. The second factor is the much higher cost of housing in the major cities as compared with the countryside. Third, in both the oil-based and the non-oil Arab countries, the higher education system is concentrated in the major cities, making for greater accessibility to higher education in those areas. The overall result is a higher than average women's educational level in the cities. Since women's educational level represents one of the two paramount factors impacting on fertility rates (see below), the increased percentage of the urban population within the total population has led to a decline in the national average fertility rates. Fourth, women's employment patterns in the cities are not conducive to taking small children with them to their jobs, as they tend to do on the household farm.

It should be emphasized, however, that in terms of the "economic cost/benefit of small families" between the urban centers and the rural areas, there are still exceptions in the lower urban strata, consisting largely of rural migrants whose children are working and serving as major contributors to their family income. These children are usually employed in the "third sector" or the "informal sector," such as shoe-shining, selling newspapers, coffee and tea in the markets, and carrying suitcases and hailing taxis for tourists in hotels. On one of my visits to Cairo, there was a little child around 10 years old in the front of my hotel who "jumped" on every visitor, offering to carry suitcases or summon a taxi. Monitoring his activities from the sidelines, I calculated that this child earned much more money in tips than the average salary for an adult man in the public sector. No doubt, this child was a major contributor to his family income. In such cases, all cost/benefit calculations of raising children in the cities are rendered totally irrelevant. According to World Bank figures, more than 18% of the children in Egypt aged 10 to 14 were working in 1980, though this rate declined to 11% in 1996.[71] Still, children's employment is a common phenomenon in the poorer Arab countries and – according to data collected by the Arab League – one that is expanding, particularly in Morocco, Tunisia, Egypt, Jordan, Yemen, Syria, and Lebanon.[72] This recent rise in child labor is the result of increasing unemployment and decreasing real wages (see Chapter 3), forcing children in the lower strata to contribute to their family income.

(d) *Improvement in female education* The sharp improvement in women's educational level in each of the Arab countries since the 1960s, as one can clearly see in tables 2.7 and 2.8, is among the most important factors accounting for the declining fertility in the Arab countries since the mid-1980s.

Table 2.7 Literacy Rates among Males and Females in Some Arab Countries, 1970, 1985, 2000–2001 (%)

Country	Year					
	1970		**1985**		**2000–2001**	
	Males	Females	Males	Females	Males	Females
Egypt	50	20	59	30	67	44
Syria	60	20	76	43	88	61
Jordan	64	29	87	63	95	84
Tunisia	44	17	68	41	81	61
Morocco	34	10	45	22	62	36
Algeria	39	11	63	37	78	57
Saudi Arabia	15	2	71	31	84	67
Kuwait	65	42	76	63	85	80
Oman	—	—	47	12	80	62

— No data available.

Sources: Population Reference Bureau, *Population Reference Bureau Data Finder* [http://www.worldpop.org/datafinder.htm]; UNDP, *Human Development Report – 1990* (Published for the UNDP by Oxford University Press, 1990).

From the population censuses and demographic surveys conducted during the past four decades in developing societies, including the Arab countries, it appears that a paramount factor determining fertility behavior is that of women's educational level. For example, according to the *Egypt Demographic and Health Survey–1995* (*EDHS–1995*), while the total fertility rate for illiterate women averaged 4.5 children per woman, this rate sharply declined to 3.0 children among women with secondary education and above.[73] A similar fertility gap in line with women's educational level appeared in the *Egypt Demographic and Health Survey–2000* (*EDHS–2000*), in which the average total fertility rate for women without any formal education averaged 4.1 children per woman, as compared with 3.2 children for women with secondary education and above (see table 2.9).

Table 2.8 Number of Enrolled Students in Universities per 100,000 in Some Arab Countries, 1965–1996

Country	1965 Males	1965 Females	1980 Males	1980 Females	1990 Males	1990 Females	1996 Males	1996 Females
Egypt	936	246	2,205	1,048	1,869	1,025	2,316 (c)	1,472 (c)
Syria	994	212	2,231	946	2,166	1,402	1,814 (b)	1,297 (b)
Jordan	215	108	1,712	1,577	2,072	2,402	2,587	2,492
Tunisia	195	45	685	297	1,005	670	1,456	1,201
Morocco	120	17	886	273	1,353	773	1,332(b)	931 (b)
Algeria	102	27	1,081	508	—	—	1,466 (c)	1,000 (c)
Saudi Arabia	103	4	863	393	955	965	1,396	1,528
Kuwait	322 (a)	395 (a)	739	1,330	—	—	1,926 (c)	2,590 (c)
Bahrain	—	—	555	542	1,071	1,859	1,056 (b)	1,972 (b)
Oman	—	—	2	3	354	340	539	524
Qatar	—	—	594	1,682	602	2,871	617	3,278

— No data available.
(a) Data related to 1970.
(b) Data related to 1994.
(c) Data related to 1995.

Sources: UNESCO, *Statistical Yearbook*, various issues, 1967–1998 (Paris).

Table 2.9 Total Fertility Rates and Mean Number of Children Ever-born in Egypt, According to Place of Residence and Female Educational Level, 2000

Background Characteristics	Total Fertility Rate (15–49)	Mean Number of Children Ever-born to Women (aged 40–49)
Place of Residence		
Urban	3.09	4.32
Rural	3.88	6.03
Female Educational Level		
No education	4.09	6.01
Primary incomplete	3.78	5.14
Primary complete/Some secondary	3.26	4.53
Secondary complete/Higher	3.22	3.01
Total	**3.53**	**5.15**

Source: Arab Republic of Egypt, Ministry of Health and Population, National Population Council and ORC Macro, *Egypt Demographic and Health Survey – 2000*, by Fatma El-Zanaty and Ann A. Way (Cairo, January 2001), p. 46, table 4.2.

A similar gap was prevalent in the other Arab countries as well. According to the *Oman Family Health Survey–1995*, while the total fertility rate among illiterate women averaged 8.6 children per woman, this rate declined to 4.8 children among women with preparatory education and even further to 3.8 children per woman among those with secondary education and above (see table 2.10). A comparable trend can also be found in the *Kuwait Child Health Survey*, conducted in 1987.[74] Thus, in terms of the huge fertility gap created by women's educational level, there were no differences between the rich-oil and the poorer Arab countries.[75]

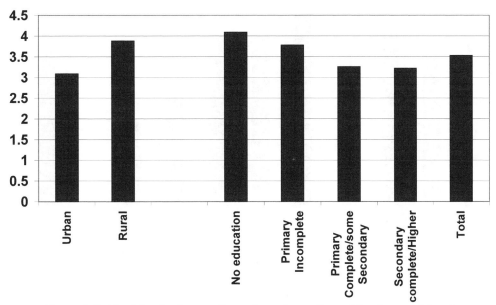

Figure 2.7   Total Fertility Rates in Egypt, According to Place of Residence and Female Educational Level, 2000

Table 2.10   Total Fertility Rate and Mean Number of Children Ever-born in Oman, According to Place of Residence and Female Educational Level, 1995

Background Characteristics	Total Fertility Rate (15–49)	Mean Number of Children Ever-born to Women (aged 40–49)
Place of Residence		
Urban	6.60	8.68
Rural	7.95	8.38
Female Educational Level		
Illiterate	8.61	8.75
Less than primary	7.59	8.39
Primary	7.51	8.14
Preparatory	4.75	5.25
Secondary and above	3.81	3.95
Total	**7.05**	**8.57**

Source: Sultanate of Oman, Ministry of Health, *Oman Family Health Survey-1995*, edited by Ali J. M. Sulaiman, Asya al-Riyami, and Samir Farid (Muscat, 1996), p. 30, table 7.3.

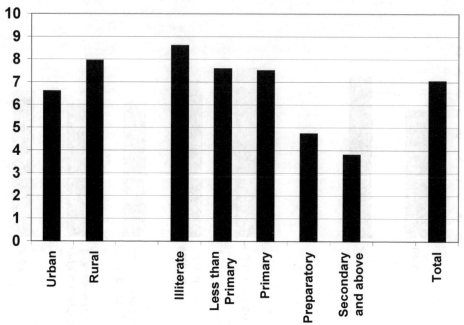

Figure 2.8   Total Fertility Rate in Oman, According to Place of Residence and Female Educational Level, 1995

The academic literature on the correlation between fertility rates and women's educational level in developing countries is immense, not only in demography and economics but also in the feminist and gender literature. Overall, the high correlation between women's educational level and fertility level is attributed mainly to the following six factors:

1   Generally speaking, the higher the woman's educational level, the greater her tendency to marry at an older age, in most cases after the completion of her education. This means that if she attended a university, she is more likely to wait at least until her mid-twenties to marry.
2   The higher the woman's educational level, the greater her tendency to work outside the home. In turn, since having a large number of small children acts as a hindrance to a woman's career, women working outside the household tend to have fewer children. According to the Syrian 1970 census, for example, the average number of children ever born to women who were economically active in non-agricultural occupations was 3.9, as compared with 5.4 on average among women who were engaged in agriculture.[76]
3   Since there is a high correlation between educational level and salary level, the "lost income" of educated women for each additional child born is higher than that of uneducated women, particularly those working in the family fields.
4   Educated women usually better understand the correlation between the number of children in the family and their standard of living. As a result, they tend to bear fewer children.
5   Educated women tend to be more aware of the option of family planning and thus have better knowledge of contraceptive methods and their proper use.[77]

6 Educated women are more competent in taking care of their children, who are, as a result, less exposed to illness. Consequently, the mortality rates among infants of educated women are considerably lower than those among infants of uneducated mothers. For example, according to the *Jordan Population and Family Health Survey–1990* (*JPFHS–1990*), while the infant mortality rate of illiterate mothers was 38.7 per 1,000 live births, this rate declined to only 23.9 per 1,000 live births among mothers with higher education.[78] Educated women are thus more inclined to have a smaller number of children because they are not as fearful about losing their offspring.

The only exception to the high correlation between women's educational level and fertility level among the non-oil Arab Middle Eastern societies is that of the Palestinians in the Occupied Territories, particularly in the Gaza Strip. Despite the average high educational level of the women there, the fertility rates remain very high – in fact the highest worldwide. According to ESCWA figures, by the year 2000 the crude birth rate in the Gaza Strip was 46.5 per 1,000, while the total fertility rate was as high as 6.93. In the West Bank, although the fertility rate is lower than in the Gaza Strip, it still remains high relative to both Arab and international averages, with a crude birth rate of 41.5 per 1,000 and a total fertility rate of 5.6 in 2000.[79]

The reasons for the continuing high fertility rates among the Palestinians in the Occupied Territories despite the marked decline in the infant and child mortality rates and the sharp rise in women's educational level are both political and economic. From the economic point of view, the aid policy of UNRWA was and still is based on the number of family members. Thus, one finds much higher fertility rates among the Palestinian refugees than among the settled population in the Palestinian Occupied Territories. According to a survey conducted by the Palestinian Central Bureau of Statistics (PCBS) in April-July 1995, while the average total fertility rate in the refugee camps (in both the West Bank and the Gaza Strip) was 6.84 children per woman, this rate declined to 6.18 among the rural population and 5.57 among the urban population.[80]

Philippe Fargues recently argued that the reason for their continuing high fertility rates among the Palestinians in the Occupied Territories is the low female labor force participation rates under the Israeli occupation, particularly since the onset of the first *Intifada* in December 1987. Since the improvement in women's educational level did not bring about an increase in their labor force participation rates, there was no subsequent decline in the fertility rates, as in other developing societies.[81] Indeed, according to the December 1997 Palestinian population census, the labor force participation rate among females 15 years of age and over was 9.3% in the West Bank and only 5.2% in the Gaza Strip[82] – lower than any of the Arab countries, even Saudi Arabia and Kuwait (see **Chapter 3**). From a political point of view, the continuing high fertility rates of the Palestinians in the Occupied Territories is attributable to the fact that the Palestinian leadership treats rapid population growth as a political asset in order to achieve an independent state – hence the absence of any kind of family planning program.

(e) Increasing employment opportunities for women   In all of the developing countries worldwide, including both the oil-based and the non-oil Arab countries, there is a marked correlation between women's employment and their fertility rates. The higher the economic active participation rate of women, the lower the fertility rate. Overall,

as will be examined in Chapter 3, during the past two decades there has been a steady rise in the economic active participation rates of women in the Arab countries. As discussed above in relation to Palestinian women in the Occupied Territories, the contradiction between the high educational level of the young GCC women, on the one hand, and their high fertility rates, on the other hand, can be explained by the various limitations, both social and legal, on women's employment. In contrast to the GCC countries, Tunisia's women have a lower educational level but a much higher crude economic active participation rate – in fact the highest among the Arab countries – thus explaining Tunisia's much lower fertility rates.

(f) Increasing family planning activities and contraceptive prevalence rates   Since the mid-1980s, following the end of the "oil decade," governmental activities in the area of family planning, both direct and indirect, were largely intensified. Even in countries such as Syria, Jordan, Oman and Algeria, which had previously implemented hidden indirect anti-natalist measures, the family planning activities became more open and targeted. The Middle Eastern experience in the area of family planning, as will be examined in Chapter 4, reveals a high correlation between the implementation of family planning programs and the rate of fertility decline.

Table 2.11   Contraceptive Prevalence Rate (all methods) among Married Women in Some Arab Countries, 1983, 1993–2001 (%)

Country	1983	1993–2001
Egypt	30	56.1(h)
Jordan	26	52.6(e)
Syria	23	39.6(a)
Tunisia	35	59.7(b)
Morocco	26	58.4(e)
Algeria	7	64.0(h)
Saudi Arabia	—	31.8(d)
Kuwait	—	52.0(g)
Bahrain	—	61.8(c)
Oman	—	23.7(c)
Qatar	—	43.2(f)

— No data available.
(a) Data related to 1993.
(b) Data related to 1994–1995.
(c) Data related to 1995 (nationals only).
(d) Data related to 1996 (nationals only).
(e) Data related to 1997.
(f) Data related to 1998 (nationals only).
(g) Data related to 1999 (nationals only).
(h) Data related to 2001.

Sources: Population Reference Bureau (PRB), *2001 World Population Data Sheets* [http://www.worldpop.org/datafinder.htm]; idem, *Family Planning Worldwide* (New York, 2002); WB, *World Development Report*, various issues (Published for the WB by Oxford University Press).

The clearest expression of the declining fertility in the Arab countries during the past two decades is the sharp increase in their contraceptive prevalence rates.[83] The highest contraceptive prevalence rate recorded among the Arab countries was 60% in Tunisia in 1994-1995. The lowest rate was 24% in Oman in 1995, though it has probably increased slightly since then as a result of the expanded anti-natalist measures taken by the Omani authorities (see Chapter 4). Also in Saudi Arabia, the contraceptive prevalence rate has remained very low, at only 32% in 1996 (see table 2.11).

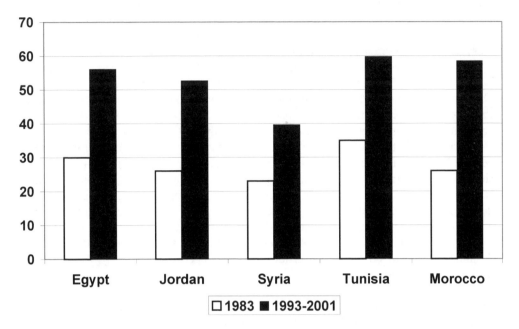

Figure 2.9 Contraceptive Prevalence Rate (all methods) among Married Women in Some Arab Countries, 1983, 1993–2001 (%)

(g) Changing socioeconomic policies The substantial macroeconomic policy changes in the entire world during the past two decades, namely, the adoption of the market economy approach at the expense of *étatism* and socialism, have constituted a major factor in fertility decline among many developing countries worldwide, including the Arab countries. The basic assumption of the capitalism approach is that the first and foremost responsibility for supporting children lies with the *parents*, as opposed to the *state* under the socialist approach. In this regard, it must be recognized that in many of the Arab countries, such as Egypt, Tunisia, and recently also Syria and Yemen, the declining fertility rates and the withdrawal from the socialist socioeconomic policy occurred simultaneously. The adoption of the market economy involved the narrowing or even complete abolishment of many state subsidies, leading to an overall increase in the cost of raising children. As a result, parents have been forced to bear fewer children in order to fulfill their responsibilities of providing for the children's basic needs.

4   The Revolution of Mortality Rates in the Arab Countries

The high natural increase rates in the Arab countries, as in other developing societies worldwide, is due to the sharp decline in death rates. The causes for the revolution in the death rates in the Middle East were many and varied. It was a process that started during the first half of the nineteenth century at a slow pace, first in Egypt and later spreading over the other regions of the Ottoman Empire in line with economic development and the adoption of market agriculture. At that time, the most important factor accounting for the declining death rates in the Middle East was the improvement in the roads, which enabled the transfer of food from one location to another in considerable quantities for the first time, thereby providing the means to overcome the starvation and accompanying disease that had previously blighted the area. Another important factor was the stabilization of the political regimes in the area, first in Egypt under the rule of Muhammad 'Ali (1805–1848) and later in the other regions of the Ottoman Empire as part of the *Tanzimat*. Overall, according to prevailing estimates, the crude death rate in the Middle East declined from 42–44 per 1,000 people at the end of the eighteenth century to 32–34 per 1,000 at the end of the nineteenth century.[84]

During the first half of the twentieth century, the rapid decline in death rates in the Middle East was, first and foremost, the result of the sharp improvement and expansion of health care services, including preventive health services. The rise in the standard of living also constituted an important factor contributing to the declining death rates in the Middle East during the first half of the twentieth century. For example, Egypt's crude death rate declined from 28.4 per 1,000 in 1907 to 21.4 per 1,000 in 1947.[85] Thus, the decline of Egypt's crude death rates was a slow but steady process. A similar process of slow decline in crude death rates occurred in other Arab countries during the Mandatory period.

During the second half of the twentieth century, however, the process of declining crude death rates strongly accelerated. By the end of the century, the crude death rates in the Arab countries, with the exception of Sudan and Yemen, were among the lowest worldwide, with a prevailing crude death rate of 5–7 per 1,000 people. Egypt's crude death rate declined from 17 per 1,000 in 1960 to 7 per 1,000 in the year 2000. In Jordan, the decline was from 20 to 5 per 1,000 and in Tunisia from 21 to 7 per 1,000 during the corresponding period. The decline in the crude death rates was the most prominent worldwide in the GCC oil countries, which turned from poor to rich states within a very short period of time of only two decades. At the same time, fertility rates have remained high, leading to a very wide-based age pyramid. In the case of Oman, the crude death rate declined from as high as 28 per 1,000 in 1960 to 13 in 1980 and only 4 in 2000. By the year 2000, Kuwait had achieved the lowest crude death rate worldwide, with only 3 per 1,000 for the indigenous population. The other GCC countries have achieved low crude death rates as well (see table 2.5).

Three components contributed to the sharp decline in the crude death rates among the Arab countries during the second half of the twentieth century. First was the marked drop in infant and child mortality rates and second was the considerable increase in life expectancy, which together constitute the two most prominent indicators for the overall health situation of any given society. Third was the very young age structure, which was a direct consequence of the prolonged high natural increase rates (see Chapter 3). In the following section, the changes in these three components during the second half of the twentieth century will be examined in more detail.

(a) The sharp decline in infant (0–1) and child (1–5) mortality rates   Until the mid-twentieth century, infant and child mortality rates in the Arab countries were very high, amounting to almost one-third of live births. Since the period 1950–1955, when the average under-5 mortality rates in the Arab countries was 312 per 1,000 live births, there has been a dramatic drop in these two indicators.[86] By 1999, the under-5 mortality

Table 2.12 Infant Mortality Rates and Life Expectancy (both sexes) in Some Arab Countries, non-Arab Developing Countries, and Developed Countries, 1960–2000

	1960		**1970**		**1980**		**1990**		**2000**	
	IM	LE	IM	LE	IM	LE	IM	LE	IM	LE
Arab Countries										
Algeria	165	47	139	53	98	59	67	65	50	70
Tunisia	159	48	127	54	72	62	44	67	22	70
Morocco	163	47	120	52	99	56	67	62	41	68
Egypt	179	46	144	51	124	55	60	66	46	67
Jordan	135	47	90	52	58	63	40	69	30	70
Syria	132	50	98	55	67	65	43	66	25	71
Iraq	139	47	104	51	78	56	63	65	103	58
Saudi Arabia	185	43	128	52	91	60	65	65	18	73
Oman	193	39	158	44	128	49	66(a)	61(a)	18	72
Kuwait	89	60	49	66	34	70	14(a)	75(a)	9	76
Bahrain	128	56	74	62	75	64	33(a)	71(a)	16	74
Non-Arab Developing Countries										
Turkey	190	50	150	57	109	62	60	65	59	70
South Korea	85	54	43	60	26	65	17	70	5	75
Brazil	116	55	95	59	67	63	57	66	32	68
Mexico	92	57	79	62	51	65	39	70	25	73
Pakistan	163	43	118	48	124	50	103	58	85	60
Developed Countries										
France	27	70	18	72	10	74	7	76	4	79
UK	22	71	18	72	12	73	8	76	6	78
Sweden	17	73	11	75	7	75	6	77	3	80
Belgium	31	70	21	71	12	73	8	75	4	78

IM = Infant mortality rate per 1,000 live births.
LE = Life expectancy at birth (both sexes).
(a) Data related to 1988 (nationals only).

Sources: WB, *World Tables, 1984–1995*, various issues (Published for the WB by Johns Hopkins University Press); idem, *World Development Report*, 1978–2002, various issues (Published for the WB by Oxford University Press); ECWA/ESCWA, *Survey of the Economic and Social Developments in the ECWA/ESCWA Region*, various issues (Baghdad, Amman, and New York); idem, *Demographic and Related Socio-Economic Data Sheets for Countries of the Economic and Social Commission for Western Asia*, 1978–2001, various issues (Beirut, Baghdad, and Amman); UNICEF, *The State of the World's Children*, various issues (Published for UNICEF by Oxford University Press); UNDP, *Human Development Report*, 1994–2002, various issues (Published for the UNDP by Oxford University Press).

rate per 1,000 live births was 62 in Morocco, 54 in Egypt, and 31 in Jordan. The highest rate among all of the Arab countries was in Yemen, with 97 deaths per 1,000 live births.[87] The major factor for the sharp decline in under-5 mortality rates was the sharp decline in infant mortality rates. Whereas the average infant mortality rate of the Arab countries during the period 1950–1955 was 181 per 1,000 live births, this rate declined to 81 on average during the years 1980–1985.[88] By the year 2000, the infant mortality rate was 46 per 1,000 live births in Egypt, 50 in Algeria, 41 in Morocco, and as high as 103 in Iraq – a direct result of the overall poor socioeconomic conditions following the sanctions imposed on the country in 1991.[89] The best achievements in this area were made in the GCC countries, whose infant mortality rates in 2000 were 16 per 1,000 live births in Bahrain and as low as 9 per 1,000 in Kuwait (see table 2.12). Thus, the infant mortality rates in the Arab countries declined from almost one-fifth of live births in the mid-twentieth century to about 4% at the end of the century and less than 1% in Kuwait!

(b) The increase in life expectancy During the 1920s and 1930s, the average life expectancy at birth in Arab Middle Eastern societies was approximately 40 years. For example, the life expectancy of the Arabs in Mandatory Palestine averaged 38 years (for men and women) during the years 1924–1926 and increased to 50 on average during the period 1940–1942. In the Hashemite Emirate of Jordan, the life expectancy at birth in 1930 was only 38 years.[90] Since then, the life expectancy at birth in all of the Arab countries, similar to many other developing societies worldwide, has sharply increased, rising to 47 years in Iraq and Jordan, 48 in Tunisia, 50 in Syria, and 60 in Kuwait by 1960. By the year 2000, life expectancy at birth reached 67 in Egypt, 68 in Morocco, 70 in Algeria, Tunisia and Jordan, and as high as 76 in Kuwait – the highest of all the Arab countries. Thus, at the end of the twentieth century, life expectancy in the Arab countries was 25 years higher on average than it had been at mid-century and more than 30 years higher than during the Mandatory period.

(c) Young age structure A direct consequence of the prolonged high natural increase rates in the Arab countries was the creation of a very young age structure. This phenomenon will be examined in greater depth in Chapter 3. The implications of a wide-based age pyramid – namely, a high percentage of the young (under-20) population in parallel to extremely low percentage of the older population (over 65) – for the crude death rates is a natural decline, given that the highest mortality rates are concentrated in the older population. The lowest worldwide crude death rate in Kuwait was a combined result of low infant and child mortality rates, high life expectancy, and above all, a wide-based age pyramid.

In addition to the overall improvement in the standard of living due to advancing socioeconomic development, the sharp decline in death rates among the Arab countries during the second half of the twentieth century was also the result of the marked improvement in health care services and facilities. This was achieved mainly through the declining ratio of both physicians/population and hospital-beds/population, despite the rapid population growth. For example, by 1995 there was one physician for every 595 people in Egypt, as compared with one for every 2,250 people in 1960. In Tunisia, the physician/population ratio declined from one physician for every 10,030 people in 1960 to one for every 1,429 people in 1998. As with the other socioeconomic indicators, the health services in the GCC oil-states were the most

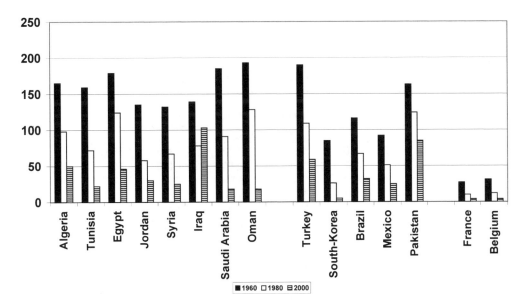

Figure 2.10 Infant mortality Rates in Some Arab Countries, non-Arab Developing Countries, and Developed Countries, 1960–2000

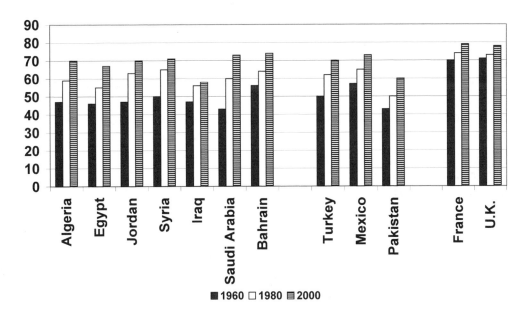

Figure 2.11 Life Expectancy at Birth (both sexes) in Some Arab Countries, non-Arab Developing Countries, and Developed Countries, 1960–2000

Table 2.13   Average Number of Persons per Physician in Some Arab Countries, non-Arab Developing Countries, and Developed Countries, 1960–1998

	1960	1970	1980	1990	1998
		Year			
Arab Countries					
Egypt	2,250	1,900	970	1,320	595(b)
Syria	4,630	3,860	2,270	1,160	694(d)
Jordan	5,800	2,480	1,700	770	602
Tunisia	10,030	5,930	3,690	1,870	1,429
Morocco	9,410	13,090	10,750	4,840	2,174
Algeria	5,530	8,100	2,630	2,330	1,182(b)
Saudi Arabia	16,370	7,460	1,670	660	602
Kuwait	1,210	1,050	570	—	529
Oman	31,180	8,380	1,900	1,060	752(d)
Non-Arab Developing Countries					
Iran	3,860	3,270	6,090	3,140	1,176(c)
Turkey	2,800	5,930	1,630	1,870	826(d)
Brazil	2,210	2,030	1,080(a)	—	786(c)
Developed Countries					
France	930	750	580	350	330
Italy	640	550	340	210	181
Sweden	1,050	730	490	370	322
Belgium	780	650	400	310	253(d)
United States	750	630	520	420	358(b)
Canada	910	680	550	450	142(b)

— No data available.

Note: The data on physicians for the period of 1995–1998 are taken from the World Health Organization database, while the population data are taken from the U.S. Census Bureau.

(a) Data related to 1984.
(b) Data related to 1995.
(c) Data related to 1996.
(d) Data related to 1997.

Sources: WB, *World Development Report*, 1978–1999/2000, various issues (Published for the WB by Oxford University Press); WHO (World Health Organization), *WHO Statistics, Estimates for Health Personnel* [http://www.who.int/whosis/health_personnel/health_personnel.cfm].

impressive following the October 1973 "oil boom." Among these countries, the most dramatic improvement was in Oman, where the physician/population ratio declined from one physician for every 31,180 people in 1960 to one for every 1,900 people in 1980 and one for every 752 people in 1997. However, as in many other social indicators, also in the area of health services, Kuwait achieved the lowest physician/population ratio, with one physician for every 529 people in 1998 (see table 2.13).

As for the hospital-beds/population ratio, the improvement was considerable as well, although less than in the physician/population ratio. In this respect as well, the best achievement was in the GCC countries. For example, there was only one hospital in Qatar in 1945 and two in Kuwait in 1949, and prior to the establishment of the UAE in 1971, health services existed only in the cities of Abu-Dhabi and Dubai.[91] By the end of the twentieth century, however, the indigenous GCC populations enjoyed one of the top health services worldwide, with health centers spread throughout the area, including hospitals with the most advanced facilities. Not less important is the wide coverage of health services provided to the indigenous populations almost free of charge, including treatments abroad in cases where the necessary treatment can not be provided in local hospitals.

5 Conclusions

The decline in the crude death rates since the nineteenth century, and particularly during the second half of the twentieth century, in parallel to the continuously high fertility rates, led to the steady increase in the natural increase rates of Arab societies through the mid-1980s. However, since the mid-1980s, the decline in the fertility rates has been sharper than the decline in the death rates, leading to a marked drop in the natural increase rates. Nevertheless, despite the considerable decline in fertility rates, by the end of the twentieth century, Tunisia and Lebanon were the only Arab countries that succeeded in reaching a natural increase rate of less than 2% and a total fertility rate close to the target of replacement-level fertility.

Thus, in the mid-twentieth century, there was great similarity among all of the Arab countries in terms of their demographic characteristics – namely, high crude birth and death rates – with only minor differences from one country to another. Yet, by the end of the century, huge demographic gaps existed between them. Thus, at the dawn of the twenty-first century, four different demographic structures prevailed in the Arab countries. The first group includes only Tunisia and Lebanon, which have achieved a total fertility rate of less than 2.5 children per woman and are approaching the target of replacement-level fertility. The second group includes Egypt, Morocco, Algeria, Syria and, recently, also Jordan – countries that have succeeded in substantially lowering their fertility rates to between 3.3 to 3.7 children per woman through mainly anti-natalist measures, either direct or indirect, combined with macroeconomic policy changes. The third group includes Sudan and Yemen, which are still characterized by high crude birth and death rates due to their poor socioeconomic condition. The fourth group includes the GCC oil-states, with the exception of Bahrain, which have created a unique demographic phenomenon of extremely low crude death rates and high fertility rates as a consequence of their unique economic and political structure following the October 1973 "oil boom." In effect, the GCC societies are rich enough to reduce the death rates at all levels, but on the other hand traditional enough to maintain high fertility rates.

In retrospect, three prominent differences in the course of the demographic transition can be identified between the developing countries, including the Arab countries, and the Western developed countries:

(a) The period the transition   In the Western European developed countries, the demographic transition "stretched" over almost two centuries, namely, from the late eighteenth century until the 1960s. In contrast, among the developing countries, including the Arab countries, the demographic transition only started in the mid-twentieth century; yet, some of the countries, such as South Korea and Singapore, had already reached the end of the third stage – namely, low natural increase rates due to both low fertility and mortality rates – by the mid-1980s, in less than three decades.[92] Among the Arab countries, Tunisia and Lebanon achieved a total fertility rate close to the replacement-level of 2.5 and 2.4 children per woman, respectively, by the year 2000, declining from 7.1 and 6.3, respectively, in 1960 (see table 2.5).

(b) The scale of the transition   In none of the Western European developed countries did the crude birth rates ever reach, in any stage of their recorded demographic history, such a high level as those prevailing in many developing countries, including all of the Arab countries, during the mid-twentieth century – namely, a crude birth rate of over 45 per 1,000 people and a total fertility rate of 7 children per woman, and in some countries even higher. For example, the crude birth rate in Britain at the beginning of the nineteenth century was estimated at 35 per 1,000.[93] A century later, during the period 1908–1913, the crude birth rate in England and Wales averaged 24.9 per 1,000 people, while the natural increase rate was slightly above 1%.[94] This means that the natural increase rates of the Western European countries at the beginning of their third stage in the Demographic Transition were only one-third those prevailing in the Arab countries in the early 1980s at the beginning of their third stage in the Demographic Transition process.

(c) Governmental involvement in family planning   Generally speaking, in the developed countries worldwide, the demographic transition process occurred without substantial state intervention. It was a long and naturally occurring process, moving from one stage of the Demographic Transition to the next purely as a result of socioeconomic and political changes. In the developing countries, on the other hand, although the changes in socioeconomic conditions and policies affected fertility patterns, a major contributor to fertility decline was the introduction of national family planning programs aimed at accelerating the pace of the fertility decline relative to that of socioeconomic development (see Chapter 4).

3 | "Jobs for the Boys (and Girls)"
The Emergence of the Employment Dilemma

"Unemployment is a bomb that will explode in the Arab region sooner or later if we are not prepared to confront it now."

Husni Mubarak, March 2001[1]

In terms of unemployment in the Arab countries, it is not hard to detect a common theme. As far back as the end of the nineteenth century, the Egyptian government considered bringing Chinese workers in order to fill a labor shortage. Since its independence and until the mid-1970s, the Syrian authorities implemented a pro-natalist policy, due at least in part to a labor shortage. Likewise, from the October 1973 "oil boom" through the 1990s, the GCC oil-states implemented a pro-natalist policy and were forced to import millions of foreign workers due to their labor shortage. In the mid-1970s, unemployment in Jordan was less than 2%, and it became a labor-importing country in order to avoid a labor shortage. During the 1980s, both Iraq and Iran implemented pro-natalist policies, and Iraq also imported more than a million Egyptian workers due to its labor shortage. By the dawn of the twenty-first century, the open unemployment rate in each of the Arab countries, both the oil-based and the non-oil, was more than 15%, and in some countries even more than 20%. This is not to mention the huge disguised unemployment and underemployment rates.

The emergence of the Arab employment dilemma can be traced to the high natural increase rates in the Arab countries during the second half of the twentieth century, with their tremendously devastating socioeconomic consequences. While these negative results affected, first and foremost, the poorer overpopulated non-oil Arab countries, the high natural increase rates became a socioeconomic problem starting from the late 1980s in the Arab oil-bases countries as well, particularly in Saudi Arabia and Oman – the two most populous GCC countries. By the end of the twentieth century, it can be said that all of the Arab countries, with the exception of the tiny GCC oil economies, namely, Qatar, Kuwait, and the United Arab Emirates, were suffering to some extent from what has been called "the overpopulation syndrome" or "the overpopulation trap." This term refers to a situation in which the population is increasing faster than the available economic resources, that is, the GDP growth rate. As a result, the per capita GDP and income decline, leading to a deterioration in the overall standard of living. This has been the situation since the 1960s in a considerable number of Arab countries, notably in Egypt, Jordan, Syria, Yemen, Sudan, Algeria, and Morocco. A "softer" variant of the "overpopulation trap" is a situation in which economic growth is still outpacing population growth, but at the same time rapid population growth is hampering faster economic development. This is the situation characterizing Saudi Arabia and, to a lesser degree, also Oman during the past decade.

The negative results of the rapid population growth in the overpopulated Arab countries were the main reasons for the creation of the "vicious circle of poverty" in these countries. The major links in this "vicious circle" are as follows: In a developing economy with high natural increase rates, the saving capability of the vast majority of the population is limited, due to a very low level of per capita income, in many cases only slightly above "the starvation line." The low income level is the consequence of a very low level of productivity in both the rural and the urban economies. The low productivity is the reflection of a low level of investment caused by low saving rates, which, in turn, leads to high fertility rates due to the low per capita income.[2]

The negative socioeconomic consequences of the rapid population growth in the Arab countries are many and varied. This chapter concentrates on the most devastating result of the high natural increase rates in the Arab countries during the second half of the twentieth century: the emergence of a "structural employment problem," referring to a situation in which the unemployment rates continue to rise even during periods of relatively high economic growth rates.

I   The Consequences of the Young Age Structure

The result of the prolonged high natural increase rates was the creation of a wide-based age pyramid.[3] Already in 1960, the under-15 population constituted 42.8% of the total population in Egypt, 46.3% in Syria, and 45.6% in Jordan in 1961. During the 1960s and the 1970s, due to the rise in natural increase rates as a result of the declining crude death rates (see Chapter 2), the percentage of the young population within the total population increased in all of the Arab countries. For example, in 1979, the percentage of the under-15 population within the total population increased to 50.7% in Jordan from 45.6% two decades earlier. A similar process, as one can see in table 3.1, occurred in the other Arab countries, with the exception of Tunisia whose fertility rates had already started to decline in the 1970s.

In the developed countries, on the contrary, the fertility rates were very low already in the 1960s and continued to decline in many of them to below replacement-level in the 1970s and the 1980s. At the same time, the life expectancy was steadily increasing. Consequently, the percentage of the young population within the total population has been gradually decreasing over the past four decades. Thus, for example, in Norway, the percentage of the under-15 population decreased from 25.8% in 1960 to 21.3% in 1982 and reached as low as 19.8% in 1998. In the other Western European countries, the same process has occurred.

Table 3.1 The Age Structure of Some Arab Countries, non-Arab Developing Countries, and Western European Countries, 1960, 1980, 2000

Country	Age Group		
	0–14	15–64	65+
	1960		
Egypt	42.8	53.7	3.5
Jordan (a)	45.6	50.6	3.8
Syria	46.3	48.9	4.8
Tunisia (c)	46.3	50.1	3.6
Morocco	44.3	51.7	4.0
Saudi Arabia	—	—	—
Oman	—	—	—
Iran (c)	46.1	50.0	3.9
Pakistan (a)	44.5	45.9	6.0 (1)
South Korea (b)	42.4	52.0	5.6 (1)
Denmark (b)	24.3	64.8	10.9
Norway	25.8	63.1	11.1
	1980		
Egypt (f)	50.8	45.6	3.6
Jordan (d)	50.7	46.6	2.7
Syria (e)	49.3	46.3	4.4
Tunisia (e)	41.8	53.8	4.4
Morocco (f)	42.2	53.9	3.9
Saudi Arabia	—	—	—
Oman	—	—	—
Iran (e)	43.2	52.7	4.1
Pakistan (e)	45.2	50.7	4.1
South Korea (g)	32.3	63.7	4.0
Denmark (f)	19.7	69.1	11.2
Norway (f)	21.3	63.6	15.1
	2000		
Egypt	34.5	61.9	3.6
Jordan	38.7	58.4	2.9
Syria	40.5	56.4	3.1
Tunisia (i)	33.4	61.0	5.6
Morocco (h)	35.4	59.9	4.7
Saudi Arabia	45.5	50.9	3.6
Oman	43.2	53.6	3.2
Iran (h)	39.5	56.1	4.4
Pakistan (k)	43.2	53.4	3.4
South Korea (k)	21.8	71.4	6.8
Denmark (j)	18.1	67.0	14.9
Norway (j)	19.8	68.6	11.6

— No available data.

(1) 60 years and over.	(d) Data related to 1979.	(h) Data related to 1996.
(a) Data related to 1961.	(e) Data related to 1981.	(i) Data related to 1997.
(b) Data related to 1962.	(f) Data related to 1982.	(j) Data related to 1998.
(c) Data related to 1966.	(g) Data related to 1983.	(k) Data related to 1999.

Sources: UN, *Demographic Yearbook,* various years (New York); ECWA/ESCWA, *Demographic and Related Socio-Economic Data Sheets,* various issues (Beirut, Baghdad, and Amman); WB, *World Tables,* various years (Published for the WB by Johns Hopkins University Press); The Kingdom of Saudi Arabia, Ministry of Planning, Central Department of Statistics, *Statistical Yearbook* – 1419 AH [1999 AD] (Riyadh, 2000); Sultanate of Oman, Ministry of National Economy, *Statistical Yearbook,* various issues (Muscat); Syrian Arab Republic, Office of the Prime Minister, Central Bureau of Statistics, *Statistical Abstract,* 1960–2001, various issues (Damascus).

However, it should be emphasized that the most dramatic age-structure change has occurred in former developing countries that have succeeded in overcoming their high natural increase rates. For example, South Korea's percentage of the under-15 population declined from 42.4% in 1962 to 32.3% in 1983 and dropped to only 21.8% in 1999 (see table 3.1). South Korea's success in reducing its fertility rates was one of the main reasons for its rapid economic expansion that entitled the country to be included in the "Asian Tigers" group. By the year 2002, South Korea's per capita GDP amounted to $16,950 (in PPP terms)[4] – five times higher than the average in the non-oil Arab countries, with the exception of Tunisia and Lebanon, which are the Arab countries with the lowest fertility rates (see Appendix 2).

Since the mid-1980s, the percentage of the young population within the total population in almost all of the Arab countries, as in many other developing countries worldwide, has steadily narrowed, due to a more rapid decline in the fertility rates than in the death rates. However, the percentages have remained very high in international comparison, with the exception of the poorest sub-Saharan African countries. Thus, for example, in the year 2000, the percentage of the under-15 population in Egypt was 34.5%, declining from 42.8% in 1960. In Syria the decline was from 46.3% to 40.5% and in Morocco from 44.3% to 35.4% during the corresponding period. At the end of the twentieth century, Tunisia achieved the lowest percentage of the under-15 population among all of the Arab countries, with 33.4% in 1997, due to its having the lowest fertility rates during the 1980s and 1990s (see table 3.1). Overall, according to UN data, by 1998 the percentage of the under-18 population of the total Middle Eastern populations (including Iran and Turkey) was 45.5%, as compared with 22.4% among the industrialized countries.[5]

The combined result of high natural increase rates and a relatively low life expectancy in the Arab countries was a narrow upper side of the age pyramid. By the year 2000, the percentage of the 65-years-and-over population in each of the Arab countries was very small, amounting to 3.6% in Egypt, 3.2% in Oman, 3.1% in Syria, and only 2.9% in Jordan. The highest percentage of the 65 years-and-over population among the Arab countries was in Tunisia, with 5.6% in 1997, as a combined result of its having the lowest fertility rates and a higher life expectancy. In the Western European countries, on the contrary, the combined result of a very high life expectancy and extremely low fertility levels for over three decades is a higher percentage of the older population. By the year 1998, the percentage of the 65-years-and-over population within the total population was 11.6% in Norway and 14.9% in Denmark – almost fivefold greater than the prevailing rates in the Arab countries (see table 3.1). In the late 1990s, Italy was the first EU country in which there were more people in the sixties age group than in the twenties.[6]

1.1   The Short- and Long-term Implications of the Demographic Momentum

The long-term demographic implication of the wide-based age pyramid is that even if the fertility rates were to decline to the replacement-level or even below it, the population would continue to grow as the number of women of reproductive age would continue to increase for some decades before finally stabilizing. Only then would the population start to decline. Thus, the younger the age pyramid, the longer the period between the achievement of replacement-level fertility and the termination of population growth. In other words, the higher the fertility rates to begin with, the longer the momentum period simply because the number of new mothers continues to increase for at least two generations. This period is called "the demographic momentum" or "the population momentum." Thus, if the world's fertility rate in 2000 was at the replacement-level, then the world's population would still grow by another 43% before stabilizing after 60 years due to the young age structure of the world's population in 2000.[7]

The implication of the almost-zero natural increase rates in the developed countries is the steady decline in their share of global population from 32% in 1950[8] to 21% in 1994.[9] This trend, of course, is intensifying due to the combined result of the differences in the age structures and the fertility rates between the developed and the developing countries. Thus, during the 1990s, among the 81 million people that were added on annual average to the worldwide population, 91.4%, or 74 million people, were in the developing countries.[10]

Since the current age structures of the Arab countries, without exception, are much younger than those of the developed countries in the 1970s, it would take much longer for the population to become stabilized at a zero growth rate even if the fertility rates were to theoretically decline to the replacement-level immediately. However, none of the Arab countries, with the exception of Tunisia and Lebanon, are even close to the target of replacement-level fertility, despite the considerable decline in fertility rates during the past two decades. In fact, in nominal numbers, their population growth during the 1990s were equal to or even higher than those of the 1980s, simply as a result of their wide-based age pyramids. Thus, for example, when Egypt's natural increase rate peaked at more than 3% in 1985, in nominal figures the population increase was 1.466 million.[11] Seventeen years later, by the year 2002, Egypt's natural increase rate had declined to 2%, but in nominal figures the population increase was 1.327 million,[12] namely, a decline of only 9.5% in nominal figures in comparison to the net population increase in 1985, despite the decline of 33% in the natural increase rate. In Jordan, Syria, Algeria, and the GCC oil-states during the 1990s, although there was a marked decline in fertility rates, in nominal figures the net population increase was much higher than ever before.

Thus, the population of the Arab countries will continue to increase rapidly during at least the first half of the twenty-first century, even if the current trend of declining fertility continues. According to the UN Population Division, by the year 2015, Egypt's population will number 84.4 million and will continue to increase to 94.8 million in 2025. Overall, during the period 2000–2025, Egypt's population is projected to increase by 40%. In the Arab countries with younger age pyramids than that of Egypt and current higher natural increase rates, the population is projected to increase by much higher rates. Thus, Syria's population is projected to increase by 43.2% during the period 2000–2015 and by as much as 69.1% during the period 2000–2025. Jordan's population is projected to increase by 46.9% and 77.6%, respectively, in the corresponding periods. The lowest population growth rate among the Arab countries is projected in Tunisia, due to its having both the lowest fertility rate and the oldest age pyramid: 18.9% during the period 2000–2015 and 29.5% during the period 2000–2025 (see table 3.2).[13] The real meaning of "the demographic momentum," wrote Michael Todaro, is that "every year that passed without a reduction in fertility means a larger multiple of the present total population size before it can eventually level off."[14]

Table 3.2 Demographic Projections for Some Arab Countries, non-Arab Developing Countries, and Western European Countries, 2000–2025

Country	Population (millions)			Growth (%)	
	2000	2015	2025	2000–2015	2000–2025
Arab Countries					
Egypt	67.9	84.4	94.8	24.3	39.6
Syria	16.2	23.2	27.4	43.2	69.1
Jordan	4.9	7.2	8.7	46.9	77.6
Tunisia	9.5	11.3	12.3	18.9	29.5
Morocco	29.9	37.7	42.0	26.1	40.5
Yemen	18.3	33.1	48.2	80.9	163.4
Non-Arab Developing Countries					
Turkey	66.7	79.0	86.6	18.4	29.8
Iran	70.3	87.1	99.3	23.9	41.3
Brazil	170.4	201.4	219.0	18.2	28.5
Argentina	37.0	43.5	47.2	17.6	27.6
Thailand	62.8	72.5	77.5	15.4	23.4
Western European Countries					
France	59.2	61.9	62.8	4.6	6.1
Italy	57.7	55.2	52.3	–4.3	–9.3
Belgium	10.2	10.3	10.2	1.0	0
Denmark	5.3	5.3	5.4	0	1.9

Source: UN, Department of Economic and Social Affairs, *World Population Prospects: The 2000 Revision* (New York, 2001), pp. 27–30, table 2.

In the Western European countries, the population growth rates are currently very low due both to old age pyramids and below-replacement-level fertility rates. In nominal figures, the natural increase of the EU population in 1999 and 2000 amounted to only 966,000 and 1.05 million, respectively.[15] In 2002, the population of the EU increased by 0.3%, representing only 2% of the world's total population growth in that year.[16] Italy is a good example for illustrating Europe's demographic situation. In 1991, the age group of 20–24, namely, those born between 1967 and 1971, numbered 4.7 million, while the age group of 0–4, namely, those born during the period 1987–1991, numbered almost half of that, only 2.8 million.[17] Overall, by the year 2000, Europe's women under the age of 20 numbered 87 million as compared with 105 million women in the age group of 20–40.[18] Thus, according to the calculations of Paul Demeny, if Europe's fertility and mortality rates in the future were to remain the same as in the year 2000, "a generation of 1,000 persons would be replaced by a second generation of 645, followed by a third generation of 416, a fourth of 268, and so on."[19] Thus, it is projected that also in the coming decades, Europe's population increase will continue to be very low and even negative in some countries that prevent immigration on a large scale. Thus, for example, Belgium's population is projected to increase by zero during the period 2000–2025. The population of Italy, the country with the lowest current fertility rate among the EU countries, is projected to decrease by 9.3% during the years 2000–2025 (see table 3.2).

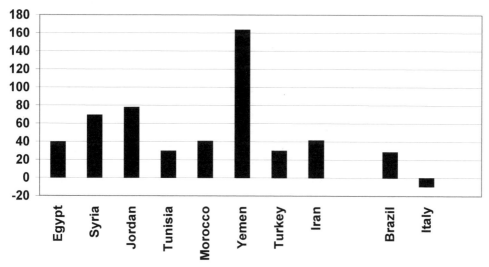

Figure 3.1 Projected Population Growth for Some Arab Countries, non-Arab Developing Countries, and Western European Countries, 2000–2025 (%)

Thus, the only two options for the EU countries to overcome their expected negative population growth rates in the coming generation are either to encourage immigration through a liberal immigration policy or to achieve higher fertility rates through pro-natalist measures. Many of these countries, such as Sweden, have been trying for some time to increase the fertility rates of their populations through substantial economic pro-natalist incentives, but without much success. Therefore, the inescapable conclusion is that the only viable option for reversing the trend toward an elderly population is to encourage large-scale immigration. This is precisely the approach being taken in the EU countries during the past three decades. Thus, while in the 1960s net immigration accounted for less than 5% of the total population growth in the EU counties, in the past decade it accounted for two-thirds of the EU net population growth, and its share is steadily increasing.[20] By the year 2002, net migration accounted for 75% of the EU population increase, while natural increase accounted for only 25%.[21] According to the projections, since the year 2000 and until the year 2050, the EU countries would need an additional 75 million foreign workers in order to compensate for their current below-replacement-level fertility.[22]

It should be emphasized, however, that the contribution of net migration to the future population growth in the EU countries should not be considered only in terms of the nominal number of immigrants. Even more important is the fact that the vast majority of the immigrants are coming from developing countries, with much higher fertility rates than those prevailing in the EU countries. Thus, the percentage of the first and second migrant generations in the overall population of the host EU countries would be much higher than their current percentage. Given that a considerable percentage of the immigrants to the EU countries are Muslims, the percentage of non-Christians in the EU countries will continue to increase in line with the pace and number of the Muslim immigrants. Since the wave of immigration to Western European countries started four decades ago, this process has had a profound effect on the ethnic composition of the EU countries. For example, at the beginning of the twenty-first century, the percentage of Muslims within the total population of France was estimated at 5% to 10%, and the percentage of non-Christians in Austria was estimated at 17%, the vast majority of them Muslims.[23]

1.2   The Effects of the Young Age Structure on Labor Force Participation

The age structure and fertility rates have a direct impact on the labor force participation rate as well as on its sex composition. In light of the young age pyramid characterizing the Arab countries, almost half of the population is typically not included in the working age group (15–65). This means that a priori the potential labor force in the Arab countries is much smaller than that of the developed countries, which have an older age structure. For example, in Oman the percentage of the working age group within the total indigenous population in 2000 was only 53.6%, whereas the corresponding figure was almost 70% in both Norway and Denmark in 1998 (see table 3.1).

In addition to the wide-based age pyramid, the overall female labor force participation rate in the Arab countries is very low, as the result of both high fertility rates and traditional limitations on female employment outside the household. The low female labor force participation rates combined with the large percentage of the population outside the working age group translate to very low overall labor force participation rates in all of the Arab countries. According to the Egyptian 1986 census, the overall labor force participation rate was recorded as 27.7% (48.1% among males and as low as 6.2% among females). Jordan's labor force participation rate in 1991 was estimated even lower than Egypt's, with only 23.8% (39.9% among males and 6.6% among females).[24] The same phenomenon prevailed in the North African countries, such as in Algeria, where the labor force participation rate in the early 1980s was less than 20%.[25]

Since the October 1973 "oil boom," and probably earlier – although reliable labor force data are not available – the lowest labor force participation rates among the Arab countries are in the GCC countries. In Kuwait, labor data are available for some time prior to the "oil boom," as such data were collected within the framework of the population censuses. In 1965, the labor force participation rate among the indigenous Kuwaiti population was recorded as low as 19.5% (37.2% among males and only 1% among women). The rate further declined to 18.8% in 1970 (36.1% among males and 1.2% among females)[26] and remained at that level during the 1970s and the 1980s as well.[27] Likewise in Qatar, the labor force participation rate of the indigenous population was very low, amounting to only 19.0% in the mid-1980s.[28]

During the 1990s, the labor force participation rates of the GCC indigenous populations, with the exception of Bahrain (see below), continued to be the lowest among the Arab countries. For example, although the Saudi authorities do not publish complete employment data on a regular basis, according to the official data, the Saudi national employees numbered 3.2 million in 1999.[29] Considering the unemployment rate of 14% among the nationals (see below), the total Saudi labor force in 1999 was approximately 3.7 million, or at best 4 million, including the Saudi women working in the informal sector. This represents a labor force participation rate of only 22%–24%.[30] A similar low labor force participation rate prevails in Kuwait, where, according to the 1995 population census, the national workforce numbered 147,768 while the total number of Kuwaiti citizens amounted to 653,616 – meaning a labor force participation rate of 22.6%.[31] It seems that the low level of labor force participation rates in the GCC countries since the October 1973 "oil boom" can be attributed to the following four factors:

(a) *An extremely wide-based age pyramid* caused by the very high fertility rates, on the one hand, and the very low infant and child mortality rates, on the other hand.

(b) *A sharp increase in the enrollment ratio* at all educational levels among both males and females, leading to a short-term decrease in the labor force participation rates. For example, despite Oman's rapid population growth, the national labor force decreased from 137,000 in 1975 to 126,000 in 1985[32]– representing a decrease of more than 8% during one decade.

(c) *Early retirement.* One of the major tools used by the GCC royal families to distribute the oil wealth among their citizens was to employ the vast majority of the indigenous labor force in the public sector (see below). Early retirement enabled them to employ new entrants to the labor market in the public sector and thus to increase the scale of the citizens enjoying public sector employment.

(d) *Very low female labor force participation rates.* None of the GCC countries, other than Saudi Arabia, have explicit legislative restrictions on women's employment. Yet, in practice, a wide variety of occupations are considered as "not suitable for women."[33] In this regard, in an interview with the economic weekly MEED in 1979, the Qatari Education Under-Secretary, 'Abd al-'Aziz 'Abdallah al-Turki, said:

> We make use of women here, but we are an Islamic country and we have special traditions. We find it very difficult, because of these traditions, to go into fields for the employment of women other than nursing and education.[34]

In Saudi Arabia, there are strict legislative restrictions affecting women's ability to work, including prohibitions on women driving or mixing together with males in the workplace.[35] These severe limitations derive from the fears of the *'ulama* that large-scale female employment will lead to cultural changes in male–female relationships and thus to a gradual change in the religious–cultural structure of the Saudi society as a whole. The Saudi royal family prefers not to confront the *'ulama* on this issue in order to maintain the status quo between them. Indeed, the political power of the *'ulama*, or the balance of power between the *'ulama* and the royal family, is the most important criterion determining the overall position of women in the GCC countries. Generally speaking, the greater the political power of the *'ulama*, the lower the position of women in the society. The resistance of the Saudi *'ulama* to female employment is so great that in May 1993 they called for firing all the women in Saudi Arabia, indigenous and foreigners alike.[36] Thus, as Peter Wilson and Douglas Graham, wrote: "women continue to serve as convenient scapegoats for the regime."[37]

The high public sector salaries paid to national employees also hamper increasing participation of women in the labor force.[38] Some researchers, such as Andrzej Kapiszewski, have argued recently that the female labor force participation rate is expected to increase in the near future.[39] However, the steady unemployment increase among GCC male nationals during the past decade casts great doubt on this optimistic projection because the paramount priority of the GCC royal families in the employment arena is to reduce the unemployment rates among male nationals and only then to increase female labor force participation. Moreover, since the females that are currently working outside the household are employed almost exclusively in the public sector, then it is reasonable to expect that those who attempt to enter the labor force, at least in the short run, would also do so primarily through the public sector and only secondarily through replacing foreign women in the private sector. This would only increase the employment pressure on the public sector, which already suffers from overstaffing and huge disguised unemployment (see below).

Table 3.3 Total Workforce and Labor Force Participation Rates in Some Arab and European Countries, 1980 and 1997

	Labor force		Labor force participation rate (LFPR)					
	Total	Annual growth	Total		Male		Female	
	1997	%	1980	1997	1980	1997	1980	1997
Country	(thousands)	1980–97						
Arab countries								
Egypt	23,817	2.6	35.0	37.0	50.7	51.4	18.9	22.1
Tunisia	3,562	2.9	34.3	38.2	48.0	52.2	20.1	23.9
Morocco	10,748	2.6	36.0	39.1	47.7	51.0	24.1	27.1
Syria	4,559	3.7	28.4	30.5	42.7	44.5	13.6	16.2
Jordan	1,671	5.3	23.8	28.9	39.2	43.8	7.2	13.4
Saudi Arabia*	6,355	4.9	29.5	32.6	50.5	50.3	4.9	10.4
Kuwait*	647	1.6	36.2	37.4	55.0	49.4	11.1	24.7
Bahrain*	260	3.8	39.4	44.6	60.3	62.5	10.3	20.6
European countries								
Germany	41,053	0.5	47.8	50.0	60.2	59.2	36.6	41.1
France	26,272	0.6	44.2	44.9	54.2	51.0	34.7	39.0
Italy	25,431	0.7	40.0	44.4	55.1	56.6	25.7	32.9
Belgium	4,225	0.4	40.1	41.5	54.2	50.4	26.6	32.9
Denmark	2,936	0.5	53.1	55.9	60.3	60.6	46.1	51.3

LFPR = defined as the ratio of the economically active population aged 10 years and over by the population of all ages.
* Including foreigner workers.
Source: International Labour Office (ILO), *World Employment Report, 1998–99* (Geneva, 1998), pp. 217–20, table 7.

Bahrain is quite different from the other GCC countries in regard to female labor force participation, as in many other socioeconomic areas. Not only are women not barred from seeking employment, they are actually encouraged to do so. Thus, according to figures published by the Bahrain Central Statistics Organization, female labor force participation increased from just over 5% in 1971 to almost 40% in 2001. However, even in Bahrain national women represented less than 1% of the private sector workforce as compared with more than 40% in the public sector.[40] The higher female labor force participation rate in Bahrain attributed to the fact that Bahrain's per capita oil revenues are the lowest among the GCC countries.[41] Thus, the Bahraini authorities cannot afford to forego half of their labor force potential and employ foreign labor instead. In addition, due to the low oil revenues, Bahrain functions the least as a *rentier* state among the GCC countries. Consequently, the salaries in the public sector are also the lowest among the GCC countries in real terms. As a result, many women must work outside the house in order to contribute to the family income. Since the early 1990s, the Omani authorities have been trying to increase female labor force participation as part of their nationalization policy of the labor force, but with only limited success thus far.[42] In the richest GCC countries, namely, Qatar and UAE, women's labor force participation rates remained very low in the 1990s as well.[43]

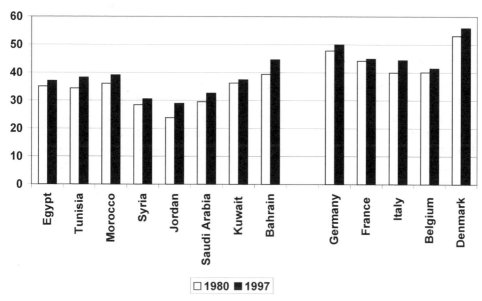

Figure 3.2 Labor Force Participation Rates in Some Arab and European Countries, 1980 and 1997 (%)

In the non-oil Arab countries, there has been some increase in the labor force participation rates in the past two decades for two main reasons. One is the increasing percentage of the working age group within the total population as a result of the fertility decline; and the second is the increase in the female labor force participation rates as a consequence of the improvement in their educational level. Thus, for example, the female labor force participation rate in Egypt increased from 9% in 1981 to 17.6% in 1993, and in Syria from 9% in 1984 to 16% in 1994.[44]

According to the ILO figures, by 1997, the overall labor force participation rate was 37% in Egypt, 38.2% in Tunisia, and 39.1% in Morocco (15 years and over). The high labor force participation rates in the GCC oil countries, including 37.4% in Kuwait and 44.6% in Bahrain (see table 3.3), can be explained by the fact that these data include the foreign labor forces as well, with their extremely high participation rates estimated at 75%–85%. Even while recognizing the increase in the overall labor force participation rates of the non-oil Arab countries since the mid-1980s, the increases are not so impressive when viewed relative to those of the developed countries. According to the ILO figures, in 1997 the overall labor force participation rate was 44.9% in France, 50.0% in Germany, and as high as 55.9% in Denmark. The much higher labor force participation rates in the developed countries are the result of two factors: higher percentages of the working age population within the total population and the much higher female labor force participation rates.

Thus, while the breadwinners/dependents ratio is 1:2 in the developed countries, the same ratio is 1:3.5–4.0 in the Arab countries, leading to what has been called the "low income trap." However, the long period below-replacement-level fertility, on the one hand, combined with the steadily increasing life expectancy, on the other hand, will serve to increase the dependency ratio and to create a "low income trap" in the Western developed countries as well, but in this case from the upper side of the age pyramid. Thus, the current fertility patterns are likely to force the EU countries to increase their reliance on immigrant laborers in the first half of the twenty-first century.

1.3   The Implications of the Young Age Pyramid for the Educational System

The wide-based age pyramid has a tremendous impact on the educational system in both the present and the future. Following independence, all of the Arab countries without exception – both those that remained monarchies and those that came to be under military rule – invested immense resources in education at all levels. Examination of the educational expenditure in the Arab countries reveals that in most of them, it was considerably higher even than in most developed countries. For example, during the years 1995–1997, the percentage of the educational expenditures of the total GNP averaged 7.9% in Jordan, 7.0% in Yemen, 5.3% in Morocco, 4.8% in Egypt, and 4.2% in Syria, as compared with 7.7% in Norway, 6.9% in Canada, 5.5% in Australia, 5.4% in the US, and 3.1% in Belgium. During the same years, the educational budget of the total governmental budget in the Arab countries was much higher than in many of the developed countries, amounting to 24.9% in Morocco, 21.6% in Yemen, and 14.9% in Egypt, as compared with 16.8% in Norway, 14.4 in the US, and 11.6% in the UK.[45]

At first glance, these data are indeed impressive, indicating the immense importance of education in the Arab countries. One would expect such a substantial investment to translate into impressive educational and scientific achievements as well. In practice, however, this is not the case because the huge investments in education were "swallowed" by the rapid increase in the number of students resulting from the wide-based age pyramid. Consequently, the challenge of keeping pace with technological advances has become even more difficult for the Arab non-oil countries to meet.[46] In the developed countries, on the other hand, the per capita educational investment increased during the second half of the twentieth century, given the relatively smaller number of students at the elementary and secondary educational levels due to the steady fertility decline.

A study conducted by the Arab League on the quantity and quality of the educational system in the Arab countries illustrates this problem. According to its results, in 1980 55 million people in all of the Arab countries were illiterate, representing 59.2% of the total adult populations. In 1995, a decade and a half later, although the average adult illiteracy rate in the Arab countries declined to 43.4%, in nominal figures their number not only did not decrease, but rather sharply increased, amounting to 65 million.[47]

The rapid increase in the number of graduates of high schools and tertiary-level educational institutions also impacts considerably on the labor market structures and unemployment rates. Since human resources have become the paramount economic resource in the modern technological world, one of the major factors accounting for the steady growth in the socioeconomic gap between the developed and the developing countries is the increasing differential in per capita investment in education due to the different age structures. An ESCWA report from 1997 noted in this regard as follows:

> Although investment in education was intensified during the past two decades, investments were concentrated on quantitative rather than qualitative growth . . . The net result was a large supply of college graduates with qualifications that do not match the requirements of the labor markets in the 1990s.[48]

1.4 The Implications of the Young Age Pyramid for Future Employment Demands

Despite the low labor force participation rates, particularly among women, the nominal number of those entering the labor force in each of the Arab countries is steadily increasing from one year to the next as a consequence of the wide-based age pyramid. This trend, it should be emphasized, will continue well into the twenty-first century even if fertility rates sharply decline. For example, in mid-2001 the Syrian population in the age group of 0–4 numbered 2.1 million, while the age group of 40–44 numbered only 731,000.[49] This means that at a constant labor force participation rate, the number of those entering the labor force during the period 2017–2021 would be three times greater than the number of those retiring.[50]

Radwan Shaban and associates argued in an article published in 1995 that: "Over the coming two decades, demographic pressures on labor markets are expected to subside somewhat in countries that have already achieved substantial reductions in fertility, such as Egypt, Lebanon, Morocco, and Tunisia."[51] However, an examination of Egypt's age structure according to the 1996 census results reveals that while the under-5 age group numbered 6.86 million, namely, 11.6% of Egypt's total population, the 40–45 age group numbered only 3.17 million, representing 5.3% of the total population. The age group of 5–10, namely, those who are expected to enter the labor market in the period 2011–2016, was almost three times higher than the 45–50 age group.[52] Thus, even if Egypt's labor force participation rate were to remain stable, the number of entrants to the labor market, at least for the coming three decades, would be at least double the number of those retiring from it. In Morocco, one can find a similar trend due to its structural similarity with Egypt's age pyramid (see table 3.1). Therein lies the true meaning and the most devastating consequence of the "demographic momentum."

Under conditions of increasing labor force participation rates due to a rise in female labor force participation rates, the gap between the number of those entering the labor force and those retiring would be much higher. For example, according to a projection of the Saudi Arabian Central Bureau of Statistics, by the year 2020 the Saudi national labor force (i.e., not including foreigners) will amount to 8.263 million, as compared with 3.173 million in 1999 – representing an increase of 160% within just two decades.[53] During the second half of the 1990s, the number of Saudis entering the labor force amounted to 120,000 on annual average.[54] According to the Saudi Seventh

Development Plan, 760,000 graduate nationals are projected to enter the labor force during the period 2000–2004.[55] Likewise, in the year 2001, the Kuwaiti labor force (i.e., not including foreign workers) increased by an unprecedented rate of 6.6%.[56] Overall, according to ESCWA figures, by the early 2000s, the region's annual labor force growth rate reached as high as 4.5% – the highest rate worldwide.[57]

From a purely demographic point of view, the future employment dilemma of the Gaza Strip Palestinians is the most acute among all the Arab Middle Eastern societies, as a result of their having the widest age pyramid. By mid-2000, the age group of 0–4 numbered 231,392, as compared with 41,235 in the age group of 40–44, meaning that the number of those entering the labor force in the period 2016–2020 will be 5.6 times higher than the number of those retiring.[58] According to the ALO (Arab Labor Organization), during the period 1998–2000, the total Arab workforce grew by an annual average of 3.3%, reaching 86.5 million in 2000. It is expected to increase annually by 4% in the coming decade and to reach 123 million by the year 2010, representing an increase of 42.2%, or 36.5 million in nominal figures, within one decade alone.[59] According to a recent study conducted by the World Bank, the workforce in the MENA region is expected to increase by 4 million on annual average during the period 2000–2010.[60]

Thus, a calculation of the historical increase in the working age populations of the Arab countries reveals that in nominal figures, the increase between the 1960s and the 1990s was hundreds of per cent in each of these countries. For example, in the case of Syria during the period 1960–1970, the working age population (15–64) increased by 688,598, representing an increase of 68,860 on annual average.[61] During the period 1991–2001, however, the net increase in the Syrian working age population amounted to 3.630 million,[62] representing an increase of 363,000 on annual average, or 5.3 times higher than the corresponding figure of three decades earlier.

The prospect of an increase in employment demands casts a "heavy shadow" on the ability of the non-oil Arab economies to supply sufficient new work opportunities for their rapidly growing workforces. Moreover, as we will see below, despite the huge number of foreign workers in the Arab oil countries, it seems that these countries can be expected to suffer from similar employment dilemmas as their non-oil counterparts, albeit to a lesser extent, due to the structure of their economies and labor markets, on the one hand, and the wide-based age pyramid, on the other hand. According to the prevailing estimates, Egypt and Jordan need a minimum annual GDP growth of 7% in order to absorb the new entrants to their labor forces (approximately half a million in Egypt and 50,000 in Jordan).[63] The World Bank report on the Jordanian economy from early 2003 claims that, "with a labor force growing at 4%–5% per annum, Jordan needs at least 6% GDP growth to stabilize unemployment."[64] An examination of the economic history of these two countries during the past two decades reveals that neither has succeeded in achieving this growth rate. The end result has been a continuing increase in unemployment (see below). The meaning of such failure to achieve the economic growth rates needed to keep unemployment at a stable level is that even higher economic growth rates will have to be achieved in the future in order to compensate for the past low economic growth. This raises the question of whether the non-oil Arab economies are, under any circumstances, capable of maintaining an economic growth rate of more than 7% on annual average for a long period time in order to eradicate the employment pressure.

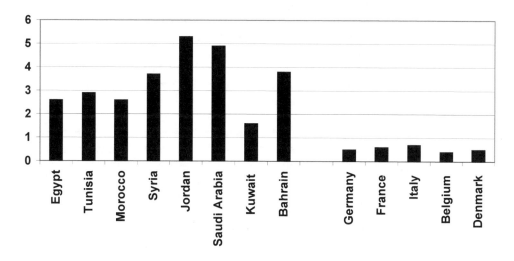

Figure 3.3 Annual Labor Force Growth Rates in Some Arab and European Countries, 1980–1997 (%)

2   Arab Employment Developments in Retrospect

In retrospect, it appears that the employment history of the Arab countries during the second half of the twentieth century can be divided broadly into four main periods, in which there was a high correlation, as will be examined in **Chapter 4**, between the employment situation and the overall governmental family planning activities. The four periods are as follows:

2.1   Rapid Employment Expansion under the Étatism

Some of the Arab countries were already plagued by high unemployment rates during the 1950s and 1960s, though short-lived in most cases, either due to internal political instability or to wars or to a combination of these two factors. For example, in Jordan during the late 1960s and the early 1970s the economy was forced to deal with both the severe economic consequences of the June 1967 War and the armed struggle between the Hashemite regime and the PLO (the Palestinian Liberation Organization). High unemployment rates also prevailed in Egypt in the period between 1965 and 1974 as a result of the four wars in which Egypt was involved during that period (the War in Yemen from 1962–1967, the June 1967 War, the War of Attrition from 1969–1970, and the October 1973 War). Generally speaking, the relatively low unemployment rates in many of the Arab countries during the 1950s and 1960s were the combined result of the following three factors:

(a) *The low scale of labor forces* due to the relatively small working age population in most of the Arab countries during that period. As one can see in **table 2.3**, among all of the Arab countries, only Egypt, Morocco and Algeria had a population of more than 10 million in 1960. In Syria, for example, the total labor force, including those in the army and the other civilian security services, amounted to a little more than one million, with a labor force participation rate of 23%–25%. This means that the civilian labor force amounted to 750,000 at the maximum. In the case of Jordan, the labor force in 1970 amounted to less than half a million, including those in the army and the civilian security forces, representing a maximum civilian labor force of 400,000. In Egypt, the labor force in 1960 amounted to approximately 7 million – a little more than one-fourth of the current Egyptian labor force.

(b) *The étatist economic approach,* which was adopted by the army officers that seized power in many of the Arab countries, held as one of its paramount aims the elimination of unemployment as a measure to eradicate poverty and reduce the wide socioeconomic gaps. The étatist policy included massive employment of the urban labor force in the rapidly growing public sector (see below).

(c) *The implementation of large-scale industrial and infrastructure projects* that contributed to the rapid increase in employment opportunities, some of them in the countryside and remote areas. These projects included, for example, the Aswan High Dam in Egypt; the massive agricultural land reclamation in Egypt and Syria; the massive industrialization projects in Egypt; and the Tabaqa Dam on the Euphrates in Syria. A similar macroeconomic policy and rapid expansion of public sector employment occurred in many other Arab countries during the 1950s and 1960s.

Thus, the employment situation in the poorer Arab countries considerably improved during the 1960s. Within the framework of Egypt's First Five-Year Plan for the period 1960–1965, more than 1 million new work opportunities were added[65] and "led to almost full employment in the 1960s . . ," as claimed by Riad El-Ghonemy.[66] According to one estimate, the number of unemployed in Egypt amounted to 175,000 in the early 1960s.[67] Overall, according to El-Ghonemy, during the Nasserite period (1952–1970), the Egyptian economy achieved an average annual real growth rate of 5.7% – more than twice the population growth rate during the corresponding period.[68]

In Syria, the economy grew rapidly during the decade following its independence (1946), based on the rapid growth in the agricultural sector.[69] The 1955 IBRD (International Bank for Reconstruction and Development) report on Syria estimated that during the period 1939–1955, Syria's national income in real terms almost doubled. Later, between 1954 and the collapse of the unification with Egypt in September 1961, its economic expansion markedly slowed to an annual average of 3.2%, which was still higher than the population growth rate during the corresponding period.[70] Overall, Syria's economic growth during the two decades of 1953–1973 was estimated at 4.5% on annual average,[71] meaning almost twice the average population growth rate during that period. Regarding that period, Yusif Sayigh wrote that: "Syria is one of the very few Arab economies which managed, on the whole, to achieve a reasonable rate of growth without the benefit of large petroleum resources and without the inflow of substantial foreign aid."[72]

However, the economic situation in the countries that were directly involved in the June 1967 War, namely Egypt, Jordan, and Syria, markedly deteriorated in the late 1960s and the early 1970s, as was examined in the Introduction. Nevertheless, this deterioration in the economic situation lasted for only a few years, with a turnaround and a rapid expansion of the economy following the October 1973 "oil boom." In the GCC oil economies, with the exception of Oman,[73] the overall economic situation largely improved during the 1950s and even more so during the 1960s and the early 1970s,[74] following the rapid increase of oil production.

2.2. The "Bonanza Period" of the "Oil Decade"

The October 1973 "oil boom" changed the socioeconomic situation in all of the Arab countries, but particularly in the oil economies, turning them into some of the richest countries worldwide in the early 1980s, with a per capita GNP well above many developed countries. By 1981, at the peak of the oil prices, Kuwait achieved a per capita GNP of $21,000 and Saudi Arabia of $16,010, which were well above that of West Germany ($13,290), Belgium ($12,060), Italy ($8,040), and Spain ($5,630).[75] The royal families in these countries now possessed the financial resources needed for the massive socioeconomic development plans that provided enormous employment opportunities to the indigenous and foreign labor forces, with the end result of negligible unemployment rates among the national labor forces of the Arab oil-states.

In retrospect, the "oil decade" (1973–1982) was the "bonanza period" not only for the Arab oil-based economies, but for the non-oil economies as well, when these countries achieved the highest economic growth rates ever in their modern history. Thus, for example, during the years 1973–1983, the GDP growth rate amounted to 8.8% on annual average in Egypt; 8.0% in Syria; and 11.1% in Jordan.[76] At the peak of the "oil decade," during the years 1976–1980, the Jordanian economy expanded by 62% in real terms[77] – higher than in any other period in its entire history. The rapid expansion of the Arab non-oil economies during the "oil decade" was due mainly to the combined result of the following three factors:

(a) *The surge of revenue increases from oil exports* of the smaller Arab oil-exporters, mainly Algeria, Egypt, and Syria, as a result of the overall increase in oil prices.

(b) *The sharp rise in aid received from the oil-rich Arab countries,* which dramatically increased after 1980 to the countries that did not enter into peace negotiations with Israel, in line with the resolutions of the Second Baghdad Arab Summit held in late March 1979 (following the Egyptian–Israeli peace treaty). In 1980, the Arab aid to Jordan peaked at $1.3 billion,[78] representing a quarter of the Jordanian GDP in that year. The Arab aid to Syria in 1979 amounted to $1.85 billion, as compared with $500–$600 million in the mid-1970s.[79]

(c) *The massive labor migration wave* from the poorer to the richer Arab oil countries in the Gulf and, to a lesser extent, also to Libya and Jordan. By 1973, on the eve of the "oil boom," the number of Egyptians working abroad was estimated at 160,000.[80] This number increased dramatically following the "oil boom," amounting to 1.365 million by early 1980.[81] Egypt's Foreign Minister estimated the number of Egyptians working in the Arab oil countries at 2.9 million in 1982,[82] representing approximately 15% of the total Egyptian labor force at that time. By mid-1983, the number of Egyptian workers in other Arab countries was estimated at approximately 3 million, of whom more than a million were in Iraq alone.[83] Although some estimates put the number of Egyptian workers abroad in the mid-1980s far below the "conventional" official Egyptian figures and the unofficial estimates (see Chapter 1), there is no doubt that the massive labor emigration wave from Egypt to the GCC countries, to Libya, and, to a lesser extent, also to Jordan totally changed the Egyptian labor market.

Following the October 1973 "oil boom," Jordan also became a major labor-exporter. According to Jordan's 1961 census, the number of Jordanian workers in other Arab countries was 15,901.[84] However, their number was estimated at 139,000 (from the East Bank of the Jordan River only) in 1975[85] and reached as high as 250,000–300,000 in 1980, representing almost 30% of the total Jordanian civilian labor force in that year.[86] By 1983, according to official Jordanian figures, the number of Jordanian workers in the other Arab countries was 271,200.[87] The third Arab major labor-exporter was North Yemen (YAR). By the mid-1980s, between 850,000 and 1.25 million North Yemenites were employed in the GCC countries, with the vast majority of them in Saudi Arabia.[88]

Overall, the poorer Arab countries not only permitted the process of labor emigration to the Arab oil states, but even encouraged it in varying degrees. The exceptional cases were South Yemen and Algeria during the 1970s and the 1980s, which almost totally prevented the temporary migration of their workers to the Arab oil states, and Syria, which maintained a restrictive migration policy until the late 1980s.[89] From the labor-exporters' point of view, the large-scale labor emigration has immense importance in three major areas:

(a) Such massive labor migration means *considerable relief of employment pressures* through both the emigration of a significant number of the local labor force, and the creation of large-scale work opportunities derived from the investments of the migrants themselves, mainly in the construction area.

(b) *The financial aid from the rich oil states* enables the authorities of the poorer countries to absorb many new employees into the public sector in order to further alleviate employment pressures. For example, 44% of the new entrants to the labor force in Egypt during the period 1976–1986 were absorbed into the public sector, and an additional 19% were absorbed into public enterprises. In Jordan, civil service employment grew by 9% on annual average during the 1970s and by 5% during the 1980s, reaching 50% of the total national labor force in 1987.[90]

(c) *The surge in hard currency resources* obtained through the workers' remittances and the financial aid from the rich oil states leads to substantial relief of the balance of payment deficits. Thus, the large-scale emigration from the poorer to the richer Arab oil states creates a "mutual dependence" whereby the oil states need the workers from the poorer countries, while the poorer countries need both the financial aid and the numerous work opportunities provided by the rich oil states.[91]

The end result of the combined rapid economic expansion and the massive labor emigration to the rich oil Arab countries was a sharp decline in unemployment rates in the poorer Arab countries. By 1982, Egypt's open unemployment rate was estimated at only 5.7%.[92] Jordan's unemployment rate declined from 14% in 1972[93] to only 1.6% in 1976 and slightly increased to 3.9% in 1981.[94] Thus, in the mid-1970s, a new problem emerged in Jordan: a labor shortage that led the Jordanian authorities to permit labor immigration. By 1975, the number of foreign workers in Jordan was estimated at 32,800,[95] increasing to almost 140,000 by the end of 1984, according to official Jordanian figures,[96] and reaching 186,506 in 1985, according to unofficial estimates.[97]

Table 3.4 Nationals and Expatriates in the GCC Labor Forces, 1975–1999 ('000)

Country	Nationals	Foreigners	Total	% Foreigners
1975				
Saudi Arabia	1,026.5	773.4	1,799.9	43.0
Kuwait	91.8	212.7	304.5	69.9
Bahrain	45.8	30.0	75.8	39.6
Oman	137.0	70.7	207.7	34.0
Qatar	12.5	53.8	66.3	81.1
UAE	45.0	251.5	296.5	84.8
Total	1,358.6	1,392.1	2,750.7	50.6
1980				
Saudi Arabia	1,220.0	1,734.1	2,954.1	58.7
Kuwait	107.8	383.7	491.5	78.1
Bahrain (a)	61.2	81.2	142.4	57.0
Oman	119.4	170.5	289.9	58.8
Qatar	14.7	106.3	121.0	87.9
UAE	53.9	470.8	524.7	89.7
Total	1,577.0	2,946.6	4,523.6	65.1
1985				
Saudi Arabia	1,440.0	2,661.8	4,101.9	64.9
Kuwait	126.4	544.0	670.4	81.1
Bahrain	72.8	100.5	173.3	58.0
Oman (b)	167.0	300.0	467.0	64.2
Qatar	17.7	155.6	173.3	89.8
UAE	71.8	612.0	683.8	89.5
Total	1,895.8	4,373.9	6,269.7	69.8
1990				
Saudi Arabia	1,934	2,878	4,812	59.8
Kuwait	118	731	849	86.1
Bahrain	127	132	259	51.0
Oman	189	442	631	70.0
Qatar	21	230	251	91.6
UAE	96	805	901	89.3
Total	2,485	5,218	7,703	67.7
1995				
Saudi Arabia (c)	2,545	3,945	6,490	60.8
Kuwait	148	614	762	80.6
Bahrain (d)	104	168	272	61.8
Oman	270	496	766	64.8
Qatar	—	—	—	—
UAE (f)	95	855	950	90.0
1999				
Saudi Arabia	3,173	4,003	7,176	55.9

Table 3.4 *(continued)*

Kuwait	221	1,005	1,226	82.0
Bahrain	113	194	307	63.2
Oman	312(g)	503	815	61.7
Qatar (e)	36	244	280	87.1
UAE (e)	124	1,165	1,289	90.4
Total	3,979	7,114	11,093	64.1

— No data available.
(a) Data related to 1981.
(b) Data related to 1986.
(c) Data related to 1994.
(d) Data related to 1996.
(e) Data related to 1997.
(f) Since the UAE authorities published data for 1995 only for the total labor force, including both nationals and foreigners without distinguishing between them, this data was divided by the author to 90% foreigners and 10% nationals, which was and still is the composition of the UAE workforce.
(g) Since the Omani authorities did not publish data on the scale of the national workforce in 1999, but only on the foreign workforce, the data on the national workforce in 1999 was calculated by the author on the basis of the 1995 data (270,000 Omani national workforce) and an annual growth rate of 3.7% since then to 1999.

Sources: The State of Kuwait, Ministry of Planning, Central Statistical Office, *Annual Statistical Abstract*, various issues (Kuwait); The State of Bahrain, Central Statistical Organization, Directorate of Statistics, *Statistical Abstract – 1992* (Manama); Sultanate of Oman, *Statistical Year-book*, various issues (Muscat); idem, Ministry of Development, *The Fifth Five-Year Development Plan, 1996–2000* (Muscat, July 1997); Central Bank of Oman, *Annual Report – 2001* (Muscat 2001); J. S. Birks and C. A. Sinclair, *International Migration and Development in the Arab Region* (Geneva: ILO, 1980); ILO, *International Migration for Employment: Manpower and Population Evolution in the GCC and Libyan Arab Jamahiriya*, World Employment Programme Research, Working Paper, by J. S. Birks and C. A. Sinclair (Geneva, October 1989); ESCWA, *Demographic and Related Socio-Economic Data Sheets for Countries of the Economic and Social Commission for Western Asia, 1978–2001*, various issues (Beirut, Baghdad, and Amman); idem, *Population Situation in the ESCWA Region, 1990* (Amman, May 1992); ESCWA, League of Arab States, and UNFPA, "Arab Labour Migration," Meeting of Senior Official and Experts, Amman, April 4–6, 1993; The Kingdom of Saudi Arabia, Ministry of Planning, *Seventh Development Plan*, 1420/21–1424/25 AH [2000–2004 AD] (Riyadh, 1999); Qatar National Bank, *Qatar Economic Review*, various issues (Doha); EIU, *Country Profile, Bahrain, Qatar, Oman, Saudi Arabia, and the United Arab Emirates*, various issues; Birks, Sinclair & Associates Ltd. *GCC Market Report*, 1990 and 1992 (Durham: Mountjoy Research Centre); Onn Winckler, "The Immigration Policy of the Gulf Cooperation Council (GCC) States," *Middle Eastern Studies*, Vol. 33, No. 3 (July 1997); Andrzej Kapiszewski, *National and Expatriates: Population and Labour Dilemmas of the Gulf Cooperation Council States* (Reading: Ithaca Press, 2001); Dawlat al-Bahrayn, al-Jihaz al-Markazi lil-Ihsa, al-Taʿdad al-ʿAmm lil-Sukan wal-Masakin wal-Mabani wal-Munshaʾat – 1991 (Manama, 1992); "al-Simat al-Asasiyya li-Sukan al-Kuwayt wa-Kuwwat al-ʿAmal fi Nihayat 1994," *al-Iqtisadi al-Kuwayti*, No. 324 (May 1995).

The tremendous increase in oil revenues following the "oil boom" led to a sharp increase in labor demand in the GCC oil economies that could not be met by local sources, due both to the small national labor forces (see table 3.4) and the low skilled and educational levels of the nationals. These countries were suffering from an almost total absence of professional and technical educational institutes. The short-term solution was to import the necessary labor, while in the longer run pro-natalist policies (see Chapter 4) combined with massive investments in educational and professional training were adopted as the means to meet the labor demand through local sources.

Figure 3.4 Nationals and Expatriates in the GCC Labor Forces, 1975–1999 ('000)

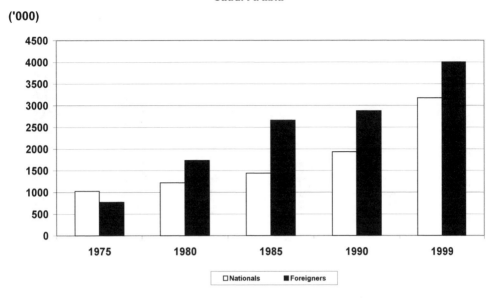

Saudi Arabia

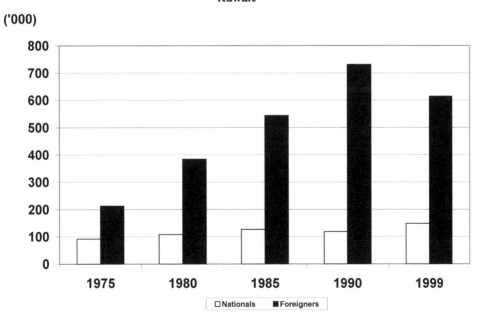

Kuwait

Oman

('000)

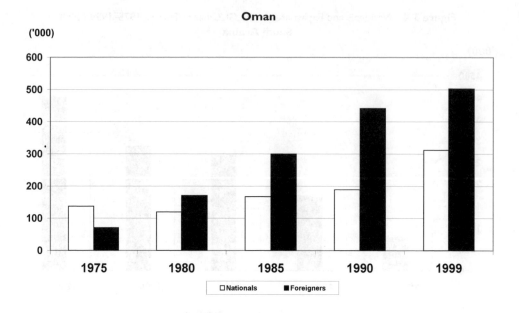

Thus, during the 1970s and the first half of the 1980s, massive numbers of foreign workers were imported to the GCC countries and Libya. The tempting salaries offered to the foreign workers,[98] together with the liberal migration policies,[99] led to the rapid increase in the number of foreign workers in the Arab oil economies. Overall, in 1985, the foreign populations in the GCC countries totaled 7.54 million, as compared with 2.76 million in 1975, representing an increase of almost threefold in one decade alone (see table 2.4). The number of foreign workers in the GCC countries increased from 1.392 million in 1975 to 4.374 million in 1985, representing an increase of more than threefold (see table 3.4).

The massive importing of labor by the GCC countries was not only a function of their real need for labor, but was also a part of their unique *rentier* nature based on their social-political structures. The term *"rentier* state" refers to an economy in which the government's revenues consist largely of external rent, such as oil and gas revenues and foreign aid.[100] For example, non-oil revenues averaged only 11.7% of Kuwait's total governmental revenues during the 1990s.[101] Likewise, in the case of Saudi Arabia, oil revenues represented 75% of the total governmental revenues in 1999.[102] In contrast to the standard model of the industrialized-democratic countries, according to which the government collects taxes in exchange for political participation, non-democratic societies in general and the GCC countries in particular are based on a model of "no taxation and no representation." The practical meaning of this system is that in exchange for "no taxation," the citizens give up their rights to political participation. Thus, citizenship in the GCC countries becomes a "welfare ticket" with no taxation on personal income and very low indirect taxes limited to only a few per cent.[103]

The *rentier* nature of the GCC countries has led to the creation of a unique pattern in their labor market structure: that of the dual labor market, with one market for nationals who are employed almost exclusively by the public sector and enjoy high salaries and improved work conditions, and the other for the private sector which employs almost exclusively foreign labor at low salaries. Peter Woodward noted on the Saudi labor market as follows:

> It is difficult to speak of a Saudi Arabian labor market in the sense of a unified, open market where a single price is paid for a specific amount of labor. Instead, the Saudi labor market is characterized by segmentation into nationalities.[104]

2.3 The "Sobering" from the "Oil boom" Illusion into a Deep Recession

The Arab economies, both the oil-based and the non-oil alike, began to rapidly deteriorate following the end of the "oil decade" in 1982, and even more so with the drop in oil prices in mid-1986 to less than $10 per barrel, as compared with $36 per barrel in 1980 (current prices). In constant prices of 1990, the decline in oil prices was from $49.6 in 1981 to $17.1 in 1986 (spot crude prices).[105] In the case of the non-oil economies, the scale of the deterioration was a function of their dependence on the oil economies.

Following the "oil boom," among the non-oil Arab countries, Jordan became the most dependent on the GCC oil-states. As Tayseer Abdel Jaber rightly noted, "Jordan became an oil economy without having oil."[106] Therefore, its economy experienced the worst deterioration as a result of the decline in aid given by the oil states, from the peak of $1.3 billion in 1980 to only $600 million in 1987,[107] and the decline in the workers' remittances from more than $1 billion in the early 1980s to $623 million in 1989.[108] This decline in remittances was mainly due to a reduction in the salaries of the foreign workers in the GCC countries.[109] The end of the Iraq–Iran War in September 1988 was also a major factor in Jordan's economic recession because during the war a considerable percentage of the activities in the 'Aqaba port were related to Iraq, while the Basra port was almost totally paralyzed. Moreover, during the war, a considerable percentage of Jordan's export of goods was to Iraq.[110] According to an IMF report: "Real GDP declined at an average rate of 6.4% during 1986–1990, with the worst recession in the recent history of Jordan occurring in 1989 when real GDP contracted by 20.9%."[111] Naturally, the severe economic recession affected the unemployment rates, which sharply increased during the second half of the 1980s, climbing to more than 10% by the end of the decade – almost threefold that of the early 1980s.[112]

The steady increase in unemployment rates in Jordan during the 1980s occurred in parallel to the steady increase in the number of foreign workers, estimated at 196,000 in early 1990.[113] The basic assumption of the Jordanian authorities had been that cheap foreign workers would replace the Jordanian nationals who had migrated to the GCC countries and that the Jordanian economy would benefit from the gap between the much higher remittances of the Jordanian workers abroad as compared to those of the foreign workers in the Kingdom. However, this assumption collapsed in the mid-1980s, when the Jordanian migrants started to return from the GCC states,[114] while the foreign workers did not leave. The attempts of the Jordanian authorities since the mid-1980s until the present to replace the foreign workers with Jordanian citizens have failed. After all, the foreign workers were and still are much cheaper than the Jordanians.[115] Thus, in the late 1980s, a new employment situation emerged in Jordan: a parallel increase in the unemployment rates of the nationals and in the number of foreign workers.

The Syrian economy also greatly deteriorated during the second half of the 1980s as a combined result of the sharp drop in oil prices and political factors. The sharp drop in oil prices led to a parallel reduction in the aid received from the oil-rich states, dropping to only $500 million on annual average during the years 1986–1988 – representing less than a third of the amount received in 1980.[116] In addition, Syria was by itself a smaller oil-exporter, meaning that the overall decline in oil prices affected Syria's revenues as well. Although from 1982 until the end of the 1980s, Iran supplied Syria with oil, this assistance did not fully compensate for the decrease in Arab aid. Another factor contributing to the economic downturn was a marked reduction in Syrian workers' remittances. The final, and the most important, factor was the huge economic burden of the "Strategic Balance Policy" with Israel that Syria adopted in the late 1970s following the Egyptian–Israeli peace treaty. By the mid-1980s, Syria's military expenditures constituted between 50%–60% of the governmental budget (see the Introduction). The end result was that by 1989, the per capita GNP was $890 (in current prices)[117] – almost half the amount in 1982. Although official unemployment figures are not published by the Syrian authorities, unofficial sources estimated Syria's unemployment rate at approximately 10% in the late 1980s.[118] The severe economic recession also began to have an impact on the stability of the Syrian regime. As Volker Perthes claimed, "for the first time since coming to power in 1970, President Hafiz al-Asad and his regime were threatened by a loss of legitimacy as the result of economic rather than political problems."[119]

Egypt, like Jordan and Yemen, also suffered from the decline of the demand for Arab labor in the Arab oil countries during the second half of the 1980s and particularly following the end of the Iraq–Iran War, which led to the return of hundreds of thousands of Egyptian workers from Iraq. According to the UNDP estimate, in mid-1990, on the eve of the Iraqi invasion of Kuwait, the number of Egyptian workers in the other Arab countries was 1.960 million,[120] as compared with approximately 3 million in the mid-1980s. It should be emphasized, however, that the decline in the number of Egyptian workers in the GCC countries and Libya during the second half of the 1980s had nothing to do with the Boycott imposed on Egypt following its March 1979 peace treaty with Israel.[121]

In addition, the February 1986 police riots led to a 18% reduction in the number of tourists in Egypt that year,[122] which led to a substantial decline in the number of available work opportunities in this sector and its related services and industries. Overall, during the years 1986–1989, Egypt's GDP shrunk by 6% (in current $US price). However, due to the continuation of the rapid population growth, the decline was 14% in per capita terms.[123] As a result, while in 1985/6 Egypt's per capita income was $750, it declined to only $600 in 1990, representing a decline of 20% in real terms in only four years.[124] At the same time, the economic recession was reflected by an increase in unemployment rates. According to the 1986 population census, the open unemployment rate in Egypt was 14%,[125] while according to unofficial estimates, Egypt's open unemployment rate in late 1988 was as high as 20%, not included underemployment and hidden unemployment.[126]

Likewise, the economic recession of the 1980s "hit" the North African countries as well. Although the factors that led to the recession in the North African countries (with the exception of Libya, which is a purely oil economy similar to the GCC countries) were quite different from those in the other Arab non-oil countries, the impact on the labor markets was the same – a steady unemployment increase.

In the case of Morocco, the recession was the combined result of a decline in the phosphate prices, droughts that hit North Africa first in the early 1980s and then again in the late 1980s, and increasing security expenditures due to the war in the Sahara.[127] The end result of the rapid growth in the labor force, on the one hand, and the shrinking economy, on the other hand, was a rapid increase in unemployment, with rates rising from 9% in 1980 to 14% in 1986 and 16% in 1989.[128] Among the Moroccan urban youth, the unemployment rate reached as high as 30% in 1989, of which 5% were university graduates, 47% were secondary education graduates, and only 7% were illiterates.[129]

The sharp drop in oil revenues[130] during the second half of the 1980s had only a minor effect on the employment situation of the GCC nationals. The GCC governments exploited their huge financial reserves from the "oil decade" to maintain the living standard of the indigenous population, including their employment in lucrative public sector positions.[131] Overall, during the second half of the 1980s, although the number of foreign workers in the GCC countries did not decline, the number of new employment opportunities for foreign workers was considerably lower than that of the previous decade. At the same time, a shift from Arab to Asian workers was enhanced in order to save money.[132] Thus, during the second half of the 1980s, the term "Arab Solidarity" became meaningless, at least in the employment arena.

2.4 The Emergence of a Structural Unemployment Problem

During the 1990s, a new unemployment pattern emerged in most of the Arab countries, both oil-based and non-oil: a structural unemployment. In contrast to previous periods when unemployment rates dropped in response to economic growth (mainly during the 1950s and the 1960s and again during the "oil decade"), during the past decade open unemployment continued to climb even in periods of relatively high economic growth. In the case of Morocco, for example, despite the fact that the real GDP growth rate in 2002 was 3.2%, more than 1% above the population growth rate, urban unemployment increased from 18.3% in 2002 to 19.3% in 2003.[133] In the case of Algeria, despite a rapid GDP growth of 4.1% in real terms in 2002, unemployment declined by only 0.5%.[134] In many other non-oil Arab countries, such as Egypt and Jordan, one can find a similar phenomenon of steadily increasing unemployment despite relatively high economic growth rates.

This phenomenon of a steady rise in unemployment, it should be emphasized, prevailed throughout the past decade not only in the non-oil Arab economies but also in the GCC countries. The SAMBA (Saudi-American Bank) report on the Saudi economy from August 2003 predicted that despite the huge expansion of the Saudi economy, which was estimated at more than 6% in 2003 in real terms due to the highest revenues from oil exports in the past two decades, [135]" it is likely that unemployment will continue to rise."[136]

Another new twist in the economic/employment situation of the non-oil Arab countries during the first half of the 1990s was that the employment pattern in each came to be primarily a function of its position regarding the Iraqi invasion of Kuwait. During the previous two decades, the overall economic/employment situation had been quite similar in all of the non-oil Arab countries, namely, high growth rates followed by recession. This qualitative change in the first half of the 1990s meant relatively high growth rates in those countries that had supported the US-led anti-Iraqi coalition in the Kuwait crisis, as opposed to severe recession, including a sharp rise in unemployment rates, in those that had not.

Thus, Jordan, which did not support the US led anti-Iraqi coalition, was forced to deal in the early 1990s with 350,000 returnees from the GCC countries (mainly from Kuwait and Saudi Arabia).[137] In addition, by 1991, Jordan's external debt amounted to $9.054 billion, of which $2.462 billion was short-term debt,[138] while Jordan's total GDP in that year was slightly above $4 billion.[139] This means that Jordan's external debt was more than twice the GDP. According to a study conducted by ESCWA, the cost of absorbing the returnees totaled $3.141 billion in the years 1992–1994 alone.[140] In other words, the cost of absorbing the returnees was about 80% of the total Jordanian GDP in 1991!. Jordan was not prepared to absorb hundreds of thousands of returnees in the space of only a few months. As such, many of the socioeconomic problems that had previously been hidden, rose to the surface, first and foremost in the employment area. By October 1991, Jordan's official unemployment rate amounted to 22.9% – more than twice that in 1990, prior to the Iraqi invasion of Kuwait. Many economists and analysts, however, believed that the actual unemployment rate in the Kingdom, including those not registered with the authorities, was about 35%.[141] This made Jordan the country with the highest unemployment rate in the entire Arab countries at that time.[142]

The high expectations for economic improvement in Jordan as a result of its October 1994 peace treaty with Israel did not materialize, at least not in the long run. The peace treaty with Israel did provide some major benefits for the Jordanian economy (see the Introduction); however, it did not bring about a revolution in the Kingdom's economy, which continued to suffered from some basic shortcomings, first and foremost high unemployment. By 1998, the official unemployment rate in Jordan was 15.2%, although according to unofficial estimates, the real rate was much higher.[143] According to an ESCWA estimate, in that year Jordan's real unemployment rate was 21%.[144] By early 2001, Jordan's official unemployment rate was 15.7% (14.4% among males and 24.1% among females),[145] declining slightly to 15.3% in December 2002. Unofficial estimates, however, claimed that the real unemployment rate by the end of 2002 "was much higher."[146]

However, as in the GCC countries, the economic recession and high unemployment rates among Jordanian citizens during the 1990s did not bring about a reduction in the number of foreign workers. All of the attempts made by the Jordanian authorities to limit the number of foreign workers failed. According to the December 1994 census data, the number of foreigners in the Kingdom was 314,965,[147] which was almost twice their number prior to the Iraqi invasion of Kuwait. By 1995, the Ministry of Labor estimated the number of foreign workers in the Kingdom at 300,000,[148] while according to unofficial estimates their number was closer to 400,000.[149] During the second half of the 1990s, despite the various attempts of the Jordanian authorities to reduce the number of foreign workers, their number remained more or less stable at the level of 250,000–300,000, the vast majority of whom were Egyptians.[150]

The main reason for the high unemployment rate in parallel to the presence of a large number of foreign workers in Jordan was the inability of the indigenous labor force to compete with the foreign labor force in the private sector. In the public sector, on the other hand, setting priorities in regard to employees and the cost of employment was regulated by the state. Thus, paradoxically, in periods of economic recession, when private employers are trying to save costs, the number of foreign workers has tended to increase, rather than decrease.

A similar process of economic recession occurred in Yemen as well due to Yemenite support of the Iraqis during the Kuwait crisis. As a result of this support, an estimated 800,000–900,000 Yemenites were forced to leave Saudi Arabia and return to Yemen.[151] The Yemenite authorities claimed that the number of returnees was actually much higher, amounting to one million workers and their accompanying family members.[152] As a result of this mass return of workers, Yemen was deprived of both workers' remittances and employment opportunities for its labor force. Thus, by 1992, Yemen's per capita GDP was only $464, as compared with $692 two years earlier, in 1990.[153] Overall, during the period 1990–1994, Yemen's real GDP growth rate reached only 1.9% on annual average, equaling half of the population growth rate during the corresponding period.[154] By 1995, Yemen's unemployment rate was the highest among the Arab countries, amounting to 30%, although it declined slightly to 25% one year later, in 1996.[155] In the year 2000, the official unemployment rate in Yemen was 20.2%,[156] climbing to approximately 25% in early 2003.[157]

The Iraqi invasion of Kuwait caused economic hardship even to those that were not directly involved in the war, through, first and foremost, the heavy labor-intensive tourism industry.[158] The combination of economic recession and a rapid increase in the demand for work opportunities led to a steady increase in unemployment rates in all of the North African countries, without exception. In Tunisia, for example, according to official figures, the average unemployment rate was more than 15% during the period 1994–2000. In addition, large numbers of people were employed on a part-time, casual or seasonal basis, particularly in agriculture.[159] In Morocco, the unemployment rate was estimated at 17.8% in 1996[160] and increased to over 20% by the end of the decade.[161] In Algeria, the unemployment rate was even higher than in Tunisia, climbing from 20.1% in 1991 to 28.0% in 1997[162] and approximately 30% in 2000[163] – representing the highest unemployment rate among all of the Arab countries (not including the Palestinians in the West Bank and Gaza Strip following the onset of *Intifadat al-Aqsa* in late September 2000).

Among the countries that supported the anti-Iraqi coalition during the Kuwait crisis, unemployment rates also increased in the following period despite the economic benefits gained from joining the anti-Iraqi coalition. In the case of Egypt, unemployment rates did not decline despite the relatively rapid economic expansion in the early 1990s, resulting mainly from substantial growth in the tourism, agricultural, construction, manufacturing, and service sectors.[164] According to research conducted by the ALO, unemployment in Egypt in 1994, adjusted for underemployment, reached as high as 21%.[165] Overall, during the period 1991–1998, although Egypt's GDP increased by 35.9% in real terms[166] – far above the population growth rates in the corresponding years – the employment pressure was not abated. Moreover, in contrast to Jordan, Yemen, and Sudan, the number of Egyptian workers in the GCC countries did not decline during the 1990s, but rather increased as part of the reward for Egypt's participation in the anti-Iraqi coalition in the Kuwait crisis. According to the December 1996 census, 2.18 million Egyptian citizens temporarily migrated abroad.[167] By early 2001, the number of Egyptian workers abroad estimated at 1.9 million.[168] Nevertheless, the unemployment rates in Egypt continued to increase because the number of new entrants to the labor force far exceeded the number of new work opportunities for Egyptians, both in Egypt itself and abroad.

Thus, while Egypt's rate of job creation was approximately 400,000 on annual average during the second half of the 1990s, the annual expansion of the workforce amounted to 500,000,[169] reflecting a 20% gap between the number of job opportunities and the expansion of the workforce. By the year 2000, while Egypt's official unemployment rate was 8%,[170] according to unofficial estimates the rate was more than double, approximately 15%–25%.[171] According to official sources, of the 18.2 million Egyptians in the labor force in early 2001, 1.5 million, or 8.2%, were unemployed.[172] In 2002, the official number of the unemployed in Egypt was 1.9 million, while unofficial sources claimed a much higher number.[173] However, even according to the official figures, net unemployment in Egypt jumped by 400,000 in 2000 alone, even though Egypt's GDP growth rate was 1.9%,[174] that is, equal to the population growth rate in that year.

During the first half of the 1990s, among the non-oil Arab economies, Syria achieved the highest economic growth rate, amounting to almost 7% on annual average, namely, approximately 4% in per capita terms.[175] This rapid growth was the combined result of increasing oil production, from 200,000 b/d to 600,000 b/d;[176] large grants from the GCC countries, which amounted to more than $3 billion during the period 1991–1993;[177] a sharp rise in the number of Syrian workers abroad, mainly in Lebanon and the GCC countries;[178] and a marked increase in agricultural production due to the good weather in the early 1990s.[179] However, starting in the mid-1990s, the Syrian economy began to deteriorate again as a result of two years of drought; low rates of private investments due to the slow privatization process; and, most importantly, the diminishing prospects for a Syrian-Israeli peace treaty. In per capita terms, the GDP growth rate was 1.8% in 1996, –1.3% in 1997, -1.5% 1998, and 0.6% in 1999.[180] The economic recession in the second half of the 1990s, combined with the inability to increase the number of Syrian workers abroad and the continued rapid expansion of the labor force, led to an increase in Syria's unemployment rate. According to official Syrian figures, by 2000, the overall unemployment rate was more than 9.5%, having increased from 7.2% in 1995.[181] However, as in the cases of Egypt and Jordan, unofficial sources claimed a much higher unemployment rate, estimating it at 15%–20% in the late 1990s.[182]

Since 2000, however, Syrian economic performance has substantially improved, due mainly to an enhanced economic relationship with Iraq that contributed to the Syrian economy in two main areas. First was the rapid increase in the export of goods to Iraq, from only $200,000 in 1995[183] to as high as $3 billion in annual terms by the end of 2002.[184] Second was the inflow of Iraqi oil, which enabled Syria to keep its oil exports at 400,000 b/d, bringing oil export revenues to a level of $1.8 billion by 2002.[185] The increase in governmental revenues led the Syrian authorities to adopt an ambitious employment program with two major provisions: mandatory retirement from the public sector at the age of 60 and acceleration in the absorption of university graduates into the public sector.[186] However, the US invasion of Iraq in March 2003 ended the economic relationship between Syria and Iraq. Thus, there is no doubt that the end of Saddam Husayn's regime represented a turning point for Syria, not only from a political point of view but also from an economic one.

Increasing unemployment rates during the 1990s have been the rule in the GCC oil economies as well, without exception. In addition to the rapid increase in employment demands due to the high natural increase rates, the prolonged low oil prices during most of the 1990s limited the ability of the GCC governments to continue with their traditional policy of absorbing the vast majority of the local labor forces into the public sector. The attempts of the GCC countries to reduce their dependence on foreign workers during the 1980s and the early 1990s failed,[187] leading to a continued increase in the number of foreign workers in each of the GCC countries during the second half of the 1980s, albeit at a slower pace than in the first half of the decade. Overall, in 1990, the total foreign labor force in the GCC countries was estimated at 5.218 million, as compared with 4.374 million in 1985, representing an increase of 19.3% (see table 3.4). Thus, the failure in the implementation of the labor force nationalization policy in all of the GCC countries led to a creation of dual labor markets, similar to the phenomenon that had emerged in Jordan a decade earlier with the end of the "oil decade": a steady increase in the number of foreign workers in parallel to a steady rise in the unemployment rates of the indigenous labor forces. By 1999, the number of foreign workers in the GCC countries was estimated at 7.114 million, as compared with 5.218 million in 1990 – representing an increase of 63.3% within less than a decade (see table 3.4).

The main factor accounting for the creation of this labor market dualism was, and still is, the huge salary gap between the nationals and the foreign labor forces. In Saudi Arabia, for example, during the mid-1990s, the gap between the salaries of the nationals and the foreigners amounted to at least 100% in all categories, from unskilled labor to the top managerial positions.[188] By 2001, while the monthly average wage for Saudi national males was SR (Saudi Riyal) 6,684, it was only SR 1,710 for foreign males, representing a gap of more than threefold. Among females, whose percentages in the labor force were marginal in any case, the wage gap between the nationals and the foreign workers was far below that of the males (SR 3,151 for nationals as compared with SR 2,403 for non-nationals).[189] In the other GCC labor markets, one can find the same wage gaps between nationals and foreigners.[190] This issue was addressed in the NCB (National Commercial Bank) report from 1995, as follows:

> Aside from certain managerial and clerical jobs, the employment of nationals in the private sector companies has been rather limited. Jobs in the public sector are still the first choice of employment . . .[191]

The main reason for the huge gap between private and public sector wages was that the GCC authorities did not impose a minimum wage rate in the private sector and left it up to negotiation between the employer and the foreign worker.[192] Thus, the wage mechanism for foreign workers in the private sector was set according to the wage levels in the home countries of those workers, rather than the salaries in the host country. This system, it should be emphasized, was part of the GCC *rentier* political system, which was and still is based on the support of the politically powerful lobbies of the larger trading families. Obviously, their aim was to pay the lowest salaries possible to the foreign workers.[193] Moreover, by not setting a minimum wage for foreign workers, the GCC royal families in effect extended to the middle classes the privilege of employing cheap foreign workers in their homes and businesses. On the other hand, the absorption of the nationals into the public sector was the major mechanism by which the authorities distributed the oil wealth to the citizenry. In other words, it was an exchange of political support for economic benefits.[194] Thus, as Hazem Beblawi noted: "Though utterly free enterprise-oriented, the number of government employees in the oil states is only matched by socialist-oriented states."[195]

Thus, the private sector in each of the GCC countries continues to rely heavily on cheap foreign labor, while the indigenous labor forces are primarily concentrated in the public sector. In fact, foreign workers can be found in any given skill category – almost without limitation on scale, skill, or nationality – from top managerial positions to unskilled agricultural jobs. In regard to the importing of labor to Saudi Arabia, Said Abdullah al-Shaikh, the Chief Economist of the Saudi NCB, claimed that:

> [It] created a wage structure that reflected the flexibility of importing different skills and not the extent of searching domestically. The relative scarcities of local labor skills did not affect the wage structure [for nationals] since demand for all needed skills could be met through imports . . . The implication of this is that both the level and the structure of wages that prevailed in Saudi Arabia have been determined independently from the supply of Saudi local labor.[196]

Hossein Askari, Vahid Nowshirvani, and Mohamed Jaber, on the other hand, claimed that: "By acting as an employer of last resort, and by setting public wages above market rates, governments have distorted the labor market."[197] Regardless of whether one subscribes to "the right wage mechanism" as that of the private sector according to Askari, Nowshirvani, and Jaber, or that of the public sector according to Said Abdullah al-Shaikh, the end result is still the same: huge wage gaps between the public and private sectors, leading to a tiny proportion of nationals in the private sector, almost solely in the top managerial positions. In 1994, foreign workers constituted only 5.5% of the total employees in the Saudi Arabian public sector, as compared with 94.5% in the private sector.[198] Conversely, the percentages of nationals employed in the private sector are very low. In Kuwait, for example, the percentage of nationals employed in the private sector in 1997 was only 7%,[199] decreasing further to only 6% in early 2003.[200] Overall, according to the ILO estimate, by the end of the 1990s: "Less than 10% of the nationals working in these countries are in the private sector."[201]

The long-term inescapable consequence of the GCC dual-labor market mechanism is a steady increase in the unemployment of nationals, due to the inability to absorb them either in the private or in the public sector. According to the Omani December 1993 population census, the unemployment rate among nationals amounted to 11.9%.[202] In Bahrain, the unemployment rate in early 1993 was estimated at 15%,[203] and in the UAE the unemployment rate among nationals in 1995 was 15%.[204] According to the Gulf Center for Strategic Studies, by the mid-1990s, the unemployment rate among Saudi nationals amounted to 20%.[205]

During the second half of the 1990s, despite some success in the implementation of the labor force nationalization policies, first and foremost in Bahrain and to a lesser extent in Oman, the number of foreign workers in each of the GCC countries continued to increase, albeit at a slower pace than previously in the cases of Saudi Arabia and Oman (see table 3.4). However, due to the dual labor market system, the unemployment rates among nationals continued to climb as well. In the case of Bahrain, the unemployment rate in 1998 reached 15%, and as high as 30% among the Shi'i rural dwellers.[206] By the year 2000, unemployment among Bahraini nationals amounted to 17%,[207] declining back again to 15% in mid-2003 due to the economic strength regained from the high oil prices in the past four years.[208] The unemployment rate among Saudi males amounted to 14% in 2000,[209] climbing to 20% in 2001 and 2002,[210] despite the rapid economic expansion as a result of the high oil prices.[211] The other GCC countries demonstrated a similar phenomenon of steadily increasing unemployment rates among nationals in parallel to a large presence of foreign workers and, in some cases, such as Qatar and Kuwait, even an increase in their numbers. In regard to the unemployment problem among the GCC nationals, Kapiszewski claimed:

> The problem of unemployment of nationals in the GCC countries is, of course, different in nature from that in most other countries in the world. It is a "masked" unemployment, since millions of foreign workers have jobs in these countries. Thus, it is more a question of integrating the national workforce into the labor market than a question of expanding the economy to create new jobs. [212]

However, from a purely economic point of view, it seems that many of the foreign workers in the GCC countries simply cannot be replaced by nationals due to the huge wage gaps between the two groups.[213] Moreover, a considerable number of the foreign workers in the GCC countries are employed in domestic services as gardeners, nannies, and drivers, the latter mainly in Saudi Arabia where women are not allowed to drive. These workers, of course, are not subject to the GCC labor force nationalization policies and cannot be replaced by nationals under any circumstances. Consequently, their effect on the national labor force employment picture is marginal, if any. For private sector employers, the replacement of foreign workers by nationals would actually mean replacing cheap employees with expensive employees. One Kuwaiti company director claimed that such a move "would be disastrous. We have already cut our margins. If we had to pay the wages Kuwaitis demand, we would not be competitive."[214] As such, the issue of national employment in the GCC countries during the 1990s, particularly during the second half, became a matter of occupational and wage structures, rather than a matter of quantity. The conclusion is that the high unemployment rate among GCC nationals represents "real," rather than "masked," unemployment.

In the mid-1990s, it appeared that addressing the employment problem in the GCC countries was comprised of two dimensions, with only a limited connection between them. One dimension was to narrow the number of foreign workers in order to decrease the huge amounts of their remittances, which constituted a substantial percentage of the GCC oil revenues. The second dimension was to provide suitable work opportunities to the rapidly growing national workforces. Consequently, similar to Jordan, the number of foreign workers in the GCC countries not only failed to decline during periods of economic recession, but rather continued to increase. Thus, during the 1990s, the GCC labor market structure changed by 180 degrees from a "resource pressure on population," as Gad Gilbar defined it in the "oil decade,"[215] to a "demographic pressure on the economy," particularly on the labor market.

Unlike the Eastern European countries, whose recent adoption of the capitalist economic approach has led to the privatization of many governmental factories and establishments, including mass dismissal of employees, the major source of unemployment in the Arab countries is the inability of new entrants to the labor force to find employment in the first place. The core of the structural unemployment problem in the Arab countries is a basic imbalance between the number of first-time job seekers and the creation of new work opportunities, due both to the wide-based age pyramids and the increasing labor force participation rates, in parallel to the insufficient number of work opportunities provided by the private sector – a direct result of the undemocratic political system in the Arab countries.

From an employment survey conducted in 11 Arab countries in the mid-1980s, it appears that 59% of the unemployed were first-time job seekers. According to the

Egyptian 1976 population census, 95% of the unemployed were first-time job seekers.[216] In 1989, while the overall unemployment in Tunisia was 14%, it was as high as 40% among the age group of 18–26.[217] Also in that year, the unemployment rate among young urban Moroccans was 30% – almost twice the national average.[218] Moreover, a major component of urban unemployment during the 1980s in both the oil and the non-oil Arab countries was made up of young women who were first-time job seekers. Thus, it can be said that the highest unemployment rates in the Arab countries, without exception, were among women in the age group of 15–24.[219]

This trend of much higher unemployment rates among the younger age groups, particularly among first-time job seekers, was even further exacerbated during the 1990s. According to ESCWA figures, in the mid-1990s, 59% of the unemployed in the member countries of the organization were young first-time job seekers.[220] By 1999, according to the ILO figures, as high as 89.4% of the unemployed in Egypt were under the age of 30, and 60.1% were under the age of 25.[221] Likewise, according to an official Omani estimate, up to 60,000 Omanis under the age of 24 were unemployed in early 2003.[222] In the case of Syria in 1999, according to an official source, the unemployment rate among the age group of 15–24 "reached an abnormally high level of 72%."[223]

Since the 1980s, paradoxically, the sector suffering the most from high unemployment in all of the Arab countries is that of young graduates from universities and other institutes of higher education.[224] This trend was even further exacerbated during the past decade. Henry Azzam recently estimated that in Egypt, Syria and Jordan, more than 50% of the unemployed are high school and higher education graduates.[225] For example, according to official Jordanian data, by the end of 2002, the unemployment rate among young Jordanian university graduates was 32.1%, while unofficial sources claimed an even higher rate.[226] One common argument for the high unemployment rates among the ranks of the young educated in the Arab countries is: "the educational system's failure to provide its students with the kinds of skills needed for private sector jobs."[227] While this argument is relevant to the Arab oil-states, it is quite irrelevant in the cases of the poorer Arab countries, considering that in these countries, with the exception of Jordan, there are no foreign workers employed in the private sector. The major factor accounting for the increasing unemployment rates among young university graduates in the poorer Arab countries is the fact that among their four main labor-absorbing options – namely, governmental employment, other public sector employment, migration to the Arab oil states, and private sector employment – the number of new employment opportunities being created were rapidly shrinking during the past two decades.[228]

In contrast, in the GCC oil economies, a major factor, and perhaps even the most important factor, accounting for the high unemployment rates among high school and university graduates is the mismatch between the demands of the labor markets, particularly the private sectors, on the one hand, and the kinds of educational and vocational training available, on the other.[229]

3   The Increase in Disguised Unemployment and Underemployment

A prominent phenomenon of the Arab labor markets found in both the oil and the non-oil economies is that of huge disguised unemployment and, in the poorer Arab countries, also underemployment. A paramount aim of "Arab Socialism" – an Arab variety of the étatism of the developing countries in the 1950s and 1960s – was to narrow the huge socioeconomic gaps between the various stratums, primarily through a reduction in unemployment. The major tool for achieving this aim was to employ the vast majority of the urban workforce in the governmental bureaucracy (mainly high school and university graduates) and state-owned establishments and factories. From a political point of view, the massive employment in the public sector, combined with the wide variety of social services and subsidies of basic foodstuffs, enhanced the identification of public sector employees with the authorities' ideologies and policies. Overall, in the early 1980s, 28% of the Egyptian workforce was employed in the public sector[230] – an extremely high percentage considering that 2.5–3 million Egyptians at that time were working abroad and approximately another 35% were working in agriculture. This means that private sector employment in the urban areas remained quite low, despite Anwar al-Sadat's *Infitah* policy.

Over time, however, due both to escalating employment pressures caused by a rapid increase in the workforces and poor performance of the private sectors, this policy led to increasing rates of disguised unemployment in the public sectors. As Rodney Wilson noted: "Underemployment remains, but in practice employees receive what amounts to part-time pay for part-time work, though that is not the official job description."[231] For example, a governmental labor survey conducted in Egypt in 1979 revealed that in Cairo alone there were 240,000 public sector employees "with nothing to do."[232] According to another estimate, the disguised unemployment in the Egyptian public sector in the late 1970s amounted to half a million employees.[233] During the 1990s, the trend of high rates of disguised unemployment continued and even accelerated. In the case of Egypt for example, in the early 1990s, disguised unemployment in the public sector was estimated at 20%.[234] A similar phenomenon of huge disguised unemployment rates is common to other Arab countries as well.

Despite the liberalization and privatization measures taken by many of the Arab countries during the 1990s, the public sector continued to be the larger employer for the urban workforces. In 1995, an estimated 35% of Egypt's total civilian workforce was employed by the public sector.[235] In 2001, the number of public sector employees in Egypt skyrocketed to 5.5 million.[236] By the year 2000, the Syrian workforce amounted to approximately 4 million, of whom 1.4 million were employed by the public sector.[237] During the past few years, the Syrian authorities have allocated a budget to absorb an additional 70,000 new employees into the public sector each year.[238] The aim of this policy is to prevent the increasing open unemployment, particularly among the educated young, to climb to a "politically dangerous" level.

Jordan is an example of a country that did not adopt the "Arab socialism" policy and has subsequently suffered from extremely high rates of disguised unemployment in the public sector. As the Jordanian Minister of Labor, 'Abd al-Hafez al-Shakhanbeh, acknowledged in April 1996:

> The administrative ranks in the government are highly bloated, as the number of civil servants totals 121,000, whereas in a country like Tunisia where the population is twice as much, the number of government workers is 50 percent less than in Jordan.[239]

Fahed al-Fanek, a leading Jordanian economist, estimated the number of governmental employees in Jordan in 1998 at 157,000. An additional 44,000 worked in other non-governmental public sector establishments and factories, and 85,000 were serving in the army. By early 1999, the number of Jordanians employed in the public sector amounted to 282,000, representing 23.5% of the total Jordanian workforce at that time.[240]

According to a recent World Bank study, the percentage of public sector employees among the total non-agricultural employees in the Middle East is the highest among the developing countries worldwide.[241] Thus, during the second half of the 1990s, public sector salaries in the Middle East represented 11% of the GDP – twice the average among the developing countries worldwide.[242] Richards and Waterbury argued that the reason a job in the public sector was and still is so attractive in the poorer Arab countries, despite its being low-paying, is that it "can easily be combined with a second job and provides a kind of 'income insurance.'"[243] Moreover, Alan Cowell claimed in 1990 that Syrian low-ranking government employees "shake down whatever they can because wages, at the black market rate, work out to only around $45 per month."[244]

Since the late 1980s, accelerating disguised unemployment in the public sector has become widespread among the GCC countries as well. However, the phenomenon of underemployment, meaning very low salaries for public sector employees, has not yet taken hold in these countries, as the GCC royal families continue to keep the salaries of the public sector national employees on a high level in order to maintain their political loyalty.

The sector that has suffered the most from disguised unemployment (and in the poorer Arab economies, also from underemployment) is that of higher education graduates. Since the late 1970s, however, and in Egypt even earlier, the balance between the supply and demand of university graduates in the Arab countries has been tipped in favor of the supply side. The major employer of graduates, that is, the public sector, could not continue to absorb additional employees. The levels of both disguised unemployment and underemployment were already high, and the governments of the non-oil Arab countries could no longer afford to increase the salary expenditures. As a *FORBES Magazine* report on the Egyptian economy stated in October 1982:

> The government promises every college-educated Egyptian a job, and piles them into offices with little to do but complicate the ministries and public companies. Such employees are not paid much . . . but they cannot be fired, either. Many hold two jobs to make ends meet. Others demand "lubrication" [*baqshish*] . . . for any effort.[245]

Equally destructive is the system of *baqshish*, which is common in other Arab countries as well. In the case of Syria, for example, David Lesch wrote in 1998 that:

> The first order of business . . . in Syria, is to choose the right local broker . . . One cannot enter into a private or public sector business situation without a local mediator [*wasta*] because the vertical patronage networks that exist in the country require it . . . [246]

From an economic point of view, such guarantees of employment in the public sector for every college and university graduate are very detrimental because rather than promoting excellence in education, they serve to discourage competition between graduates. In any case, due to the rapid expansion of the labor forces on the one hand, and the private sector weakness on the other hand, the Arab governments are not able to live up to their promises. It is not surprising that in 2001, the waiting time required of higher education graduates on the waiting list for public sector employment in Egypt amounted to 11 years![247]

One of the most devastating consequences of the large-scale disguised unemployment in the public sectors of the Arab countries is their low labor productivity. Egypt, Algeria, and Jordan have the lowest rates of labor productivity growth in the region and are also the ones with the largest share of governmental employment among the non-agricultural labor force.[248] In the EIU's 1985 Annual Supplement, it was argued that: "Rapid growth in population and the creation of unproductive jobs under social and political pressure have given rise to a declining trend in labor productivity."[249] Large-scale underemployment in the Arab countries prevails not only in the public sector but in the private sector as well, particularly among those who make their living in the agriculture and tourism sectors, due to the seasonal nature of these occupations.[250] The underemployment in tourism and its related services and industries is attributable not only to the seasonal nature of this sector but also to the security-political instability affecting the number of tourists in the region. In the agriculture sector, the underemployment is concentrated mainly among those cultivating non-irrigated lands. This problem is particularly severe in Syria, where only 22.6% of the total cultivated lands were irrigated in 2000.[251] Many of the Syrians who make their living from the non-irrigated lands are forced to work in neighboring Lebanon and Jordan during the intervening periods between agricultural seasons.

From a purely political point of view, however, the policy of absorbing the vast majority of the higher education graduates into the public sector proved to be very useful because the major supporters of the Arab revolutionary/military regimes were, in addition to the rural populations, the students and graduates who were employed by the public sector and provided the "ideological" support for these regimes. This, it appears, was and still is one of the paramount factors contributing to the stability of the Arab regimes.

4 Unemployment as a Differentiating Factor between the Arab Countries and the Developed Countries

Overall, it seems that the differences in the unemployment patterns between the Arab countries, particularly the non-oil economies, and the developed countries can be summarized in the following six factors:

(a) *Scale of unemployment.* The open unemployment rates in each of the Arab countries in the early 2000s were above 15%, and in many of the non-oil countries even above 20%, whereas in the developed countries the open unemployment rates were much lower, amounting in 2001 to 7.4% on average in the EU countries and less than 6% in both Japan and the US .[252]

(b) *"Unemployment by choice."* In almost all of the developed countries worldwide, unemployment payments are provided by the government, thus allowing the labor forces in these countries, particularly the unmarried young, to be more selective in choosing work. Many jobs that are considered to be unattractive, due to either their low social status or their low wages, are in most cases filled by foreign workers, such as Turks in Germany, North Africans in France, Albans in Italy, Indians and

Pakistanis in the UK, and so forth. Thus, "long-term unemployment"[253] in the EU countries represents as much as 45% of total unemployment,[254] with the labor market mismatch apparently lying between the market demands and the types of jobs available on the one hand, and the desires and expectations of the indigenous labor forces on the other hand.

Like their developed counterparts, during the 1970s and 1980s, a large percentage of unemployment among the GCC nationals, particularly among the young, was a matter of "unemployment by choice." In the non-oil Arab countries, on the other hand, the huge rates of unemployment, particularly among the young, were a result of the mismatch between the number of new available work opportunities and the number of new entrants to the labor force.

(c) The scale of disguised unemployment and underemployment. In the Arab countries, in both the oil and the non-oil economies, the scale of disguised unemployment is far beyond that found in the developed countries, due mainly to two factors. First, the growth of the labor supply has greatly outpaced economic growth and the creation of new work opportunities in productive areas. This has left the Arab governments with no other choice, particularly following the end of the "oil decade," but to absorb a huge percentage of the urban workforce into the public sector, mainly through declining real wages. A high rate of disguised unemployment, particularly in the poorer overpopulated Arab countries, also prevails in the private sector due to the low wages and low productivity. In the developed countries, on the other hand, economic growth rates and the pace of creation of new work opportunities tend to be higher than the growth of the labor force. Together with much higher salaries, this trend reduces the rates of disguised unemployment, in both the private and the public sectors.

The second major factor accounting for the difference in the scale of disguised unemployment between the Arab countries and the developed countries is the difference in their socioeconomic policies. All of the Arab countries, with the exception of Lebanon, have adopted a state economic policy of étatism, with one of its main characteristics being a wide scale of public sector employment. This is in contrast to the developed countries, where capitalism is the prevailing policy and thus the percentage of public sector employment within the total employment is considerably lower than in the Arab countries. The fact that disguised unemployment prevails on a much larger scale in the public sector than in the private sector has contributed to the much higher disguised unemployment rates in the Arab countries.

(d) The age composition of the unemployed. As already discussed, the vast majority of the unemployed in both the oil and the non-oil Arab economies are young. In the developed countries, although the percentage of the young among the total population of the unemployed is higher than their percentage in the labor force, it is still considerably lower than the corresponding percentage in the Arab countries. For example, in 2000, the percentage of the under-30 age group within the total population of the unemployed was 30.9% in Austria[255] and 43.4% in Belgium,[256] as compared with almost 90% in Egypt for example.[257]

This difference in the age composition of the unemployed population is mainly the result of the following three factors. First, due to the wide-based age pyramid, the overall percentage of the young within the total labor forces of the Arab countries is much higher than in the developed countries, which are characterized by a much older age structure. Second, the already high female labor force participation rates in the developed countries contribute to preserving stable overall labor force participation rates. In the non-oil Arab countries, on the other hand, the steady increase in female labor force participation rates, particularly since the mid-1980s, is creating a situation in which the growth rates of the workforces are far above the growth rates of the working age population. Third, despite privatization measures, the public sector is still the largest employer in the Arab countries, making it natural for unemployment to be more widespread among the young, many of whom are waiting for a job in the public sector. Since it is almost impossible to fire an employee from the public sector in the Arab countries, in both the oil and the non-oil economies, the percentage of unemployment in old age is relatively small. In contrast, a considerable number of the unemployed in the developed capitalist economies are older workers who have been laid off from the traditionally heavy labor-intensive industries (such as textile, wood, steel, etc.) and who are not equipped with the necessary skills to integrate into modern technological industries and services.

(e) *The educational and professional levels of the unemployed.* While in the Arab countries a significant percentage of the unemployed are higher education graduates, in the developed countries the vast majority of the unemployed are uneducated, due mainly to the economic structure of these countries. In the case of the EU countries, for example, almost 90% of the new jobs created during the period 1995–2001 were concentrated in the high-tech sector (almost 20%) and the knowledge-intensive service and industrial sectors (approximately 70%).[258] Thus, in each of the EU countries, the unemployment rate among those with a tertiary educational level was one-third that of individuals with less than a secondary educational level.[259] In other developed countries worldwide, one can find a similar trend of increasing unemployment in line with decreasing educational level. In the case of the US, for example, in 1997 the unemployment rates among those with a professional degree or a doctorate were 1.3% and 1.4%, respectively, whereas this rate sharply increased to 7.1% among those with less than a secondary educational level.[260]

(f) *The geographical concentration of the unemployment.* While in the developed countries the unemployment rates, in most cases, are much higher in the remote areas than in the major urban centers, the opposite is true in the Arab countries where the unemployment rates in the major cities far exceed those in the countryside.[261] The much higher unemployment rates in the major cities than in the rural areas in the poorer Arab countries can be attributed to the following two factors: First, until today, the agricultural employment pattern in the Arab countries is characterized in most cases by "household production," meaning that the entire family works together on cultivating the family fields. Thus, in effect, all of the family members are employed, including the women and children. Although this mode of employment creates a large scale of disguised unemployment and underemployment, open unemployment in the rural areas is much lower than in the major cities.

Second, there is an absence of employment opportunities in the countryside in the Arab countries other than in agriculture. Consequently, those who lose their means of livelihood as a result of scarcity in agricultural lands[262] are forced to migrate to the major cities, where employment options, mainly in the informal sector, are much more flexible and varied. In the developed countries, on the other hand, the extremely high cost of city living, particularly housing, combined with the more flexible employment options available in the countryside and the remote areas, in parallel to the governmental allowances to the unemployed, "keep" many of the unemployed in the remote areas.

More recently, however, there has also been further acceleration of economic hardships and unemployment in the peripheral areas in the poorer Arab countries. This is the case in Egypt, where the poorest areas are in Upper Egypt, as well as in Jordan, where the unemployment rates in 2002 in Ma'an, Tafila, Mafraq, and Madaba were considerably higher than in the capital Amman.[263] The political implications of the deteriorating economic conditions in the southern region of Jordan were manifested by the demonstrations against the Hashemite regime in this area, in which the Islamist opposition played a major part. Thus, whereas in the past the main activities of Islamist opposition groups were concentrated in the major cities, a new politically dangerous phenomenon is emerging in some of the non-oil Arab countries: that of increasing Islamist opposition in the remote and peripheral areas.

5 Conclusions

Until now, the non-oil Arab regimes have succeeded in avoiding a major political crisis on socioeconomic grounds through a series of temporary and unpredictable events leading to sharp economic growth and a rapid increase in employment opportunities within a relatively short period time. The first event was the "oil boom" of October 1973, which led to rapid economic expansion until the mid-1980s.

The second event was the Iraqi invasion of Kuwait, which served as an economic "spring-board" for the Arab countries that supported the US-led anti-Iraqi coalition, first and foremost for Egypt and Syria. In the case of Egypt, a major part of the "reward" for their support of the anti-Iraqi coalition was the considerable increase in the number of Egyptians working in the GCC countries, particularly in Saudi Arabia and Kuwait, in addition to the huge US financial aid and soft loans from the IMF. In the case of Syria, the "reward" was in both cash and soft loans from the GCC countries. Thus, the economies of these countries recovered to a large extent during the first half of the 1990s after the deep recession of the second half of the 1980s.

The third event was the improvement in Arab–Israeli relations during the 1990s, which included the September 1993 Israeli–Palestinian Oslo Accords, the October 1994 Jordanian-Israeli peace agreement, and the Syrian-Israeli peace negotiations. These political developments led to sharp growth in the tourism industry as well as expansion of foreign investments in the region. In 1999, the number of tourists in Egypt climbed to 4.8 million, of whom 66% were from Europe. During the 1990s, the tourism industry became the largest private sector employer (direct and indirect) in Egypt,[264] and tourism receipts reached more than $4 billion – higher than ever before.[265] In 1999, the number of tourists in Jordan reached 1.35 million, exceeding all previous record numbers.[266] Also in the North African countries, the tourism industry prospered during the 1990s. Since the tourism industry is a heavy labor-intensive, its expansion added a substantial number of new work opportunities.

The fourth event was the UN boycott on Iraq, which not only led to an increase in oil revenues but also to a surge in Arab exports to Iraq. Thus, the Iraqi crisis actually benefited most of the non-oil Arab economies and more than compensated for the economic losses in tourism revenues caused by the Palestinian *Intifadat al-Aqsa* and the Iraqi crisis.

However, all of these events led to only temporary relief. Following the American invasion of Iraq and the removal of Saddam Husayn's regime, the non-oil Arab countries must now find other sources for their exports, without which their economies will again deteriorate and unemployment will surge even further, particularly among the young educated first-time job seekers. Although in May 2003 Jordan received an extraordinary cash grant of $500 million from the US as compensation for the losses incurred from the war in Iraq and in 2004 is expected to receive another $200 million, in 2005 the US aid to Jordan is expected to drop back to its normal level of $250 million annually.[267] In any case, it seems that the additional US grants still did not compensate for the overall Jordanian losses incurred from the overthrow of Saddam Husayn's regime.

Moreover, the ups and downs in the GDP growth rates of many Arab countries during the 1990s, in both the oil-based and the non-oil based economies, did not have a great influence on the employment situation, as these fluctuations occurred in response to changing oil prices rather than to alterations in the mode of production or the pattern of labor migration. In late 1988, George Alan, a reporter of the monthly The Middle East, wrote an article about the Syrian economy entitled "An Economy Saved by Circumstances."[268] It seems that this title is also fitting for most of the non-oil Arab economies during the past three decades.

In the 91st Session of the ILO, held in Geneva on June 12, 2003, Jordan's King 'Abdallah, clearly underscored the connection between political stability and the employment situation by saying that: "Young people, who desperately need opportunities and hope, see themselves and their societies held back by poverty, health crises, illiteracy and more . . . Is it any surprise that these communities can become recruiting grounds for extremist ideologies?"[269]

4 | Between Pro-Natalist and Anti-Natalist in the Arab Countries

"Egypt with 20 million people could have been a Mediterranean country, a Greece or Portugal. Egypt with 70 million people will be Bangladesh."

Boutros Boutros-Ghali[1]

I   The Attitudes Toward Population Growth in Historical Perspective

Michael Todaro raised the basic demographic dilemma: "is rapid population growth per se as serious a problem as many people believe, or is it a manifestation of more fundamental problems of underdevelopment and the unequal utilization of global resources between rich and poor nations, as others argue?"[2] The growing emphasis on "globalization," or the "new world economic order," on the one hand, and the steadily increasing socioeconomic gaps between the OECD countries (see Appendix 2),[3] and the developing countries, on the other hand, have only intensified the dispute over the issue of population growth and its socioeconomic effects in the developing countries for both the short and the long terms.

Until the mid-twentieth century, with very few exceptions, the conventional world-wide attitude toward the new phenomenon of rapid accelerated population growth was positive and was even viewed as an important advantage from both political-security and economic perspectives. The arguments for supporting rapid population growth as a positive phenomenon were, respectively, that a large nation is a strong nation and that rapid population growth would facilitate the adoption of modern mass production techniques and advanced technology in both agriculture and industry. In contrast to this conventional positive attitude toward rapid population growth, were the few economists and philosophers, starting in the late eighteenth century, who argued that in the long run, rapid population growth would have devastating economic as well as political consequences and that this new phenomenon should be curbed or at least controlled.

Among these, one of the first and certainly the most famous, was an English reverend and philosopher, Thomas Malthus (1766–1834),[4] who in 1798 published a book entitled *An Essay on the Principle of Population.*[5] Malthus' basic argument was that while population increases in a geometric ratio,[6] the means of subsistence increases in an arithmetic ratio.[7] Thus, the inevitable result would be a steady decrease of per capita agricultural land and eventually a steady decrease in the marginal food production for every additional agricultural laborer, in line with the law of diminishing marginal productivity. Malthus' conclusion was that in order to avoid conflicts over the means of production, people should limit the number of their offspring. This theory was entitled "the Malthusian Population Trap," or "the Low Level Equilibrium Population Trap."[8] Immediately following the publication of the first version of *An Essay on the Principle of Population*, Malthus was harshly criticized by many of his time. Eventually, the support for Malthus' theory came from an unexpected direction: from feminists and from other organizations promoting the use of contraceptives. Thus, ironically, "the father" of the modern family planning programs was a reverend who personally rejected the use of contraceptives from a religious point of view.

Since the 1960s, but more so since the 1970s, when worldwide natural increase rates peaked at more than 2% annually, the "neo-Malthusians" warned of global catastrophe if the current population growth rates would not be sharply reduced. They pointed to the starvation epidemics and the overall poor socioeconomic conditions in Sub-Saharan Africa as a "Malthusian Population Trap." They advocated, in contrast to Malthus himself, the use of modern contraceptives, including free abortions in public hospitals, in order to bring about a fertility decline within the shortest amount of time possible.[9] The basic argument of the "neo-Malthusians" is that rapid population growth has a detrimental effect on environmental conditions and quality of life, thereby "echoing Malthus' original concerns."[10] Their major argument is that the planet is close to the upper limit of its ecology caring-capacity and that a reduction in population growth rates is crucial for the basic survival of the planet. Thus, while in the past the debate on the validity of Malthus' theory was concentrated on the issue of the ability to produce sufficient food for the rapidly growing population, the modern debate, since the 1970s, has been more focused on the environmental and ecological arenas.

In contrast to Malthus' pessimistic attitude regarding the caring-capacity limit of the planet was that of the French mathematician and philosopher, Marie Jean Antoine Nicolas Caritat, the Marquis de Condorcet (1743–1794). In a book entitled *Esquisse d'un Tableau Historique des Progrès de l'Esprit Humain* [*Sketch for a Historical Picture of the Progress of the Human Mind*], published in 1795, three years before Malthus' first version of *An Essay on the Principle of Population*, Condorcet argued that modern technologies and new methods for agricultural production would increase the level of food production. At the same time, reforms in the educational system would bring education to the lower stratums. Thus, fertility decline would ensue and the problem of overpopulation would be solved voluntarily without the use of coercive means by the authorities.[11]

The modern criticism of Malthus' theory is that he disregarded the most important dimension of the Industrial Revolution – the huge technological progress that led to a steady increase in the ability to produce food. Overall, although the world's population increased fourfold during the twentieth century, the world's GDP increased 20 to 40 times during the corresponding period, leading to a sharp increase in the standard of living throughout the world, even in the least developed Sub-Saharan African countries.[12] The meaning of the steady technological advancement is that much more food can be produced with substantial less water and agricultural lands. Overall, the per capita food available for direct human consumption increased by 24% during the period 1961–1998, despite the rapid population growth.[13] As a result, during the second half of the twentieth century the prices of basic food items decreased steadily.

In fact, the decrease in the past three decades has been so sharp that all of the industrial countries, without exception, are being forced to subsidize the agricultural sector on a large scale; otherwise, the prices would be so low that it would become economically infeasible for the farmers to continue to produce basic food items due to a huge surplus of production. Thus, the famine and even starvation diseases that occurred in some of the sub-Saharan African countries during the second half of the twentieth century should not be attributed to the "Malthusian Population Trap," but rather to economic underdevelopment resulting from political instability, including numerous civil wars.

In any case, the dispute over the socioeconomic consequences of rapid population growth is still ongoing. As Steven Wisensale and Amany Khodair wrote in the late 1990s, "In many respects the echoes of Malthus' pessimism and Condorcet's optimism are heard clearly today as the great demographic debate of the 20th century moving into the 21st."[14] However, many people, and not only those from the religious establishments, are not convinced that rapid population growth is by itself at the core of the poverty and underdevelopment in the developing countries. Rather, they point to many other factors, first and foremost to the favorable conditions accorded to the developed countries in international trade – a new variant of the "Dependency Theory." The basic argument of the neo-Marxist economists during the 1960s and 1970s, for example, was that in many rural areas, mainly in sub-Saharan Africa, much arable land was left unused due to shortages of labor. Others argued that rapid population growth would promote technological developments and cost-saving production methods through free-market mechanisms and increasing governmental infrastructure investments.[15]

Some, although small in number, of those dealing with Middle Eastern economic development have argued along the same lines of the neo-Marxist economists. For example, although there was a seven-fold increase in Egypt's population during the twentieth century, yet, the living standard of the Egyptian population considerably improved during this time, as manifested by the sharp rise in life expectancy, the marked reduction in infant and child mortality rates, the improvements in educational level for the whole population, and above all, the substantial per capita GDP growth in real terms.[16] The mistake of these researchers is that the improvement in the Egyptian standard of living during the twentieth century – although it certainly is "an unarguable fact" – *was not because of* Egypt's rapid population growth, *but in spite of it*. Otherwise, the improvement would have been much sharper and, by the end of the century, Egypt's per capita GDP would have been much higher than $1,350.

Thus, the debate about the socioeconomic consequences of rapid population growth is basically a "chicken and egg" question. Are the poor conditions of the sub-Saharan African countries, as well as other less-developed countries in Asia, including some Arab countries, mainly the result of their high natural increase rates, or are the conditions a consequence of misleading socioeconomic policies in parallel to political-security instability, with the high natural increase rates only an outcome or reflection of their underdevelopment? The answer is becoming increasingly clear that rapid population growth is one of, if not the most, important factors accounting for underdevelopment. At least in the case of the Arab countries, no one has succeeded in proving that rapid population growth has any economic advantage in and of itself. Moreover, in many countries with small populations, such as Norway (4.5 million in 2000) and Sweden (8.9 million in 2000),[17] the technological improvements in production, in both agriculture and industry, during the second half of the twentieth century were very impressive without the need for large indigenous populations, simply because the "markets" for local products were expanded to an international, rather than just a local, level. The process of removing barriers from international trade as part of ongoing globalization has served to abolish the meaning of the amount or even the purchasing power of the local population. Consequently, during the second half of the twentieth century, the pace of economic development was highly correlated with low fertility rates. That is, the higher the fertility rate, the lower the pace of economic development. This has proven to be an almost universal fact, with very few exceptions.

2   The "Population Policy" Definitions

What is the meaning of "population policy"? When can it be said that a government is implementing any kind of population policy and, even more importantly, how can it be clarified as to which policy is implemented in cases when the policy is hidden due to the extremely sensitive religious-political nature of the demographic issue? The US National Academy of Sciences defined the term "population policy" as "policies related to change in the quality and quantity of the population and its geographical distribution . . ."[18] According to the official definition of the UN, which was adopted prior to the 1974 First World's Population Conference in Bucharest, population policy includes "all policies and programs – including social and economic policies – concerned with the major population variables: fertility, mortality, internal migration and geographical distribution of population, and international migration."[19] Allan Findlay and Anne Findlay defined "population policy" as "those policies that seek in a deliberate way to change the size, growth, composition or distribution of a country's population."[20] From these and other definitions, it appears that population policy, both pro- and anti-natalist alike, is a part of the broader socioeconomic policies of any given government.

In general, there are two components of "population policy." The first is that of *population-responsive policy*, which attempts to counter the negative consequences of rapid population growth, mainly in the areas of food supply, housing, work opportunities, and basic public services, such as health care, education, transportation, sanitation, water, and electricity. The second component of population policy is that of *population-influencing policy* ("natalist policy"), which aims to influence the fertility behavior itself, either through direct measures (such as family planning policy, children's allowances, minimum age at first marriage, and a ban on polygamy), or through indirect measures (mainly by encouraging women's education and employment outside the household or by preventing their employment as a pro-natalist measure).[21] Since births, deaths, immigration (in-migration), emigration (out-migration), and urbanization (internal migration) are the basic demographic factors responsible for the changes in both the scale of the population and its spatial distribution in any given country, the definition of "population policy" could be limited only to the *direct measures* taken by any government in order to influence one or more of the above-mentioned factors.

However, it should be emphasized that almost any governmental action has an influence of some kind, whether direct or indirect, on at least one of the demographic characteristics of any given population. For example, the provision of full governmental subsidies for education, particularly for women, has an immense influence on fertility patterns, as was illustrated in Chapter 2. However, during the past few decades, at least elementary and secondary education is universally provided almost free of charge, even in countries that are trying to promote higher fertility rates, such as the GCC states, Israel, and Sweden. On the other hand, the provision of free or heavily subsidized health care services leads to a marked decline in infant and child mortality rates – a prominent factor contributing to fertility decline. Again, these services are highly subsidized in both anti-natalist and pro-natalist countries.

As previously discussed in Chapter 2, the fertility rates in the Western countries have declined throughout the past two centuries without any direct governmental involvement. This begs the question as to why the governments of developing countries, including the overpopulated Arab countries, would implement direct anti-natalist measures, first and foremost national family planning polices, which demand huge resources, if declining fertility occurs naturally in response to macro-socioeconomic changes? Rather than concentrate on the area of direct anti-natalist policy, would it not be better to invest their limited financial resources in promoting socioeconomic conditions that eventually would lead to fertility decline?

The answer to this crucial question is that the aim of direct anti-natalist policy is to enhance the process of fertility reduction when the basic socioeconomic conditions in the country, by themselves, are not favorable for lowering fertility, due to the low per capita income, the low female labor force participation rates outside of agriculture, and the non-existent or insufficient social security benefits provided by the state to the elderly population. In other words, the aim of the national family planning program is to overcome the socioeconomic barriers to fertility decline. It is obvious, however, that if per capita income is high, infant and child mortality rates are low, female educational level and labor force participation rates are high, and social security for the elderly population is sufficient, then fertility rates will be low, even in countries implementing pro-natalist policies.[22]

3   The Natalist Approach of the Arab Countries:
A Historical Analysis

In the following section, the natalist approach of the Arab countries since the mid-twentieth century, at the time that many of them achieved independence, until present will be examined in line with the changing global natalist approach.

3.1   The 1950 and Early 1960s: "Population Growth by Itself is not at the "Core of Poverty"

At the beginning of the process of accelerated natural increase rates in the 1950s and early 1960s, the leaders of many developing countries perceived this process to be in line with the positive traditional attitude toward population growth and therefore made no attempts to limit it. The attempts made by Western leaders to convince them of the need to curb the accelerating population growth rates were in most cases unsuccessful because the majority of the developing countries' regimes, as well as the public, considered the Western attempts as an "imperialist conspiracy" and a variant of "neo-colonialism."[23] It should be taken into account that many of the developing countries had received independence from the "West" only a decade earlier, following World War II, and that in many cases, this independence was achieved only after a long struggle against the Western imperialist countries. Thus, the Western idea of family planning in developing countries was totally rejected by almost all of the developing countries' leaders.

At that time, it should be emphasized, the "dependency theory"[24] was widely accepted in the developing countries. Accordingly, it was believed by many that the end of the Western colonialism, combined with the adoption of socialist-étatist socioe-conomic policies, would bring about rapid economic development. In other words, the poor economic condition in the developing countries was not an outcome of the rapid population growth, but rather the result of a long period colonialism and exploitation by the Western colonial countries. India, it should be noted, was an exception in this regard, and adopted a national family planning policy already in 1951.[25]

In line with the common approach among developing countries' leaders during the 1950s, many Arab leaders also viewed the new phenomenon of rapid population growth as a blessing and therefore made no attempt to limit it. From their perspective, the "Malthusian Population Trap" was not relevant to their own countries. Thus, not only did they not act to limit the scale of population growth, but rather some even adopted pro-natalist policies.[26] Within the framework of the pro-natalist approach, in the former French colonial North African countries, the 1920 French law forbidding both abortions and the promotion and use of contraceptives was still in force.[27]

Although the overall approach among the Arab leaders was pro-natalist, in prac-tice only Syria implemented specific pro-natalist measures. In 1949, the propaganda, distribution, or use of contraceptives was forbidden. Two additional regulations were ratified in 1952: The first determined that families with more than three children would be granted discounts on pubic transportation; and the second was that these families would enjoy a special government bonus. Another decree in 1952 entitled state employees to a government subsidy in addition to their salary according to their number of children. Originally, this subsidy was meant to subsidize education costs for families with many children, but it soon became an instrument for encouraging higher birth and fertility rates among state employees.[28] It seems that the reason behind Syria's pro-natalist policy during that period was the feeling of the Syrian leadership that the Syrian population was too small in comparison to the country's economic and espe-cially military needs, as it only numbered less than 3.3 million in 1950 (see table 2.3).

In the case of Egypt, there were some who warned that the rapid population growth in Egypt would lead to a Malthusian population trap. Following publication of the 1917 census results, Dr. Levi, Chief of the Department of Statistics, wrote that: "Given the state of its economic organization, the density of the population has reached a level that is only surpassed perhaps by China and certain parts of India."[29] However, the most famous document published during the Monarch period that warned against the economic consequences of the rapid population growth was Wendell Cleland, *The Population Problem in Egypt*.[30] Despite these warnings, the Monarchy regime not only did not promote fertility decline, but actually adopted a pro-natalist approach. However, in contrast to Syria, the Egyptian authorities did not implement specific pro-natalist measures, though contraceptives were not prohibited for distribution. Dr.

Muhammad al-Razaq, a senior official in the Egyptian bureaucracy, argued in 1962 that under the Monarchy regime, he delivered a memo to the Minister of Health on the urgent need to narrow the fertility rates. In response, the Minister rebuked him, stating that: "the King [Faruq] wants to be a king of 100 million people regardless of whether they are naked or starving."[31] In addition to the traditional pro-natalist approach of the Monarchy regime, the economic interests of the industrialists and big landlords, who ruled not only the economy but politics as well, lay in the continued supply of cheap labor to both the rural and the urban areas.[32]

In order to promote family planning activities in developing countries, the International Planned Parenthood Federation (IPPF) was established as an NGO in 1952 with funding from private foundations as well as some Western governments. The first members of the organization came from the US, the Netherlands, Sweden, West Germany, Singapore, and Hong Kong.[33] The aims of the IPPF were to increase awareness about the issue of family planning, to enhance family education, and to support family planning services in developing countries. In order to achieve these goals, the IPPF encouraged the establishment of a parallel national association in each developing county that would pioneer family planning activities and bring about a climate in public opinion that would be favorable to adopting a national family planning program. The basic assumptions of the organization were that knowledge of family planning methods is a basic human right and that a balance between worldwide population and natural resources is a preliminary condition for achieving economic prosperity, political stability, and peace.[34]

The first among the Arab leaders to become aware of the devastating long-term results of rapid population growth was the Egyptian leader, 'Abd al-Nasser. Already in early 1953, a short time after the "Free Officer" Revolution (July 23, 1952), a parliamentary committee for population affairs was established in order to investigate Egypt's demographic developments – a move that reflected official recognition of the existence of a demographic problem in Egypt. At that time, the new regime began to operate in the area of demography in two arenas: One was the encouragement of the emigration of *fellahin* (peasants) from Egypt to other Arab countries; and the second was the introduction of preliminary measures in the area of family planning,[35] including the establishment of 20 experimental family planning clinics in 1958.[36] Additionally, a voluntary family planning association, the Egyptian Association for Population Studies, was established.[37] Muhammad Nagib, Egypt's first President following the "Free Officer" Revolution, was also worried about Egypt's demographic pressure, arguing that Egypt should act in two major areas: enlarging the cultivated area and narrowing the high fertility rates.[38]

Toward the end of the 1950s, however, 'Abd al-Nasser changed his basic demographic concept and started to advocate the approach that rapid economic development could raise the current low living standard and lead to fertility decline without the need for direct governmental involvement in family planning activities. This approach was evident in an interview he gave to the *Christian Science Monitor* in October 1959: "I am not a believer in calling on people to exercise birth control by decrees or persuasion. . . . Instead of teaching people how to exercise birth control, we would do better to teach them how to increase their land production. . . ."[39]

'Abd al-Nasser himself never explained the reasons for the change in his fertility approach. Charles Issawi claimed that this change was caused by an accelerating sense of nationalism in Egypt following the October 1956 Suez War and the conception that a large population would provide a source of military strength for the continuing military conflict with Israel.[40] Hussein Abdel-Aziz Sayed argued that Egypt's unification with Syria in February 1958 raised strong feelings for overall Arab unity, which included sharing in the oil resources and redistributing the whole Arab population throughout the Arab territories.[41] Saad Eddin Ibrahim wrote that: "Some observers at the time suspected that Nasser, himself a father of five children, felt that a bigger population gave Egypt much greater weight in Arab, Middle Eastern, and international affairs."[42]

In addition to the above-mentioned factors, one might speculate that another purely political factor accounting for 'Abd al-Nasser's changing demographic concept in the second half of the 1950s, was the struggle with Iraq for seniority in the Arab world, though there is no official or even unofficial evidence to that effect. Official adoption of a national family planning program, aiming to reduce Egypt's fertility rates, could serve the Iraqi propaganda against 'Abd al-Nasser himself, accusing him, personally, of acting against the "Arab cause" and serving the "Western neo-colonialism." In light of 'Abd al-Nasser's aspirations for seniority in the Arab world, he could not risk the adoption of an official anti-natalist policy, even if he was personally convinced of the need to reduce the population growth rates in Egypt.

Although the 20 family planning clinics that were established in 1958 continued to operate, it was on an experimental basis only and under specific restrictive conditions.[43] The overall approach of the "Free Offices" regime during the first decade of the Revolution was to leave this issue to the public itself without direct governmental involvement. Thus, we can conclude by saying that despite the awareness of the Nasserite regime of the devastating socioeconomic results of the country's rapid population growth, they preferred not to adopt a national direct family planning program and instead took an "economic development approach," which, of course, did not arouse any opposition, religious or otherwise. From short-term political point of view, this way was the "easy way," but certainly not the best way in light of Egypt's accelerating demographic problems. Moreover, following Egypt's victory in the Suez War, when 'Abd al-Nasser's popularity among the Egyptian people and beyond began to skyrocket, he still chose not to use his immense popularity to promote fertility decline or to implement the economic reforms needed to boost Egypt's economy. As part of his populist style of leadership, 'Abd al-Nasser continued to operate within the broadest consensus in the socioeconomic arena, including in the area of family planning.[44] In the words of Fouad Ajami: "Under Nasser . . . the state tried to be many things to many groups."[45]

In the other Arab countries, the issue of population pressure or the need for direct governmental family planning activities in order to curb high fertility rates did not arise at all simply because, with the exception of Egypt, the population of the other Arab countries during the 1950s was quite low, below 10 million (see table 2.3).

3.2 The Changing Approach in the mid-1960s: "Rapid Population Growth is the Core of Underdevelopment"

The results of the population censuses that were conducted in many developing countries in the late 1950s and early 1960s, including in many Arab countries, showed that the natural increase rates in many developing countries were actually higher than previously assumed. In parallel, many leader of developing countries became increasingly aware of the negative correlation between the pace of "economic development" and the rate of population growth. When they realized that much of the economic development was actually being "swallowed" by the rapid population growth, the traditional positive approach of large population began to change. In addition, the adoption of socialist-étatist socioeconomic policies, including a wide variety of public subsidies, has led to a steady increase in public spending and budgetary deficits in line with the population growth rates.

Thus, some of these developing countries have adopted national family planning programs in order to achieve two primary goals: first, a decline in fertility rates, and second, a more balanced age pyramid as a result of those declining fertility rates. In so doing, they should be able to overcome the "low income trap" caused by low labor force participation rates. The change in the demographic perception first began in Asia, with South Korea adopting a national family planning program as early as 1961, Singapore in 1965, Indonesia and Taiwan in 1968, and Thailand and the Philippines in 1970.[46] It later moved to some South American countries as well as some, albeit very few, Arab countries (see below).

Following the election of John F. Kennedy as President in 1962, the US began to be involved in worldwide demographic issues and became the largest donor to the UN Fund for Population Activities (UNFPA).[47] By channeling the funds through the UN and not directly to the countries themselves, the US administration was trying to avoid charges of "neo-imperialism," "racism," and "genocide," for which Western countries, particularly the US, were often accused by developing countries.[48] In 1965, the US Agency for International Aid (USAID) also got involved in demographic issues and started to support demographic researches and the implementation of national family planning programs in developing countries.[49]

In the early 1960s, the Catholic Church was also forced to deal with the issue of rapid population growth in the developing countries. Two major factors, it seems, forced the Catholic Church to change its traditionally negative attitude toward the use of contraceptives. The first was the rampant poverty in Latin American countries, and the second was the innovation of the birth control pill, which was from the beginning a cheap and easy contraceptive method. Thus, in 1962, the Vatican Council II decreed that from now on, couples are autonomous in determining the number of their offspring.[50]

Also in the early 1960s, the traditional pro-natalist approach among some of the Arab countries began to change as well. The publication of the census results from the late 1950s and early 1960s (see table 1.1) highlighted the trend of accelerating natural increase rates resulting, first and foremost, from the sharp decline in the crude death rates. At the same time, accelerating pressures from Western governments on developing countries led to the adoption of national family planning programs in some of the overpopulated Arab countries. The initiative for adopting family planning programs in the Arab countries, it should be emphasized, came from the political elite and not from "grassroots sources." In other words, it was not a natural reaction of the population to long-term and broad socioeconomic changes, but purely a leadership initiative. Based on the results of a comparative study on the decision-making processes among the political elite in the area of family planning in 17 countries, including Egypt, John Thomas and Merilee Grindle reached the conclusion that: "Rarely, in fact, does population policy become an agenda item through social mobilization and pressure . . ."[51]

In the case of Egypt, this was clearly illustrated by the fact that women's organizations and physicians had been trying to promote family planning measures since the early 1930s without much success. In the other Arab countries as well, whenever anti-natalist measures have been adopted, either formally or informally, they have always been initiated by the political leadership upon the realization that continued high natural increase rates would seriously hamper further socioeconomic development, rather than by any efforts on the part of the population itself. Although the family planning associations established in the Arab countries were formally NGOs, in practice they were governmental initiatives and enjoyed governmental financial support. The reasons for this is quite simple: the weakness of the Arab "civil society" at that time.

Among the Arab leaders, the first to go beyond paying lip service in the area of family planning was Tunisia's President, Habib Bourguiba. In March 12, 1962, Bourguiba stated:

> With our rapidly growing population, the rising generations are exerting pressure on us. If we are not careful now, in ten to twenty years' time, there will be a marked disproportion between the national income and the number of people we have to feed. A race against the clock is going on between our economic development and the demographic increase. Unless we take, as of today, the necessary measures, the country in a few decades will experience convulsions.[52]

Fertility rates in Tunisia, as in Egypt, continued to be high despite the overall socioeconomic improvement in the late 1950s and early 1960s. Thus, it became clear to the Tunisian authorities that in order to substantially reduce fertility rates, direct anti-natalist measures would have to be taken immediately.[53] In 1961, Tunisia was the first among the former French colonial North African countries to abolish the 1920 French law forbidding abortions and the promotion and use of contraceptives.[54] Three years latter, in June 1964, Tunisia officially adopted a national family planning program – the first among the Arab countries. The direct measures of the national family planning program in Tunisia included the provision of information and services within the existing network of the mother-and-child health care clinics, as well as sterilization procedures in public health clinics and hospitals.[55]

In contrast to 'Abd al-Nasser's concern about Egypt's rapid population growth, which was natural considering the obvious nature of Egypt's demographic problem, Bourguiba's anti-natalist perception in the early 1960s is quite surprising, given the small size of Tunisia's population at that time – amounting to only 4.533 million according to the 1966 census results.[56] Thus, although small in number, Bourguiba realized the true meaning of the long-term implications of the "demographic momentum."

On May 21, 1962, 'Abd al-Nasser presented the National Charter [*al-Mithaq al-Watani*] in which he stated that the population growth "constitutes the most dangerous obstacle that faces the Egyptian people in their drive toward raising the standard of production . . . Attempts at family planning deserve the most sincere efforts . . ."[57] It is widely accepted in the academic literature on Egypt's demographic policy, that the National Charter was "a turning point." However, it seems that this approach should be re-examined. If the National Charter were indeed "a turning point" in 'Abd al-Nasser's family planning perception, then why did it take more than three years, until mid-1965, when the Nasserite regime actually started to implement a national direct family planning program? If the demographic pressure was so great and constituted "the most dangerous obstacle" to further economic development, as he claimed in the National Charter, then one would have expected his government to immediately implement a national direct family planning program, despite the opposition of the "Muslim Brothers."

It seems that one major factor accounting for the delay was the rapid economic progress achieved in the first four years of the First Five-Year Economic Plan, 1960–1965, namely, from 1960 until 1963. This progress was reflected in the number of new work opportunities created, the construction of the Aswan High Dam, the establishment of heavy industries, and the steady improvement in relations with the Soviet Union. These developments all contributed to 'Abd al-Nasser's feelings that, at least for the moment, he could avoid implementing direct governmental anti-natalist measures. To this "economic factor" one should also add a purely political factor: the collapse of the union with Syria in September 1961, which was the first "political defeat" to 'Abd al-Nasser since the July 1952 "Free Officers" Revolution.[58] The collapse of the unification with Syria cracked, to a large extent, 'Abd al-Nasser's image and prestige among the "masses" in Egypt and in the other Arab countries alike. Thus, it is reasonable to believe that he preferred to avoid taking any controversial steps such a short time after the collapse and that the National Charter served his purposes of regaining popularity and prestige. Overall, however, Egypt was not unique in this respect. As John Thomas and Merilee Grindle observed: "Periods of several years passed in many cases between a governmental decision to do something about population growth and the introduction of substantive measures to accomplish this goal."[59]

In the mid-1960s, it appeared that the socioeconomic problems caused by Egypt's rapid population growth had intensified even further. At the same time, it was quite clear that the Second Five-Year Plan for the years 1966–1970 would not even get off the ground due to the inability of the Egyptian authorities to raise the capital needed, given the great extent of the external debt. Thus, in 1965, after 13 years in power, 'Abd al-Nasser eventually adopted a national family planning program – when he finally realized that in the current Egypt's socioeconomic situation he could no longer avoid it.[60] The stated aim of the program was to reduce the crude birth rate from 41 per 1,000 in 1966 to 30 per 1,000, 12 years later, in 1978.[61]

A year later, in 1966, Morocco also adopted a national family planning program because of the devastating consequences of the high natural increase rates. As it was written in the Moroccan Second Five-Year Development Plan, lest they "give rise to an unfavorable demographic situation, not only because of the rate of increase, but also because it brings about an age pyramid in which the dependent population constitutes a large proportion of the total population."[62]

Several patterns were common to the national family planning programs implemented in Tunisia, Egypt, and Morocco during the 1960s. The first pattern was that they emphasized the supply side so as to fulfill the perceived "unmet demand" for contraceptives among young couples. It was assumed at that time that the newly invented birth control pill and intrauterine device (IUD) would serve as "magic bullets" to bring about fertility decline.[63] These contraceptives and related medical services were distributed mainly through the existing framework of mother-and-child health care clinics, which was already well established in these countries, even in the remote rural areas. In the case of the Egyptian program, the Ministry of Health clinics were used to save time and money, as well as to benefit from the established confidence between the community and the health staff. These clinics, under the jurisdiction of the "Executive Board of Family Planning," generally consisted of a physician and a nurse who provided information and supplied contraceptives.[64]

The second pattern common to the national family planning programs in the Arab countries during the 1960s was to mobilize the *'ulama* to support the national family planning policies in order to overcome the religious opposition of the "Muslim Brothers." Since the early stages of the family planning programs in the 1960s, the authorities of Tunisia, Egypt, and Morocco made use of the most prominent official *Muftis* to publish numerous *fatwas* in the mass media, emphasizing that the use of contraceptives is not contradictory to the Islamic *Shari'a* [*halal*]. It was quite clear from the beginning that without the support of the *'ulama*, the programs would not succeed.

The third common pattern was the establishment of family planning associations as voluntary organizations in order to achieve three main goals: to coordinate between all of the bodies involved in the various aspects of family planning; to promote cooperation with the IPPF; and to "somewhat cut" the direct relationship between the authorities themselves and the sensitive issue of family planning.

Although these three Arab countries were among the first developing countries worldwide to officially adopt family planning programs in the mid-1960s, only in Tunisia the issue of fertility decline actually received top governmental priority. In the case of Egypt, the program did not receive high governmental priority from the outset and was particularly ignored following the defeat in the June 1967 War when the demographic issue, as one among other socioeconomic areas, was almost totally abandoned by the Egyptian authorities. During his last three years in power (1967–1970), 'Abd al-Nasser concentrated mainly on the ongoing military conflict with Israel and even initiated the War of Attrition in early 1969, that ended only in August 1970, just prior to his death on September 28, 1970. Other major obstacles to implementing the Egyptian family planning program during the late 1960s were limited financial resources; lack of coordination between the various bodies involved in the implementation of the programs; lack of staff training in the clinics; and shortages of contraceptives, ending in poor services.[65]

In retrospect, neither 'Abd al-Nasser nor King Hassan II of Morocco were willing to risk their political position by publicly voicing strong support for the family planning issue. In the case of Morocco, Robert Lapham wrote in 1977 that: "It is not surprising that not much happened in terms of a vigorous family planning program, especially since in the background Hassan II remained silent on the question of family planning . . ."[66] In the other Arab countries at that time, it was not only a question of almost nothing happening in the area of family planning, but rather of active pro-natalist attitudes emerging. For example, in Algeria, President Houari Boumedienne declared in his Independence Day speech of 1972 that the country's population was too small in comparison to its large territory and natural resources and that increasing the size of the population would represent "a long-term investment."[67]

The end result was that during the 1960s and early 1970s, fertility rates remained high – with a crude birth rate of around 40 per 1,000 people (see table 2.5) – in the Arab countries that had officially adopted national family planning programs, with the exception of Egypt. However, in the case of Egypt, it is widely agreed that this reduction was not brought about by the family planning program, but rather by the economic hardship endured in Egypt following the June 1967 War, combined with the fact that over one million Egyptians were in military service at that time.[68]

During the second half of the 1960s and the early 1970s, the overall international activities in the area of family planning were rapidly enhanced. In 1966, 12 countries, including three Arab countries (Sweden, Columbia, Finland, Malaysia, Nepal, Singapore, South Korea, Yugoslavia, India, Egypt, Tunisia, and Morocco) submitted a document to the UN calling for a reduction in the fertility rates of developing countries, given the various devastating socioeconomic consequences of the current high fertility rates. This document constituted "a cornerstone" in the changing demographic approach of the major international organizations. On December 17, 1966, the UN General Assembly adopted resolution 2211, calling on the UN Secretary-General to enhance population programs in developing countries, to support demographic research, and to disseminate demographic knowledge worldwide.[69]

As a result, in 1967, the UNFPA was established with the aims of assisting developing countries to implement family planning programs, expanding the overall activities of the UN on demographic issues, and pursuing new demographic programs for developing countries. Other UN agencies operating in the areas of labor, women, children, and other related issues since the early 1970s include: the International Labour Office (ILO), the United Nations Children's Fund (UNICEF), the United Nations Development Programme (UNDP), the Food and Agricultural Organization (FAO), and the World Health Organization (WHO). In addition, the Population Division of the UN Department of International Economic and Social Affairs is responsible for collecting and analyzing worldwide demographic data.[70] However, the population censuses that were conducted in many Arab countries during the late 1960s and the early 1970s (see table 1.1) pointed to substantial increases in the natural increase rates during the 1950s and 1960s. This was the result of a sharp decline in the crude death rates and a stability of the crude birth rates, or even an increase in some cases, such as that of Syria. The first in many cases to become aware of the long-term implications of the continuing high natural increase rates were the professionals in the Departments of Statistics or other governmental branches dealing with demographic and related issues.[71] Thus, for example, in a report of the Syrian Central Bureau of Statistics from 1973, it was written that:

> It seems that high population growth rates have adversely affected the efforts exerted for securing [a] better life for all members of the population. Despite the high economic development rates which were achieved during the last decade, such rates are still not sufficient to meet basic population needs, and especially in the fields of education, health, housing and transportation. The high percentages of dependent children have led to increased consumer expenditure and a decreased volume of savings . . .[72]

As a result, in the early 1970s, prior to the "oil boom," the Syrian traditional pro-natalist approach began to change. Although the Syrian population at that time was still quite small in number, amounting to 6.3 million according to the 1970 census results (see table 2.3), the Syrian authorities began to become aware of the long-term implications of the continuing high natural increase rates, although at that stage they did not implement any specific anti-natalist measures.

As in Syria, the Jordanian authorities also became aware in the early 1970s about the severity of the high natural increase rates. In 1972, the Department of Statistics initiated a conference of demographic experts, with the intention of drawing up a comprehensive demographic policy for the Kingdom.[73] Several months later, in 1973,

Chart 4.1 The Natalist Perception of the non-Oil Arab Countries during the 1950s and 1960s

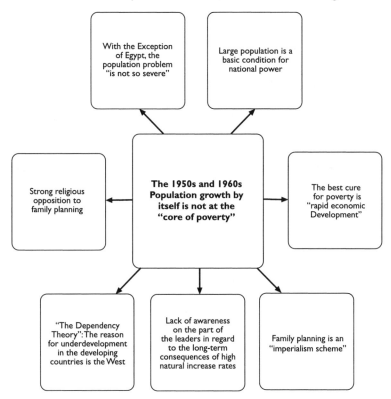

the National Population Commission was established, with the aim of advising the authorities in the area of population policies.[74] However, as in the case of Syria, although the authorities in Jordan became aware of the long-term implications of the high fertility rates, this awareness did not result in the formulation of a precise anti-natalist measures.

Overall, by 1973, of 117 developing countries worldwide, 32 countries had implemented a national family planning program, including three Arab countries: Tunisia, Egypt, and Morocco.[75]

3.3   The "Illusion Oil Decade" (1973–1982): "Awareness without Activity"

During the 1970s, however, in line with the acceleration of the devastating results of the high natural increase rates in the developing countries, international awareness of the crucial need to curb the high fertility rates also moved forward. The most important indication of this increasing international awareness was the initiation of the First World Population Conference in Bucharest, Romania in 1974. It is widely acknowledged that this conference constituted a turning point in the world's family planning history. It was the first world conference dealing with population policy itself, rather than with demographic research, as did the first two UN demographic conferences (Rome in 1954 and Belgrade in 1965).[76] Moreover, the Bucharest conference led to widespread awareness of the importance of the population issue and its socioeconomic implications in developing countries and was extensively covered by the media. This increasing awareness gave political legitimacy to many other leaders of developing countries to begin with the implementation of national family planning programs in their own countries.

During the conference itself, however, a crucial "chicken and egg" debate arose between the US and many developing countries regarding the role of national family planning programs within the broader approach to socioeconomic development. While the US suggested that the developing countries should implement comprehensive national family planning programs as a major means by which to overcome their socioeconomic problems, most developing countries, including China and India, argued that the optimal way to solve their demographic problem was by changing the "world economic order" by improving the ability of these countries to export their products and raw materials to the developed countries, and not through aggressive family planning programs. A substantial economic expansion, they claimed, would lead to a decline in fertility rates, meaning that the harsh demographic situation is only a reflection of the overall socioeconomic condition.[77] Thus, it is not surprising that the slogan of the conference was that "development is the best contraceptive,"[78] representing a shift in approach to the demographic issue from the 1950s and 1960s, when it was treated as a separate and isolated issue rather than as part of the broader scope of overall socioeconomic development strategies.

This change in the perception of the role of family planning programs was part of a new demographic perspective taking hold in the first half of the 1970s. This view maintained the futility of investing the scarce resources of developing countries in family planning programs, given that fertility decline could be achieved only through improvement in socioeconomic indicators, such as improvement in women's educational level and labor force participation rates, sharp declines in infant and child mortality rates, and above all, a substantial improvement in the overall standard of living. Thus, achieving lower fertility rates could only be accomplished by concentrating governmental efforts and financial resources in creating favorable socioeconomic conditions that promote fertility decline.[79]

A major factor in the insistence of many developing countries' leaders, including the non-oil Arab countries, on the "indirect approach" to the issue of fertility reduction was their fear about the continued stability of their regimes due to the immense sensitivity of the family planning issue. In this respect, Peter Donaldson wrote that: "Third world leaders worry first about staying alive and in command and then, as time allows, about development."[80] The overpopulated Arab countries, similar to many other developing countries worldwide, also adopted the indirect approach to fertility decline, as it was very convenient from a political point of view.

Nevertheless, the most important single event that shaped the fertility approach of the Arab countries in the second half of the twentieth century – both the oil and the non-oil countries – was the October 1973 "oil boom," which not only led to the adoption of extremely pro-natalist measures in the Arab oil states, but also was responsible for the spread of the feeling among the non-oil Arab leaders that the demographic issue, although important, was not so severe, at least not in the short run. In retrospect, the "oil boom," more than any other factor, was responsible for the indirect fertility approach that prevailed in the non-oil Arab countries until the mid-1980s. As a result of the high economic growth rates during the "oil decade" (see **Chapter 3**), they were provided with a "shelter," albeit a temporary one, from dealing with this politically sensitive issue.

Thus, although the Syrian authorities had already become aware of the long-term devastating consequences of the high natural increase rates in the early 1970s, the tremendous improvement in the country's economic and employment conditions following the onset of the "oil boom" (see Chapter 3) stopped this awareness from being translated into an explicit and direct governmental anti-natalist measures. Furthermore, the "oil boom" was used as an excuse for the *Ba'thi-'Alawi* regime[81] to avoid taking any unpopular measures in order to keep its legitimacy among the Muslim majority. Since the mid-1970s, the Syrian *Ba'thi-'Alawi* regime and the "Muslim Brothers" had clashed over popular support for legitimacy and control in the country, and the implementation of a national family planning program by the *Ba'thi-'Alawi* regime could have been used by the "Muslim Brothers" as a propaganda tool.[82]

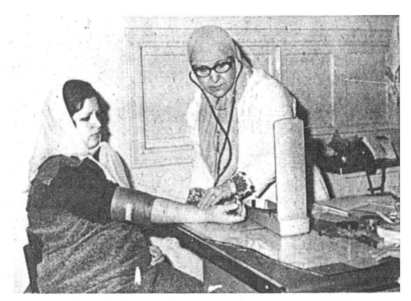

Picture 4.1 A Syrian woman receives service in a family planning clinic
Source: Tishrin, August 23, 1982

In an attempt to maintain a low profile, the Syrian authorities adopted an indirect approach to fertility decline and established the Syrian Family Planning Association in 1974 as a voluntary organization which was financially supported by the government. In addition, the Syrian press began to publish reports, articles, and cartoons about the socioeconomic consequences of rapid population growth, not only on the national level but also on the family level. Through the mass media, the Syrian authorities consistently stressed the strong connection between planning birth intervals and maintaining the health of mothers and children.

Yet, in all of their official statements published in the official newspapers, the government tried to hide its intentions, emphasizing that the aim of distributing birth control was not to reduce fertility rates.[83] By presenting this kind of unofficial anti-natalist policy, they thought to achieve more cooperation from the population. However, following the publication of the 1981 census results, the Syrian official press started to direct more attention to the demographic issue. The following anti-natalist cartoon, published in mid-1987, shows a very poor family with a large number of children, illustrating "the difficulty of bringing bread to a large family."

Cartoon 4.1
Source: al-Thawra, May 28, 1987

These indirect anti-natalist steps notwithstanding, it must be emphasized that the pro-natal regulations were not cancelled.[84] Overall, during the "oil decade," the decline in fertility level in Syria was quite minor. In 1986, Syria's crude birth rate was 42.4 per 1,000 and the total fertility rate was 7.1 children per woman,[85] declining from 48 per 1,000 and 7.6, respectively, in 1970 (see table 2.5).

As in Syria, Jordan adopted an indirect approach to fertility decline for very similar reasons: on the one hand, high economic growth rates and the substantial alleviation of employment pressures due to massive labor migration to the Arab oil states following the "oil boom" (see Chapter 3), and on the other hand, the escalation of internal Islamic opposition. As Asher Susser stated, the Hashemite regime "strove to deepen its Islamic legitimacy in light of the new reality in the region."[86] In order to avoid further confrontation with the Islamists, the Hashemite regime chose to operate through various indirect measures in the area of family planning. First, financial assistance was provided for NGO activities in the area of family planning. Second, family planning services were offered through the Maternal and Child Health clinics. However, these clinics did not actively promote the use of contraceptives, but rather supplied them upon request. Third, the option of sterilization was given as a legal birth control method.[87]

It should be emphasized, however, that in contrast to Syria, the Hashemite regime neither financed active pro-natalist measures, on the one hand, nor prohibited the use of contraceptives, on the other hand. Thus, the transition to an unofficial anti-natalist approach did not involve any legislative changes. However, the effect of the indirect anti-natalist measures in Jordan during the 1970s and 1980s, as in Syria, was quite minor. In the late 1980s, Jordan's fertility rate remained very high by any international comparison, with a crude birth rate of 38.7 per 1,000 in 1988 and a total fertility rate of 6.4 children per woman.[88]

In Egypt, Anwar al-Sadat, who took power following the death of 'Abd al-Nasser, also preferred to operate through an indirect approach to family planning. In 1973, a new family planning plan was initiated by the Supreme Council for Population and Family Planning [*al-Majlis al-A'la lil-Sukan wa-Tanzim al-Usra*] for a period 10 years, with the overall aim of reducing the crude birth rate from 34 per 1,000 in 1973 to 24 per 1,000 in 1982 through an increase in the contraceptive prevalence rate from 16% to 35%. The long-term goal of the plan was that Egypt's population would not exceed more than 60 million by the year 2000. In order to implement the new plan, a Department of Population was established in the Ministry of Health in June 1973. The new plan emphasized indirect measures to fertility decline, mainly in the areas of improving women's educational level and employment opportunities; increasing agricultural mechanization in order to diminish the need for children's employment; and reducing infant mortality in order to increase parents' confidence in the survival chances of their offspring. In addition, in 1974, within the framework of the new plan, population concepts were introduced into intermediate and secondary school textbooks.[89]

Sadat's adoption of the indirect approach was motivated by both political and economic considerations. From a political point of view, similar to Jordan and Syria at that time, Sadat preferred to take the indirect approach as part of its overall policy of rapprochement toward the Muslim Brothers.[90] From an economic point of view, Sadat was "dazzled" by the rapid economic growth following the "oil boom" and the alleviation of employment pressures due to the large-scale labor-emigration to the Arab oil countries during the "oil decade" (see **Chapter 3**). He thus chose to "escape" from the unpopularity of direct family planning measures and, as Saad Eddin Ibrahim claimed, he "hardly paid any attention to the problem."[91] Likewise, Thomas Lippman wrote in this regard that: "Sadat and his prime ministers hardly even gave lip service to birth control, despite all their speeches about the demands posed by the rising population. They did not hide their embarrassment at the dogged, outspoken support for family planning by the only prominent figure to make that commitment – Sadat's wife, Jihan."[92]

During Sadat's 11 years in power (October 1970–October 1981), Egypt's fertility rates not only failed to decline, but on the contrary, started to increase again in 1974 with the improvement in both the economic and the political–security situations following the October 1973 War. The crude birth rate climbed to 37.0 per 1,000 in 1981,[93] as compared with 35.1 per 1,000 in 1971.[94] Overall, during Sadat's rule, Egypt's population increased from 33.807 million in 1971[95] to 43.322 million in 1981,[96] representing an increase of 28.1% within 11 years – a net increase of 9.5 million people. However, for the long run, even more severe than the rapid population growth during this time was the widening of the age pyramid. By 1982, the percentage of the under-15 population within Egypt's total population amounted to almost 51%, as compared with less than 43% in 1960 (see **table 3.1**).

The ascendancy of Husni Mubarak to the presidency, following the murder of Sadat by the *Gama'at al-Islamiyya* on October 6, 1981, did not lead to a change in the Egyptian government's family planning approach. In fact, during the first four years of his presidency, the demographic area was almost totally ignored.[97] As in the case of Sadat, Mubarak preferred not to confront the "Muslim Brothers" also on the issue of family planning. In addition, rapid economic growth continued, with the real GDP growth rate reaching 7.9% by the fiscal year of 1982/83, meaning a net increase of more than 5% in per capita terms. At the same time, the current account deficit narrowed from over $2 billion in the fiscal year of 1981/82 to around $1 billion in the fiscal year of 1983/84.[98] Thus, in retrospect, it seems that like his two predecessors, Mubark also decided to "sacrifice" Egypt's long-term socioeconomic development so as to avoid posing a threat to his own personal regime in the short-term. Thus, in the first half of the 1980s, Egypt's fertility rate continued to accelerate, amounting to a total fertility rate of 6.9 children per woman, according to a survey conducted in 1984,[99] and a crude birth rate of 39.8 per 1,000 in 1985[100] – a higher rate than in the early 1960s – prior to the adoption of the official family planning program.

In addition to the rapid economic expansion and the alleviation of employment pressures, the relatively high grants given by the rich Arab oil-states to the poorer Arab countries (see Chapter 3) served to enhance the feelings of "Arab Unity" [*al-Wahda al-'Arabiyya*], or at least "Arab Solidarity" [*al-Tadamun al-'Arabi*]. Accordingly, it was understood by many of the poorer Arab countries that the rich Arab oil-states would provide them with substantial economic assistance through generous grants, soft loans and other financial measures, together with employment of their surplus labor forces. These feelings were enhanced by a reduction in the tension between the "revolutionary" regimes and the Gulf oil monarchies following the death of 'Abd al-Nasser. In an article published in 1988, Riad Tabbarah used the term "The United Arab States" as follows:

> The area of this country is 14 million square kilometers; it is the second largest country in the world in area, after the Soviet Union . . . and before Canada, China and the Unites States . . . The per capita GNP was $2,000 in 1985, which means that the United Arab States is a developing country, but one which occupies a relatively high rank among those countries, similar to Mexico, Portugal or the Republic of Korea . . .[101]

Thus, in light of the huge oil revenues that would be distributed among the various Arab countries, the issue of rapid population growth during the "oil decade" was viewed as posing a challenge only in the longer run and was not deemed to warrant direct governmental involvement in the area of family planning. As Hassan Yousif and Ahmad Hammouda noted: "population growth and its ramifications were seen as long-term problems which were undeniably important but neither pressing nor urgent. Population issues were of secondary importance."[102]

In addition to the "oil boom" effects, there was also a widespread feeling in the overpopulated Arab countries that the demographic trends for the short run, namely, for the coming generation, were already set and that the ability to change them, even through an extensive national family planning program, was quite minor. As an advisor to the Egyptian Prime Minister, Hilmi 'Abd al-Rahman, stated in 1975:

> The development of the population for the next 25 years has already been determined . . . Our population will double in the next 25 years with only a 20% possibility of variation . . . Therefore, for the next 20 or 25 years the problem in Egypt is mainly to meet the requirements of an increase in population.[103]

In addition, the World Bank staff that evaluated Egypt's demographic policy in August 1978 was very optimistic in regard to Egypt's future demographic characteristics and the successful outcome of the indirect family planning program being implemented at that time by Sadat's regime. They projected that by the year 2000 Egypt's population would amount to 59.374 million, while during the second half of the 1990s the crude birth rate would average 23.3 per 1,000 and the total fertility rate would average 2.9 children per woman.[104] This projection, in retrospect, proved to be totally unrealistic.

To the general optimistic feelings that the demographic issue was not so severe and that there was almost nothing to be done about it in the short run anyway, at least in the case of Egypt, another factor accounting for the low level of family planning activity in the overpopulated Arab countries during the first half of the 1980s should be added: the change in the US international demographic policy. During the 1960s and 1970s, the US promoted a direct family planning approach in the developing countries. However, in the 1980s, following the ascendancy to political power of Ronald Reagan and the conservatives, who opposed abortions and family planning from a religious point of view, the US demographic approach in the developing countries was to adopt a liberal economic policy that would bring about economic prosperity and thereby alleviate the demographic pressure and decrease the fertility rates without direct governmental involvement.[105] Thus, in practice, the new US demographic approach was reminiscent of the 1974 Bucharest Population Conference slogan that "development is the best contraceptive." At the Second World Population Conference held in Mexico City in 1984, the US delegation presented their platform that "the relationship between population growth and economic development is not necessarily a negative one" and that "governmental control of economies," or "economic statism," had caused population growth in developing countries to change from an "asset" to a "peril."[106]

It is clear that all of the above-mentioned factors for not implementing direct and explicitly anti-natalist measures were first and foremost "excuses" to avoid dealing with the Islamists and the traditional norms of life, particularly among the rural dwellers. In retrospect, it is quite hard to believe that Anwar al-Sadat, Husni Mubarak, Hafiz al-Asad, and King Husayn of Jordan truly thought that the high fertility rates in their countries could be reduced without intensive direct governmental involvement or that the demographic problem was not so severe. It seems that they preferred to delay the implementation of a direct national family planning program for the longest period possible due to short-term political calculations.

Among the non-oil Arab countries, Tunisia was the only exceptional because even during the "oil decade," it did not abandon its direct and explicitly national family planning policy. One major reason for this continuation was that the economic growth rates in Tunisia during the "oil decade" were lower than during the prior decade, due to a relatively low amount of workers' remittances combined with a low level of financial aid from the rich Arab oil states.[107]

In sharp contrast to the overpopulated Arab countries, the family planning activities in many developing countries worldwide during the late 1970s and throughout the first half of the 1980s were substantially expanded. This phenomenon was attributable to two main factors. First, the socioeconomic problems resulting from the high natural increase rates were steadily worsening, including employment pressures, inadequate public services, housing problems in the major cities that were forced to absorb the bulging number of rural migrants, and above all, relatively low GDP growth rates during the "oil decade," due part to the sharp increase in oil prices following the October 1973 "oil boom" (see below). The second factor was that the socioeconomic improvement of the 1960s and 1970s did not bring about a substantial decline in fertility, despite the widespread belief that "the best contraceptive is economic development." Thus, for example, the crude birth rate in Ecuador was 46 per 1,000 in 1960 and 45 per 1,000 in 1975. Likewise, in Peru, the crude birth rate in 1960 was 43 per 1,000 and 42 per 1,000 in 1975.[108]

Regarding the demographic perception of the developing countries during the 1980s, Jason Finkle and Barbara Crane wrote that: "They no longer spoke of international population assistance as racist, genocidal, or imperialistic, or accused Western nations of advocating population control as a substitute for foreign aid."[109] Thus, the demographic slogan of the 1980s returned to that which had prevailed in the late 1960s, namely that "the best contraceptive is a contraceptive." The practical meaning of the renewed slogan was the promotion of direct family planning activities in many developing countries. In 1983, 76% of developing populations worldwide were living in countries that had an official national family planning program aimed at curbing the high fertility rates, and an additional 17% were living in countries that officially supported family planning programs, but only to improve the health and welfare situation and not to reduce the fertility rates.[110]

Without entering into the endless debate on the role of direct national family planning programs in fertility decline,[111] in retrospect, one thing is undisputed: In many developing countries that adopted national family planning programs, the fertility rates did substantially decline. Thus, for example, by 1986, the crude birth rate in India was 29 per 1,000 as compared to 42 in 1960. In Indonesia, the decline in the corresponding period was from 44 to 29; in Brazil from 43 to 29; in the Philippines from 46 to 31; in Mexico from 54 to 32; and in South Korea from 43 to 23.[112] On the contrary, in the overpopulated Arab countries, with the exception of Tunisia, the fertility rates had not declined during the 1970s and the early 1980s, but rather had even increased or at least maintained their previous high level. It can be said that, from a purely demographic point of view, the "oil decade" was also a "lost demographic decade" for the overpopulated Arab countries, with huge implications for their future demographic and socioeconomic profiles well into the twenty-first century.

In sharp contrast to the overpopulated Arab countries, a new demographic situation emerged in the rich Arab oil-states following the October 1973 "oil boom." Prior to the "oil boom," one can hardly talk about any demographic policy in the Gulf oil-states. Even basic demographic data constituting a preliminary pre-condition for the formulation of any policy, either pro-natalist or anti-natalist, were non-existent, with the exception of Bahrain and Kuwait (see Chapter 1). The announcement by the ministers of the Organization of Petroleum Exporting Countries (OPEC) of their decision to double the prices of all types of crude oil brought about a surge in income from oil exports. This "oil boom" transformed the GCC countries, within a short period time of only a few years, into the wealthiest countries in the Arab region as well as worldwide. In 1974, the oil revenues of the GCC countries amounted to $52.4 billion, as compared with less than $10 billion only two years earlier, in 1972. By 1981, the GCC oil revenues had skyrocketed to $157.8 billion (current prices).[113] In 1982, the Saudi Arabia per capita GNP amounted to $15,270, as compared with $830 only one decade earlier, in 1972.[114] In 1981, Kuwait's per capita GNP exceeded $20,000 – the highest worldwide that year and more than five times that of 1972.[115] No doubt, the economic development of these countries was indeed unique by any international comparison.

The tremendous increase in oil revenues following the "oil boom" led to a sharp increase in labor demand in the Arab oil states that could not be met by local sources. Thus, the short-term strategy adopted by these countries regarding the supply of

Chart 4.2 The Natalist Perception of the non-Oil Arab Countries during the "Oil Decade"

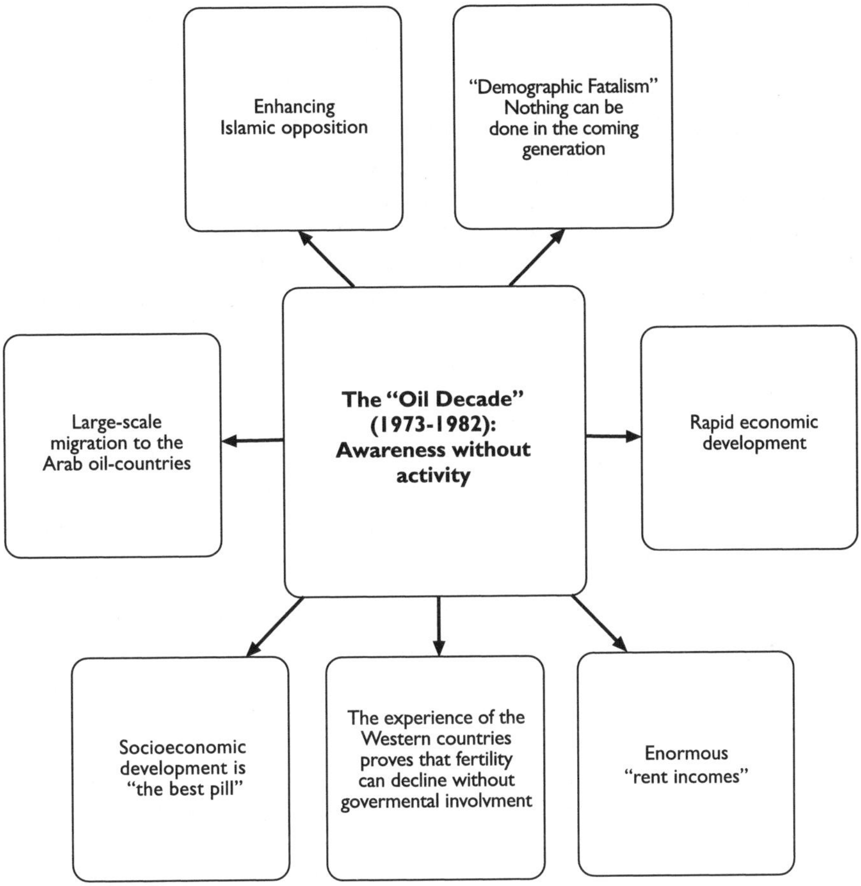

sufficient labor was to import large numbers of temporary foreign workers (see Chapter 3). The long-term goal was to supply the necessary workforce from local sources through a tremendous improvement in the educational and professional training systems for the nationals, in parallel to adopting pro-natalist policies.[116] In Bahrain, for example, the authorities chose not to adopt anti-natalist measures despite the high fertility rate "because it was considered necessary to hasten the process of replacing immigrants with an indigenous labor force..."[117]

According to the Demographic Transition theory, fertility rates could be expected to drop naturally, without any direct governmental involvement, following a prolonged decline in infant and child mortality rates, combined with a surge in economic development and women's educational level. Thus, the GCC pro-natalist policies were aimed at changing this "natural" evolutionary demographic process by granting various financial benefits to large families, in the same way that anti-natalist policies were intended to overcome the basic pro-natalist factors in developing societies.

Overall, various pro-natalist measures have been taken by the GCC governments in order to maintain the high fertility rates. The intensity of the measures taken varied from one country to another in accordance with the per capita oil revenues. Thus, the most intensive measures were taken in Kuwait and Qatar, the richest among the GCC oil-states in per capita terms, and the least intensive measures were taken in Bahrain and Oman, the poorest among these countries. One of the main measures taken was the initiation of public housing projects whereby the government sold housing at cost or provided land for building while offering long-term loans at very low interest rates.[118] Besides encouraging high fertility rates, the policy of distributing land to the population also had a political target: to increase support for the royal families as part of the GCC *rentier* political system. In Kuwait, during the 1950s, this policy constituted one of the major channels used by the regime to distribute oil revenues to the merchant elite and tribal notables. The regimes of Qatar and UAE also adopted a similar policy, and in Saudi Arabia the system of land gifts has been in force since the beginning of the Ibn Sa'ud regime.[119] Other major pro-natalist measures included the encouragement of early marriage through large marriage allowances;[120] full governmental subsidies for education (including books, clothing, etc.) provided from the first grade through the university level; and children's allowances for each child of nationals employed in the public sector.[121] Overall, in can be said that during the "oil decade," the GCC countries implemented the most extreme pro-natalist measures known worldwide during the second half of the twentieth century.

However, it should be emphasized that, with the exception of Saudi Arabia, the pro-natalist policies in the other GCC countries were implemented on a voluntary basis and that although the distribution and use of contraceptives were allowed, there was no direct governmental involvement. In Saudi Arabia on the contrary, contraceptives were pronounced as contradiction to the teaching of Islam and their import and use were banned in 1975.[122] A clear sign of the Saudi pro-natalist approach is the fact that the *Saudi Arabia Child Health Survey*, conducted in 1987, did not include a chapter on family planning and contraceptive use. However, even in Saudi Arabia, despite the restrictions on contraceptive use, they were still available during the 1970s at least in the major cities.[123]

In retrospect, this policy achieved its primary goal: While the educational level of the entire GCC indigenous population, including the women, tremendously improved and the death rates radically declined, particularly among infants and children (see **Chapter 2**), the fertility levels remained very high during the "oil decade," without significant changes in comparison to the previous decades. In 1985, the crude birth rate and total fertility rate were 44.7 per 1,000 and 5.9 children per woman, respectively, in Bahrain; 46.9 and 7.2, respectively, in Qatar; 46.3 and 7.5, respectively, in the UAE; and 46.0 and 7.5, respectively, in Saudi Arabia.[124]

The option of supplying the necessary workforce through mass naturalization of foreign workers and their families, as done in Canada, the US, Australia, and other developed countries worldwide, was never even viewed as a viable alternative in any of the GCC countries, due mainly to two political considerations. First and foremost, the unique tribal social structure of the GCC societies could be damaged through the naturalization of a large number of outsiders, thus clearly working against the basic political interests of the GCC royal families. The second factor was that the major possible sources for large-scale naturalization of Arabs were from Egypt, Algeria, Sudan and Syria, which all had "revolutionary" regimes and political identities that could threaten their current monarchy political structure. The large-scale naturalization of non-Arabs was also not considered as an option in the interests of preserving the Islamic-Arabic culture of the GCC societies.

3.4 The mid-1980s Onward: "The Sobriety": Direct Family Planning Programs is the Only Solution

The end of the "oil decade" in 1982, and more so the drop in oil prices in mid-1986 to less than $10 per barrel, led to a deterioration in all of the Arab economies, both oil and non-oil alike (see **Chapter 3**). As a result, the natalist approach in the Arab over-populated countries dramatically changed, heralding a new period that can be called the "Demographic Sobriety." Since the mid-1980s, and especially during the past decade, the family planning programs and the anti-natalist measures introduced in the overpopulated Arab countries have been intensified, either officially by the state itself or by NGOs with governmental financial support.

The first country that changed its natalist approach following the end of the "oil decade" was Egypt. In 1985, the National Population Council, headed by Mubarak himself, was established.[125] A year later, in 1986, a new family planning program was announced with the aim of reducing the natural increase rate from 2.8% in 1986 to 2.1% in 2001. There were two basic assumptions of the new plan. First, rapid population growth by itself constitutes a major socioeconomic problem, and thus a comprehensive national family planning program is necessary to reduce the high fertility levels in preparation for transforming Egyptian society into an industrialized one. Second, a sharp fertility decline should bring about certain structural changes that will help to raise the standard of living and enhance Egypt's industrialization process.[126] Although the new plan included many elements from the previous plans, it reflected change in two critical areas. First, the demographic problem was given top governmental priority, and second, emphasis was placed on both the supply and the demand measures simultaneously.[127] The new emphasis on the supply side was the result of pressure from the USAID that there was a 15%–20% unmet need for contraceptives in Egypt, particularly in the countryside and remote areas.[128] Thus, in early 1987, the ministerial committee for social services decided to establish one family planning unit to serve every 2,000 families throughout the country.[129]

Besides Egypt, new family planning activities were also initiated in other Arab countries. In 1987, the Tunisian authorities limited children's allowances to families with a maximum of four children and one year later, in 1988, to only three children. A maternity leave of two months at full pay, followed by four months at half pay, was also limited in 1988 to the first three children.[130] The year 1987 also marked a turning point in the Syrian demographic policy as a direct outcome of the deep recession. In that year, the financial benefits given to large families were cancelled. At the same time, the Ministry of Health appealed to young families through the mass media to take family planning steps, while the range of activities of the Syrian Family Planning Association was expanded.[131]

What were the major factors that led to the intensified family planning activities in many of the Arab countries starting in the mid-1980s?

(a) *The collapse of the "economic development" thesis.* In the mid-1980s, the leaders of the Arab overpopulated countries began to grasp the misguided nature of their belief that prolonged economic improvement would bring about fertility decline without direct governmental involvement. Not only did fertility rates fail to decline, but in some countries, such as Egypt and, to a lesser extent, Syria, they even increased despite the substantial socioeconomic improvement.

(b) The collapse of the inter-Arab migration option. The leaders of the largest Arab labor-exporting countries realized in the mid-1980s that alleviating the employment pressure in their own countries through large-scale labor-emigration to the Arab oil countries was no longer a realistic option, given the recession in the oil countries and the growing preference of employers for Asian workers over Arab workers (see **Chapter 3**).

(c) The sharp cut in the grants from the Arab oil-states. Although even in the mid-1980s there were some who continued to believe in Arab unity, it was quite clear that the Arab oil-states would not continue to back the overpopulated Arab countries and that each country would have to operate according to its own interests. Thus, it became more expedient for these countries to promote direct and extensive family planning activities in order to compensate for the lack of financial backing from the rich Arab oil-states.

(d) The success of family planning programs in many developing countries worldwide. In the mid-1980s, it became clear that a growing number of developing countries, such as South Korea, China, Singapore and Thailand, were succeeding to reduce their high fertility rates through comprehensive national family planning programs.[132] This led to an increase in the number of developing countries that actually supported either direct or indirect anti-natalist measures. By 2001, according to the UN data, 91% of the world's countries supported either direct or indirect family planning methods.[133]

(e) The change in the global political economy. In the second half of the 1980s, an increasing number of developing countries fell into an economic recession and became increasingly dependent on Western and international financial institutions aid, forcing them to adopt macroeconomic reforms that were more conducive to creating a better environment for implementing family planning programs.[134]

During the 1990s, there was a further increase in the direct governmental anti-natalist activities in many of the Arab countries. In 1991, the government of Yemen[135] adopted a long-term family planning program aimed at reducing the total fertility rate from 7 children per woman in the early 1990s to 4 in 2018[136] and raising the contraceptive prevalence rate to 50% so as to reach a natural increase rate of 2% by the year 2023.[137] The short-term aims were to reduce the total fertility rate to 6 children per woman and to increase the contraceptive prevalence rate to 35% by the year 2000.[138] Actually, by 1997, the contraceptive prevalence rate in Yemen amounted to 21%, as compared with 10% in 1991/2.[139]

In Egypt, the family planning activities were also expanded during the 1990s. In 1991, the Egyptian government's demographic targets were that the contraceptive prevalence rate would increase to 65% and that the crude birth rate would decline to 25 per 1,000 by the year 2007.[140] The increasing attention being devoted to the demographic issue within Egypt's overall socioeconomic development strategy was reflected by the fact that the Five-Year Development Plan for 1992/3–1996/7 contained, for the first time, a separate chapter on the demographic challenge.[141] In October 1993, Mubarak set seven national priorities for the new cabinet, and "for the first time ever, the population problem was among them."[142] During the 1990s, cartoons illustrating the devastating consequences of rapid population growth were appearing not only in the press but also in official governmental publications, such as the following two.[143]

Cartoon 4.2

Cartoon 4.3

The setting for the 1994 World Population Conference in Cairo was an international acknowledgement of Egypt's successful family planning efforts. Within the framework of the new family planning concept, adopted following the 1994 World Population Conference, the national family planning services were integrated into the broader mother-and-child health services, and greater emphasis was placed on the rural areas, where fertility rates were traditionally much higher than in the major cities.[144] Overall, by 1996 the number of family planning units operating throughout the country was 4,733, of which 62.1% were in rural areas.[145]

In Jordan, following the return of some 350,000 Jordanian citizens from the GCC countries, the authorities realized that the only viable option for reducing the country's socioeconomic burden, particularly the subsidy pressures in the short run and the employment pressures in the longer run, was through a sharp decline in fertility. Thus, in 1993, within the framework of the Five-Year Development Plan for 1993–1997, the Jordanian authorities officially adopted a national family planning program.[146] The plan contained very similar components, in terms of both supply and demand family planning characteristics, to those of the family planning programs implemented in other Arab countries.[147] The target set by the plan was to reduce the crude birth rate by 1 per 1,000 each year.[148] Recently, due to the increasing burden of rapid population growth, the issue of family planning has received even higher governmental attention. In a meeting of the Jordanian Higher Population Council, held in May 26, 2003, Jordan's Prime Minister, 'Ali 'Abd al-Ragheb, called for initiating a detailed action program in the demographic area, claiming that Jordan's rapid population growth "has an adverse impact on various aspects of life since it is disproportionate to growth in the available national resources."[149] The *Jordan Times* reported lately that: "Population challenges currently top the government's list of priorities . . ."[150]

Family planning activities in Syria were intensified during the 1990s, starting with conferences on the population problem and the need for family planning. By receiving broad press coverage, these conferences were designed to highlight the dangers to Syrian society from uncontrolled population growth and to convince the masses that there was no religious restrictions on contraceptives.[151] By mid-1993, the overall number of family planning clinics in Syria was 552, about two-thirds of which were in the rural areas.[152] However, it should be emphasized that despite the abolishment of financial and other benefits to large families, in contrast to Jordan, the Syrian anti-natalist approach also during the 1990s remained unofficial. We cannot find any expression of Hafiz al-Asad himself or any other senior officials in the Syrian regime publicly advocating an official family planning program. Thus, for example, in the conference "Economic and Investment Policies in Syria," held at the University of Damascus in March 1997, the Syrian Minister of Economy and Foreign Trade, Muhammad al-'Imadi, said that the demographic challenge of Syria "can only find its response in constant work, in the optimum use of the innovations of science and technology, and in a development policy that is compatible with the labor market."[153] The Minister did not even mention the need for a comprehensive national direct family planning program in order to curb the country's high fertility rates.

In May 2002, however, the Syrian authorities made a dramatic step toward promoting fertility decline by announcing that henceforth children's allowances would be paid according to the number of children in each family, rather than according to a fixed amount for each child, as was previously paid. The highest allowance of 200 Syrian pound (S£) would be paid for the first child, S£150 for the second child, S£100 for the third child, and another S£25 for families with more than three children. The maximum for children's allowances was set at S£475. Thus, the higher the number of children in a family, the lower the average allowances paid for each child.[154]

Algeria was also forced to intensify its family planning activities during the 1990s in response to the increasing economic burden caused by the country's rapid population growth. First and foremost among these problems was the sharp rise in unemployment to a dangerous level from a political point of view. Thus, in 1997, the Comité National de la Population was established in order to promote family planning activities in the country.[155]

A major characteristic of the anti-natalist measures implemented in the Arab countries during the 1990s, particularly during the second half of the decade, was that the activities, in contrast to the past, were carried out in the open. Many Arab governments, particularly those of Syria, Jordan and Algeria, stopped trying to hide their ambitions to reduce fertility rates, and family planning and fertility decline became legitimate governmental goals. It seems that several major factors contributed to making these activities an official policy, or at least a "visible policy."

(a) Worsening of the socioeconomic consequences of rapid population growth. The severity of these socioeconomic consequences became overwhelming, even in countries that were relatively not so populous until the 1970s, such as Jordan, Syria, and Yemen. The leaders of the more populous Arab countries, namely, Egypt, Morocco and Algeria, reached the inescapable conclusion that they were facing real political threats to the fundamental legitimacy of their regimes as a result of these severe consequences. Indeed, from the 1950s until the mid-1980s, there had been a steady improvement in the standard of living in all of the Arab countries, even in the poorer ones. In this respect, the revolutionary regimes had "delivered the goods" by living up to their promises for "a better life." However, the economic recession that started in the mid-1980s and continued during the 1990s, in parallel to the changing dynamics in the inter-Arab economic relationships and the new "world economic order," forced the governments of the overpopulated Arab countries to make corresponding adjustments in their socioeconomic policies, including in the area of fertility. The paradox of these developments is that until the late 1980s, the initiation of governmental activities in the area of family planning had been considered politically dangerous, whereas in past few years the greater danger seemed to lie in the failure to act in this area.

(b) The declining threat of the Islamic fundamentalist opposition. One of the most important factors that prevented massive governmental activities in the area of family planning in many Arab countries until the second half of the 1980s was the fear of confrontation with the Islamic fundamentalist opposition. However, it seems that this threat was largely diminished starting in the mid-1980s, and even more so during the 1990s. Moreover, in 1989, the Islamic Republic of Iran started to implement an official family planning program and justified it religiously, which in turn provided "religious validation" to the Arab-Islamic countries as well.[156] In the 1994 Cairo Population and Development Conference, the Iranian government went even further by publicly supporting the implementation of governmental family planning programs in order to reduce fertility rates.[157]

(c) The diminishing of the Arab–Israeli conflict. A major argument of those who were opposed to family planning in Egypt during the 1960s and 1970s was the continuation of the Arab–Israeli military conflict. However, the diminishing of the conflict, starting with the March 1979 Egyptian–Israeli peace treaty and followed by the October 1991

Madrid Conference, the September 1993 Palestinian–Israeli Oslo Accords, the October 1994 Jordanian–Israeli peace treaty, and the peace talks between Syria and Israel, all contributed to reducing the conflict from an overall Arab–Israeli conflict to a Palestinian–Israeli conflict. Thus, the Arab–Israeli conflict could no longer constitute a cause or an "excuse" for failing to take action in the area of family planning. Among the Palestinians and the Israelis, however, the fertility attitude has indeed remained pro-natalist on both sides (see the Introduction).

(d) The collapse of the Soviet Union. The demise of Communist ideology in the late 1980s led to the creation of one superpower, not only in the political dimension but also in the economic arena. This factor constituted a major lever for enhancing family planning activities in many developing countries worldwide, including the Arab countries. The collapse of the Soviet Union, it should be remembered, was brought about on purely economic grounds and was not the result of war or any other kind of international conflict. As such, Communist socioeconomic ideology, which was not supportive of national family planning programs, was rendered irrelevant. It was quite apparent then that the only economic policy which could be of any use in the modern economy was that of capitalism, which supported national family planning programs as the best option for curbing the rapid population growth in overpopulated developing countries.

(e) The reversal in the US demographic policy. Following the ascendancy of Bill Clinton to the office of US President in January 1993, the US reversed its demographic policy toward developing countries to that which had prevailed prior to the ascendancy of Ronald Reagan.[158] This renewed support, it seems, also contributed to enhancing anti-natalist activities in many developing countries worldwide, including the Arab countries that had become increasingly dependent on US and IMF financial support.

(f) Ease of access to the target population. During the 1990s, more than ever before, it was much easier for the Arab governments to act in the area of family planning and related issues, due mainly to two factors. First, the sharp and steady improvement in women's educational levels since the 1960s meant that the women who were the target of the governmental family planning policies in the 1990s were much more educated than were those of previous periods. Since women's educational level constitutes one of the two most important factors shaping fertility rates, then the likelihood of women availing themselves of the contraceptives being offered by governmental family planning programs in the 1990s was greater than ever before. Second, the widespread use of mass media, particularly electronic media and mainly television, enabled the Arab governments to disseminate their messages in the area of family planning and related issues more effectively than in the 1960s and 1970s, when such media were either scarce or not available at all.

(g) The falsehood of "Arab unity." At least in the economic meaning of "Arab Unity," it became clear that the rich Arab oil-states were not willing to share their oil revenues with the poorer Arab countries, as the scale of aid sharply declined during the 1990s. The only exception was the one-time aid given to the countries that supported the anti-Iraqi coalition in the 1990–1991 Kuwait Crisis. Thus, the leaders of the poorer Arab countries were forced to confront the inescapable reality that their socioeconomic

problems would not be resolved through massive Arab aid, but only through substantial socioeconomic reforms, including the adoption of direct and effective anti-natalist measures. This realization, it should be emphasized, occurred in parallel to steady increasing pressure from the IMF and the World Bank to implement substantial economic reforms in line with the "Washington Consensus."

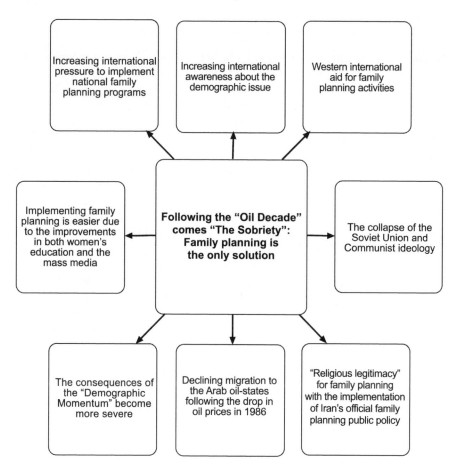

Chart 4.3   The Natalist Perception of the non-Oil Arab Countries following the "Oil Decade"

The most dramatic natalist perception change during the 1990s occurred in the two most populated GCC states, namely, Oman and, to a lesser extent, Saudi Arabia, which gradually moved away from their traditional pro-natalist approach and started to advocate fertility decline. The change in the natalist approach of Sultan Qabus of Oman was the outcome of several factors. First, the continued high natural increase rates, combined with the increasing female labor force participation rates, ensured a steady increase in the potential indigenous labor force for the foreseeable future. Second, the prolonged low oil prices until April 1999 led to economic stagnation and even decline in per capita terms. Third, the various obstacles to implementing the Omanization labor policy resulted in an increase in the number of foreign workers in parallel to rising unemployment among nationals.[159] Thus, following the publication of the 1993 census results, Sultan Qabus attempted to convince the public that there were no Islamic restrictions against the use of contraceptives in order to control fertility:

> We need to take another look at family planning. The recommended figure in the world as a whole is five members per family. When we see that the Omani family averages seven members, and that there is a strong belief that the creator will provide, we should also realize that almighty God has also given us intelligence and urged us to use it.[160]

Within the framework of the Omani long-term socioeconomic development plan, which was published in 1995 and entitled "Oman 2020," the demographic issue was given high priority. The first dimension noted as part of the human resource development strategy was: "To achieve a balance between population and economic growth by reducing the current population growth rate to less than 3% by 2020, through reasoning and enlightenment."[161]

Oman became the first among the GCC countries that not only practically but also officially promoted fertility reduction and the use of contraceptives. In October 1994, the Birth Spacing Services Program was incorporated into the governmental Maternal and Child Health clinics, where contraceptives are distributed free of charge.[162] Overall, by the year 2000, the percentage of married Omani women using family planning methods was 32%, as compared with 9% in the late 1980s.[163]

In the case of Saudi Arabia, it seems that the authorities eventually reached the inescapable conclusion that their former demographic approach was misguided, both in terms of foreign labor and the desired fertility rates of the indigenous population. It became clear that the high fertility rates of the indigenous population were not bringing about a decline in the need for foreign labor; on the contrary, the rapid increase in the indigenous population was only leading to an increase in the demand for foreign labor. Thus, the Saudi Sixth Development Plan for the years 1995–2000 acknowledged that: "Although the rapid growth of the Saudi population is not an entirely new phenomenon, it has now reached the stage of exerting considerable influence on many aspects of economic and social policy."[164]

A clear indicator of the changing Saudi demographic approach was the abolishment in 1996 of the 1975 law forbidding the promotion, distribution or use of contraceptives.[165] Another indicator of the Saudi authorities' changing approach to fertility is their public admission of the existence of a serious demographic problem in the Kingdom, in contrast to their previous representation of the high fertility rates as an outcome of their successful socioeconomic policy.[166] In the past few years, the Saudi authorities have become particularly concerned about the wide-based age pyramid of the indigenous population and the need to create an increasing number of new work opportunities for the rapidly growing national workforce. For example, the Saudi Arabian Monetary Agency reported in 2002 that:

> A major challenge facing the Saudi economy is the high rate of population growth and related demographic profile [i.e. the age structure] and their implications for economic growth and job opportunities . . . High population growth is straining public services such as education, health, municipalities, water, electricity, roads and housing with adverse effects on the standard of living and economic and social well-being.[167]

However, it should be emphasized that the change in the Saudi fertility approach is very slow, in line with the overall "Saudi pace" in many other aspects, political and socioeconomic alike. This slow progress is a reflection of the paramount aim of the al-Saʿud royal family not to shake the current political order in the Kingdom.

The indigenous populations of the other four GCC countries are very small and, with the exception of Bahrain, foreigners constituted more than 70% of the total population and more than 80% of the labor force (see tables 2.4 and 3.4). Given this demographic profile, the promotion of anti-natalist policy in order to bring about a fertility decline was not so relevant in their case. Although the basic fertility orientation of these countries, other than Bahrain,[168] remained pro-natalist during the 1990s, family planning services were still available through the public health clinics within the framework of the overall health services offered by the authorities to the indigenous populations. Thus, whereas in the 1970s and 1980s, the GCC countries were all overtly pro-natalist, at the dawn of the twenty-first century only three of the six countries remained pro-natalist, while the other three promoted fertility decline in some way.

In an article published in 1988, J. S. Birks raised a rhetorical question about whether it would be possible for the GCC countries to implement anti-natalist measures sometime in the future. His answer was definitively negative due to three main factors. First, the GCC rulers believed that the international and security positions of their countries would be too vulnerable with extremely small populations. Second, the impact of family planning activities can be felt only after a period of one to two generations, and the perspective of the GCC rulers was much shorter. Third, the GCC rulers traditionally considered rapid population growth as a lever for enhancing economic development.[169]

4 Evaluation of the Family Planning Programs in the Arab Countries

As the data reveal, fertility rates in all of the Arab countries, even in the rich oil-states, have substantially declined during the past two decades. However, by international comparison, this decline started two decades after that of many other developing countries and the pace of decline has been much slower. Thus, while Turkey's crude birth rate in 1960 was higher than Egypt's, in the year 2000 Turkey's total fertility rate was 2.2 children per woman in comparison to 3.3 in Egypt and almost 4 in both Jordan and Syria. Non-Middle Eastern developing countries achieved even lower total fertility rates by the year 2000, including 1.5 in South Korea, 2.1 in Brazil, and 2.7 in Mexico (see table 2.5).

Although Egypt is considered as a "success story" in the area of fertility decline and its family planning policy as exemplary,[170] the fact is that during the past decade, the country's fertility rates have remained almost unchanged. According to the *EDHS–2000*, the average total fertility rate in Egypt during the period 1997–2000 was 3.5 children per woman, representing an insignificant decline from 3.6 in the period 1992–1995. The Survey's data also reveal that Egypt's main demographic problem is in the rural areas of Upper Egypt, where fertility rates remain very high at an average of 4.7 children per woman.[171] There are three major factors contributing to the much higher fertility rates in the rural areas of Upper Egypt in comparison to the national average. First, Upper Egypt considered by experts to be a more "tradition" in comparison to other parts of the country.[172] Second, the availability of family planning services in these areas does not approach the same standard as in other areas of the country, particularly in the major cities, leaving the need for contraceptives there largely unmet. Third, the indirect factors that contribute to lower fertility, mainly women's educational level and employment opportunities, in addition to the enforcement of the prohibition on child labor, are not as strong in these areas as in the rest of the country. According to the *EDHS–1995* data, the mean age for first marriage of women aged 25–29 was only 17.8 years in Upper Egypt.[173] This means that a considerable percentage of women in this area are still getting married below the minimum age permitted by law.

Despite the overall increase in Egypt's contraceptive prevalence rates (see table 2.9), it should be noted that even in the major cities of Egypt, where the fertility rates are considerably lower than those in the countryside, the goal of replacement-level fertility is still far from being achieved. According to the *EDHS–2000* data, the total fertility rate in the major cities in the period 1997–2000 averaged 2.9 children per woman, as compared with 2.7 children during the period 1990–1992, representing an increase of almost 10%.[174] In 2001, Egypt's overall crude birth rate was 26.7 per 1,000, as compared with 27.7 per 1,000 in 1992, representing an insignificant decline of only 1 per 1,000 in almost a decade. Moreover, whereas during the period 1986–1992, Egypt's crude birth rate steadily declined from 40.0 to 27.7 per 1,000, since 1993 it has been fluctuating upward and downward from one year to another.[175]

In Syria, according to the 1999 Multiple Survey, the average total fertility rate was 4.2 children per women – the same rate as in the *SMCHS–1993*. Thus far, the governmental anti-natalist measures did not appear to be bringing about a substantial fertility decline, particularly not in the rural areas where the total fertility rate was as high as 4.4, according to the 1999 Multiple Survey.[176] The changes made in the children's allowances system in 2002 did not yet appear to be affecting the fertility rates.

In the case of Jordan, according to the *JPFHS–1997*, only 45.3% of currently married women in the rural areas were using contraceptives (both modern and traditional), although almost 100% were knowledgeable about contraceptive methods.[177] This means that more than one half of rural married women in Jordan chose not to use contraceptives despite being familiar with them. However, despite the fact that the "unmet need" for contraceptives in Jordan remained quite high in the early 2000s at the level of 11%,[178] fertility rates in Jordan, in contrast to Egypt and Syria, continued to steadily decline during the past decade: from 4.4 children per woman according to the *JPFHS–1997*,[179] to 3.7 children per woman in 2003.[180] At the same time, it should be remembered that despite the marked fertility decline, still the meaning of a total fertility rate at the level of 3.7 children per woman is almost twice the replacement-level rate.

Overall, the situation in almost all of the other Arab countries was quite similar at the end of the twentieth century, with very high fertility rates in the countryside and remote areas that had a substantial impact on the national average. Thus, the crucial question in this regard is why the fertility levels in almost all of the Arab countries remained so much higher than the average level among developing countries worldwide with similar socioeconomic characteristics? Many researchers attribute the late fertility decline in the Arab countries to two main factors: Islam and the low status of women.[181] However, one should not ignore the presence of many other long-term socio-political factors that contributed to the late fertility decline in the vast majority of the Arab countries. Whereas the short-term factors have already been examined, following is a brief outline of the most prominent long-term factors that should be considered:

(a) The first factor was, and to a large extent still is, *low awareness* of the extremely important role played by fertility decline in advancing socioeconomic development. This low awareness not only led to delays in the implementation of family planning programs until the mid-1980s and in some countries until the 1990s, but also to their insignificance in the overall development policy, even in those countries that had officially adopted an anti-natalist policy.

Lack of awareness was typical not only of politicians but also of academicians, as reflected in the absence of the issue of family planning from the famous *Arab Human Development Report–2002*.[182] Another example in this regard is that in a recently published article, Mustapha Nabil, the Chief Economist for MENA in the World Bank, said that: "if the [economic] environment is constrained, a potential demographic gift could turn into a demographic curse and give way to a social crisis."[183] In line with the current and future prospects for labor force growth rates, it no longer seems appropriate to refer to any kind of "demographic gift" in this part of the world.

(b) *The prolonged Arab–Israeli conflict* also hampered the adoption of comprehensive family planning programs in the countries that were directly involved in the conflict. By devoting their attention and resources to the conflict itself, the Arab leaders failed to deal with issues that could affect fertility levels, either directly or indirectly. One of these issues was the "pro-natalist environment" created by the prolonged conflict, in which, as argued by many, a quantitative demographic advantage over Israel constituted an important factor in winning the conflict.[184] The continuation of the Arab–Israeli conflict, it should be emphasized, serves as an obstacle not only to the promotion of the family planning concept, but also to the introduction of structural macroeconomic reforms. As Gred Nonneman claims: "a combination of political-economic and related political-cultural factors, added to by the Arab–Israeli conflict, continues to hamper political and economic development in the Middle East."[185]

(c) The third factor was *the prevailing pan-Arab concept* that ruled Arab politics, at least officially, until the 1980s, namely, that substantial help would be available from the rich Arab oil-states. The millions of workers exported from the poorer Arab countries to the GCC countries and Libya during the 1970s and 1980s, as well as the sharp rise in the scale of trade between the Arab countries themselves,[186] fuelled this feeling. However, if the pan-Arab system ever had any meaning, in the 1990s it was definitely defunct. The only exception was the priority given by Saddam Husayn to other Arab countries that were exporting their goods and products to Iraq within the framework of the "oil-for-food" program, which was in operation from December 1996 until the collapse of his regime in March 2003 (see Chapter 3).

(d) The Arab states, both poorer and richer alike, were characterized by their "*soft state*" nature.[187] This was reflected not only in the high subsidies on basic food items, electricity, fuel, gas, housing, and public services, including health care and education, but also in the low enforcement of basic laws that related directly and indirectly to fertility patterns, mainly the minimum age at first marriage for women and restrictions on children's employment. This form of socioeconomic policy, it should be emphasized, was part of the political approach of the Arab regimes, namely, to enhance their political legitimacy and prevent political participation in exchange for promises of a "better life," particularly for the lower stratums. In other words, it was a "populist socioeconomic policy" whereby the population is not forced to "sacrifice" by paying higher taxes or by shouldering any other *personal* economic burden in order to support the rapid population growth. Therefore, financing the accelerating population growth is viewed as "the problem of the authorities," rather than of the "masses" themselves. In democratic countries, where the public is forced to finance the economic burden of rapid population growth through higher taxation, the pressure for adopting anti-natalist measures is more likely to come from public organizations and political parties that oppose the prevailing pro-natalist policies.[188]

(e) The "Dutch Disease" syndrome[189] led many of the Arab leaders in the 1970s and 1980s to believe that they could succeed in achieving considerable economic expansion and substantial improvement in the standard of living in parallel to rapid population growth. Viktor Lavy and Eliezer Sheffer argued that the massive aid and the workers' remittances received by Jordan and Egypt had an overall negative effect on their economies insofar as they did not see the need to implement structural economic reforms in line with the changing world economic order.[190] The failure to adopt a comprehensive family planning program was part and parcel of this overall socioeconomic shortsightedness, as indicated by Alan Richards:

> The worst legacy of the oil boom is not that the benefits were not widely shared but that they *were* widely shared: Labor exporters as well as oil producers caught the Dutch Disease, leaving the Arab world poorly equipped to face the challenge of an increasingly competitive international economy.[191]

Many other developing countries worldwide had already started to implement both comprehensive family planning programs and wider macroeconomic reforms during the 1970s in response to the sharp increase in oil prices and the subsequent economic recession.[192] However, the non-oil Arab countries, began to implement such reforms only in the late 1980s and early 1990s, neglecting to do so earlier also because of the sharp increase in oil prices. Thus, there is no doubt that the labor migration from the poorer to the rich oil Arab countries was a "blessing" from the individual point of view. The migrants earned more money in a few years than what they could ever have earned even in a lifetime in their home countries. Nevertheless, one would have to say that from a macroeconomic as well as demographic points of view, the 1970s and 1980s were "two lost decades" for the Arab labor-exporting countries and that in the long run, the "oil boom" was more of a "curse" than a "blessing."

5   Why Tunisia and Lebanon?

As the data reveal, at the beginning of the twenty-first century, among all of the Arab countries only Tunisia and Lebanon had reached a fertility rate that is close to the replacement-level. Although the result was the same, namely, low fertility rates, the reasons for the sharp fertility decline in each of these two countries during the past four decades were quite different. While in Tunisia the fertility decline was a direct outcome of the comprehensive family planning program, in Lebanon such a policy was never implemented and the pattern of fertility decline resembled that of the "Western pattern," meaning without direct governmental involvement.

5.1 Tunisia[193]

In the case of Tunisia, several major factors were responsible for the sharp fertility decline during the past three decades, the most important of which are:

(a) First and foremost was *the high governmental priority given to fertility decline* by the authorities since the mid-1960s. The 2001 ECA Demographic Report noted specifically that two of the main factors accounting for Tunisia's family planning success were "implication of a clear, well-designed and well-planned family planning and health program" and "political support for the population policy at the highest level."[194]

(b) In contrast to the other Arab countries, the Tunisian anti-natalist measures were accompanied since their inception in the mid-1960s by *a promotion of the status of women* through high enrollment rates in education, higher labor force participation rates, greater accessibility to legal abortion, and personal status in both family and public life.[195]

(c) Unlike many other Arab countries, whose long-standing political agenda included "Western hostility," Tunisia continued to *maintain close relations with Western governments* since gaining its independence peacefully from France. Due to the identification of family planning with Western governments, "family planning tended to come onto the policy agenda earlier in those countries which had closer relations with the West."[196]

(d) In Tunisia, *the Islamic opposition never constituted a real threat to the regime.* Thus, from the onset, it was much easier for the Tunisian authorities to implement a comprehensive national family planning policy without fear of the Islamic opposition.[197]

5.2. Lebanon

In the case of Lebanon, the low fertility rates were attributable to two major factors. The first is that Lebanon, in contrast to other Arab countries, was never a "soft state," meaning that it never guaranteed public employment for its citizens and never offered a wide variety of free or even highly subsidized public services. This was not only an outcome of the Lebanese "Western" socioeconomic culture since its establishment in 1920, but also of its political instability and weak central authority that prevented any implementation of socialist measures. Thus, in contrast to all of the other Arab countries, parents in Lebanon were forced to support their own children, rather than depending on massive subsidies provided by the state. As a result, they were more motivated to maintain a low fertility level. The second factor was the "shaky" political situation in the country since the onset of the second Civil War. When a country is involved in consecutive wars, as in Egypt during the period 1967–1973, the political-security instability has an impact on the personal level by lowering fertility. Thus, while in Tunisia the sharp fertility decline during the past three decades can be attributed to "good governance," in the case of Lebanon the low fertility rates should be attributed to "no governance."

6 Conclusions

During the 1990s, with the exception of the smaller GCC oil-states, the governmental family planning activities of the Arab countries were greatly enhanced following the realization of the authorities that the only viable option for relief of widespread poverty and other socioeconomic problems was through the introduction of family planning activities and substantial macroeconomic reforms. However, while many of the other developing countries worldwide had already started to implement comprehensive anti-natalist measures in the 1960s and 1970s, the Arab countries, with the exception of Tunisia, started to do so only in the second half of the 1980s or during the 1990s. Even in Egypt, the most populated of the Arab countries, it was not until the mid-1980s that the demographic issue assumed top priority in the political agenda.

In hindsight, if the non-oil Arab countries had initiated a comprehensive anti-natalist measures in the 1950s and 1960s instead of waiting until the 1980s and 1990s, then they could possibly have reached a stable population level by the early twenty-first century. Egypt's population would then have numbered 75 to 80 million in 2025, rather than the 100 million as it looks today. This is true also in the case of the other Arab countries. It can be concluded that the failure of the Arab leaders until very recently to deal seriously with the demographic problem is responsible for prolonging the poverty and low standard of living of their populations well into the twenty-first century.

Conclusions and Prospects

The demographic and socioeconomic history of the Middle East during the twentieth century reveals that despite the huge unprecedented rapid population growth, "the Malthusian population trap" thesis has proved to be mistaken. The latest starvation disease in this part of the world occurred in Iran during the years 1869–1871.[1] Moreover, in the parts of the world where starvation diseases and epidemics did occur during the twentieth century, mainly in the sub-Saharan African countries, they were caused by political-security instability in those countries that prevented overall socioeconomic development, rather than by a limited supply of water or arable land, as the Malthusian thesis would explain it. In retrospect, during the twentieth century, particularly in the second half of the century, the increase in food production worldwide far exceeded the population growth rates as a direct result of technological advances – namely, the "missing link" in the "Malthusian population trap" theory. In the case of the Arab countries, during the second half of the twentieth century, life expectancy at birth increased by 25 years on average and the child mortality rate declined from almost one-third of live births to 4%–5%. These developments are indicative of the overall improvement in the standard of living in the Arab countries, even in the two poorest among them – Yemen and Sudan.

However, despite the refutation of the "Malthusian population trap" theory, the "mega-question" of the "worldwide demographic carrying capacity" has become the subject of debate between demographers, economists, sociologists, environmentalists, and the like, with many arguing that the world is approaching the point at which population density will considerably hamper further socioeconomic development. The neo-Malthusian pessimists argue that the world is facing the threat of ecological catastrophe if the current population growth rates are not controlled, whereas the optimists point to the sharp rise in the standard of living during the second half of the twentieth century despite the rapid population growth. The "big change," however, is that during the past generation, even the optimists have come to realize that the rapid population growth in the developing countries constitutes an economic burden rather than an asset. The common perception of the 1950s and 1960s among many leaders of developing countries, including some of the Arab leaders, that rapid population growth would bring about technological improvements and the development of more efficient production methods was almost totally debunked in the early 1980s.

The significant change in demographic perception served to pave the way for the adoption of efficient family planning programs in many developing countries world-wide, which have in turn led to the rapid fertility decline of the past two decades. This process is still ongoing and is playing a major role in global economic development. As one UN demographic report from 1992 noted: "In a number of Asian countries, notably South Korea, Taiwan and Thailand, success in boosting family planning and lowering fertility has preceded economic booms."[2]

Although the fertility rates in the Arab countries have declined considerably in the past two decades, they still remain very high. This constitutes a paramount barrier to boosting economic development in the non-oil Arab countries. A comparison between the socioeconomic development of these Arab countries and other developing coun-tries worldwide that have succeeded in substantially reducing fertility rates during the second half of the twentieth century is not flattering to the Arab countries.[3] Thus, Lebanon and Tunisia, the countries with the lowest fertility rates among the Arab countries, are ranked higher than any other non-oil Arab countries in the HDI (Lebanon is ranked 75 and Tunisia is ranked 96). The other Arab countries, as one can see in Appendix 2, are ranked below 100 – far behind countries such as South Korea (27), Thailand (70), and Brazil (73), whose socioeconomic condition in the 1950s and 1960s was quite similar or even worse than that prevailing in the non-oil Arab coun-tries. Thus, the most crucial question is: What went wrong? Why were the non-oil Arab economies unable to achieve the same degree of socioeconomic development as many other developing countries around the world that started in the mid-twentieth century from a very similar starting point?

In retrospect, it seems that the same factors which hampered the implementation of an effective family planning policy in the non-oil Arab countries prevented the adop-tion of the necessary macroeconomic reforms, namely, the rapid economic expansion during the "oil decade" that seemed to obviate the need for macroeconomic reforms; the prevailing illusion of "Arab Unity;" the ongoing Arab–Israeli conflict that not only demanded immense financial allocations for security, but also diverted the leadership's attention away from the socioeconomic development arena; and the constant "balance of fright" between the regimes and the Islamic opposition.

Thus, during the 1970s and 1980s, and in some countries, such as Syria, even into the 1990s, all of the Arab countries, with the exception of Lebanon and Tunisia, remained basically Myrdal's "soft states" and Beblawi's "*rentier* states," with all the various long-term devastating socioeconomic consequences. Thus, it appears that the demographic and the macroeconomic issues were two sides of the same coin. Only in the second half of the 1980s and more so during the 1990s did it become clear, beyond any doubt, that the natalist approach and the macroeconomic policy alike must be changed in order to avoid economic catastrophic. Then, and only then, were macro-economic reform programs and anti-natalist measures adopted almost simultaneously in the vast majority of the Arab countries in coordination with the IMF and the World Bank in line with the "Washington Consensus."

However, severe public opposition to these reforms was generated, particularly in the lower stratums, because public sector employment and governmental subsidies on basic foodstuffs, energy products, and public services were crucial for their basic sur-vival. Thus, large-scale demonstrations against the reforms were staged in many Arab countries, including the January 1977 "food riots" in Egypt,[4] in Morocco during the early 1980s,[5] in April 1989 and again in August 1996 in Jordan,[6] and in 1998 in Yemen.[7]

Although the reforms were crucial in order to revive the non-oil Arab economies, they failed, at least until the present, to bring about relief in two paramount areas. The first area in which the macroeconomic reforms did not live up to their initial aims was in the eradication of poverty. The initial assumption upon which the reforms were based was that economic liberalization would be for the benefit of all, including the lower stratums. However, this did not materialize in most countries, with the exception of Tunisia, where damage from the liberalization measures was minimized through governmental aid to poor families and support of the NGO activities among the lower stratums.[8] Tunisia was able to achieve this, *inter alia*, because of its much smaller population in the 1990s – a direct consequence of its successful anti-natalist policy in the 1970s and 1980s.

The second area in which the macroeconomic reforms did not bring relief was in unemployment. Whereas previously increases and decreases in unemployment rates had been a function of overall economic development, starting in the early 1990s steady increases in unemployment rates were occurring in all of the Arab countries, in both the oil and the non-oil economies, even during periods of substantial economic expansion of more than 4% on annual average. This new phenomenon developed when the number of new work opportunities available could not match the number of new entrants to the labor forces, thereby "fuelling" the already high employment pressures. As described in the 2004 ESCWA socioeconomic report:

> The region now faces the highest global rate of new entrants into the labor market, the highest unemployment rate and, when calculated over the past two decades, the lowest global rate of per capita GDP growth.[9]

Moreover, a central part of the economic reforms was massive privatization of public sector companies. In the case of Egypt, the privatization scheme adopted in 1991 in coordination with the IMF included 314 governmental companies, which employed over a million employees at that time. Ten years later, in 2001, the number of employees in these companies had been reduced to less than half a million.[10] Thus, at least in the short run, the process of privatization has involved the massive dismissal of employees. Similar to the demonstrations staged against the cuts in governmental subsidies, so have there been recent protests of Bahraini nationals in response to the unemployment situation.[11]

Thus, the Arab governments are being forced to operate in an unfavorable economic environment. On the one hand, enhancing privatization and economic liberalization is crucial to further economic development and constitutes a precondition to IMF support. On the other hand, it is politically untenable to dismiss a huge number of employees from the public sector when the private sector cannot possibly absorb them. Moreover, all of the non-oil Arab governments, without exception, are facing a "growth trap" by investing a huge percentage of their limited budgets to support their bulging populations through subsidies of basic foodstuffs, electricity, water, and public services. These subsidies practically support the continuation of high fertility rates, or at least do not support fertility limitation, as well as constitute an ongoing increasing burden on governmental budgets and come at the expense of investments in more productive sectors that promote economic expansion, such as infrastructure, support of foreign investment, tax reduction, and the like.

The continuing high natural increase rates have created a situation in which any annual GDP growth rate of less than 3% is, in effect, a stagnation in per capita terms. The economic history of the Arab countries since the end of the "oil decade" reveals that for most of the past two decades, even this minimum of a 3% annual GDP growth rate has not always been achieved. This was particularly the case in Jordan and Syria, which at the dawn of the twenty-first century did not achieve the per capita GDP that had prevailed in these countries in the early 1980s, not even in nominal terms. In the GCC oil-states, almost the sole factor responsible for their economic development during the second half of the twentieth century was and still is the oil revenues. Thus, the overall decline in oil prices since the end of the "oil decade," on the one hand, and the extremely rapid growth of the indigenous populations, on the other hand, have led to a sharp decline in their per capita GDP – simply because a much higher number of nationals are now "sharing" the "petrodollars." Nathan Keyfitz illustrated the overall demographic paradox of developing countries worldwide by saying that "population growth prevents the development that would slow population growth."[12] In sum, this is the core of the demographic, economic, and political "Catch 22" facing the Arab countries, both the oil-based and the non-oil alike, today.

Appendix 1

Basic Economic Indicators for the Arab Countries, 2002

Country	Total GNI (Atlas method, current $US, billions)	Per capita GNI (Atlas method, $US)	Per capita GDP (PPP, $US)
Non-Oil Countries			
Lebanon	17.3	3,900	4,360
Tunisia	19.5	1,990	6,760
Jordan	9.1	1,760	4,220
Algeria	58.3	1,720	5,760
Syria	18.5	1,090	3,620
Egypt	97.8	1,470	3,810
Morocco	34.7	1,170	3,810
Sudan	13.2	400	1,820
Yemen	9.1	490	870
Oil-Countries			
Bahrain	7.6	11,260	17,170
Kuwait	38.0	16,340	16,240
UAE	—	—	22,420
Qatar	—	—	19,844
Libya	—	—	7,570
Saudi Arabia	186.8	8,530	12,650
Oman	19.9	7,830	13,340

— No data available.

GNI (Gross National Income). The sum of value added by all resident producers plus any product taxes (less subsidies) not included in the valuation of output plus net receipts of primary income (compensation of employees and property income) from abroad.

PPP (Purchasing Power Parity). A rate of exchange that accounts for different prices for goods and services in various countries worldwide, thus enabling an international comparison of real outputs and incomes.

Sources: WB, *World Development Indicators Database* [http://www.worldbank.org]; UNDP, *Human Development Report – 2004*, pp. 139–42, table 1.

Appendix 2

UNDP Human Development Index for Some Arab Countries, non-Arab Developing Countries, and Developed Countries, 1975–2000

Country	Year 1975	1980	1985	1990	1995	2000
Developed Countries						
Norway (1)	0.859	0.877	0.888	0.901	0.925	0.942
Sweden (2)	0.863	0.872	0.883	0.894	0.925	0.941
United States (6)	0.863	0.884	0.898	0.914	0.925	0.939
Japan (9)	0.854	0.878	0.893	0.909	0.923	0.933
Switzerland (11)	0.874	0.886	0.893	0.905	0.914	0.928
France (12)	0.848	0.863	0.875	0.897	0.914	0.928
Arab Oil-Countries						
Bahrain (39)	—	—	—	—	—	0.831
Kuwait (45)	0.753	0.773	0.777	—	0.812	0.813
UAE (46)	—	—	—	—	—	0.812
Qatar (51)	—	—	—	—	—	0.803
Libya (64)	—	—	—	—	—	0.773
Saudi Arabia (71)	0.587	0.646	0.670	0.706	0.737	0.759
Oman (78)	—	—	—	—	—	0.751
Arab non-Oil Countries						
Lebanon (75)	—	—	—	0.680	0.730	0.755
Tunisia (97)	0.514	0.566	0.613	0.646	0.682	0.722
Jordan (99)	—	0.636	0.658	0.677	0.703	0.717
Algeria (106)	0.501	0.550	0.600	0.639	0.663	0.697
Syria (108)	0.538	0.580	0.614	0.634	0.665	0.691
Egypt (115)	0.435	0.482	0.532	0.574	0.605	0.642
Morocco (123)	0.429	0.474	0.508	0.540	0.569	0.602
Sudan (139)	0.346	0.374	0.395	0.419	0.462	0.499
Yemen (144)	—	—	—	—	—	—
Non-Arab Developing Countries						
South Korea (27)	0.691	0.732	0.774	0.815	0.852	0.882
Thailand (70)	0.604	0.645	0.676	0.713	0.749	0.762
Brazil (73)	0.644	0.679	0.692	0.713	0.737	0.757
Philippines (77)	0.652	0.684	0.688	0.716	0.733	0.754
Turkey (85)	0.593	0.617	0.654	0.686	717	0.742

The number in the parentheses indicates the range of the country in the year 2000.
— No data available.

The **Human Development Index (HDI)** is a summary measure of human development. The index measures the average achievement of the countries in three basic components of human development. The first indicator is the **life expectancy at birth**, which indicates, together with infant and child mortality rates, the health condition of any given society. The second indicator is the rate of **adult literacy** and the **combined primary, secondary and tertiary gross enrollment ratio**. The third indicator is the **per capita GDP** (in PPP US$ terms), which indicates the overall standard of living. The combined result of these three indicators is the HDI.

Source: UNDP, *Human Development Report – 2002*, pp. 153–56, table 2.

Notes

Introduction: *The Methodological Framework*

1   Kuwait and Libya were relatively rich countries already in the 1960s, with a per capita GNP of \$3,650 in Kuwait and \$1,490 in Libya in 1968. This was due to their small indigenous populations, on the one hand, and their relatively large oil exports on the other.

2   The World Bank (WB), *World Tables, 1989–90 Edition* (Published for the World Bank by the Johns Hopkins University Press, Baltimore and London, 1990).

3   The two common names to this part of the Middle East are the "Arabian Gulf," used, naturally, by the Arabs, and the "Persian Gulf," used by the Persians. In order to avoid political connotation, I decided to use the neutral name of "the Gulf."

4   Gad G. Gilbar, *The Middle East Oil Decade and Beyond* (London and Portland: Frank Cass, 1997), p. 1.

5   WB, *World Development Report–1983* (Published for the World Bank by Oxford University Press, Oxford and New York, 1983), pp. 148–49, table 1.

6   Eliyahu Kanovsky, *Economic Development of Jordan* (Tel-Aviv University, the David Horovitz Institute for the Research of Developing Countries, 1974), p. 63.

7   On the economic damage to Egypt resulting from the June 1967 War, see: Eliyahu Kanovsky, *The Economic Impact of the Six-Day War: Israel, The Occupied Territories, Egypt, Jordan* (New York: Praeger Publishers, 1970), pp. 279–86.

8   Osama Hamed, "Egypt's Open Door Economic Policy: An Attempt at Economic Integration in the Middle East," *IJMES*, Vol. 13, No. 2 (May 1981), p. 1.

9   On the Syrian defence burden, see: Volker Perthes, *The Political Economy of Syria under Asad* (London and New York: I. B. Tauris, 1995), pp. 31–32; Paul Rivlin, "The Syrian Economy in the 1990s," *Data and Analysis* (Tel Aviv University, The Moshe Dayan Center, June 1999), pp. 53–54; Onn Winckler, "Hafiz al-Asad's Socio-Economic Legacy: The Balance of Achievements and Failures," *Orient*, Vol. 42, No. 3 (September 2001), p. 451.

10   All in all, Egypt's direct economic dividends from the peace treaty with Israel amounted to more than \$12 billion annually on average since 1979 until present. On the contribution of the peace agreement with Israel to the Egyptian economy, see: Gad G. Gilbar, *Kalkalat ha-Mizrah ha-Tikhon ba-'Et ha-Hadasha* (Tel Aviv: Ministry of Defense, 1990), pp. 202–3.

11   On the contribution of the peace agreement with Israel to the Jordanian economy, see: Onn Winckler, "The Economic Factor of the Middle East Peace Process: The Jordanian Case," in Joseph Ginat and Onn Winckler (eds.), *The Jordanian–Palestinian–Israeli Triangle: Smoothing the Path to Peace* (Brighton and Portland: Sussex Academic Press, 1998), pp. 170–73. By 2002, the total Jordanian exports to the US amounted to JD (Jordanian Dinar) 304.4 million, increasing from only JD5.6 million in 1998. Source: Jordan, *Statistical Yearbook–2002*, p. 200, table 10.1.2.

12   *MEED*, May 31, 2002, p. 25.

13   *MEED*, August 1, 2003, p. 6.

14   See on this regard: Steven Heydemann, "Taxation without Representation: Authoritarianism and Economic Liberalization in Syria," in Ellis Goldberg, Reşat Kasaba, and Joel Migdal (eds.), *Rules and Rights in the Middle East: Democracy, Law, and Society* (Seattle and London: University of Washington Press, 1993), pp. 69–80.

15   A "soft state," a term initiated by Gunnar Myrdal, refers to countries in which "policies decided on are often not enforced, if they are enforced at all, and in that the authorities, even when framing policies, are reluctant to place obligations on people." *Asian Drama: An Inquiry into the Poverty of Nations*, Vol. 1 (New York: Pantheon, Random House, 1968), p. 66.

16   Iliya Harik, "Privatization: The Issue, the Prospects, and the Fears," in Iliya Harik and Denis J. Sullivan (eds.), *Privatization and Liberalization in the Middle East* (Bloomington, IN: Indiana University Press, 1992), p. 16.

17   By the years 2000 and 2001, foreign direct investment (FDI) in Tunisia amounted to $1.265 billion – the highest among all the Arab countries in per capita terms. Source: UNDP and Arab Fund for Economic and Social Development, *Arab Human Development Report–2003* (Amman: SYNTAX, 2003), p. 102, table 5.1.

18   Clement M. Henry and Robert Springborg, *Globalization and the Politics of Development in the Middle East* (Cambridge: Cambridge University Press, 2001), p. 99.

19   On the meaning of the PPP term regarding the Middle Eastern countries, see: Alan Richards and John Waterbury, *A Political Economy of the Middle East*, second edition (Boulder: Westview Press, 1996), pp. 11–13.

20   The World Bank Group [http://www.worldbank.org/data].

21   WB, *World Tables, 1995 Edition*, p. 648.

22   Charles B. Nam and Susan G. Philliber, *Population: A Basic Orientation*, second edition (Englewood Cliffs, New Jersey: Prentice Hall, Inc., 1984), p. 2.

23   On the traditional demographic perception of the PLO, see: Matti Steinberg, "Lir'ot et ha-Nolad: ha-Gorem ha-Demography be-Re'iyat Asha"f," in Ami Ayalon and Gad G. Gilbar (eds.), *Demographya ve-Politiqa be-Medinot 'Arav* (Tel Aviv: Hakibbutz Hameuchad, 1995), pp. 153–89 (Hebrew). On the Israeli pro-natalist concept and policy, see: Onn Winckler, "Fertility Transition in the Middle East: The Case of the Israeli-Arabs," *Israel Affairs*, Vol. 9, Nos. 1&2 (Autumn/Winter 2003), pp. 49–53.

24   I would like to thank Ms. Irit Rosenblum, Advocate, the founder and chairperson of the New Family organization, for the data on the survey. Some of the survey's results were published in *Ma'ariv*, February 26, 2004.

25   André Burguière, "Demography," in Jacques Le Goff and Pierre Nora (eds.), *Constructing the Past: Essays in Historical Methodology* (Cambridge: Cambridge University Press, 1985), p. 99.

Chapter 1   *Sources for Demographic Research of the Arab States*

1   Georges Sabagh, "The Demography of the Middle East," *Middle East Studies Association Bulletin*, Vol. 4, No. 2 (May 15, 1970), pp. 1–2.

2   The *Iltizam* system was based on renting the right of tax collection from a specific area on an annual basis in exchange for a fixed amount of tax that must be delivered to the central authorities. The revenues of the tax collector, the *Multazim*, consisted of the gap between the amount that he succeeded to collect and the amount that he was obligated to deliver to the regime.

3   Stanford J. Shaw, "The Ottoman Census System and Population, 1831–1914," *IJMES*, Vol. 9 (1978), p. 325.

4   Haim Gerber, "The Population of Syria and Palestine in the Nineteenth Century," *Asian and African Studies*, Vol. 13, No. 1 (1979), p. 58.

5   Shaw, "The Ottoman Census," pp. 325–27; Bernard Lewis, *The Emergence of Modern Turkey*, second edition (Oxford and New York: Oxford University Press, 1968), p. 90.

6   Kemal H. Karpat, "Ottoman Population Records and the Census of 1881/82–1893," *IJMES*, Vol. 9 (1978), p. 242.

7   Uri M. Kupferschmidt, "A Note on the Muslim Religions Hierarchy Towards the End of the Ottoman period," in David Kushner (ed.), *Palestine in the Late Ottoman Period* (Jerusalem: Yad Yzhak Ben-Zvi Press, 1986), p. 123.

8   On the problematic nature of the Lebanese demographic data, see, e.g., Gad G. Gilbar, "Mavo: Beyn Demographya ve-Politiqa ba-Mizrah ha-Tikhon," in Ami Ayalon and Gad G. Gilbar (eds.), *Demographya ve-Politiqa be-Medinot 'Arav* (Tel Aviv: Hakibbutz Hameuchad, 1995), pp. 12–13 (Hebrew).

9   The organization of the Gulf Cooperation Council (GCC) was established in 1981 and includes the following countries: Saudi Arabia, Kuwait, Oman, Qatar, Bahrain, and the United Arab Emirates (UAE).

10   Few, if any, countries in the world have such a long population records history as Egypt, dating back to BC 3340. In modern times, the population censuses in Egypt started in 1800 under the French occupation, followed by a census conducted by the British rule in 1882 after their invasion of Egypt. During the period from 1897 to 1947, Egypt conducted a population census every 10 years. The next censuses were conducted in 1960, 1966, 1976, 1986 and the latest in 1996. On the history of population censuses in Egypt, see: Arab Republic of Egypt, Central Agency for Public Mobilisation and Statistics (CAPMAS), *The Statistical Yearbook, 1987* (Cairo, 1988), pp. 3–6.

11   Republique Tunisienne, Ministère du Développement Economique, Institut National de la Statistique, *Annuaire Statistique de la Tunisie*, chapter 2.

12   ECWA, *The Population Situation in the ECWA Region-Jordan* (Beirut, 1979), p. 2.

13   *Jordan Times*, December 29–30, 1994.

14   *Jordan Times*, September 16, 2003.

15   On the 1921–1922 census, see: Mohamed Chafic Dibbs, "The Relationship Between Censuses and Civil Registration in the Syrian Arab Republic," *Population Bulletin of ECWA*, No. 18 (June 1980), p. 82.

16   Robert Widmer, "Population," in Said B. Himadeh (ed.), *Economic Organization of Syria* (Beirut: The American University of Beirut Press, 1936), p. 3.

17   Bent Hansen, *Economic Development in Syria* (California: The Rand Corporation Resources for the Future, December 1969), p. 16.

18   Eliane Domschke and Doreen S. Goyer, *The Handbook of National Population Censuses, Africa and Asia* (New York, Westport, Connecticut and London: Greenwood Press, 1986), p. 835.

19   The unification between Egypt and Syria started in February 1958 and ended in September 1961, with the Syrian withdrawal from the union.

20   Domschke and Goyer, *The Handbook of National Population Censuses, Africa and Asia*, p. 838; Syrian Arab Republic, State Planning Commission and Central Bureau of Statistics (CBS), in collaboration with the Population Council, by M. Nader Hallak, *Rates of Natural Increase in the Syrian Regions* (Damascus, December 1979), pp. 1–2.

21   ECWA, *The Population Situation in the ECWA Region-Syrian Arab Republic* (Beirut, 1980), p. 2.

22   Domschke and Goyer, *The Handbook of National Population Censuses, Africa and Asia*, p. 838.

23   Farid el-Boustani, "The levels of Demographic Data in the Syrian Arab Republic and Future Trends," in Syrian Arab Republic, Office of the Prime Minister, CBS, *Factors of Population Growth and Their Future Trends,* Papers Presented at a Seminar Held in Damascus, September 16–20, 1978, under the auspices of the Syrian CBS and UNFPA (Damascus: Central Bureau of Statistics Press, 1979), p. 5.

24   On the preparation for the census, see: Eyal Zisser, "Syria," *MECS*, Vol. 18 (1994), p. 619.

25   See M. N. al-Hallak, "Demographic Situation in the Syrian Arab Republic," Expert Group

Meeting on the Application of Demographic Data and Studies in Development Planning of the UN Economic and Social Office in Beirut, Beirut, December 7–12, 1970, pp. 7–8.

26 WB, *World Development Report–1992*, p. 271, table 27.

27 WB, *World Development Report–1996*, p. 199, table 6.

28 ESCWA, *Demographic and Related Socio-Economic Data Sheets for Countries of the Economic and Social Commission for Western Asia*, No. 8 (1995), p. 62, table 3.

29 *Ibid.*, p. 130, table 3.

30 *Al-Sharq al-Awsat*, October 20, 1999, p. 7.

31 UNDP, *The Arab Human Development Report–2002* (New York, 2002), p. 99.

32 ESCWA is a UN regional organization, currently based in Beirut, and its members include: Egypt, Syria, Lebanon, Iraq, Yemen, the Palestinians, and the GCC countries. The organization is part of the Secretariat of the UN and is one of the five regional commissions that report to the UN Economic and Social Council. The funding of the organization is mainly from the member states. In many cases, the data provided by ESCWA is the only available information source regarding GCC demographic trends and developments.

33 ECWA, *The Population Situation in the ECWA Region-Saudi Arabia* (Beirut, 1979), p. 2.

34 Gilbar, "Mavo: Beyn Demographya ve-Politiqa ba-Mizrah ha-Tikhon," p. 14.

35 ECWA, *The Population Situation-Saudi Arabia*, p. 2.

36 *Ibid.*, p. 6, table 11.3; J. S. Birks and C. A. Sinclair, *International Migration Project, Country Case Study: The Kingdom of Saudi Arabia* (Durham: The University of Durham, Department of Economics, 1979), p. 4, table 4.

37 Peter W. Wilson, and Douglas F. Graham, *Saudi Arabia: The Coming Storm* (New York: M.E. Sharpe, 1994), p. 33, note 8.

38 Gilbar, "Mavo: Beyn Demographya ve-Politiqa ba-Mizrah ha-Tikhon," pp. 14–15.

39 EIU (Economist intelligence Unit), *Country Profile, Saudi Arabia, 1987–88*, p. 7.

40 EIU, QER (Quarterly Economic Review), *Saudi Arabia, Annual Supplement, 1985*, p. 7.

41 See, e.g., the estimate of Birks and Sinclair from May 1992 that the total number of Saudi nationals was 8,066,400. Source: Birks Sinclair & Associates Ltd., *GCC Market Report–1992* (Durham: Mountjoy Research Centre, May 1992), p. 100, table 2.2.

42 The *GFHS*, conducted in each of the GCC countries during the years 1995–1998, collected data in the fields of marriage patterns, fertility behaviors, and contraceptive prevalence rates. On the characteristics of all the surveys conducted within the *GFHS*, including the number of the surveyed population, their sex, age, spatial distribution, and the like, see: al-Lajna al-Iqtisadiyya wal-Ijtima'iyya li-Gharbi Asia, *al-Nashra al-Sukaniyya* [*Population Bulletin of ESCWA*], No. 49 (2000), p. 31, table 1 (Arabic).

43 *Ibid.*, p. 35, table 4.

44 UN, Population Division and UNFPA, *Population Policy Compendium-Bahrain* (New York, 1981), p. 2; ESCWA, *Population Situation in the ESCWA Region, 1990* (Amman, May 1992), p. 25.

45 On the project of the *GCHS*, see: Ayman Gaafar Zohry and Lee L. Been, "Infant Mortality and Health Care in the Arabian Gulf Region," in Cairo Demographic Centre (CDC), *CDC 24th Annual Seminar on Population Issues and the Challenges of the 21st Century in the Middle East, Africa, and Asia*, Research Monograph Series, No. 24 (Cairo, 1995), pp. 487–507.

46 Mustafa al-Shalkani, "A System for Collecting Vital Statistics in Gulf Cooperation Council Countries," *Population Bulletin of ESCWA*, Nos. 35–37 (December 1989 – December 1990), p. 47.

47 Allan G. Hill, "The Demography of the Kuwaiti Population of Kuwait," *Demography*, Vol. 12, No. 3 (August 1975), p. 537.

48 Al-Shalkani, "A System for Collecting Vital Statistics," pp. 49–50.

49 Dale F. Eickelman, *The Middle East: An Anthropology Approach*, second edition (Englewood Cliffs, N.J.: Prentice-Hall, 1989), p. 368. See also: John E. Peterson, *Oman in*

the Twentieth Century: Political Foundations of an Emerging State (London: Croom Helm, 1978), p. 136.

50 ECWA, Directorate General of National Statistics Department Council, Technical Secretariat, "Achievements, Plans and Recommendations Relating to Population and Housing Censuses in the Sultanate of Oman," Economic Commission for Western Asia, Expert Group Meeting on Census Techniques, December 12–16, 1977, Beirut, pp. 1–2.

51 See: the Sultanate of Oman, Ministry of National Economy, *Statistical Yearbook–2001* (Muscat, August 2002), pp. 416–17.

52 *Ibid.*, pp. 40–41, 47.

53 ECWA, *The Population Situation in the ECWA Region-Qatar* (Beirut, 1980), p. 8.

54 Al-Shalkani, "A System for Collecting Vital Statistics," p. 48; ESCWA, *Population Situation in the ESCWA Region, 1990*, p. 153.

55 The British Embassy of Beirut, Middle East Development Division, by N. B. Hudson, *The First Population Census of Qatar*, April/May 1970 (Beirut, October 1970), pp. 3–4; ECWA, *The Population Situation-Qatar*, p. 2.

56 Al-Shalkani, "A System for Collecting Vital Statistics," pp. 46, 53.

57 The EIU rightly claimed in this regard that: "no breakdown between expatriates and locals is available." EIU, *Country Profile–Qatar, 1999–2000*, p. 42.

58 EIU, *Country Profile–Qatar, 2003*, p. 12.

59 State of Qatar, Presidency of the Council of Ministers, Central Statistical Organization, *Annual Statistical Abstract–1999* (Doha, October 1999), p. 17, table 6.

60 *Ibid.*, p. 66, table 37.

61 On the religious composition of the Israeli-Arabs since the establishment of the state of Israel and until the year 2000, see: Winckler, "Fertility Transition in the Middle East: The Case of the Israeli-Arabs," p. 56, table 1.

62 Arnon Soffer, "Lebanon – Where Demography is the Core of Politics and Life," *Middle Eastern Studies*, Vol. 22, No. 2 (1986), p. 199, table 2.

63 On the Lebanese 1943 National Pact political arrangements, see, e.g., Kamal S. Salibi, *The Modern History of Lebanon* (London: Weindenfeld and Nicolson, 1965), pp. 187–88; Itamar Rabinovich, *The War for Lebanon, 1970–1985* (Ithaca and London: Cornell University Press, 1985), pp. 24–26.

64 Colbert C. Held, *Middle East Patterns: Places, Peoples, and Politics*, second edition (Boulder: Westview Press, 1994), p. 221.

65 According to UNRWA data, by June 30, 2003, the number of Palestinian refugees in Lebanon was 391,679. See the official UNRWA website [http://www.un.org/unrwa].

66 The Palestinian refugees in Lebanon, as in the other Arab countries, with the exception of Jordan, are not enjoying the privilege of citizenship in the host countries.

67 M. E. Sales, *International Migration Project: Syrian Arab Republic* (Durham: The University of Durham, Department of Economics, October 1978), p. 59; *al-Khalij*, January 11, 1985.

68 The Yazidi religion has elements of Judaism, Christianity, and Islam, as well as of Paganism, and the Bible and the Qur'an are considered as sacred. In 1964, there were approximately 10,000 Yazidis in Syria. Source: Library of Congress Country Studies [http://lcweb2loc.gov].

69 Held, *Middle East Patterns*, pp. 208–9; EIU, *Country Profile–Syria, 2000–2001*, p. 10.

70 CIA, *The World Factbook–2003* [http://www.cia.gov/publications/factbook].

71 W. B. Fisher, "Jordan: A Demographic Shatter-Belt," in J. I. Clarke and W. B. Fisher (eds.), *Populations of the Middle East and North Africa: A Geographical Approach* (London: University of London Press, 1972), pp. 211–12.

72 Insight Guides [http://www.insightguides.com]; EIU, *Country Profile–Jordan, 1993–94*, p. 11.

73 See the official UNRWA website: [http://www.un.org/unrwa].

74 Peter Gubser, *Jordan: Crossroads of Middle Eastern Events* (Boulder: Westview Press, and

London: Croom Helm, 1983), p. 12; Asher Susser, "Demographya ve-Politiqa be-Yarden," in Ayalon and Gilbar (eds.), *Demographya ve-Politiqa be-Medinot 'Arav*, p. 131 (Hebrew).

75 Jordan, *Statistical Yearbook–2002*, p. 5, table 2.1.

76 EIU, *Country Profile-Egypt, 1999–2000*, p. 12.

77 A.S.M. Kashef, "Egypt," in John Dixon (ed.), *Social Welfare in the Middle East* (London: Croom Helm, 1987), p. 1.

78 CIA, *The World Factbook–2003*.

79 EIU, *Country Profile-Egypt, 1999–2000*, p. 12; Held, *Middle East Patterns*, p. 90; Ami Ayalon, "Egypt's Coptic Pandora's Box," in Ofra Bengio and Gabriel Ben-Dor (eds.), *Minorities and the State in the Arab World* (Boulder: Lynne Rienner Publishers, 1999), p. 53.

80 Under the name of the founder of this sect, Muhammad al-Wahhab (1703–1791), Wahhabism began in the Arabian Peninsula in the eighteenth century in reaction to the popular practice of *Sufism*. On the Wahhabism, see: Ewan W. Anderson, *The Middle East: Geography and Geopolitics* (London and New York: Routledge, 2000), p. 142.

81 *Gulf States Newsletter*, May 2, 2003, p. 6.

82 U.S. Department of State, *International Religious Freedom Report–2002*, "Saudi Arabia" [http://www.state.gov].

83 EIU, *Country Profile–Saudi Arabia, 2003*, p. 10. In regard to the dispute on the number of Shi'is in Saudi Arabia, see also: Graham E. Fuller and Rend Rahim Francke, *The Arab Shi'a: The Forgotten Muslim* (New York: St. Martin's Press, 1999), p. 180.

84 May Seikaly, "Women and Social Change in Bahrain," *IJMES*, Vol. 26 (1994), p. 418; Fuller and Francke, *The Arab Shi'a*, p. 120.

85 On the clashes between the Shi'a activists and the security forces, see: Dore Gold, "Bahrain," *MECS*, Vol. 18 (1994), pp. 253–56; Joshua Teitelbaum, "Bahrain," *MECS*, Vol. 20 (1996), pp. 250–53; Uzi Rabi and Joseph Kostiner, "The Shi'is in Bahrain: Class and Religious Protest," in Bengio and Ben-Dor (eds.), *Minorities and the State in the Arab World*, p. 172.

86 Richards and Waterbury, *A Political Economy of the Middle East*, second edition, p. 134.

87 Rodney Wilson, *Economic Development in the Middle East* (London and New York: Routledge, 1995), p. 65.

88 ESCWA, *Survey of Economic and Social Developments in the ESCWA Region, 2002–2003, Summary* (New York, 2003), p. 5.

89 *The Middle East*, February 2003, p. 47.

90 Eliyahu Kanovsky, "What's Behind Syria's Current Economic Problems?" *Occasional Papers* (The Moshe Dayan Center, Tel Aviv University, May 1985), p. 45. On the accuracy of the Syrian official economic data, see also: Perthes, *The Political Economy of Syria under Asad*, pp. 13–14.

91 ESCWA, *Survey of Economic and Social Developments in the ESCWA Region, 2004, Summary* (New York, 2004), p. 8.

92 Dawn Chatty, "Women Working in Oman: Individual Choice and Cultural Constraints," *IJMES*, Vol. 32, No. 2 (2000), p. 251.

93 *MEED*, September 20, 2002, p. 39.

94 *MEED*, June 27, 2003, p. 7.

95 *MEED*, September 20, 2002, p. 39.

96 The Kingdom of Saudi Arabia, Ministry of Planning, *Seventh Development Plan, 1420/21–1424/25 AH* [2000–2004] (Riyadh, 1999), p. 158.

97 ESCWA, *Survey, 2001–2002*, p. 19.

98 See: *MEED*, September 26 – October 2, 2003, p. 38.

99 *MEED*, December 11, 1998, p. 31.

100 *MEED*, September 28, 2001, p. 28. In April 2001, the official unemployment rate among

Bahraini nationals was 3.1%, increasing from 2.5% at the end of 1999. Source: ESCWA, *Survey, 2001–2002*, p. 19.

101 *MEED*, September 28, 2001, p. 28.

102 EIU, *Country Profile–Bahrain, 2003*, p. 20.

103 See: *Ibid*.

104 *Jordan Times*, November 18, 1999; ESCWA, *Survey, 1998-1999*, p. 51.

105 ESCWA, *Survey, 2000–2001*, pp. 30–31; *MEED*, April 20, 2001, p. 28.

106 EIU, *Country Profile–Egypt, 2001*, p. 33.

107 *Al-Ahram Weekly*, February 27 – March 5, 2002.

108 ESCWA, *Survey, 2001–2002*, p. 18.

109 Edward Gardner, "Wanted: More Jobs," *Finance and Development*, Vol. 40, No. 1 (March 2003). [http://www.imf.org/external/pubs/ft/fandd/fda].

110 ILO, *World Employment Report–2001* (Geneva, 2001), p. 361, table 4.

111 Eliyahu Kanovsky, "Egypt's Troubled Economy: Mubarak's Inheritance," in *MECS, 1981–82*, p. 416.

112 See, e.g., *The Egyptian Gazette*, August 23, 1985. On the various estimates regarding the number of Egyptian workers in other Arab countries in the early 1980s, see: Gil Feiler, "The Number of Egyptian Workers in the Arab Oil Countries, 1974–1983: A Critical Discussion," *Occasional Papers* (The Moshe Dayan Center, Tel Aviv University, October 1986); Galal A. Amin and Elizabeth Awny, *International Migration of Egyptian Labor: A Review of the State of Art*, International Development Research Centre (Canada, May 1985), p.25, table 6.

113 *MEED*, February 24, 1984, p. 55.

114 Arab Republic of Egypt, Central Agency for Public Mibilisation and Statistics (CAPMAS), *External Migration As a Demographic Phenomenon* (Cairo, 1994), p. 14.

115 HRD Base, *Socio-Demographic Profiles of Key Arab Countries* (Newcastle: Lloyds Bank Chambers, May 1987).

116 EIU, QER, *Egypt*, No. 3 (1984), p. 10.

117 See in this regard: ILO, *International Migration for Employment: Manpower and Population Evolution in the GCC and Libyan Arab Jamahiriya*, World Employment Programme Research, Working Paper by J. S. Birks and C. A. Sinclair (Geneva, October 1989), p. 2.

118 "Kuwait: Expatriate Workers Outnumber Nationals," *The Arab Economist* (April 1979), p. 32.

119 Michael E. Bonine, "Population Growth, the Labor Market and the Gulf Security," in David E. Long and Christian Koch (eds.), *Gulf Security in the Twenty-First Century* (Abu-Dhabi: The Emirates Center for Strategic Studies and Research, 1997), p. 227.

120 Roger Owen and Şevket Pamuk, *A History of Middle East Economies in the Twentieth Century* (Cambridge, Mass.: Harvard University Press, 1999), p. 208.

121 On the informal economy in developing countries, see: Philip Harding and Richard Jenkins, *The Myth of the Hidden Economy: Towards a New Understanding of Informal Economic Activity* (Milton Keynes: Open University Press, 1989); Edgar L. Feige (ed.), *The Underground Economies: The Evasion and Information Distortion* (Cambridge: Cambridge University Press, 1989).

122 Delwin A. Roy, "The Hidden Economy in Egypt," *Middle Eastern Studies*, Vol. 28, No. 4 (October 1992), p. 689.

123 ILO, *World Employment Report–2001*, p. 37.

124 ILO, *International Migration for Employment: The Jordanian Migration System in Transition*, by Allan M. Findlay (Geneva, March 1987), p. 2.

125 See: WB, *World Tables, 1984–1995*, various editions; idem, *World Development Report, 1994–2002*, various issues; IMF, *International Financial Statistics Yearbook*, various issues (Washington, D.C.).

126 In the case of Egypt, for example, while the official rate in late 1983 was $1=£E (Egyptian

Pound) 0.84, the unofficial rate was $1=£E 1.12–1.20, meaning roughly a 20% gap between the official and the "black market" rates. Source: *MEED*, December 2, 1983, p. 11. In late 1985, while the official exchange rate was $1=£E1.35, the free market rate was as high as $1=£E1.85, representing a gap of 37%. Source: *MEED*, December 7, 1985, p. 12; "MEED Special Report-Egypt," June 1986, p. 8. In the case of Syria, while the official rate in 1993 was $1=£S (Syrian Pound)11.2, the unofficial rate available in Lebanon and Jordan was more than four times that of the official rate. Source: *Financial Times*, May 11, 1993.

127 Nazli Choucri, "The Hidden Economy: A New View of Remittances in the Arab World," *World Development*, Vol. 14, No. 6 (1986), p. 697. See also in this regard: Robert. L. Looney, "Patterns of Remittances and Labor Migration in the Arab World," *International Migration*, Vol. 24, No.4 (1989), pp. 565–67.

128 Nazli Choucri, "Migration in the Middle East: Old Economics Or New Politics?" *Journal of Arab Affairs*, Vol. 7, No. 1 (Spring 1988), p. 12. See also on Egypt's real workers' remittances during the past three decades: Elie Podeh and Onn Winckler, "The Boycott that Never Was: Egypt and the Arab System, 1979–1989," *Durham Middle East Papers*, No. 72 (December 2002), pp. 36–39; ESCWA, *Return Migration: Profiles, Impact and Absorption in Home Countries* (New York, December 1993), p. 36; Dan Tschirgi, "Egyptian Labor Migration: Social, Political and Economic Effects," in Shtayyeh (ed.), *Labor Migration: Palestine, Jordan, Egypt and Israel*, pp. 55–56.

129 WB, *World Tables, 1995 Edition*, pp. 258–59.

130 Roy, "The Hidden Economy in Egypt," p. 691.

131 WB, *World Tables, 1995 Edition*, p. 650.

132 On the case of the Syrian workers' remittances, see: Onn Winckler, *Demographic Developments and Population Policies in Ba'thist Syria* (Brighton and Portland: Sussex Academic Press, 1999), p. 106.

133 WB, *World Tables, 1995 Edition*, p. 386.

134 Musa Samha, "Population Spatial Distribution Policies in Jordan," in ESCWA, *Population Spatial Distribution* (Amman, August 1993), p. 93

135 WB, *World Development Report–1996*, p. 218, table 16.

136 CAPMAS, *Statistical Yearbook, 1992–1998*, p. 11, table 1–15.

137 Richards and Waterbury, *A Political Economy of the Middle East*, second edition, p. 140.

138 WB, *Labor Market Reforms, Growth and Unemployment in Labor-Exporting MENA Countries*, by Pierre-Richard Agénor, Mustapha K. Nabli, Tarik Yousef, and Henning T. Jensen (Washington, D.C., 2003), p. 6.

139 EIU, *Country Profile–Egypt, 1989–90*, p. 16. According to other estimates, Egypt's hidden economy in 1988 was running between 35% and 55% of the recorded (official) GNP. See: Roy, "The Hidden Economy in Egypt," p. 707.

140 National Bank of Egypt, *The Underground Economy with Special Reference to the Case of Egypt*, by Ibrahim M. Oweiss (Cairo, December 1994), p. 21.

Chapter 2   *Beyond the Expectations: Arab Population Growth in the Twentieth Century*

1 Cited from Saad M. Gadalla, *Is There Hope? Fertility and Family Planning in a Rural Egyptian Community* (Cairo: American University in Cairo Press, 1978), p. 212.

2 Allan Findlay and Anne Findlay, *Population and Development in the Third World* (London and New York: Methuen, 1987), p. 1.

3 The Black Death was one of the worst natural disasters in worldwide history, decimating about one-third of Europe's population.

4 John Durand, "Historical Estimates of World Population: An Evaluation," *Population and Development Review*, Vol. 3, No. 3 (September 1977), p. 259, table 2.

5 WB, *World Development Report–1992*, p. 271, table 27.

6 The academic literature on the Demographic Transition theory is immense. A summary of the Demographic Transition concept and the Demographic Transition theory appears in

John B. Casterline, "Demographic Transition," in Paul Demeny and Geoffery McNicoll (eds.), *Encyclopedia of Population* (New York: Macmillan Reference USA, 2003), pp. 210–16; Ronald Pressat, *The Dictionary of Demography* (Oxford: Clarendon Press, 1985), pp. 52–55; Michael S. Teitelbaum, "Relevance of Demographic Transition Theory for Developing Countries," *Science*, Vol. 188 (May 2, 1975), p. 421; Ibrahim Bushnaf Bendardaf, *Socioeconomic Modernization and Demographic Changes in Syria* (Unpublished Ph.D. Thesis, University of Missouri, 1988), pp. 1–6.

7 Frank W. Notestein, "Population – The Long View," in Theodore W. Schultz (ed.), *Food for the World* (Chicago: University of Chicago Press, 1945), pp. 36–57.

8 Warren S. Thompson, "Population," *The American Journal of Sociology*, Vol. 34, No. 6 (May 1929), pp. 959–75.

9 An autarky economy refers to economic self-sufficiency with minimal trade on both domestic and international levels. On the concept of autarky economy, see: John Eatwell, Murray Milgate, and Peter Newman, *The New Palgrave: A Dictionary of Economics*, Vol. 1 (London: The Macmillan Press Limited, 1987), pp. 151–52.

10 John Cleland, "Marital Fertility Decline in Developing Countries: Theories and the Evidence," in John Cleland and John Hobcraft (eds.), *Reproductive Change in Developing Countries* (Oxford: Oxford University Press, 1985), pp. 225–28.

11 Notestein, "Population – The Long View," p. 40.

12 *Ibid.*, p. 41.

13 Shirley Forster Hartley, *Population – Quantity vs. Quality: A Sociological Examination of the Causes and Consequences of the Population Explosion* (New Jersey: Prentice Hall, Inc. Englewood Cliffs, 1972), p. 4.

14 *Ibid.*

15 For example, during the period 1908–1913, the annual average natural increase rate was 1.3% in Germany, 1.2% in Italy, 1.1% in England, and 1% in Swaziland and Spain. Source: Thompson, "Population," pp. 960–61, table 1.

16 Michael P. Todaro, *Economic Development*, seventh edition (Reading, Mass.: Addison-Wesley, 1999), p. 222, figure 6.6.

17 Even under conditions of low mortality, replacement-level fertility is considered to be 2.1 children per woman rather than 2.0. This is both because in any given society (without migration) there are slightly more males than females and because not all children will survive up to the end of their childbearing period (normally age 45). Thus, a total fertility rate of 2.1 children per woman corresponds to an NRR (Net Reproductive Rate) of 1. In developing countries, due to much higher infant and child mortality rates, the replacement-level fertility is higher than 2.1 children per woman, varying from one society to another in accordance with the different death rates.

18 A wide discussion on the phenomenon of below-replacement-level fertility and its factors in Western-European countries appears in: Dirk J. van de Kaa, *The Past of Europe's Demographic Future*, Uhlenbeck Lecture 17 (Wassenaar 1999).

19 *The New York Times*, July 10, 1998.

20 *Ibid.*

21 The percentage of the urban population within the total population in Europe increased from 52.4% in 1950 to 67.3% in 1975 and reached 73.4% in 2000. UN, Department of Economic and Social Affairs, Population Division, *World Urbanization Prospects: The 2001 Revision* (New York, March 2002), p. 5, table 2.

22 The Population Reference Bureau, *Population Handbook*, fourth edition, by Arthur Haupt and Thomas T. Kane (New York, 1997), p. 49.

23 WB, *World Development Report–1978*, p. 105, table 15.

24 WB, *World Development Report–1982*, p. 145, table 18.

25 WB, *World Development Report–1992*, p. 271, table 27.

26 The U.S., Department of Commerce, U.S. Census Bureau [http:/www.census.gov].

27 "First Results of the Demographic Data Collection for 2002 in Europe," p. 3, table 1 [http://europa.eu.int].
28 *Ibid.*, p. 5, table 3.
29 The data related to North Yemen. UNICEF (United Nations Children's Fund), *The State of the World's Children–1988* (Published for UNICEF by Oxford University Press, 1998), p. 72, table 5. See also: Nam and Philliber, *Population*, p. 45.
30 The data related to the united Yemen. ESCWA, *Demographic and Related Socio-Economic Data Sheets*, No. 11 (2001), p. 178, table 5.
31 See, Winckler, "Fertility Transition in the Middle East: The Case of the Israeli-Arabs," pp. 42–43.
32 United Nations, Economic Commission for Africa (ECA), *The State of Demographic Transition in Africa* (Addis Ababa, December 2001), p. 1; Teitelbaum, "Relevance of Demographic Transition Theory for Developing Countries," p. 422; Peter N. Hess, *Population Growth and Socioeconomic Progress in Less Developed Countries: Determinants of Fertility Transition* (New York and London: Praeger, 1988), pp. 13–14.
33 See in this regard: Teitelbaum, "Relevance of Demographic Transition Theory for Developing Countries," p. 422.
34 See, e.g., Lant H. Pritchett, "Desired Fertility and the Impact of Population Policies," *Population and Development Review*, Vol. 20, No. 1 (1994), pp. 1–55.
35 See e.g., Robert J. Lapham and Parker Mauldin, "Family Planning Program Effort and Birthrate Decline in Developing Countries," *International Family Planning Perspectives*, Vol. 10, Issue 4 (1984); pp. 109–18; Susan H. Cochrane and David K. Guilkey, "The Effects of Fertility Intensions and Access to Services on Contraceptive Use in Tunisia," *Economic Development and Cultural Change*, Vol. 43, No. 4 (1995), pp. 779–804.
36 Hartley, *Population*, p. 4.
37 UNICEF, *The State of the World's Children–2000*, p. 103, table 5.
38 Population Reference Bureau, *2003 World Population Data Sheets* (New York, 2003), p. 3.
39 Todaro, *Economic Development*, seventh edition, p. 210.
40 UNICEF, *The State of the World's Children–2000*, pp. 100–3, table 5.
41 Charles Issawi, *An Economic History of the Middle East and North Africa* (New York: Columbia University Press, 1982), p. 93.
42 *Ibid.* See also: Abdel R. Omran and Farzaneh Roudi, "The Middle East Population Puzzle," *Population Bulletin*, Vol. 47 (July 1993), p. 5.
43 The data for the Arab oil-states refer only to the indigenous populations (i.e., not including foreign workers and their accompanying family members, who constitute a considerable percentage of the total population in these countries). Sources: UNDP, *Human Development Report–2002*, pp. 162–65, table 5; ESCWA, *Demographic and Related Socio-Economic Data Sheets*, No. 11 (2001); Issawi, *An Economic History of the Middle East*, p. 93, table 6.1.
44 A. M. Abdelghany, "Evaluating the Application of the Stable Population Model of the Population of Egypt," *Population Bulletin of ECWA*, No. 21 (December 1981), p. 109, table 3. See also: Robert Mabro, *The Egyptian Economy, 1952–1972* (Oxford: Clarendon Press, 1974), p. 29, table 2.2.
45 See, e.g., Omran and Roudi, "The Middle East Population Puzzle," p. 12.
46 On the issue of women's status in the Middle East, see: Dale F. Eickelman, *The Middle East and Central Asia: An Anthropological Approach*, fourth edition (Upper Saddle River, NJ.: Prentice Hall, 2002), pp. 180–86.
47 In the case of the Arab countries, see in this regard: John R. Weeks, "The Demography of Islamic Nations," *Population Bulletin*, Vol. 43, No. 4 (December 1988), p. 25; Carla Makhlouf Obermeyer, "Islam, Women and Politics: The Demography of Arab Countries," *Population and Development Review*, Vol. 18, No. 1 (1992), pp. 45–56.
48 Laurie Ann Mazur, "Beyond the Numbers: An Introduction and Overview," in Laurie Ann

Mazur (ed.), *Beyond the Numbers: A Reader on Population, Consumption, and Environment* (Washington, D.C.: Island Press, 1994), pp. 14–15.

49   Weeks, "The Demography of Islamic Nations," p. 21.

50   Winckler, *Demographic Developments and Population Policies in Ba'thist Syria*, pp. 46–47.

51   In the early 1990s, 99% of the women in Yemen aged 15–19 were already married. Source: ESCWA, *Survey, 1996–1997*, p. 137.

52   Roderic Beaujot and Mongi Bchir, *Fertility in Tunisia: Traditional and Modern Contrasts* (Washington, D.C., Population Reference Bureau, Inc., 1984), p. 21, table 3.

53   ECA, *The State of Demographic Transition in Africa*, p. 36.

54   Syrian Arab Republic, Office of the Prime Minister, Central Bureau of Statistics and League of Arab States, Pan-Arab Project for Child Development, *Syrian Maternal and Child Health Survey–1993* (Damascus, 1999), p. 220.

55   UN, Social Development Division, Women Empowerment and Gender Mainstreaming, *Country Profile–Bahrain*.

56   *Syrian Maternal and Child Health Survey–1993*, p. 220.

57   See also: Weeks, "The Demography of Islamic Nations," p. 21.

58   Winckler, *Demographic Developments and Population Policies in Ba'thist Syria*, p. 49.

59   The Kingdom of Saudi Arabia, Ministry of Health, *Saudi Arabia Child Health Survey*, edited by Yagob al-Mazrou and Samir Farid (Riyadh, 1991), p. 269.

60   Valentine M. Moghadam, *Modernizing Women: Gender and Social Change in the Middle East* (Boulder and London: Lynne Rienner Publishers, 1993), p. 119. Specifically in the case of Egypt, see: Uri M. Kupferschmidt, "Nasserist and Post-Nasserist Elites in an Official Biographical Lexicon," in Elie Podeh and Onn Winckler (eds.), *Rethinking Nasserism: Revolution and Historical Memory in Modern Egypt* (Gainesville: University Press of Florida, 2004), p. 171.

61   See in this regard: Mohammad Taghi Sheykhi, "The Socio-Psychological Factors of Family Planning with Special Reference to Iran: A Theoretical Appraisal," *International Sociology*, Vol. 10, No. 1 (March 1995), p. 72.

62   Peter J. Donaldson, *Nature Against Us: The United States and the World Population Crisis, 1965–1980* (Chapel Hill and London: The University of North Carolina Press, 1990), pp. 114–15.

63   See in this regard: Hess, *Population Growth and Socioeconomic Progress in Less Developed Countries*, p. 17.

64   UNDP, *The Arab Human Development Report–2002*, p. 39.

65   See, e.g., Moghadam, *Modernizing Women*, pp. 116–17.

66   Sultanate of Oman, Ministry of Health, *Oman Child Health Survey*, edited by Murtadha J. Suleiman, Ahmed al-Ghassany, and Samir Farid (Muscat, 1992), p. 246.

67   *Syrian Maternal and Child Health Survey–1993*, p. 169, table 12.11.

68   Syrian Arab Republic, Office of the Prime Minister, Central Bureau of Statistics, *Statistical Abstract–2001* (Damascus, 2002), p. 62, table 6/2.

69   The Kingdom of Morocco, Ministry of Public Health, *National Survey on Population and Health – Morocco, 1992* (Rabat, 1992), figure 2, no page.

70   Royaume du Maroc, Ministère de la Santé Publique and Macro International Inc., *Enquête de Panel sur la Population et la Santé (EPPS)-1995* (Rabat, Janvier 1996), p. 24, table 3.1.

71   WB, *African Development Indicators, 1998/99* (Washington, D.C., 1998), p. 284, table 11–2. See also in this regard: Hayam El-Beblawi and Azza Mohamed Abedo, "Some Aspects of Child Labor in Egypt," *CDC Working Paper*, No. 41 (1999); Mohamed Abdel Rahman, "Socio-Demographic Aspects of Child Labor in Egypt," in CDC, *Population & Sustainable Development*, Research Monograph Series, No. 5 (Cairo, 1998), pp. 349–68.

72   *Gulf News*, November 13, 2003.

73   Arab Republic of Egypt, National Population Council and Macro International Inc. (Calverton, Maryland USA), *Egypt Demographic and Health Survey–1995* (Cairo, September 1996), p. 39, table 3.2.

74 State of Kuwait, Ministry of Health, *Kuwait Child Health Survey*, edited by Rashid al-Rashoud and Samir Farid (Kuwait, 1991), p. 216, table 11.4.

75 See: Anne Valia Goujon, "Population and Education Prospects in the Arab Region," in Ismail Sirageldin (ed.), *Human Capital: Population Economics in the Middle East* (Cairo: The American University in Cairo Press, 2002), p. 117, table 5.1.

76 Mahmoud Farag, "Differences in Age at Marriage in Syria," in S. H. Huzayyin and G. T. Acsadi (eds.), *Family and Marriage in some African and Asiatic Countries*, Research Monograph Series, No. 6 (Cairo: Cairo Demographic Centre, 1976), p. 503, table 24.7.

77 Hamed Abu-Gamrah, "Fertility Levels and Differentials by Mother's Education in some Countries of the ECWA Region," in CDC, *Determinants of Fertility in some African and Asian Countries*, Research Monograph Series, No. 10 (Cairo, 1982), pp. 199–201; ESCWA, Population Section, *Gender and Population Dynamics in the ESCWA Region*, By Batool Shakoori (Beirut, 2000), pp. 6–7; Goujon, "Population and Education Prospects in the Arab Region," p. 118, figure 5.1; Richards and Waterbury, *A Political Economy of the Middle East*, second edition, p. 83.

78 The Hashemite Kingdom of Jordan, Department of Statistics, *Jordan Population and Family Health Survey–1990* (Amman, 1992), p. 79, table 7.2.

79 ESCWA, *Demographic and Related Socio-Economic Data Sheets*, No. 11 (2001), pp. 102–3, tables 4 and 5.

80 PCBS, *The Demographic Survey in the West Bank and Gaza Strip*, final report (Ramallah, 1997), p. 123, table 57.

81 Philippe Fargues, "Protracted National Conflict and Fertility Change: Palestinians and Israelis in the Twentieth Century," *Population and Development Review*, Vol. 26, No. 3 (September 2000), pp. 464–66.

82 *Ibid.*, p. 466, table 5. On the overall demographic developments of the Palestinians in the Occupied Territories since the Israeli occupation in the June 1967 War, see: Marwan Khawaja, "The Recent Rise in Palestinian Fertility: Permanent or Transient?" *Population Studies*, Vo. 54 (2000), pp. 331–46.

83 Contraceptive prevalence rate is defined as the percentage of marries women currently using contraceptives.

84 Gilbar, *Kalkalat ha-Mizrah ha-Tikhon ba-'Et ha-Hadasha*, pp. 30–31.

85 Abdelghany, "Evaluating the Application of the Stable Population Model of the Population of Egypt," p. 109, table 3.

86 UN, Department of International Economic and Social Affairs, "Mortality of Children Under Age 5: World Estimates and Projections, 1950–2025," *Population Studies*, No. 105 (New York, 1988), p. 32, table A.1.

87 WB, *World Development Report–2002*, pp. 232–33, table 1.

88 UN, "Mortality of Children Under Age 5," p. 38, table A.2.

89 On the increase of the death rates in Iraq, particularly infant mortality rates, following the sanctions imposed by the UN in 1991, see: Amatzia Baram, "The Effect of Iraqi Sanctions: Statistical Pitfalls and Responsibility," *Middle East Journal*, Vol. 54, No. 2 (Spring 2000), pp. 194–223.

90 Allan G. Hill, "Population Growth in the Middle East since 1945 with Special Reference to the Arab Countries of West Asia," in John I. Clarke and Howard Bowen-Jones (eds.), *Change and Development in the Middle East* (London and New York: Methuen, 1981), p. 132, table 8.1.

91 K. L. Kohli and Musa'ad al-Omaim, "Mortality Levels, Trends and Differentials in Kuwait, 1957-1983," *Population Bulletin of ESCWA*, No. 28 (June 1986), p. 119; State of Qatar, Ministry of Information, *Qatar into the Seventies* (Doha, May 1973), p. 79; Jacqueline Ismael and Tareq Y. Ismael, "Social Policy in the Arab World," *Cairo Papers in Social Science*, Vol. 18, Monograph 1 (Spring 1995), p. 68.

92 By 1990, South Korea's natural increase rate was only 1%, declining from almost 3% in 1960 (see table 2.5).

93 Teitelbaum, "Relevance of Demographic Transition Theory for Developing Countries," p. 422.

94 Thompson, "Population," pp. 960–61, table 1.

Chapter 3 *"Jobs for the Boys (and Girls)": The Emergence of the Employment Dilemma*

1 *Al-Ahram*, March 23, 2001. Quoted from: *MEED*, April 20, 2001, p. 24.

2 Gilbar, *Kalkalat ha-Mizrah ha-Tikhon ba-'Et ha-Hadasha*, p. 40.

3 On the process of the development of a wide-based age pyramid due to high natural increase rates, see, e.g., Ismail Sirageldin, "Population Dynamics, Environment, and Conflict," in Ismail Sirageldin and Eqbal al-Rahmani (eds.), *Population and Development Transformations in the Arab World*, Research in Human Capital and Development (Greenwich, Connecticut and London: JAI Press INC., 1996), pp. 189–96.

4 UNDP, *Human Development Report–2004* (Published for the UNDP by Oxford University Press, Oxford and New York, 2004), p. 139, table 1.

5 UNICEF, *The State of the World's Children–2000*, p. 87, table 1; p. 103, table 5.

6 See *Ha'aretz*, July 22, 1998 (Hebrew).

7 John Knodel, "Deconstructing Population Momentum," *Population Today*, Vol. 27, No. 3 (March 1999), p. 2.

8 UN, Department of Economic and Social Affairs, Population Division, *World Population Monitoring–2001: Population, Environment and Development* (New York, 2001), p. 1.

9 Wolfgang Lutz, "The Future of World Population," *Population Bulletin*, Vol. 49, No. 1 (June 1994), pp. 4–6.

10 Todaro, *Economic Development*, seventh edition, p. 210.

11 CAPMAS, *Statistical Yearbook*, 1952–1992, p. 28, table 1–18.

12 *Al-Ahram Weekly*, February 27 – March 5, 2003.

13 On the projected population growth rates in the Arab countries during the first half of the twenty-first century, see: Philippe Fargues, "Demographic Explosion or Social Upheaval?" in Ghassan Salamè (ed.), *Democracy without Democrats? The Renewal of Politics in the Muslim World* (London and New York: I.B. Tauris, 1994), pp. 157–65.

14 Todaro, *Economic Development*, Seventh edition, p. 221

15 Statistical Office of the European Union, *Eurostat Yearbook–2002* (Luxembourg, 2003), p. 2.

16 Eurostat News Release, "European Population Trends in 2002," 92/2003 – August 8, 2003 [http://europa.eu.int/comm/eurostat].

17 Jean-Claude Chesnais, "The Demographic Sunset of the West? *Population Today*, Vol. 25, No. 1 (January 1997), p. 5.

18 Paul Demeny, "Population Policy Dilemmas in Europe at the Dawn of the Twenty-First Century," *Population and Development Review*, Vol. 29, No. 1 (March 2003), p. 2.

19 *Ibid.*, p. 3.

20 EU, *Eurostat Yearbook–2002*, p. 2.

21 Eurostat News Release, "European Population Trends in 2002," 92/2003 – August 8, 2003 [http://europa.eu.int/comm/eurostat].

22 See: *Ha'aretz*, December 25, 2000.

23 CIA, *The World Factbook–2002* [http://www.cia.gov/cia/publications/factbook].

24 ILO, *Yearbook of Labour Statistics*, various issues (Geneva).

25 Euromonitor Publications Limited, *Middle East Economic Handbook* (London: Euromonitor Publications Ltd., 1986), p. 81.

26 Shamlan Y. Alessa, *The Manpower Problem in Kuwait* (London and Boston: Kegan Paul International, 1981), p. 17, table 2.4.

27 See: ESCWA, *Survey of the Economic and Social Developments in the ESCWA*

Region–1995, p. 40, table 12; Robert E. Looney, *Manpower Policies and Development in the Persian Gulf Region* (Westport and London: Praeger, 1994), p. 30, table 3.2.

28 *MEED*, January 27, 1989, p. 3; Looney, *Manpower Policies and Development*, p. 30, table 3.2.

29 Saudi Arabia, *Seventh Development Plan*, p. 62, table 2.1.

30 See also in this regard, a report of the Saudi Arabian Monetary Agency in *Saudi Economic Survey*, December 15, 1999, p. 18.

31 The State of Kuwait, Ministry of Planning, Statistics and Information Center, *Annual Statistical Abstract–2000* (Kuwait, 2001), p. 91, table 76.

32 Onn Winckler, "The Challenge of Foreign Workers in the Persian/Arabian Gulf: The Case of Oman," *Immigrants & Minorities*, Vol. 18, No. 2 (July 2000), p. 28, table 2.

33 In regard to Kuwait, see, e.g., Alessa, *The Manpower Problem in Kuwait*, p. 16.

34 *MEED*, "Special Report-Qatar," November 1979, p. 11.

35 During the past few years, however, a slow and gradual change in the area of women driving has occurred in Saudi Arabia, with a very limited number of Saudi women now allowed to drive under strict limitations.

36 Wilson and Douglas, *Saudi Arabia*, p. 246.

37 *Ibid.*, p. 250.

38 See in this regard: Adil Osman Gebriel, "Overview of Major Issues in the Development of National Human Resources in the Gulf," in Abbas Abdelkarim (ed.), *Change and Development in the Gulf* (London: Macmillan Press, and New York: St. Martin's Press, 1999), pp. 152–53.

39 Andrzej Kapiszewski, *National and Expatriates: Population and Labour Dilemmas of the Gulf Cooperation Council States* (Reading: Ithaca Press, 2001), p. 112.

40 *The Middle East*, January 2003, p. 23.

41 By 2001, Bahrain's oil exports amounted to only 37,000 b/d and its oil revenues in this year amounted to $1.788 billion – the lowest among the GCC countries. Source: The Cooperation Council of the Arab States of the Gulf, Secretarial General, Statistical Department, *Statistical Bulletin*, No. 12 (2003), tables 144 and 148 [http://www.gcc-sg.org/STATISTICS].

42 On the participation of the Omani women in the labor market, see: Chatty, "Women Working in Oman," pp. 241–54.

43 In regard to the UAE, see: Fatma al-Sayegh, "Domestic Politics in the United Arab Emirates: Social and Economic Policies, 1990–2000," in Joseph A. Kechichian (ed), *Iran, Iraq, and the Arab Gulf States* (New York: Palgrave, 2001), pp. 172–73.

44 ESCWA, *Survey, 1998–1999*, pp. 173–74.

45 UNDP, *Human Development Report–2002*, pp. 178–81, table 9.

46 See, e.g., Onn Winckler, "The Demographic Dilemma of the Arab World: The Employment Aspect," *Journal of Contemporary History*, Vol. 37, No. 4 (October 2002), p. 621.

47 *Jordan Times*, November 14–15, 1996.

48 ESCWA, *Survey, 1996–1997*, p. 38, box 5.

49 Syria, *Statistical Abstract–2001*, p. 65, table 9/2.

50 See also on this regard: Winckler, "The Demographic Dilemma of the Arab World," p. 621.

51 Radwan A. Shaban, Ragui Assaad, and Sulayman S. al-Qudsi, "The Challenge of Unemployment in the Arab Region," *International Labour Review*, Vol. 134, No. 1 (1995), p. 69.

52 CAPMAS, *Statistical Yearbook, 1992–1998*, p. 20, table 1–9.

53 Saudi Arabia, *Seventh Development Plan*, p. 78, table 3.1.

54 *MEED*, September 15, 2000, p. 29.

55 Saudi Arabian Monetary Agency, *Thirty-Eighth Annual Report-1423* [2002] (Riyadh, 2003), p. 56.

56   *MEED*, June 28, 2002, p. 20.
57   ESCWA, *Survey, 2004, Summary*, p. 7.
58   ESCWA, *Demographic and Related Socio-Economic Data Sheets*, No. 11 (2001), p. 99, table 1.
59   Henry T. Azzam, *The Arab World Facing the Challenge of the New Millennium* (London and New York: I. B. Tauris, 2002), p. 5.
60   The World Bank, "Expanded Trade and Investment Needed in MENA," [http://www.worldbank.org].
61   UN, *Demographic Yearbook–1970*, pp. 296–97; *1975*, pp. 240–41.
62   Syria, *Statistical Abstract–1991*, p. 60, table 10.2; *2001*, p. 65, table 9/2.
63   ESCWA, *Survey, 1996–1997*, p. 36; *Jordan Times*, October 27, 1996.
64   WB, *Hashemite Kingdom of Jordan*, A Quarterly Publication of the Jordan Country Unit, First Quarter 2003 (Washington, D.C., 2003), p. 8.
65   Moshe Efrat, "Tokhnit he-'Asor ve-Totzoteha," in Shimon Shamir (ed.), *Yeridat ha-Nasserism, 1965–1970: Shqi'ata shel Tenu'a Meshikhit* (Tel Aviv: Mif'alim Universitayim, 1978), p. 66 (Hebrew).
66   M. Riad El-Ghonemy, "An Assessment of Egypt's Development Strategy, 1952–1970," in Podeh and Winckler (eds.), *Rethinking Nasserism*, p. 258.
67   *Al-Mussawar*, No. 3377, June 30, 1989, p. 17.
68   El-Ghonemy, "An Assessment of Egypt's Development Strategy," p. 257.
69   Hansen, *Economic Development in Syria*, p. 13.
70   Foreign Areas Studies Division, *Area Handbook for Syria* (Washington, D.C.: The American University, July 1965), p. 236.
71   Yusif A. Sayigh, *The Economies of the Arab World: Development Since 1945* (London: Croom Helm, 1978), p. 229.
72   *Ibid.*
73   Oman remained a poor country also during the 1960s due both to the overall socioeconomic approach of the Sultan Sa'id bin Taymur and the fact that oil export started only in 1967. Thus, according to the World Bank figures, Oman's per capita GNP in 1968 amounted to only $250. WB, *World Tables, 1989–90 Edition*, p. 432.
74   For example, Saudi Arabia's per capita GNP increased from $500 in 1968 to $830 in 1972, the last year prior to the "oil boom," while that of Libya increased from $1,490 to $1,980 in the corresponding years. Kuwait's per capita GNP was already high in the early 1970s, amounting to $3,700 in 1972 (current prices). WB, *World Tables, 1989–90 Edition*, pp. 344, 356, 472. Specific and accurate data for Bahrain, UAE, and Qatar are not available.
75   WB, *World Tables, 1989–90 Edition*.
76   WB, *World Development Report–1985*, pp. 175–76, table 2.
77   *Middle East International*, February 22, 1985, p. 16.
78   Eliyahu Kanovsky, "Jordan's Economy: From Prosperity to Crisis," *Occasional Papers*, No. 106 (The Moshe Dayan Center for Middle Eastern and African Studies, Tel Aviv University, May 1989), p. 41.
79   *MEED*, April 11, 1987, p. 36.
80   J. S. Birks, C. A. Sinclair, and J. A. Socknat, "The Demand for Egyptian Labor Abroad," in Alan Richards and Philip L. Martin (eds.), *Migration, Mechanization, and Agricultural Labor Markets in Egypt* (Boulder: Westview Press, 1983), p. 118.
81   *The Arab Economist*, April 1980, p. 25; *al-Ahram*, January 14, 1980.
82   Ralph R. Sell, "Egyptian International Labor Migration and Social Processes: Toward Regional Integration," *International Migration Review*, Vol. 22, No. 3 (March 1988), p. 91.
83   *MEED*, September 16, 1983, p. 22; EIU, *Country Profile–Egypt, 1986–87*, p. 8; Gil Feiler, "Migration and Recession: Arab Labor Mobility in the Middle East, 1982–1989," *Population and Development Review*, Vol. 17, No. 1 (March 1991), p. 136.
84   M.A.J. Share, "The Use of Jordanian Workers' Remittances," in Bichara Khader and

Adnan Badran (eds.), *The Economic Development of Jordan* (London: Croom Helm, 1987), p. 33, table 3.1.

85 J. S. Birks and C. A. Sinclair, *International Migration Project: Country Case Study: The Hashemite Kingdom of Jordan* (Durham: The University of Durham, Department of Economics, November 1978), p. 9, table. 3; Ian J. Seccombe, "Labour Emigration Policies and Economic Development in Jordan: From Unemployment to Labour Shortage," in Khader and Badran (eds.), *The Economic Development of Jordan*, p. 120.

86 J. S. Birks, I. Seragelding, C. A. Sinclair, and J. A. Socknat, "Who is Migrating Where? An Overview of International Labor Migration in the Arab World," in Richards and Martin (eds.), *Migration, Mechanization, and Agricultural Labor Markets in Egypt*, p. 115, table 2; Share, "The Use of Jordanian Workers' Remittances," p. 34, table 3.2; *al-Dustur*, March 24, 1981.

87 Jordan, *Statistical Abstract–1989*, p. 83, table 4/2/3.

88 Allan M. Findlay, "Return to Yemen: The End of the Old Migration Order in the Arab World," in W. T. S. Gould and A. M. Findlay (eds.), *Population Migration and the Changing World Order* (Chichester: John Wiley & Sons, 1994), p. 214.

89 See in this regard: Ian J. Seccombe and R. I. Lawless, "State Intervention and the International Labour Market: A Review of Labour Emigration Policies in the Arab World," in Reginald Appleyard (ed.), *The Impact of International Migration on Developing Countries* (Paris: Development Centre of the Organization for Economic Co-Operation and Development, 1989), pp. 69–78.

90 Bayan Tabbara, "Labour Markets in the ESCWA Region During the Past 25 Years," in ESCWA, *Proceedings of the Expert Group Meeting on Assessment of Economic and Social Developments in the ESCWA Region During the Last 25 Years and Priorities for the Next Decade*, 1999–2009 (New York, 1999), pp. 109–10.

91 On the development of the intra-Arab "mutual dependence" following the "oil boom," see: Saad Eddin Ibrahim, "Oil, Migration, and the New Arab Social Order," in Malcolm H. Kerr and El Sayed Yassin (eds.), *Rich and Poor States in the Middle East: Egypt and the New Arab Order* (Boulder: Westview Press and Cairo: The American University in Cairo Press, 1982), pp. 17–70.

92 M. Riad El-Ghonemy, *Affluence and Poverty in the Middle East* (London and New York: Routledge, 1998), p. 183.

93 Tayseer Abdel Jaber, "Jordanian Labor Migration: Social, Political and Economic Effects," in Shtayyeh (ed.), *Labor Migration*, p. 85.

94 Muhammad Sa'ad 'Amirah, "Waqi' al-Bitala fi al-Urdun wa-Nazara Nahwa al-Mustaqbal," in Mustafa al-Hamarneh (ed.), *al-Iqtisad al-Urduni: al-Mushkilat wal-Afaq* (Amman: Markaz al-Dirasat al- Istratigiyya, 1994), p. 224, table 2.

95 J. S. Birks and C. A. Sinclair, *International Migration and Development in the Arab Region* (Geneva: ILO, 1980), p. 135, table 10.

96 *Al-Ra'y*, November 21, 1984.

97 HRD base Ltd., *Socio-Demographic Profiles of Key Arab Countries*, p. 44, table 3.2.

98 During the "oil decade," the salaries offered to foreign workers in the GCC countries were several times higher than those received in their home countries. See in this regard, e.g., Roger Owen, *Migrant Workers in the Gulf* (London: The Minority Rights Group, 1985), p. 4; Richards and Waterbury, *A Political Economy of the Middle East*, second edition, p. 369; Saad Eddin Ibrahim, *The New Arab Social Order: A Study of the Social Impact of the Oil Wealth* (Boulder: Westview Press and London: Croom Helm, 1982), p. 69; *al-Thawra* (Damascus), January 23, 1980.

99 On the GCC liberal employment and immigration policies during the "oil decade," see, e.g., Winckler, "The Immigration Policy of the Gulf Cooperation Council," p. 483.

100 The term "rental revenues" refers to a situation by which increasing revenues are not derived from greater efficiency or from the introduction of new technologies and invest-

ments. Thus, the sharp increase in oil prices following the October 1973 "oil boom" was not an outcome of increasing production costs, but rather resulted from changes in the oil market despite the decline in oil production costs. See: Richards and Waterbury, *A Political Economy of the Middle East*, second addition, p. 16. On the GCC *Rentier* state, see: Hazem Beblawi and Giacomo Luciani (eds.), *The Rentier State*, Vol. II (London: Croom Helm, 1987); Hazem Beblawi, "The Rentier State in the Arab World," in Giacomo Luciani (ed.), *The Arab State* (London: Routledge, 1990), pp. 85–98; Nazih Ayubi, *Over-Stating the Arab States: Politics and Society in the Middle East* (London and New York: I.B. Tauris, 1995), pp. 224–40; F. Gregory Gause III, *Oil Monarchies: Domestic and Security Challenges in the Arab Gulf States* (New York: Council on Foreign Relations Press, 1994), pp. 42–77; Uzi Rabi, "Majlis al-Shura and Majlis al-Dawla: Weaving Old Practices and New Realities in the Process of State Formation in Oman," *Middle Eastern Studies*, Vol. 38, No. 4 (October 2002), pp. 41–42.

101 Central Bank of Kuwait, *Economic Report–2000* (Kuwait, 2001), p. 198 .
102 *Saudi Economic Survey*, September 27, 2000, p. 15.
103 On the strategies employed by the GCC rulers in order to preserve the political system, see: Abdulhadi Khalaf, "What the Gulf Ruling Families Do when They Rule," *Orient*, Vol. 44, No. 4 (2003), pp. 537–54.
104 Peter N. Woodward, *Oil and Labor in the Middle East: Saudi Arabia and the Oil Boom* (New York: Praeger, 1988), p. 19.
105 Paul Rivlin, *World Oil and Energy Trends: Strategic Implications for the Middle East*, Memorendum No. 57 (Tel Aviv: Jaffee Center for Strategic Studies, Tel Aviv University, September 2000), p. 17, table 1.
106 Abdel Jaber, "Jordanian Labor Migration," p. 83.
107 Kanovsky, "Jordan's Economy: From Prosperity to Crisis," p. 41.
108 WB, *World Tables, 1995 Edition*, pp. 386–87.
109 See, e.g., Feiler, "Migration and Recession," p. 139.
110 On the economic relationship between Jordan and Iraq prior to the Iraqi invasion of Kuwait, see: Amatzia Baram, "Ba‘thi Iraq and Hashemite Jordan: From Hostility to Alignment," *Middle East Journal*, Vol. 45, No. 1 (Spring 1991), pp. 56–58.
111 IMF, *Jordan: Background Information on Selected Aspects of Adjustment and Growth Strategy* (Washington, D.C., August 29, 1995), p. 16.
112 'Amirah, "Waqi‘ al-Bitala fi al-Urdun," p. 224, table 2; *Middle East International*, January 9, 1987, p. 14.
113 *Al-Dustur*, April 17, 1990.
114 See, e.g., Feiler, "Migration and Recession," p. 142.
115 On the Jordanian immigration policy during the 1980s and the first half of the 1990s, see: Abdel Jaber, "Jordanian Labor Migration," pp. 91–95; Onn Winckler, *Population Growth and Migration in Jordan, 1950–1994* (Brighton and Portland: Sussex Academic Press, 1997), pp. 84–86.
116 Raymond A. Hinnebusch, "Syria," in Tim Niblock and Emma Merphy (eds.), *Economic and Political Liberalization in the Middle East* (London and New York: British Academic Press, 1993), p. 188.
117 WB, *World Tables, 1995 Edition*, p. 649.
118 *Al-Hayat*, January 26, 1992.
119 Volker Perthes, "The Syrian Economy in the 1980s," *Middle East Journal*, Vol. 46, No. 1 (Winter 1992), p. 37.
120 ESCWA, *Return Migration*, p. 20, table 6.
121 In this regard, see: Podeh and Winckler, "The Boycott that Never Was," pp. 32–36.
122 EIU, *Country Report-Egypt*, No. 3 (1987), p. 14.
123 WB, *World Tables, 1995 Edition*, pp. 4–5, table 2; pp. 28–29, table 7.
124 El-Ghonemy, *Affluence and Poverty in the Middle East*, p. 182.

125 ESCWA, *Return Migration*, p. 17.
126 EIU, *Country Report-Egypt*, No. 4 (1988), p. 10.
127 Bruce Maddy-Weitzman, "Masoret, Gidul Okhlosiya, ve-Tikhnun Mishpaha be-Marocco" in Ayalon and Gilbar (eds.), *Demographya ve-Politiqa be-Medinot 'Arav*, p. 58 (Hebrew).
128 El-Ghonemy, *Affluence and Poverty in the Middle East*, p. 188.
129 Mohamed Farid Azzi, "Maghrebi Youth: Between Alienation and Integration," in Yahia H. Zoubir (ed.), *North Africa in Transition: State, Society, and Economic Transformation in the 1990s* (Gainesville: University Press of Florida, 1999), pp. 113–14.
130 The GCC oil revenues declined from a peak of $157.8 billion in 1981 to $38.3 billion in 1986 – the lowest level ever since the "oil boom" – and increased slightly to $50.78 billion in 1989 (in current $US). Source: ESCWA, *Survey, 1998–1999*, pp. 44–45.
131 For example, the Saudi foreign currency reserves declined from $125 billion in 1980 to $65 in 1990 and reached as low as $7–$15 billion in 1993. Source: *Middle East International*, September 24, 1993, p. 20.
132 On the wage gaps between Asian and Arab foreign workers in the GCC countries, see, e.g., Nazli Choucri, "Asians in the Arab World: Labor Migration and Public Policy," *Middle Eastern Studies*, Vol. 22, No. 2 (1986), p. 254; *MEED*, December 11, 1998, p. 32.
133 *Africa Monitor*, July 2004, p. 3.
134 *Ibid.*, p. 5.
135 By 2003, according to the EIA (Energy Information Administration, US Department of Energy) estimate, Saudi oil revenues amounted to $81 billion – the highest amount ever since the peak of the "oil boom" in 1981. Source: EIA, "OPEC Revenues: Country Details," January 2004 [http://www.eia.dov.gov].
136 Saudi-American Bank (SAMBA), *The Saudi Economy: Mid-Year 2003* (Riyadh, August 2003), p. 6.
137 *MEED*, August 14, 1992, p. 19.
138 ESCWA, *Survey, 1994*, p. 65, table 38.
139 WB, *World Tables, 1995 Edition*, p. 29, table 7.
140 *MEED*, November 8, 1991, p. 17.
141 *Jordan Times*, October 14, 1991.
142 On the economic situation in Jordan during 1991, see: Asher Susser, "Jordan," *MECS*, Vol. 15 (1991), pp. 486–88.
143 *Jordan Times*, November 18; December 28, 1999.
144 ESCWA, *Survey, 1998–1999*, p. 51.
145 The Hashemite Kingdom of Jordan, Department of Statistics, *Employment and Unemployment Survey*, February 2001, Principal Report (Amman, April 2001), p. 23.
146 *Jordan Times*, July 10, 2003.
147 The Hashemite Kingdom of Jordan, Department of Statistics [http://www.dos.gov.jo].
148 *Jordan Times*, August 7, 1996; [http://www.migrationint.com.au/news/paris/dec 1996–27 mn.asp].
149 See, e.g., http://www.migrationint.co.au/news/paris/dec_1996–27mn.asp.
150 See, e.g., ESCWA, *Survey, 2000–2001*, p. 31.
151 *The Middle East*, October 1991, p. 36; Nicholas Van Hear, *New Diaspora: The Mass Exodus, Dispersal, and Regrouping of Migrant Communities* (London: UCL Press, 1998), p. 87.
152 Findlay, "Return to Yemen," p. 218.
153 ESCWA, *National Accounts Studies of the ESCWA Region*, Bulletin No. 17 (New York, 1997), p. 9.
154 http://www.al-bab.com/yemen/econ/maitami2.htm. In regard to the overall socioeconomic impact of the mass return on the Yemenite economy, see: Nicholas Van Hear, "The Socio-Economic Impact of the Involuntary Mass Return to Yemen in 1990," *Journal of Refugee Studies*, Vo. 7, No. 1 (March 1994), pp. 18–38.

155 ESCWA, *Survey, 1996–1997*, p. 36.

156 ESCWA, *Survey, 2000–2001*, p. 33.

157 *Gulf States Newsletter*, April 18, 2003, p. 19.

158 See, e.g., *Middle East International*, May 3, 1991, p. 22.

159 EIU, *Country Profile–Tunisia, 1999–2000*, pp. 22; 41, table 2; *2001*, p. 25; IMF, *Tunisia: Recent Economic Developments*, IMF Stuff Country Report 00/37 (Washington, D.C. March 2000), pp. 17–18.

160 IMF, *International Financial Statistics Yearbook–1999*, p. 665.

161 Nora Ann Colton, "The Maghrebi Economies as Emerging Markets?" in Zoubir (ed.), *North Africa in Transition*, p. 162; *Azzam, The Arab World Facing the Challenge of the New Millennium*, p. 118; ILO, *World Employment Report–2001*, p. 361, table 4.

162 IMF, *Algeria: Selected Economic Issues*, Stuff Country Report 98/87 (Washington, D.C. 1998), p. 49, table 15; No. 96/71 (Washington, D.C., 1996), p. 35, table 6. According to the ILO figures, the unemployment rate in Algeria was 28.7% by 1997. ILO, *World Employment Report–2001*, p. 361, table 4.

163 EIU, *Country Profile–Algeria, 2001*, p. 32.

164 ESCWA, *Survey, 1994*, p. 15.

165 ESCWA, *Social Impact of Reconstructing with Special Reference to Employment* (New York, 1999), p. 34. On the development of unemployment in Egypt during the first half of the 1990s, see: Hesham Mohamed Shaker, "Main Features of Unemployment in Egypt (1990–1995)," in CDC, *28th Annual Seminar on Population Issues in the Middle East, Africa and Asia*, pp. 515–33.

166 ESCWA, *National Accounts Studies*, Bulletin 19, pp. 3–4; *MEED*, April 16, 1999, p. 18.

167 CAPMAS, *Statistical Yearbook, 1992–1998*, p. 11, table 1-15.

168 EIU, *Country Profile–Egypt, 2001*, p. 15.

169 EIU, *Country Profile–Egypt, 1999–2000*, p. 28.

170 ESCWA, *Survey, 2000–2001*, pp. 30–31; *MEED*, April 20, 2001, p. 28.

171 EIU, *Country Profile–Egypt, 2001*, p. 33.

172 ESCWA, *Survey, 2001–2002*, p. 16.

173 *Al-Ahram Weekly*, February 27 – March 5, 2003.

174 ESCWA, *Survey, 2002–2003*, Summary, p. 3.

175 *MEED*, February 9, 1996, p. 2.

176 ESCWA, *Survey, 1995*, p. 159, table 81.

177 *MEED*, November 18, 1994, p. 10.

178 By the mid-1990s, the number of Syrian workers in other Arab countries totaled about 800,000, representing more than 15% of the total Syrian workforce and approximately 20% of the civilian workforce.

179 By the early 1990s, the agricultural sector represented approximately 30% of the Syrian GDP. *Syria, Statistical Abstract–2000*, pp. 536–37, table 29/16.

180 ESCWA, *National Accounts Studies of the ESCWA Region*, Bulletin 19, p. 6; ESCWA, *Survey, 2002–2003*, Summary, p. 3.

181 ESCWA, *Survey, 2001–2002*, p. 17.

182 EIU, *Country Profile–Syria, 2000–2001*, p. 20.

183 ESCWA, *External Trade Bulletin of the ESCWA Region*, eleventh edition (New York, 2002), pp. 84–86, table II-4.

184 Eyal Zisser, *Be-Shem ha-Av: Bashar al-Asad: Shanim Rishonot ba-Shilton* (Tel Aviv: Tel Aviv University Press, 2004), p. 200 (Hebrew); "Oil for Food: Impact on Iraq and its Main Arab Trading Partners," p. 6 [WSCWA Website, [http://www.escwa.org].

185 EIA, "Major Non-OPEC Countries Oil Revenues," (June 2003), EIA website [http://www.eia.doe.gov].

186 ESCWA, *Survey, 2001–2002*, p. 18.

187 On the GCC nationalization policies and causes for its failure during the second half of the

1980s and the first half of the 1990s, see: Onn Winckler, "Gulf Monarchies as Rentier States: The Nationalization Policies of the Labor Force," in Joseph Kostiner (ed.), *Middle East Monarchies: The Challenge of Modernity* (Boulder: Lynne Rienner Publishers, 2000), pp. 247–50.

188 See, e.g., *MEED*, April 5, 1996, p. 56; Said Abdullah al-Shaikh, "Demographic Transitions in Saudi Arabia and Their Impact on Economic Growth and the Labor Market," *Saudi Economic Survey*, September 13, 2000, p. 20, tables 3 and 4.

189 Saudi Arabian Monetary Agency, *Thirty-Eighth Annual Report 1423* [2002], p. 321, table 18.9.

190 See, e.g., Hossein Askari, Vahid Nowshirvani, and Mohamed Jaber, *Economic Development in the GCC: The Blessing and Curse of Oil* (Greenwich and London: JAI Press, 1997), pp. 66–68.

191 "Gulf Population and Labour Force Structure," *The NCB* [National Commercial Bank] *Economist*, Vol. 5 (June/July 1995), p. 8.

192 On the nature of the negotiations between the GCC employers and the foreign workers, see: Woodward, *Oil and Labor in the Middle East*, pp. 135–44.

193 See in this regard: Kapiszewski, *Nationals and Expatriates*, p. 208.

194 See in this regard: Mahmoud Abdel-Fadil, "The Macro-Behaviour of Oil-Rentier States in the Arab Region," in Hazem Beblawi and Giacomo Luciani (eds.), *The Rentier State*, Vol. II (London: Croom Helm, 1987), pp. 84–86.

195 Hazem Beblawi, "The Rentier State in the Arab World," in Giacomo Luciani (ed.), *The Arab State* (London: Routledge, 1990), p. 91.

196 Al-Shaikh, "Demographic Transitions in Saudi Arabia," pp. 15, 21.

197 Askari, Nowshirvani, and Jaber, *Economic Development in the GCC*, p. 22.

198 *Saudi Economic Survey*, December 13, 1995, p. 6.

199 *MEED*, August 14, 1998, p. 2; Azzam, *The Arab World Facing the Challenge of the New Millennium*, p. 176.

200 *Gulf States Newsletter*, February 21, 2003, p. 15.

201 ILO, *World Employment Report–2001*, pp. 37–38.

202 Sultanate of Oman, Ministry of Development, *General Census of Population, Housing and Establishments, 1993* (Muscat 1995), p. 55.

203 *MEED*, March 12, 1993, p. 8.

204 *Gulf States Newsletter*, April 8, 1996.

205 Kapiszewski, *Nationals and Expatriates*, p. 233.

206 *MEED*, December 11, 1998, p. 31.

207 *MEED*, September 28, 2001, p. 28.

208 *Gulf States Newsletter*, July 11, 2003, p. 14.

209 *MEED*, March 16, 2001, p. 24.

210 *Gulf States Newsletter*, February 21, 2003, p. 5; ESCWA, *Survey, 2001–2002*, p. 19.

211 By 2002, Saudi Arabian oil revenues climbed to $55 billion (current prices). Source: *Middle East International*, June 27, 2003, p. 17.

212 Kapiszewski, *National and Expatriates*, pp. 210-11.

213 In Oman, for example, in 1998, 80% of the foreign workers earned less than $200 per month. Source: EIU, *Country Profile–Oman, 1998–99*, p. 12; *MEED*, December 11, 1998, p. 32.

214 *MEED*, February 23, 1996, p. 8.

215 Gad G. Gilbar, "Introduction: The Policies of Demographic Change," in his *Population Dilemmas in the Middle East* (London and Portland: Frank Cass, 1997), p. 4.

216 Kashef, "Egypt," p. 26; Shaban, Ragui, and al-Qudsi, "The Challenge of Unemployment in the Arab Region," p. 75.

217 EIU, *Country Profile–Tunisia, 1989–90*, p. 10. See also: Euromonitor Publications Limited, *Middle East Economic Handbook*, p. 381.

218 Azzi, "Maghrebi Youth: Between Alienation and Integration," pp. 113–14.

219 See: Shaban, Ragui, and al-Qudsi, "The Challenge of Unemployment in the Arab Region," p. 75; Richards and Waterbury, *A Political Economy of the Middle East*, second edition, pp. 136–38.

220 ESCWA, *Survey, 1998–1999*, p. 177.

221 ILO, *Yearbook of Labour Statistics–2002*, pp. 487–88, table 3B.

222 *MEED*, May 2, 2003, p. 23.

223 ESCWA, *Survey, 2001–2002*, p. 17.

224 Richards and Waterbury, *A Political Economy of the Middle East*, second edition, pp. 136–37.

225 Azzam, *The Arab World Facing the Challenge of the New Millennium*, p. 11.

226 *Jordan Times*, July 10, 2003.

227 Edward Gardner, "Wanted: More Jobs," *Finance and Development*, Vol. 40, No. 1 (March 2003).

228 See, e.g., ESCWA, *Social Impact of Reconstructing*, p. 39.

229 On the mismatch between the GCC educational systems and the labor market demands, see: Hamad al-Sulayti, "Education and Training in GCC Countries: Some Issues of Concern," in The Emirates Center for Strategic Studies and Research, *Education and the Arab World: Challenges of the Next Millennium* (Abu Dhabi, 1999), p. 275.

230 EIU, QER, *Egypt – Annual Supplement, 1985*, p. 30.

231 Wilson, *Economic Development in the Middle East*, p. 65.

232 Henry J. Bruton, "Egypt's Development in the Seventies," *Economic Development and Cultural Change*, Vol. 33, No. 4 (July 1983), p. 690.

233 *Ibid.*

234 Salwa Soliman et al., *Population and Development in Egypt* (Cairo: Cairo Demographic Center, 1994), p. 51.

235 ESCWA, *Survey, 1998–1999*, pp. 174–75.

236 EIU, *Country Profile–Egypt, 2001*, p. 14; *Ha'aretz*, May 1, 2002.

237 ESCWA, *Survey, 2000–2001*, p. 23.

238 *Ha'aretz*, May 1, 2002.

239 *Jordan Times*, April 20, 1996.

240 *Jordan Times*, February 21, 1999.

241 WB, *Labor Market Reforms, Growth and Unemployment in Labor-Exporting MENA Countries*, p. 6.

242 Adam Bennett, "Failed Legacies," *Finance and Development*, Vol. 40, No. 1 (March 2003).

243 Richards and Waterbury, *A Political Economy of the Middle East*, second edition, p. 120. See also: *Ibid.*, p. 140–41.

244 Alan Cowell, "Trouble in Damascus," *The New York Times Magazine* (April 1, 1990), p. 33.

245 *FORBES*, October 25, 1982, p. 48.

246 David W. Lesch, "History and Political Culture in Syria: Obstacles to Integration in the Global Economy After the Gulf War," in Moshe Ma'oz, Joseph Ginat, and Onn Winckler (eds.), *Modern Syria: From Ottoman Rule to Pivotal Role in the Middle East* (Brighton and Portland: Sussex Academic Press, 1999), pp. 57-58.

247 EIU, *Country Profile–Egypt, 2001*, p. 33.

248 Edward Gardner, "Wanted: More Jobs," *Finance and Development*, Vol. 40, No. 1 (March 2003).

249 EIU, QER, *Egypt – Annual Supplement, 1985*, p. 14.

250 See, e.g., *The Middle East*, February 2003, p. 47.

251 Syria, *Statistical Abstract–2001*, p. 109, table 6/4.

252 European Commission, Directorate-General for Employment and Social Affairs, *Employment in Europe 2002: Recent Trends and Prospects* (Luxembourg, July 2002), p. 16.

253 Long-term unemployment is defined as the state of being unemployed for one year or more and looking for a job.
254 EU, *Eurostat Yearbook–2002*, p. 17.
255 ILO, *Yearbook of Labour Statistics–2002*, pp. 509–10, table 3B.
256 *Ibid.*, pp. 510–11, table 3B.
257 *Ibid.*, pp. 487–88, table 3B.
258 European Commission, *Employment in Europe 2002*, p. 29.
259 See, e.g., http://europa.eu.int/comm/regional_policy, which provides data for 1999.
260 US Department of Labor, Bureau of Labor Statistics [http://www.bls.gov/opub/ooq/1999/Fall/oochart/pdf].
261 In the oil-rich Arab countries, the percentage of the rural population within the total population is in any case marginal.
262 In the case of Egypt, for example, the per capita rural cropped area declined from 0.63 *feddan* (one *feddan* is 4,200 square meters) in 1960 to 0.37 *feddan* in 1996. CAPMAS, *Statistical Yearbook*, various issues. In the case of Syria, the per capita rural cropped area declined from 1.21 hectares (10,000 square meters) in 1960 to 0.67 hectares in 2000. Syria, *Statistical Abstract*, various issues.
263 *Jordan Times*, July 10, 2003.
264 Cassandra, "The Impending Crisis in Egypt," *Middle East Journal*, Vol. 49, No. 1 (1995), p. 19.
265 IPR Strategic Business Information Database, May 21, 2000 – LEXIS-NEXIS Academic Universe – file:///A/egypt2.htm; The National Bank of Egypt, *The Egyptian Economy in Brief–2000* (Cairo, 2001).
266 *The Middle East*, March 2000, p. 21.
267 *Jordan Times*, October 20, 2003.
268 George Alan, "Syria: An Economy Saved by Circumstances," *The Middle East*, December 1988, pp. 27–29.
269 The official website of the ILO, Press Release [http://www.ilo.org].

Chapter 4 *Between Pro-Natalist and Anti-Natalist in the Arab Countries*

1 Thomas W. Lippman, *Egypt After Nasser: Sadat, Peace and the Mirage of Prosperity* (New York: Paragon Press, 1989), p. 164.
2 Todaro, *Economic Development*, seventh edition, p. 209.
3 According to UN data from the early 1990s, only 25% of the total worldwide population living in developed countries were responsible for 85% of all forest products consumed, 72% of steel products, and 75% of worldwide energy use. Mazur, "Beyond the Numbers," p. 3.
4 On Thomas Malthus' personal life, education, etc., see: www.blupete.com/Literature/Biographies/Philosophy/Malthus/htm.
5 Thomas Robert Malthus, *An Essay on the Principle of Population*, edited by Philip Appleman (New York: W. W. Norton, 1976).
6 Geometric ratio: 2, 4, 8, 16, 32 etc.
7 Arithmetic ratio: 2, 4, 6, 8, 10, etc.
8 Todaro, *Economic Development*, seventh edition, pp. 224–26; Gilbar, *Kalkalat ha-Mizrah ha-Tikhon*, pp. 39–40.
9 On the neo-Malthusianism doctrine, see: Pressat, *The Dictionary of Demography*, pp. 157–58.
10 UN, *World Population Monitoring–2001*, p. 28.
11 Steven K. Wisensale and Amany A. Khodair, "The Two-child Family: The Egyptian Model of Family Planning," *Journal of Comparative Family Studies*, Vol. 29, No. 3 (Autumn 1998), p. 503; Nam and Philliber, *Population*, p. 38.
12 UN, *World Population Monitoring–2001*, p. 1.

13 *Ibid.*, p. 16.

14 Wisensale and Khodair, "The Two-child Family," p. 503.

15 Todaro, *Economic Development*, seventh edition, p. 234–38; "Links between Population and Economic Growth," *Population Today*, Vol. 14, No. 2 (March 1986), pp. 3, 8.

16 See: Richards and Waterbury, *A Political Economy of the Middle East*, second edition, p. 89.

17 The US, Department of Commerce, US Census Bureau, *International Data Base* [http:/www.census.gov].

18 National Academy of Sciences, *Rapid Population Growth: Consequences and Policy Implications* (Baltimore and London: Johns Hopkins University Press, 1971), p. 70.

19 UN, Department of Economic and Social Affairs, Population Division, *National Population Policies* (New York, 1998), p. 1.

20 Findlay and Findlay, *Population and Development in the Third World*, p. 67. Another two definitions, one of a UN demographic expert group and the second of Bernard R. Berelson, the President of the Population Council in New York (1968–1974), appear in Hanna Rizk, "Population Policies: Scope, Goals, Means and Problems," *Population Bulletin of ECWA*, No. 7 (July 1974), pp. 132–34.

21 See in this regard: National Academy of Sciences, *Rapid Population Growth*, p. 70.

22 See, e.g., UN, Department of International Economic and Social Affairs, Population Division, *Fertility, Contraception and Population Policies* (New York, 2003), p. 7.

23 "Neo-Colonialism" is a political term that was adopted by many developing countries during the 1950s and the 1960s by which the Western political-military dominance over the developing countries was simply replaced by Western "economic dominance."

24 The "Dependency Theory" maintains that the increasing economic gaps between the "central countries," i.e., the Western developed countries, and the "peripheral countries," i.e., the developing countries, were caused, first and foremost, by the former's use of the latter's natural resources during the colonial period.

25 See: Joseph Chamie, "Trends, Variations, and Contradictions in National Policies to Influence Fertility," in Jason L. Finkle and C. Alison McIntosh (eds.), *The New Politics of Population: Conflict and Consensus in Family Planning*, Supplement to Vol. 20 of *Population and Development Review* (New York: The Population Council, 1994), p. 37; Kelley Lee and Gill Walt, "Linking National and Global Population Agendas: Case Studies From Eight Developing Countries," *Third World Quarterly*, Vol. 16, No. 2 (1995), p. 259.

26 Gabriel Baer, *'Arviyey ha-Mizrah ha-Tikhon*, second edition (Tel Aviv: Hakibbutz Hameuchad, 1973), p. 39 (Hebrew).

27 UN, *Fertility, Contraception and Population Policies*, p. 20.

28 Adnan Habbab, "Family Planning in the Syrian Arab Republic," Paper presented at the First Regional population Conference of ECWA, Beirut, February 18 – March 1, 1974, pp. 5–6.

29 I. Lévi, "Le Recensement de la Population de l'Egypte de 1917," *L'Egypte Contemporaine*, Vol. 13, No. 67 (1922). Quoted from: Philippe Fargues, "State Policies and the Birth Rate in Egypt: From Socialism to Liberalism," *Population and Development Review*, Vol. 23, No. 1(1997), p. 116.

30 Wendell Cleland, *The Population Problem in Egypt* (Lancaster, PA: Science Press Printing Company, 1936).

31 Azriel Karni, "Temurot be-Yahas la-Piquah 'al ha-Yeluda ba-Mizrah ha-Tikhon," *Hamizrah Hehadash*, Vol. 17 (1967), p. 230 (Hebrew).

32 Baer, *'Arviyey ha-Mizrah ha-Tikhon*, p. 39.

33 Peter J. Donaldson and Amy Ong Tsui, "The International Family Planning Movement," *Population Bulletin*, Vol. 45, No. 3 (November 1990), pp. 9–10.

34 Stanley P. Johnson, *World Population – Turning the Tide: Three Decades of Progress*

(London, Dordrecht, and Boston: Graham & Trotman/Martinus Nijhoff, 1994), pp. 103–4.

35 Karni, Temurot be-Yahas la-Piquah 'al ha-Yeluda ba-Mizrah ha-Tikhon," p. 231.

36 J. Mayone Stycos, Hussein Abdel Aziz Sayed, Roger Avery, and Samuel Fridman, *Community Development and Family Planning: An Egyptian Experiment* (Boulder and London: Westview Press, 1988), p. 14.

37 Khalid Ikram, *Egypt: Economic Management in a Period of Transition*, A World Bank Country Economic Report (Baltimore and London: The Johns Hopkins University Press, 1980), p. 110.

38 Mohammed Neguib, *Egypt's Destiny* (London: Victor Gollancz Ltd., 1955), pp. 158–62; Nazek Nosseir, "Egypt: Population, Urbanization, and Development," in Dan Tschirgi (ed.), *Development in the Age of Liberalization: Egypt and Mexico* (Cairo: The American University in Cairo Press, 1996), p. 191.

39 Cited from: Gadalla, *Is There Hope?*, p. 212.

40 Charles Issawi, *Egypt in Revolution* (London: Oxford University Press, 1963), p. 302.

41 Hussein Abdel-Aziz Sayed, "The Population Family Planning Program in Egypt: Structure and Performance," *Population Studies*, Vol. 11, No. 70 (July–September 1984), p. 7.

42 Saad Eddin Ibrahim, "State, Women, and Civil Society: An Evaluation of Egypt's Population Policy," in Carla Makhlouf Obermeyer (ed.), *Family, Gender, and Population in the Middle East* (Cairo: The American University in Cairo Press, 1995), pp. 59–60.

43 Stycos et al., *Community Development and Family Planning*, p. 14; Sayed, "The Population Family Planning Program in Egypt," p. 7.

44 On 'Abd al-Nasser's populism leadership style, see: Elie Podeh and Onn Winckler, "Introduction: Nasserism as a Form of Populism," in Podeh and Winckler (eds.), *Rethinking Nasserism*, pp. 18–28.

45 Ajami quoted in the Preface of Gouda Abdel-Khalek and Robert Tignor (eds.), *The Political Economy of Income Distribution in Egypt* (New York: Holmes and Meier, 1982), p. 9.

46 Donaldson, *Nature Against Us*, p. 117.

47 Other major donors to the UNFPA were Japan and Sweden.

48 Jason L. Finkle and C. Alison McIntosh, "The New Politics of Population," in Finkle and McIntosh (eds.), *The New Politics of Population*, pp. 8–9.

49 Donaldson, *Nature Against Us*, p. 42; p. 48, table 3.1.

50 Nam and Philliber, *Population*, p. 299.

51 John W. Thomas and Merilee S. Grindle, "Political Leadership and Policy Characteristics in Population Policy Reform," in Finkle and McIntosh (eds.), *The New Politics of Population*, p. 53.

52 IBRD, *The Population Program of the Government of Tunisia: A Second Review*, Report No. 651–TUN (February 27, 1975), p. 6.

53 G. M. Stubbs, "Population Policy in the Arab Countries," in Abdel-Rahim Omran, *Population in the Arab World: Problems and Prospects* (London: Croom Helm, 1980), p. 181.

54 UN, *Fertility, Contraception and Population Policies*, p. 20.

55 On the earlier stages of the Tunisian family planning program, see: International Planned Parenthood Federation-Middle East and North Africa Region, "Family Planning and Population Policies in the Middle East and North Africa," in James Allman (ed.), *Women's Status and Fertility in the Muslim World* (New York and London: Praeger, 1978), pp. 42–43; Robert J. Lapham, "Population Policies in the Middle East and North Africa," *Middle East Studies Association Bulletin*, Vol. 11, No. 2 (May 1, 1977), pp. 7–8.

56 IBRD, *The Population Program of the Government of Tunisia*, p. 3.

57 For the Arabic version of the National Charter, see: *al-Ahram*, May 22, 1962. The English translation appears in: Nissim Rejwan, *Nasserist Ideology: Its Exponents and Critics* (New York: John Wiley & Sons, 1974), pp. 195–265.

58 On the factors for the collapse of the unification between Egypt and Syria, see: Elie Podeh, *The Decline of Arab Unity: The Rise and Fall of the United Arab Republic* (Brighton and Portland: Sussex Academic Press, 1999), pp. 110–58.

59 Thomas and Grindle, "Political Leadership and Policy Characteristics in Population Policy Reform," p. 60.

60 On Egypt's family planning program during the second half of the 1960s, see: Gad G. Gilbar, "Family Planning Under Mubarak," in his *Population Dilemmas in the Middle East*, pp. 117–19; Gadalla, *Is There Hope?* pp. 213–19.

61 Wisensale and Khodair, "The Two-child Family," p. 505.

62 International Planned Parenthood Federation-Middle East and North Africa Region, "Family Planning and Population Policies in the Middle East and North Africa," p. 37.

63 Muhammad Faour, "Fertility Policy and Family Planning in the Arab Countries," *Studies in Family Planning*, Vol. 20, No. 5 (September/October 1989), p. 256; Mazur, "Beyond the Numbers," p. 11.

64 Sayed, "The Population Family Planning Program in Egypt," pp. 9–12. See also: WB, *Egypt: Staff Appraisal of A Second Population Project* (Washington, D.C., August 14, 1978), p. 4.

65 On the problems with the implementation of the Egyptian family planning program during the second half of the 1960s and early 1970s, see: Gadalla, *Is there Hope?*, pp. 215–19; Mahasen Mostafa Hassanin, Amany Mousa Mohamed, and Galaa Helmy Selem, "Estimating Family Planning Target Population of Egypt in 1997," in *CDC 24th Annual Seminar on Population Issues and the Challenges of the 21st Century in the Middle East, Africa, and Asia*, Research Monograph Series, No. 24 (Cairo, 1995), p. 441.

66 Lapham, "Population Policies in the Middle East and North Africa," p. 6.

67 Chamie, "Trends, Variations, and Contradictions," p. 37.

68 Gad G. Gilbar, "Nasser's Soft Revolution," in his *Population Dilemmas in the Middle East*, pp. 84–85.

69 Hartley, *Population: Quantity vs. Quality*, pp. 310–11; Johnson, *World Population*, p. 93.

70 Johnson, *World Population*, pp. 93–94.

71 Also in the case of Iran, the initiative to adopt a family planning program in the late 1980s was made by professionals in the Central Bureau of Statistics who conducted the 1986 population census and by professionals in the Ministries of Health and Education. See in this regard: Homa Hoodfar and Samad Assadpour, "The Politics of Population Policy in the Islamic Republic of Iran," *Studies in Family Planning*, Vol. 31, No. 1 (March 2000), pp. 22-24.

72 Syrian Arab Republic, Office of the Prime Minister, Central Bureau of Statistics, *Socio-Economic Development in Syria, 1960–1970*, Studies Series, No. 73 (Damascus, 1973), p. 47.

73 Charles W. Warren et al., "Fertility and Family Planning in Jordan: Results from the 1985 Jordan Husbands' Fertility Survey," *Studies in Family Planning*, Vol. 21, No. 1 (1990), pp. 33–34.

74 ESCWA, *Population Situation, 1990*, p. 101.

75 Ronald Freedman and Bernard Berelson, "The Record of Family Planning Programs," *Studies in Family Planning*, Vol. 7, No. 1 (1976), p. 5.

76 UN, *Fertility, Contraception and Population Policies*, p. 16.

77 Donaldson and Tsui, "The International Family Planning Movement," p. 11; Godfrey Roberts, "Population Policy Issues in Selected Asian Countries," in Godfrey Roberts (ed.), *Population Policy: Contemporary Issues* (New York: Praeger, 1990), p. 86.

78 WB, *Population and Development: Implications for the World Bank* (Washington, D.C., 1994), pp. 51–52.

79 See, e.g., ECA, "Population Policy Overview" [http://www.uneca.org].

80 Donaldson, *Nature Against Us*, p. 114.

81 On the nature of the Syrian *Ba'thi-'Alawi* regime, see: Eyal Zisser, *Paneha shel Surya: Hevra, Mishtar, ve-Medina* (Tel Aviv: Hakibbutz Hameuchad, 2003), pp. 127–87 (Hebrew).

82 On the confrontation between the *Ba'thi-'Alawi* regime and the "Muslim Brothers" since the mid-1970s, see, e.g., Raymond A. Hinnebusch, *Authoritarian Power and State Formation in Ba'thist Syria* (Boulder: Westview Press, 1990), pp. 291–99; Moshe Ma'oz, *Asad: The Sphinx of Damascus: A Political Biography* (New York: Weidenfeld & Nicholson, 1988), pp. 159–63.

83 See, e.g., *Tishrin*, June 22, 1980.

84 A broader discussion on the Syrian natalist policy of that period appears in: Winckler, *Demographic Developments and Population Policies in Ba'thist Syria*, pp. 111–14.

85 ESCWA, *Demographic and Related Socio-Economic Data Sheets*, No. 5 (1987), p. 204, table 2.

86 Asher Susser, "ha-Ahim ha-Muslemim be-Yarden: Du-Qiyum ve-'Imut Mevuqar," in Meir Litvak (ed.), *Islam ve-Demoqratyya ba-'Olam ha-'Aravi* (Tel Aviv: Hakibbutz Hameuchad, 1997), pp. 125–26 (Hebrew).

87 On the Jordanian anti-natalist measures, see: Gad G. Gilbar, "Jordan's Road to Family Planning Policy," in his *Population Dilemmas*, pp. 73–76; Winckler, *Population Growth and Migration in Jordan,* pp. 82–84.

88 ESCWA, *Population Situation, 1990*, p. 94, table 5.4.

89 Charles F. Gallagher, "Population and Development in Egypt, Part 1: Birth and Death on the Nile," *American University Field Stuff Report*, No. 31 (1981), p. 11; Sayed, "The Population Family Planning Program in Egypt," p. 19; WB, *Egypt: Staff Appraisal of A Second Population Project* (August 14, 1978), pp. 5, 8; Stycos et al., *Community Development and Family Planning*, p. 15.

90 On the relationship between Sadat and the Islamic opposition in Egypt, see: Raymond A. Hinnebusch, *Egyptian Politics Under Sadat: The Post-Populist Development of an Authoritarian-Modernizing State* (Cambridge: Cambridge University Press, 1985), pp. 206–8.

91 Saad Eddin Ibrahim, "State, Women, and Civil Society," p. 65.

92 Lippman, *Egypt After Nasser*, p. 162.

93 CAPMAS, *Statistical Yearbook, 1952–1992*, p. 28, table 1–18.

94 CAPMAS, *Statistical Yearbook, 1952–1984*, p. 30.

95 *Ibid.*, p. 8.

96 CAPMAS, *Statistical Yearbook, 1952–1992*, p. 28, table 1–18.

97 Ami Ayalon, "Demographya, Politiqa, ve-Masoret be-Mitzrayim shel Mubarak," in Ayalon and Gilbar (eds.), *Demographya ve-Politiqa be-Medinot 'Arav*, p. 32 (Hebrew).

98 *MEED*, December 2, 1983, p. 10; August 10, 1984, p. 10.

99 *Population Today*, Vol. 15, No. 5 (May 1987), p. 5.

100 CAPMAS, *Statistical Yearbook, 1952–1992*, p. 28, table 1–18.

101 Riad Tabbarah, "Challenges in Arab Demography," *Population Bulletin of ESCWA*, No. 33 (December 1988), pp. 3–4.

102 Hassan M. Yousif and Ahmad A. Hammouda, "Alternative Population Projection Scenarios by Education Attainment for Egypt, the Sudan and Tunisia," *Population Bulletin of ESCWA*, No. 43 (1995), p. 68. See also in this regard: Jeffrey G. Williamson and Tarik M. Yousef, "Demographic Transitions and Economic Performance in the Middle East and North Africa," in Sirageldin (ed.), *Human Capital*, p. 17.

103 Cited from John Waterbury, *The Egypt of Nasser and Sadat: The Political Economy of Two Regimes* (Princeton: Princeton University Press, 1983), p. 44.

104 WB, *Egypt: Staff Appraisal of A Second Population Project* (August 14, 1978), p. 4, table 2.

105 On the change in the US' approach toward family planning in developing countries

following the ascendancy of Reagan, see: Jason L. Finkle and Barbara B. Crane, "Ideology and Politics at Mexico City: The United States at the 1984 International Conference on Population," *Population and Development Review*, Vol. 11, No. 1 (March 1985), pp. 11–16; Donaldson and Tsui, "The International Family Planning Movement," pp. 12–14.

106 Finkle and Crane, "Ideology and Politics at Mexico City," p. 11.

107 During the period 1965–1973, the GDP growth rate in Tunisia was 6.5% on annual average, as compared with 4.1% during the decade of 1973–1983. WB, *World Development Report*, various issues.

108 WB, *World Development Report–1978*, pp. 104–5, table 15.

109 Finkle and Crane, "Ideology and Politics at Mexico City," p. 1.

110 Ronald Freedman, "Family Planning Programs in the Third World," *The Annals of the American Academy*, No. 510 (July 1990), p. 34.

111 The journal *Population and Development Review* devoted Vol. 20 (1994) to this debate. See the various articles in this volume.

112 UNICEF, *The State of the World's Children–1988*, pp. 72–73, table 5.

113 ESCWA, *Survey, 1998–1999*, pp. 45–46.

114 WB, *World Tables, 1989–90 Edition*, pp. 472–73.

115 *Ibid.*, pp. 344–45.

116 See in this regard: Faour, "Fertility Policy and Family Planning in the Arab Countries," p. 261.

117 Stubbs, "Population Policy in the Arab Countries," p. 173.

118 Baquer Salman al-Najjar, "Population Policies in the Countries of the Gulf Cooperation Council: Politics and Society," *Immigrants & Minorities*, Vol. 12, No. 2 (July 1993), p. 212.

119 Gause, *Oil Monarchies*, p. 54.

120 Thus, for example, despite the severe damage to the Kuwaiti economy caused by the Iraqi invasion, a large increase in the marriage grant to Kuwaiti nationals was approved by the Council of Ministers at the beginning of 1992. According to this decision, eligible Kuwaiti males were entitled to receive $14,000 (half as a grant and half as a loan) for their marriage to Kuwaiti women. This amount was twice the previous sum. The reason for such a large increase, according to the Kuwaiti Minister of Finance, Nasser 'Abdullah al-Roudhan, was "to encourage Kuwaiti youths to marry." Source: *Gulf States Newsletter,* April 6, 1992, p. 5.

121 UN Department of International Economic and Social Affairs, Population Division, "World Population Policies-Qatar," Vol. III (1990), pp. 39–40; Gause, *Oil Monarchies*, pp. 60–61; al-Najjar, "Population Policies in the Countries of the Gulf Cooperation Council," p. 212.

122 Allan G. Hill, "Population Growth in the Middle East and North Africa: Selected Policy Issues," in A. L. Udovich (ed.), *The Middle East: Oil, Conflict and Hope* (Lexington: Lexington Books, 1976), p. 36; James Allman "The Demographic Transition in the Middle East and North Africa," in Allman (ed.), *Women's Status and Fertility in the Muslim World*, pp. 24–25.

123 Shirley Kay, "Social Change in Modern Saudi Arabia," in Tim Niblock (ed.), *State, Society and Economy in Saudi Arabia* (London: Croom Helm, 1982), p. 180.

124 ESCWA, *Demographic and Related Socio-Economic Data Sheets*, No. 5 (1987), p. 4, table 2; p. 164, table 2; p. 184, table 2; p. 224, table 2.

125 Gilbar, "Family Planning Under Mubarak," p. 120; ESCWA, *Population Situation, 1990*, p. 96.

126 Kamran Asdar Ali, *Planning the Family in Egypt: New Bodies, New Selves* (Austin: University of Texas Press, 2002), pp. 30–31.

127 Mona A. Khalifa, "Family Planning and Sustainable Development in Egypt," *CDC Series on Population and Development*, No. 5 (Cairo, 1994), pp. 4–5; Gilbar, "Family Planning Under Mubarak," p. 120.

128 Ali, *Planning the Family in Egypt*, p. 33; Khalifa, "Family Planning and Sustainable Development in Egypt," pp. 12–13. According to the 1984 Egypt Contraceptive Prevalence Survey, the "ideal" or the desired number of children was 3.3, but the actual total fertility rate was much higher as a result of the considerable unmet need for contraceptives. *Population Today*, Vol. 15, No, 5 (May 1987), p. 5.

129 *The Egyptian* Gazette, February 11; July 23, 1987.

130 UN Department of International Economic and Social Affairs, "World Population Policies," Vol. III, pp. 159–60; Faour, "Fertility Policy and Family Planning in the Arab Countries," p. 260.

131 ESCWA, *Population Situation, 1990*, p. 192.

132 In 1990, the total fertility rate in China was 2.5 children per woman as compared with 6.4 in 1965. In Singapore and South Korea the total fertility rate declined to below replacement-level in the second half of the 1980s as compared with a total fertility rate of 4.7 and 4.9, respectively, in 1965. See: WB, W*orld Development Report–1992*, pp. 271–72, table 27. The Chinese family planning slogan was: "One is best, at most two, never a third." On the Chinese "one-child policy," see: UN, Department of International Economic and Social Affairs, *Case Studies in Population Policy: China*, Population Policy Paper, No. 20 (New York, 1989), pp. 37–45; Susan E. Short and Fengying Zhai, "Looking Locally at China's "One-child Policy," *Studies in Family Planning*, Vol. 29, No. 4 (December 1998), pp. 373–85; Edwin A. Winckler, "Chinese Reproductive Policy at the Turn of the Millennium: Dynamic Stability," *Population and Development Review*, Vol. 28, No. 3 (2001), pp. 379–418. On Singapore's family planning program, see: UNFPA, *Singapore*, Population Profile, No. 1 (New York, 1977); J. John Palen, "Population Policy: Singapore," in Roberts (ed.), *Population Policy*, pp. 168–69.

133 UN, *Fertility, Contraception and Population Policies*, p. 28.

134 See in this regard: Lee and Walt, "Linking National and Global Population Agendas," p. 264.

135 In May 1990, North and South Yemens were united again into one country.

136 Nazy Roudi, "Population Policies Vary in Middle East," *Population Today*, Vol. 21 (April 1993), p. 10.

137 Gihan A. Shawky, "Detecting Changes in Fertility in Algeria, Egypt and Yemen," *CDC Working Paper*, No. 42 (1999), pp. 36–37; ESCWA, *Population Policies and Programmes in the Arab World*, by Hussein A. Sayed. Arab Population Conference, Amman, April 4–8, 1993, p. 5.

138 UN Department of International Economic and Social Affairs, Population Division, "Levels and Trends in Fertility in Oman and Yemen," by Eltigani E. Eltigani, *Workshop on Prospects for Fertility Decline in High Fertility Countries*, New York, July 9–11, 2001, p. 9.

139 *Ibid.*, p. 5.

140 Mohamed Kamel Marwan (Assistant General Secretary of the NPC), "Population Strategy, 1992/2007," *Population Studies*, Vol. 14, No. 75 (July-September 1992), pp. 113–15.

141 Mahasen Mostafa Hassanin, Amany Mousa Mohamed, and Galaa Helmy Selem, "Estimating Family Planning Target Population of Egypt in 1997," in *CDC 24th Annual Seminar on Population Issues and the Challenges of the 21st Century in the Middle East, Africa, and Asia*, Research Monograph Series, No. 24 (Cairo, 1995), p. 442.

142 Saad Eddin Ibrahim, "State, Women, and Civil Society," p. 62.

143 Arab Republic of Egypt, National Population Information Center, special issue, October 14, 1991.

144 *Egypt Demographic and Health Survey–2000*, p. 4.

145 Naguib Ghita (Consultant of Statistics and Information at the National Population Council), "A Seminar on the Preliminary Results of the 1996 Census on Population,

Housing and Establishments in the Light of the National Population Strategy," *Population Studies*, Vol. 16, No. 81 (January-March 1998), p. 103.

146 The Hashemite Kingdom of Jordan, Ministry of Planning, *Plan for Economic and Social Development, 1993–1997* (Amman, 1993), p. 155.

147 *Jordan Population and Family Health Survey–1997*, pp. 2–3.

148 The Hashemite Kingdom of Jordan, Ministry of Planning, Economic Aid Coordination Unit, *Partners in Development*, No. 31 (December 1999), p. 5.

149 *Jordan Times*, May 27, 2003.

150 *Jordan Times*, July 23–24, 2004.

151 See: Eyal Zisser, "Syria," *MECS*, Vol. 18 (1994), p. 619.

152 *Syrian Maternal and Child Health Survey–1993*, p. 177.

153 Mohammed al-Imadi, "The Economic and Investment Policies in Syria," in Hans Hopfinger and Raslan Khadour (eds.), *Economic Development and Investment Policies in Syria* (Neustadt an der Aisch: Verlagsdrucherei Schmidt, 1998), p. 22.

154 *Tishrin*, May 19, 2002.

155 EIU, *Country Profile–Algeria, 2001*, p. 17.

156 On the changing Iranian natalist approach and the adoption of official family planning program in 1989, see, WB, *Fertility and Family Planning in Iran*, by Rodolfo A. Bulatao and Gail Richardson, Discussion Paper Series, No. 13 (December 1994); Hoodfar and Assadpour, "The Politics of Population Policy in the Islamic Republic of Iran," pp. 19–34. Iran, it should be noted, is the only Middle Eastern country that promotes sterilization for both females and males. Farzaneh Roudi, "Surprising Decline in Iran's Growth Rates," *Population Today*, Vol. 25, No. 11 (November 1997), p. 4.

157 The Islamic Republic of Iran, *National Report on Population, The Islamic Republic of Iran*. Submitted to the International Conference on Population and Development, Cairo, 1994, pp. 12-15.

158 McIntosh and Finkle, "The Cairo Conference on Population and Developmen," p. 240; Mazur, "Beyond the Numbers," p. 12-13.

159 On the failure of the Omanization policy during the 1980s and the early 1990s, see: Winckler, "The Challenge of Foreign Workers in the Persian/Arabian Gulf: The Case of Oman," pp. 39–41.

160 International Republican Institute, *Oman: Political Development & the Maglis Ash'Shura* (Washington, D. C., July 1995), pp. 26–27. See also the speech of Sultan Qabus in his annual meet-the-people tour of January 1994 – *al-Wasat* (London), January 24, 1994.

161 Sultanate of Oman, Ministry of Development, *The Fifth Five-Year Development Plan, 1996–2000* (Muscat, July 1997), p. 192.

162 ESCWA, *Survey, 1996–1997*, p. 133; UN, "Levels and Trends in Fertility in Oman and Yemen," by Eltigani E. Eltigani, p. 9.

163 *Ibid.*, p. 5.

164 The Kingdom of Saudi Arabia, Ministry of Planning, *Sixth Development Plan, 1415–1420* [1995–2000] (Riyadh, 1996), p. 89.

165 UN, *Fertility, Contraception and Population Policies*, p. 23.

166 Thus, for example, in the 2000 report of the Saudi Arabian Monetary Agency, it was written that the high fertility rate was "due to the rise in the standard of living in the Kingdom . . ." (p. 261).

167 Saudi Arabia Monetary Agency, *Thirty-Eighth Annual Report 1423* [2002] (Riyadh, 2003), pp. 52, 56.

168 The Bahraini government offers subsidized family planning services through the public health clinics. See: Population Reference Bureau, *Country Profiles for Population and Reproductive Health: Policy Developments and Indicators–2003*, p. 176 [http://www.prb.org]. Indeed, as indicated in table 2.5, the fertility rates of the indigenous Bahraini population are the lowest among the GCC countries.

169 J. S. Birks, "The Demographic Challenge in the Arab Gulf," in B.R. Pridham (ed.), *The Arab Gulf and the Arab World* (London: Croom Helm, 1988), pp. 136–37.

170 Thus, for example, Steven Wisensale and Amany Khodair ended their article, "The Two-child Family," by stating that: "Although Egypt's experience in family planning has not been flawless, it represents one model from which other nations can learn" (p. 513).

171 *Egypt Demographic and Health Survey–2000*, p. 48, table 4.4.

172 Ali, *Planning the Family in Egypt*, pp. 42–43.

173 ECA, *The State of Demographic Transition in Africa*, p. 40.

174 *Egypt Demographic and Health Survey–2000*, p. 48, table 4.4.

175 CAPMAS, *Statistical Yearbook, 1994–2001*, p. 30.

176 Syria, *Statistical Abstract–2001*, p. 62, table 6/2.

177 *Jordan Population and Family Health Survey–1997*, p. 36, table 4.2; p. 41, table 4.7.

178 *Jordan Times*, August 4, 2004.

179 *Jordan Population and Family Health Survey–1997*, p. 28, table 3.3.

180 *Jordan Times*, July 7, 2004.

181 See, e.g., Obermeyer, "Islam, Women and Politics," p. 33.

182 UNDP, *The Arab Human Development Report–2002* (New York, 2002).

183 WB, "Expanded Trade and Investment Needed in MENA," [http://www.worldbank.org].

184 See in this regard the interviews conducted by John Waterbury during the 1970s with Egyptian intellectuals and politicians regarding their views on family planning in Egypt. *Egypt: Burdens of the Past – Options for the Future* (Indiana: American University Field Stuff, 1978), p. 61.

185 Gred Nonneman, "Rentiers and Autocrats, Monarchs and Democrats, State and Society: The Middle East Between Globalization, Human 'Agency,' and Europe," *International Affairs*, Vol. 77, No. 1 (2001), p. 159.

186 On the sharp increase of intra-Arab trade following the "oil boom," see, e.g., Wilson, *Economic Development in the Middle East*, pp. 171–75.

187 On 'Abd al-Nasser's "soft economic approach," Khalid Muhi al-Din wrote that 'Abd al-Nasser thought that he could raise sufficient financial resources for implementing the massive development plans, for improving and expanding public services, and for increasing consumption by massive subsidies through the nationalization of the Suez Canal company and the nationalization of foreign assets. See: Leonard Binder, "Gamal 'Abd al-Nasser: Iconology, Ideology and Demonology," in Podeh and Winckler (eds.), *Rethinking Nasserism*, p. 57. Regarding Egypt's "soft state" and its overall macroeconomic implications, see: John Waterbury, "The 'Soft State' and the Open Door: Egypt's Experience with Economic Liberalization, 1974–1984," *Comparative Politics*, Vol. 18 (October 1985), pp. 65–83; Gilbar, "Nasser's Soft Revolution," pp. 86–87.

188 Israel under the Ariel Sharon government constitutes as a perfect example for this political process.

189 The term "Dutch Disease" is connected to the term "*rentier* state" and refers to a situation in which a country enjoys large revenues from the export of certain natural resources and then deteriorates into a deep recession following a sharp decline in those revenues. This economic phenomenon is known as the "Dutch Disease" because its existence was first noted in the Netherlands in the 1960s following the discovery of North Sea gas. After a relatively short period of high revenues from the gas exports, the Dutch economy entered into a deep recession.

190 Victor Lavy and Eliezer Sheffer, *Foreign Aid and Economic Development in the Middle East: Egypt, Syria, and Jordan* (New York: Praeger Publishers, 1991).

191 Alan Richards, "Oil Wealth in the Arab World: Whence, to Whom, and Whither?" in Dan Tschirgi (ed.), *The Arab World Today* (Boulder and London: Lynne Rienner Publishers, 1994), p. 68.

192 Thus, for example, while the annual GDP growth rate in Turkey averaged 6.5% during the

years 1965–1973, it declined to 4.1% during the decade of 1973–1983. In Brazil, the annual average GDP growth in 1965–1973 was 9.8%, and it declined to 4.8% during the decade of 1973–1983. In Argentina, the rates were 4.3% and 0.4%, respectively. In many other developing countries worldwide, one can find very similar economic growth patterns during the 1960s and 1970s. See: WB, *World Development Report–1985*, pp. 176–77, table 2.

193 The following section on Tunisia family planning policy is based on Gad G. Gilbar and Onn Winckler, "Nasser's Family Planning Policy in Perspective," in Podeh and Winckler (eds.), *Rethinking Nasserism*, pp. 296-98.

194 ECA, *The State of Demographic Transition in Africa*, p. 3. See also: Youssef Courbage, "Issues in Fertility Transition in the Middle East and North Africa," *Economic Research Forum*, Working Paper 9903 (Cairo, 1999), p. 7.

195 See: London School of Hygiene & Tropical Medicine and United Nations Population Fund, by Kelley Lee, Gill Walt, Louisiana Lush, and John Cleland, *Population Policies and Programmes: Determinants and Consequences in Eight Developing Countries* (London, 1995), p. 41; Foreign Area Studies, the American University, edited by Harold D. Nelson, *Tunisia: A Country Study* (Washington, D.C., 1979), p. 86.

196 Lee and Walt, "Linking National and Global Population Agendas," p. 259. See also in this regard: Ali, *Planning the Family in Egypt*, p. 154.

197 See in this regard: K. L. Brown, "The Campaign to Encourage Family Planning in Tunisia and Some Responses at the Village Level," *Middle Eastern Studies*, Vol. 17, No. 1 (January 1981), p. 82; Beaujot and Bchir, *Fertility in Tunisia*, pp. 36-37.

Conclusions and Prospects

1 Gilbar, *Kalkalat ha-Mizrah ha-Tikhon*, pp. 40–41.

2 UN, Department of International Economic and Social Affairs, Population Division, *Population Growth and Economic Development*. Report on the Consultative Meeting of Economists Convened by the United Nations Population Fund (New York, September 28–29, 1992), p. 9.

3 See, e.g., Paul Rivlin, "Nasser's Egypt and Park's Korea: A Comparison of their Economic Achievements," in Podeh and Winckler (eds.), *Rethinking Nasserism*, pp. 264–81.

4 On the January 1977 "food riots" in Egypt, see, e.g., Gilbar, *Kalkalat ha-Mizrah ha-Tikhon*, p. 201.

5 See: Colton, "The Maghrebi Economies as Emerging Markets?" p. 160.

6 See: Asher Susser, "Jordan," *MECS*, Vol. 20 (1996), pp. 425–32.

7 See: Joseph Kostiner, "Yemen," *MECS*, Vol. 22 (1998), pp. 664–65.

8 El-Ghonemy, *Affluence and Poverty in the Middle East*, pp. 178–80; 200–5.

9 ESCWA, *Survey, 2004, Summary*, p. 1.

10 *The Middle East*, April 2003, pp. 54–55.

11 EIU, *Country Profile–Bahrain, 2003*, p. 20.

12 UN Population Fund, *Population and the Environment: The Challenges Ahead* (New York 1991), p. 21. Cited from Mazur, "Beyond the Numbers," p. 8.

Bibliography

Official Publications

The State of Bahrain

Central Statistics Organization, Directorate of Statistics. *Statistical Abstract*, various issues, 1980–2002. Manama.

Al-Jihaz al-Markazi lil-Ihsa. *Al-Ta'dad al-'Amm lil-Sukan wal-Masakin wal-Mabani wal-Munsha'at–1991*. Manama, 1992 (Arabic).

Ministry of Health. *Bahrain Child Health Survey–1989*. Manama, 1992.

Arab Republic of Egypt

CAPMAS (Central Agency for Public Mobilisation and Statistics). *Statistical Yearbook*, various issues, 1960–2002. Cairo.

—— *External Migration As A Demographic Phenomenon*. Cairo, 1994.

Ministry of Waqfs and Ministry of Information, State Information Service, Information, Education and Communication Center. *Islam's Attitude Towards Family Planning*. Cairo, 1994.

National Bank of Egypt. *The Underground Economy with Special Reference to the Case of Egypt*. By Ibrahim M. Oweiss. Cairo, 1995.

—— *The Egyptian Economy in Brief–2000*. Cairo, 2001.

Supreme Council for Family Planning and Population. "National Strategy Framework of Population, Human Resource Development and the Family Planning Program." *Population Studies*, No. 56 (January–March 1981).

National Population Council and Macro International Inc. (Calverton, Maryland USA) and Ministry of Health and Population. *Egypt Demographic and Health Survey–1995*. Cairo, September 1996.

—— *Egypt Demographic and Health Survey–2000*. Cairo, January 2001.

The European Union (the EU)

European Commission, Directorate-General for employment and Social Affairs. *Employment in Europe 2002: Recent Trends and Prospects*. Luxembourg, July 2002.

Statistical Office of the European Union. *Eurostat Yearbook–2002*. Luxembourg, 2003.

The Islamic Republic of Iran

National Report on Population, The Islamic Republic of Iran. Submitted to the International Conference on Population and Development, Cairo 1994.

The Hashemite Kingdom of Jordan

Department of Statistics. *Statistical Yearbook*, various issues, 1980–2002. Amman.
—— *Jordan Population and Family Health Survey–1990*. Amman, 1992.
—— *Jordan Population and Health Survey–1997*. Amman, 1998.
—— *Employment and Unemployment Survey*. February 2001, Principal Report. Amman, April 2001.
Ministry of Planning. *Plan for Economic and Social Development, 1993–1997*. Amman, 1993.
—— Economic Aid Coordination Unit. *Partners in Development*, No. 31, December 1999.
Central Bank of Jordan, Research Department. *Annual Report*, various issues. Amman.

The State of Kuwait

Ministry of Planning. Statistics and Information Center. *Annual Statistical Abstract*, various issues, 1966–2001. Kuwait.
Ministry of Health. *Kuwait Child Health Survey*. Edited by Rashid al-Rashoud and Samir Farid. Kuwait, 1991.
Central Bank of Kuwait. *Economic Report*, various issues, 1990–2001. Kuwait.

Kingdom of Morocco

Ministry of Public Health. *National Survey on Population and Health – Morocco, 1992*. Rabat, 1992.
—— and Macro International Inc. *Enquête de Panel sur la Population et la Santé* (EPPS), *1995*. Rabat, Janvier 1996.

Sultanate of Oman

Ministry of National Economy. *Statistical Yearbook*, various issues, 1980–2002. Muscat.
—— *Facts & Figures on Development Efforts, 1970–2000*. Muscat: Information and Public Center, November 2000.
Ministry of Development. National Statistical Department. *General Census of Population, Housing, and Establishments, 1993*. Muscat, 1995.
Development Council. *The Second Five-Year Development Plan, 1981–1985*. Muscat, 1981.
—— *The Fifth Five-Year Development Plan, 1996–2000*. Muscat, July 1997.
Ministry of Health. *Oman Child Health Survey*. Edited by Murtadha J. Suleiman, Ahmed al-Ghassany, and Samir Farid. Muscat, 1992.
—— *Oman Family Health Survey, 1995*. Edited by Ali J. M. Sulaiman, Asya al-Riyami, and Samir Farid. Muscat, 1996.
Ministry of Information. *The Speeches of H. M. Sultan Qaboos, 1970–1990*. Muscat, n.d.
Central Bank of Oman. *Annual Report–2001*. Muscat 2001.

Palestinian National Authority (PNA)

Central Bureau of Statistics. *The Demographic Survey in the West Bank and Gaza Strip*, final report. Ramallah, 1997.

State of Qatar

Presidency of the Council of Ministers, Central Statistical Organization. *Annual Statistical Abstract*, various issues, 1980–2000. Doha.
Ministry of Health. *Qatar Child Health Survey*. Edited by Abdul-Jalil Salman, Khalifa al-Jaber, and Samir Farid. Doha, 1991.
Ministry of Information. *Qatar into the Seventies*. Doha, May 1973.
Qatar National Bank. *Qatar Economic Review*, various issues, 1995–2001. Doha.

The Kingdom of Saudi Arabia

Ministry of Planning, Central Department of Statistics. *Statistical Yearbook*, various issues, 1995–2000. Riyadh.
—— *Sixth Development Plan, 1415–1420* AH [1995–2000]. Riyadh, 1996.

—— *Seventh Development Plan, 1420/21–1424/25* AH [2000–2004] Riyadh, 1999.
Ministry of Health. *Saudi Arabia Child Health Survey*. Edited by Yagob Al-Mazrou and Samir Farid. Riyadh, 1991.
Saudi Arabian Monetary Agency. Research and Statistics Department. *Annual Report*, various issues, 1985–2002. Riyadh.

Syrian Arab Republic

Office of the Prime Minister, Central Bureau of Statistics (CBS). *Statistical Abstract*, 1960–2002, various issues. Damascus.
—— *Socio-Economic Development in Syria, 1960–1970*, Studies Series, No. 73. Damascus, 1973.
—— and State Planning Commission in collaboration with the Population Council. *Rates of Natural Increase in the Syrian Region*. By M. Nader Hallak. Damascus, September 1979.
Factors of Population Growth and Their Future Trends. Paper Presented at a Seminar Held in Damascus, September 16–20, 1978, under the auspices of the Syrian CBS and UNFPA. Damascus, 1979.
—— and League of Arab States, Pan-Arab Project for Child Development. *Syrian Maternal and Child Health Survey–1993*. Principal Report. Damascus, 1999.

Tunisian Republic

Ministère du Développement Economique, Institut National de la Statistique. *Annuaire Statistique de la Tunisie*, various issues. Tunis.

United Kingdom (UK)

The British Embassy of Beirut, Middle East Development Division. By N. B. Hudson. *The First Population Census of Qatar*. April/May 1970. Beirut, October 1970.

The Cooperation Council of the Arab States of the Gulf (GCC)

Secretarial General, Statistical Department. *Statistical Bulletin*, No. 12 (2003).

Publications of Official International Organizations

The World Bank (WB)

World Development Report, various issues, 1978–2002. Published for the World Bank by Oxford University Press, Oxford and New York.
World Tables, various issues, 1984–1995. Published for the World Bank by Johns Hopkins University Press, Baltimore and London.
African Development Indicators, various issues. Washington, D.C.
Egypt: Staff Appraisal of A Second Population Project. Washington, D.C., August 14, 1978.
Population Change and Economic Development. Published for the World Bank by Oxford University Press, Oxford and New York, 1985.
Population and Development: Implications for the World Bank. Washington, D.C., 1994.
Fertility and Family Planning in Iran. By Rodolfo A. Bulatao and Gail Richardson. Discussion Paper Series, No. 13. December 1994.
Hashemite Kingdom of Jordan. A Quarterly Publication of the Jordan Country Unit, First Quarter 2003. Washington, D.C., 2003.
Labor Market Reforms, Growth and Unemployment in Labor-Exporting MENA Countries. By Pierre-Richard Agénor, Mustapha K. Nabli, Tarik Yousef, and Henning T. Jensen. Washington, D.C., 2003.

International Bank For Reconstruction and Development (IBRD)

The Population Program of the Government of Tunisia: A Second Review. Report No. 651–TUN. February 27, 1975.

International Monetary Fund (IMF)

International Financial Statistics Yearbook, various issues, 1990–2002. Washington, D.C.

Finance and Development (quarterly) [http://www.imf.org/external/pubs/ft/fandd/fda].

Economic Development of the Arab countries. Paper presented at a Seminar held in Bahrain, February 1–3, 1993. Edited by Said El-Naggar. Washington, D.C., 1993.

Jordan: Background Information on Selected Aspects of Adjustment and Growth Strategy. Washington, D.C., August 29, 1995.

Algeria: Selected Economic Issues. Stuff Country Report, No. 96/71. Washington, D.C., 1996.

Demography, Capital Dependency and Growth in MENA. By Tarik M. Yousef, African Department. January 31, 1998.

Algeria: Selected Economic Issues. Stuff Country Report, No. 98/87. Washington, D.C. 1998.

Tunisia: Recent Economic Developments. IMF Stuff Country Report 00/37. Washington, D.C. March 2000.

The United Nations (UN)

Department of Economic and Social Affairs, Population Division

Demographic Yearbook, various issues, 1970–1999. New York: UN Publications.

—— and UNFPA. *Population Policy Compendium–Bahrain*. New York, 1981.

Case Studies in Population Policy: Kuwait. Population Policy Paper, No. 15. New York, 1988.

"Mortality of Children Under Age 5: World Estimates and Projections, 1950–2025." *Population Studies*, No. 105. New York, 1988.

Case Studies in Population Policy: China. Population Policy Paper, No. 20. New York, 1989.

"World Population Policies." *Population Studies*, 3 Vols. New York, 1990.

Population Growth and Economic Development. Report on the Consultative Meeting of Economists Convened by the United Nations Population Fund. New York, September 28–29, 1992.

National Population Policies. New York, 1998.

World Population Prospects: The 2000 Revision. New York 2001.

World Population Monitoring–2001: Population, Environment and Development. New York, 2001.

"Levels and Trends in Fertility in Oman and Yemen." By Eltigani E. Eltigani, *Workshop on Prospects for Fertility Decline in High Fertility Countries*. New York, July 9–11, 2001.

World Urbanization Prospects: The 2001 Revision. New York, March 2002.

Fertility, Contraception and Population Policies. New York, 2003.

United Nations Economic Commission for Africa (ECA)

The State of Demographic Transition in Africa. Addis Ababa. December 2001.

United Nations Development Programme (UNDP)

Human Development Report, various issues, 1994–2004. Published for the UNDP by Oxford University Press, Oxford and New York.

The Arab Human Development Report–2002. Published for the UNDP by Oxford University Press, Oxford and New York, 2002.

—— and Arab Fund for Economic and Social Development. *Arab Human Development Report–2003*. Amman: SYNTAX, 2003.

United Nations Educational, Scientific, and Cultural Organization (UNESCO)

Statistical Yearbook, various issues, 1967–1998. Paris.

United Nations Economic and Social Office in Beirut (UNESOB)

"Demographic Situation in the Syrian Arab Republic." By M. N. al-Hallak. Expert Group

Meeting on the Application of Demographic Data and Studies in Development Planning of the UN Economic and Social Office in Beirut. Beirut, December 7–12, 1970.

UN Economic (and Social) Commission for Western Asia (ECWA/ESCWA)

Demographic and Related Socio-Economic Data Sheets for Countries of the Economic and Social Commission for Western Asia, various issues, 1978–2001.Beirut, Baghdad, and Amman.
National Accounts Studies of the ESCWA Region, various issues. 1995–2001. New York.
Statistical Abstract of the ESCWA Region, various issues, 1979–2001. New York.
Survey of Economic and Social Developments in the ESCWA Region, various issues, 1982–2004. New York.
Habbab, Adnan. "Family Planning in the Syrian Arab Republic." Paper presented at the First Regional Population Conference of ECWA. Beirut, February 18 – March 1, 1974.
Technical Secretariat. "Achievements, Plans and Recommendations Relating to Population and Housing Censuses in the Sultanate of Oman." Economic Commission for Western Asia, Expert Group Meeting on Census Techniques. Beirut December 12–16, 1977.
The Population Situation in the ECWA Region–Jordan. Beirut, 1979.
The Population Situation in the ECWA Region–Saudi Arabia. Beirut, 1979.
The Population Situation in the ECWA Region–Qatar. Beirut, 1980.
The population Situation in the ECWA Region–Syrian Arab Republic. Beirut, 1980.
Infant and Childhood Mortality in Western Asia. Baghdad, December 1989.
Population Situation in the ESCWA Region, 1990. Amman, May 1992.
Population Policies and Programmes in the Arab World. By Hussein A. Sayed. Arab Population Conference. Amman, April 4–8, 1993.
—— and League of Arab States, and UNFPA. "Arab Labour Migration." Meeting of Senior Official and Experts. Amman, April 4–6, 1993.
Population Spatial Distribution. Amman, August 1993.
Compendium of Social Statistics and Indicators, third issue. New York, December 1993.
Return Migration: Profiles, Impact and Absorption in Home Countries. New York, December 1993.
Arab Women in ESCWA Member States. New York, 1994.
Social Impact of Reconstructing with Special Reference to Employment. New York, 1999.
Proceedings of the Expert Group Meeting on Assessment of Economic and Social Developments in the ESCWA Region During the Last 25 Years and Priorities for the Next Decade, 1999–2009. New York, 1999.
Population Section. *Gender and Population Dynamics in the ESCWA Region*. By Batool Shakoori. Beirut, 2000.
Al-Nashra al-Sukaniyya [Population Bulletin of ESCWA], No. 49, 2000 (Arabic).

United Nations Funds for Population Activities (UNFPA)

Singapore. Population Profile, No. 1. New York, 1977.

United Nations Children's Fund (UNICEF)

The State of the World's Children, various issues, 1984–2001. New York.

International Labour Office (ILO)

Yearbook of Labour Statistics, various issues, 1980–2002. Geneva.
International Migration and Development in the Arab Region. By J. S. Birks and C. A. Sinclair. Geneva, 1980.
International Migration for Employment: The Jordanian Migration System in Transition. By Allan M. Findlay. Geneva, March 1987.
International Migration for Employment: Manpower and Population Evolution in the GCC and Libyan Arab Jamahiriya. World Employment Programme Research, Working Paper. By J. S. Birks and C. A. Sinclair. Geneva, October 1989.

World Employment Report, various issues, 1998–2001. Geneva.

World Tourism Organization (WTO)

Yearbook of Tourism Statistics, various issues, 1980–2000. Madrid.

Dissertations (Ph.D Thesis)

Bendardaf, Ibrahim Bushnaf. *Socioeconomic Modernization and Demographic Changes in Syria*. Unpublished Ph.D. Thesis, University of Missouri, 1988.

Publications of Commercial Companies and Banks

Birks, Sinclair & Associates Ltd. *GCC Market Report*, 1990 and 1992. Durham: Mountjoy Research Centre.
Euromonitor Publications Limited. *Middle East Economic Handbook*. London: Euromonitor Publications Ltd., 1986.
HRD base Ltd., Lloyds Bank Chambers. *Socio-Demographic Profiles of Key Arab Countries*. Newcastle, May 1987.
The NCB Economist (National Commercial Bank-Saudi Arabia). "Gulf Population and Labour Force Structure." Vol. 5 (June/July 1995).
Saudi-American Bank (SAMBA). *The Saudi Economy: Mid-Year 2003*. Riyadh, August 2003.

Books

Arabic and Hebrew

Ayalon, Ami and Gad G. Gilbar (eds.). *Demographya ve-Politiqa be-Medinot 'Arav* [Demography and Politics in the Arab States]. Tel Aviv: Hakibbutz Hameuchad, 1995. (Hebrew).
Baer, Gabriel. *'Arviyey ha-Mizrah ha-Tikhon* [The Arabs of the Middle East], second edition. Tel Aviv: Hakibbutz Hameuchad, 1973 (Hebrew).
Gilbar, Gad G. *Kalkalat ha-Mizrah ha-Tikhon ba-'Et ha-Hadasha* [The Economic Development of the Middle East in Modern Times]. Tel Aviv: Ministry of Defense, 1990 (Hebrew).
Al-Hamarneh, Mustafa (ed.). *Al-Iqtisad al-Urduni: al-Mushkilat wal-Afaq* [The Problems and Future Options of the Jordanian Economy]. Amman: Markaz al-Dirasat al-Istratigiyya, 1994 (Arabic).
Litvak, Meir (ed.). *Islam ve-Demoqratyya ba-'Olam ha-'Aravi* [Islam and Democracy in the Arab World]. Tel Aviv: Hakibbutz Hameuchad, 1997 (Hebrew).
Shamir, Shimon. (ed.). *Yeridat ha-Nasserism, 1965–1970: Shqi'ata shel Tenu'a Meshihit* [The Decline of Nasserism 1965–1970: The Waning of a Messianic Movement]. Tel Aviv: Mif'alim Universitayim, 1978 (Hebrew).
Zisser, Eyal. *Paneha shel Surya: Hevra, Mishtar, ve-Medina* [Faces of Syria: Society, Regime and State]. Tel Aviv: Hakibbutz Hameuchad, 2003 (Hebrew).
—— *Be-Shem ha-Av: Bashar al-Asad: Shanim Rishonot ba-Shilton*. Tel Aviv: Tel Aviv University Press, 2004.

English

Abdelkarim, Abbas (ed.). *Change and Development in the Gulf*. London: Macmillan Press, and New York: St. Martin's Press, 1999.
Abdel-Khalek, Gouda and Robert Tignor (eds.). *The Political Economy of Income Distribution in Egypt*. New York: Holmes and Meier, 1982.
Alessa, Shamlan Y. *The Manpower Problem in Kuwait*. London and Boston: Kegan Paul International, 1981.
Ali, Kamran Asdar. *Planning the Family in Egypt: New Bodies, New Selves*. Austin: University of Texas Press, 2002.
Allen, Calvin H. and W. Lynn Rigsbee. *Oman Under Sultan Qaboos: From Coup to Constitution, 1970–1996*. London and Portland: Frank Cass, 2000.

Allman, James (ed.). *Women's Status and Fertility in the Muslim World.* New York and London: Praeger Publishers, 1978.

Amin, Galal A. *Egypt's Economic Predicament: A Study in the Interaction of External Pressure, Political Folly and Social Tension in Egypt, 1960–1990.* Leiden: Brill, 1995.

—— and Elizabeth Awny. *International Migration of Egyptian Labour: A Review of the State of Art.* International Development Research Centre. Canada, May 1985.

Anderson, Ewan W. *The Middle East: Geography and Geopolitics.* London and New York: Routledge, 2000.

Appleyard, Reginald (ed.). *The Impact of International Migration on Developing Countries.* Paris: Development Centre of the Organization for Economic Co-Operation and Development, 1989.

Askari, Hossein. *Saudi Arabia's Economy: Oil and the Search for Economic Development.* Greenwich and London: JAI Press, 1990.

—— and John Thomas Cummings. *Middle East Economies in the 1970s: A Comparative Approach.* New York: Praeger, 1976.

—— and Vahid Nowshirvani, and Mohamed Jaber. *Economic Development in the GCC: The Blessing and the Curse of Oil.* Greenwich and London: JAI Press, 1997.

Ayubi, Nazih N. *Over-Stating the Arab State: Politics and Society in the Middle East.* London and New York: I. B. Tauris Publishers, 1995.

El-Azhary, M. S. (ed.). *The Impact of Oil Revenues on Arab Gulf Development.* London: Croom Helm, and Boulder: Westview Press, 1984.

Azzam, Henry T. *The Arab World Facing the Challenge of the New Millennium.* London and New York: I. B. Tauris, 2002.

Beaujot, Roderic and Mongi Bchir. *Fertility in Tunisia: Traditional and Modern Contrasts.* Washington, D.C., Population Reference Bureau, Inc., 1984.

Beblawi, Hazem and Giacomo Luciani (eds.), *The Rentier State,* 2 Vols. London: Croom Helm, 1987.

Bengio, Ofra and Gabriel Ben-Dor (eds.). *Minorities and the State in the Arab World.* Boulder: Lynne Rienner Publishers, 1999.

Birks, J. S. and C. A. Sinclair. *International Migration Project, Country Case Study: The Sultanate of Oman,* Part One. The University of Durham, Department of Economics, July 1977.

—— *International Migration Project: Country Case Study: The Hashemite Kingdom of Jordan.* Durham: The University of Durham, Department of Economics, November 1978.

—— *International Migration Project, Country Case Study: The Kingdom of Saudi Arabia* Durham: The University of Durham, Department of Economics, 1979.

Bonine, Michael E. (ed.). *Population, Poverty, and Politics in Middle East Cities.* Gainesville: University Press of Florida, 1997.

Cairo Demographic Center (CDC). *Demographic Aspects of Socio-Economic Development in some Arab and African Countries.* Edited by S. A. Huzayyin and T. E. Smith. Research Monograph Series, No. 5. Cairo, 1974.

—— *Family and Marriage in some African and Asiatic Countries.* Edited by S. A. Huzayyin and G. T. Acsadi. Research Monograph Series, No. 6. Cairo, 1976.

—— *Determinants of Fertility in some African and Asian Countries.* Research Monograph Series, No. 10. Cairo, 1982.

—— *Population & Development.* Population & Development Research Monograph Series, No. 1. Cairo, 1994.

—— *Population & Development.* Research Monograph Series, No. 2. Cairo, 1995.

—— *CDC 24th Annual Seminar on Population Issues and the Challenges of the 21st Century in the Middle East, Africa, and Asia.* Research Monograph Series, No. 24. Cairo, 1995.

—— *Population & Sustainable Development.* Research Monograph Series, No. 5. Cairo, 1998.

—— *CDC 28th Annual Seminar on Population Issues in the Middle East, Africa and Asia.* Research Monograph Series, No. 28. Cairo, 1999.

Choueiri, Youssef M. *Arab Nationalism: A History*. Oxford: Blackwell, 2000.

Clarke, J. I. and W. B. Fisher (eds.). *Populations of the Middle East and North Africa: A Geographical Approach*. London: University of London Press, 1972.

Clarke, J. I and Howard Bowen-Jones (eds.). *Change and Development in the Middle East*. London and New York: Methuen, 1981.

Cleland, John and John Hobcraft (eds.). *Reproductive Change in Developing Countries: Insights from the World Fertility Survey*. Oxford: Oxford University Press, 1985.

Cleland, Wendell. *The Population Problem in Egypt*. Lancaster, PA: Science Press Printing Company, 1936.

Cordesman, Anthony H. *Bahrain, Oman, Qatar, and the UAE: Challenges of Security*. Boulder: Westview Press, 1997.

Demeny, Paul and Geoffrey McNicoll (eds.). *Encyclopedia of Population*. New York: Macmillan Reference USA, 2003.

Dixon, John (ed.). *Social Welfare in the Middle East*. London: Croom Helm, 1987.

Domschke, Eliance and Doreen S. Goyer. *The Handbook of National Population Censuses, Africa and Asia*. New York, Westport and London: Greenwood Press, 1986.

Donaldson, Peter J. *Nature Against Us: The United States and the World Population Crisis, 1965–1980*. Chapel Hill and London: The University of North Carolina Press, 1990.

Eatwell, John, Murray Milgate, and Peter Newman. *The New Palgrave: A Dictionary of Economics*. London: The Macmillan Press Limited, 1987.

Eickelman, Dale F. *The Middle East: an Anthropology Approach*, third edition. Englewood Cliffs, N.J.: Prentice Hall, 1989.

—— *The Middle East and Central Asia: An Anthropological Approach*, fourth edition. Upper Saddle River, NJ.: Prentice Hall, 2002.

The Emirates Center for Strategic Studies and Research. *Education and the Arab World: Challenges of the Next Millennium*. Abu Dhabi, 1999.

Feige, Edgar L. (ed.). *The Underground Economies: The Evasion and Information Distortion*. Cambridge: Cambridge University Press, 1989.

Feiler, Gil. *Economic Relations Between Egypt and the Gulf Oil States, 1967–2000*. Brighton and Portland: Sussex Academic Press, 2004.

Findlay, Allan and Anne Findlay. *Population and Development in the Third World*. London and New York: Methuen, 1987.

Finkle, Jason L. and C. Alison McIntosh (eds.). *The New Politics of Population: Conflict and Consensus in Family Planning*. Supplement to Vol. 20 of *Population and Development Review*. New York: The Population Council, 1994.

Foreign Areas Studies Division. *Area Handbook for Syria*. Washington, D.C.: The American University, July 1965.

Foreign Area Studies, The American University. *Tunisia: A Country Study*. Edited by Harold D. Nelson. Washington, D.C., 1979.

Fuller, Graham E. and Rend Rahim Francke. *The Arab Shi'a: The Forgotten Muslim*. New York: St. Martin's Press, 1999.

Gadalla, Saad M. *Is there Hope? Fertility and Family Planning in a Rural Egyptian Community*. Cairo: American University in Cairo Press, 1978.

Gause, Gregory III. *Oil Monarchies: Domestic and Security Challenges in the Arab Gulf States*. New York: Council on Foreign Relations, 1994.

El-Ghonemy, M. Riad. *Affluence and Poverty in the Middle East*. London and New York: Routledge, 1998.

Gilbar, Gad G. *The Middle East Oil Decade and Beyond*. London and Portland: Frank Cass, 1997.

—— *Population Dilemmas in the Middle East*. London and Portland: Frank Cass, 1997.

Ginat, Joseph and Onn Winckler (eds.). *The Jordanian–Palestinian–Israeli Triangle: Smoothing the Path to Peace*. Brighton and Portland: Sussex Academic Press, 1998.

Le Goff, Jacques and Pierre Nora (eds.). *Constructing the Past: Essays in Historical Methodology*. Cambridge: Cambridge University Press, 1985.

Goldberg, Ellis, Reşat Kasaba, and Joel Migdal (eds.). *Rules and Rights in the Middle East: Democracy, Law and Society*. Seattle and London: University of Washington Press, 1993.

Gould, W. T. S. and A. M. Findlay (eds.). *Population Migration and the Changing World Order*. Chichester: John Wiley & Sons, 1994.

Hansen, Bent. *Economic Development in Syria*. California: The Rand Corporation Resources for the Future, December 1969.

Harding, Philip and Richard Jenkins. *The Myth of the Hidden Economy: Towards a New Understanding of Informal Economic Activity*. Milton Keynes: Open University Press, 1989.

Harik, Iliya and Denis J. Sullivan (eds.). *Privatization and Liberalization in the Middle East*. Bloomington, IN: Indiana University Press, 1992.

Hartley, Shirley Forster. *Population – Quantity vs. Quality: A Sociological Examination of the Causes and Consequences of the Population Explosion*. New Jersey: Prentice-Hall, Inc. Englewood Cliffs, 1972.

Held, Colbert C. *Middle East Patterns: Places, Peoples, and Politics*, second edition. Boulder: Westview Press, 1994.

Henry, Clement M. and Robert Springborg. *Globalization and the Politics of Development in the Middle East*. Cambridge: Cambridge University Press, 2001.

Hess, Peter N. *Population Growth and Socioeconomic Progress in Less Developed Countries: Determinants of Fertility Transition*. New York and London: Praeger, 1988.

Himadeh, Said B. (ed.). *Economic Organization of Syria*. Beirut: The American University of Beirut Press, 1936.

Hinnebusch, Raymond A. *Egyptian Politics under Sadat: The Post-Populist Development of an Authoritarian-Modernizing State*. Cambridge: Cambridge University Press, 1985.

—— *Authoritarian Power and State Formation in Ba' thist Syria*. Boulder: Westview Press, 1990

Hopfinger, Hans and Raslan Khadour (eds.). *Economic Development and Investment Policies in Syria*. Neustadt an der Aisch: Verlagsdrucherei Schmidt, 1998.

Hopkins, Nicholas S. and Saad Eddin Inrahim (eds.). *Arab Society: Class, Gender, Power, and Development*, third edition. Cairo: The American University in Cairo Press, 1997.

Ibrahim, Saad Eddin. *The New Arab Social Order: A Study of the Social Impact of the Oil Wealth*. Boulder: Westview Press and London: Croom Helm, 1982.

Ikram, Khalid. *Egypt: Economic Management in a Period of Transition*, A World Bank Country Economic Report. Baltimore and London: The Johns Hopkins University Press, 1980.

International Republican Institute. *Oman: Political Development & the Maglis Ash-Shura*. Washington, D.C., July 1995.

Issawi, Charles. *Egypt in Revolution*. London: Oxford University Press, 1963.

—— *An Economic History of the Middle East and North Africa*. New York: Columbia University Press, 1982.

Johnson, Stanley P. *World Population – Turning the Tide: Three Decades of Progress*. London, Dordrecht, and Boston: Graham & Trotman/ Martinus Nijhoff, 1994.

van de Kaa, Dirk J. *The Past of Europe's Demographic Future*, Uhlenbeck Lecture 17. Wassenaar 1999.

Kanovsky, Eliyahu. *The Economic Impact of the Six-Day War: Israel, The Occupied Territories, Egypt, Jordan*. New York: Praeger Publishers, 1970.

—— *Economic Development of Jordan*. Tel-Aviv University, The David Horovitz Institute for the Research of Developing Countries, 1974.

Kapiszewski, Andrzej. *National and Expatriates: Population and Labour Dilemmas of the Gulf Cooperation Council States*. Reading: Ithaca Press, 2001.

Kechichian, Joseph A. (ed). *Iran, Iraq, and the Arab Gulf States*. New York: Palgrave, 2001.

Kelley, Allen C. Atef M. Khalifa, and M. Nabil El-Khorazaty. *Population and Development in Rural Egypt*. Durham, N. C.: Duke Press Policy Studies, Studies in Social and Economic Development, 1982.

Kerr, Malcolm H. and El Sayed Yassin (eds.). *Rich and Poor States in the Middle East:Egypt and the New Arab Order*. Boulder: Westview Press and Cairo: The American University in Cairo Press, 1982.

Khader, Bichara and Adnan Badran (eds.). *The Economic Development of Jordan*. London: Croom Helm, 1987.

Kostiner, Joseph (ed.). *Middle East Monarchies: The Challenge of Modernity*. Boulder: Lynne Rienner Publishers, 2001.

Kushner, David (ed.). *Palestine in the Late Ottoman Period*. Jerusalem: Yad Yzhak Ben-Zvi Press, 1986.

Lavy, Victor and Eliezer Sheffer. *Foreign Aid and Economic Development in the Middle East: Egypt, Syria, and Jordan*. New York: Praeger Publishers, 1991.

Lewis, Bernard. *The Emergence of Modern Turkey*, second edition. Oxford and New York: Oxford University Press, 1968.

Lippman, Thomas W. *Egypt After Nasser: Sadat, Peace and the Mirage of Prosperity*. New York: Paragon Press, 1989.

London School of Hygiene & Tropical Medicine and United Nations Population Fund. *Population Policies and Programmes: Determinants and Consequences in Eight Developing Countries*. By Kelley Lee, Gill Walt, Louisiana Lush, and John Cleland. London, 1995.

Long, David. E. *The Kingdom of Saudi Arabia*. Gainesville: University Press of Florida, 1997.

—— and Christian Koch (eds.). *Gulf Security in the Twenty-First Century*. Abu-Dhabi: The Emirates Center for Strategic Studies and Research, 1997.

Looney, Robert E. *Manpower Policies and Development in the Persian Gulf Region*. Westport and London: Praeger, 1994.

Luciani, Giacomo (ed.). *The Arab State*. London: Routledge, 1990.

Mabro, Robert. *The Egyptian Economy, 1952–1972*. Oxford: Clarendon Press, 1974.

Malthus, Thomas Robert. *An Essay on the Principle of Population*. Edited by Philip Appleman. New York: W. W. Norton, 1976.

Ma'oz, Moshe. *Asad: The Sphinx of Damascus: A Political Biography*. New York: Weidenfeld & Nicholson, 1988.

——, Joseph Ginat, and Onn Winckler (eds.). *Modern Syria: From Ottoman Rule to Pivotal Role in the Middle East*. Brighton and Portland: Sussex Academic Press, 1999.

Mazur, Laurie Ann (ed.). *Beyond the Numbers: A Reader on Population, Consumption, and Environment*. Washington, D.C.: Island Press, 1994.

Moghadam, Valentine M. *Modernizing Women: Gender and Social Change in the Middle East*. Boulder and London: Lynne Rienner Publishers, 1993.

Myrdal, Gunnar. *Asian Drama: An Inquiry into the Poverty of Nations*, 2 Vols. New York: Pantheon, Random House, 1968.

Nam, Charles B. and Susan G. Philliber. *Population: A Basic Orientation*, second edition. Englewood Cliffs, New Jersey: Prentice Hall, Inc., 1984.

National Academy of Sciences. *Rapid Population Growth: Consequences and Policy Implications*. Baltimore and London: Johns Hopkins University Press, 1971.

Neguib, Mohammed. *Egypt's Destiny*. London: Victor Gollancz Ltd., 1955.

Niblock, Tim (ed.). *Social and Economic Development in the Arab Gulf*. London: Croom Helm, 1982.

—— (ed.). *State, Society and Economy in Saudi Arabia*. London: Croom Helm, 1982.

—— and Emma Merphy (eds.). *Economic and Political Liberalization in the Middle East*. London and New York: British Academic Press, 1993.

—— and Rodney Wilson (eds.). *The Political Economy of the Middle East*, 6 Vols. Cheltenham, UK: Edward Elgar, 1999.

Obermeyer, Carla Makhlouf (ed.). *Family, Gender, and Population in the Middle East*. Cairo: The American University in Cairo press, 1995.

Omran, Abdel-Rahim. *Population in the Arab World: Problems and Prospects*. London: Croom Helm, 1980.

—— *Family Planning in the Legacy of Islam*. London and New York: Routledge, 1992.

Oweiss, Ibrahim M. (ed.), *The Political Economy of Contemporary Egypt*. Washington, D.C.: Center for Contemporary Arab Studies, Georgetown University, 1990.

Owen, Roger. *Migrant Workers in the Gulf*. London: Minority Rights Group, 1985.

—— and Şevket Pamuk. *A History of Middle East Economies in the Twentieth Century*. Cambridge, Mass.: Harvard University Press, 1999.

Perthes, Volker. *The Political Economy of Syria under Asad*. London and New York: I. B. Tauris, 1995.

Peterson, John E. *Oman in the Twentieth Century: Political Foundations of an Emerging State*. London: Croom Helm, 1978.

Podeh, Elie. *The Decline of Arab Unity: The Rise and Fall of the United Arab Republic* Brighton and Portland: Sussex Academic Press, 1999.

—— and Onn Winckler (eds.). *Rethinking Nasserism: Revolution and Historical Memory in Modern Egypt*. Gainesville: University Press of Florida, 2004.

The Population Reference Bureau. *Population Handbook*, fourth edition. By Arthur Haupt and Thomas T. Kane. New York, 1997.

—— *World Population Data Sheets*, various issues, 2000–2003. New York.

Pressat, Ronald. *The Dictionary of Demography*. Oxford: Clarendon Press, 1985.

Pridham, B. R. (ed.). *The Arab Gulf and the Arab World*. London: Croom Helm, 1988.

Rabinovich, Itamar. *The War for Lebanon, 1970–1985*. Ithaca and London: Cornell University Press, 1985.

Radwan, Samir. *Towards Full Employment: Egypt into the 21st Century*. Cairo: Egyptian Center for Economic Studies, 1998.

Rejwan, Nissim. *Nasserist Ideology: Its Exponents and Critics*. New York: John Wiley& Sons, 1974.

Richards, Alan and Philip L. Martin (eds.). *Migration, Mechanization, and Agricultural Labor Markets in Egypt*. Boulder: Westwiew Press, 1983.

Richards, Alan and John Waterbury. *A Political Economy of the Middle East*, second edition. Boulder: Westview Press, 1996.

Rivlin, Paul. *World Oil and Energy Trends: Strategic Implications for the Middle East*, Memorendum No. 57. Tel Aviv: Jaffee Center for Strategic Studies, Tel Aviv University, September 2000

—— *Economic Policy and Performance in the Arab World*. Boulder and London: Lynne Rienner Publishers, 2001.

Roberts, Godfrey (ed.). *Population Policy: Contemporary Issues*. New York: Praeger, 1990,

Salamé, Ghassan (ed.). *Democracy without Democrats? The Renewal of Politics in the Muslim World*. London and New York: I. B. Tauris, 1994.

Sales, M. E. *International Migration Project: Syrian Arab Republic*. Durham: The University of Durham, Department of Economics, October 1978.

Salibi, Kamal S. *The Modern History of Lebanon*. London: Weidenfeld and Nicolson, 1965.

Sayigh, Yusif A. *The Economies of the Arab World: Development Since 1945*. London: Croom Helm, 1978.

Schultz, Theodore W. (ed.). *Food for the World*. Chicago: University of Chicago Press, 1945.

Shaw, Paul R. *Mobilizing Human Resources in the Arab World*. London: Kegan Paul International, 1983.

Shtayyeh, Mohammad (ed.). *Labor Migration: Palestine, Jordan, Egypt and Israel*. Jerusalem: Palestine Center for Regional Studies, 1998.

Sirageldin, Ismail. (ed.). *Human Capital: Population Economics in the Middle East*. Cairo: The American University in Cairo Press, 2002.

—— and Eqbal al-Rahmani (eds.). *Population and Development Transformations in theArab World*. Research in Human Capital and Development. Greenwich, Connecticut and London: JAI Press INC., 1996.

Soliman, Salwa et al. *Population and Development in Egypt*. Cairo: CDC, 1994.

Stycos, J. Mayone, Hussein Abdel Aziz Sayed, Roger Avery, and Samuel Fridman. *Community Development and Family Planning: An Egyptian Experiment*. Boulder and London: Westview Press, 1988.

Todaro, Michael P. *Economic Development*, seventh edition. Reading, Mass.: Addison-Wesley, 1999.

Tschirgi, Dan (ed.). *The Arab World Today*. Boulder and London: Lynne Rienner Publishers, 1994.

—— *Development in the Age of Liberalization: Egypt and Mexico*. Cairo: The American University in Cairo Press, 1996.

Udovich, A. L. (ed.). *The Middle East: Oil, Conflict and Hope*. Lexington: Lexington Books, 1976.

Van Hear, Nicholas. *New Diaspora: The Mass Exodus, Dispersal, and Regrouping of Migrant Communities*. London: UCL Press, 1998.

Waterbury, John. *Egypt: Burdens of the Past – Options for the Future*. Indiana: American University Field Stuff, 1978.

—— *The Egypt of Nasser and Sadat: The Political Economy of Two Regimes*. Princeton: Princeton University Press, 1983.

Wilson, Peter W. and Douglas F. Graham. *Saudi Arabia: The Coming Storm*. New York: M. E. Sharpe, 1994.

Wilson, Rodney. *Economic Development in the Middle East*. London and New York: Routledge, 1995.

Winckler, Onn. *Population Growth and Migration in Jordan, 1950–1994*. Brighton and Portland: Sussex Academic Press, 1997.

—— *Demographic Developments and Population Policies in Ba'thist Syria*. Brighton and Portland: Sussex Academic Press, 1999.

Woodward, Peter N. *Oil and Labor in the Middle East: Saudi Arabia and the Oil Boom*. New York: Praeger, 1988.

Yamani, Mai. *Changed Identities: The Challenge of the New Generation in Saudi Arabia*. London: The Royal Institute of International Affairs, 2000.

Zoubir, Yahia H. (ed.). *North Africa in Transition: State, Society, and Economic Transformation in the 1990s*. Gainesville: University Press of Florida, 1999.

Articles

Arabic and Hebrew

'Amirah, Muhammad Sa'ad. Waqi' al-Bitala fi al-Urdun wa-Nazara Nahwa al-Mustaqbal." [The Employment Situation in Jordan and its Future Prospect]. In Mustafa al-Hamarneh (ed.). *Al-Iqtisad al-Urduni: al-Mushkilat wal-Afaq*. Amman: Markaz al-Dirasat al-Istratigiyya, 1994, pp. 206–26 (Arabic).

Ayalon, Ami. "Demographya, Politiqa, ve-Masoret be-Mitzrayim shel Mubarak." [Demography, Politics, and Tradition in Mubarak's Egypt]. In Ami Ayalon and Gad G. Gilbar (eds.). *Demographya ve-Politiqa be-Medinot 'Arav*. Tel Aviv: Hakibbutz Hameuchad, 1995, pp. 29–50 (Hebrew).

Efrat, Moshe. "Tokhnit ha-'Asor ve-Totzoteha." [The Ten-Year Plan and its Consequences] in Shimon Shamir (ed.). *Yeridat ha-Nasserism, 1965–1970: Shqi'ata shel Tenu'a Meshikhit*. Tel Aviv: Mif'alim Universitayim, 1978, pp. 61–78 (Hebrew).

Gilbar, Gad G. "Mavo: Beyn Demographya ve-Politiqa ba-Mizrah ha-Tikhon" [Introduction: Between Demography and Politics in the Middle East]. In Ami Ayalon and Gad G. Gilbar (eds.). *Demographya ve-Politiqa be-Medinot 'Arav*. Tel Aviv: Hakibbutz Hameuchad, 1995, pp. 11–28 (Hebrew).

Karni, Azriel. "Temurot be-Yahas la-Piquah 'al ha-Yeluda ba-Mizrah ha-Tikhon" [Trends in

Fertility Control in the Middle East]. *Hamizrah Hehadash*, Vol. 17 (1967), pp. 222–41 (Hebrew).

Maddy-Weitzman, Bruce. "Masoret, Gidul Okhlosiyya, ve-Tikhnun Mishpaha Be-Marocco" [Tradition, Population Growth, and Family Planning in Morocco]. In Ami Ayalon and Gad G. Gilbar (eds.). *Demographya ve-Politiqa be-Medinot 'Arav*. Tel Aviv: Hakibbutz Hameuchad, 1995, pp. 51–67 (Hebrew).

"Al-Simat al-Asasiyya li-Sukan al-Kuwayt wa-Kuwwat al-'Amal fi Nihayat 1994." *Al-Iqtisadi al-Kuwayti*, No. 324 (May 1995), pp. 24–30 (Arabic).

Steinberg, Matti. " Lir'ot et ha-Nolad: ha-Gorem ha-Demography be-Re'iyat Asha"f" [To Foresee the Events: The Demographic Factor in the PLO Perception]. In Ami Ayalon and Gad G. Gilbar (eds.). *Demographya ve-Politiqa be-Medinot 'Arav*. Tel Aviv: Hakibbutz Hameuchad, 1995, pp. 153–89 (Hebrew).

Susser, Asher. "Demographya ve-Politiqa be-Yarden" [Demography and Politics in Jordan]. In Ami Ayalon and Gad G. Gilbar (eds.). *Demographya ve-Politiqa be-Medinot 'Arav*. Tel Aviv: Hakibbutz Hameuchad, 1995, pp. 131–51 (Hebrew).

—— "ha-Ahim ha-Muslemim be-Yarden: Du-Qiyum ve-'Imut Mevuqar" [The Muslim Brothers in Jordan: Coexistence and Controlled Confrontation]. In Meir Litvak (ed.). *Islam ve-Demoqratyya ba-'Olam ha-'Aravi*. Tel Aviv: Hakibbutz Hameuchad, 1997, pp. 123–46 (Hebrew).

English and French

Abdel-Fadil, Mahmoud. "The Macro-Behaviour of Oil-Rentier States in the Arab Region." In Hazem Beblawi and Giacomo Luciani (eds.). *The Rentier State*, Vol. II. London: Croom Helm, 1987, pp. 83–107.

Abdelghany, A. M. "Evaluating the Application of the Stable Population Model of the Population of Egypt." *Population Bulletin of ECWA*, No. 21 (December 1981), pp. 105–16.

Abdel-Jaber, Tayseer. "Jordanian Labor Migration: Social, Political and Economic Effects." In Mohammad Shtayyeh (ed.). *Labor Migration: Palestine, Jordan, Egypt and Israel*. Jerusalem: Palestine Center for Regional Studies, 1998, pp. 81–105.

Abdel Rahman, Mohamed. "Socio-Demographic Aspects of Child Labor in Egypt." In CDC, *Population & Sustainable Development*. Research Monograph Series, No. 5. Cairo, 1998, pp. 49–68.

Abu-Gamrah, Hamed. "Fertility Levels and Differentials by Mother's Education in some Countries of the ECWA Region." In CDC. *Determinants of Fertility in some African and Asian Countries*. Research Monograph Series, No. 10. Cairo, 1982, pp. 191–211.

Allman, James. "The Demographic Transition in the Middle East and North Africa." In James Allman (ed.). *Women's Status and Fertility in the Muslim World*. New York and London: Praeger Publishers, 1978, pp. 3–32.

Ayalon, Ami. "Egypt's Coptic Pandora's Box." In Ofra Bengio and Gabriel Ben-Dor (eds.). *Minorities and the State in the Arab World*. Boulder: Lynne Rienner Publishers, 1999, pp. 53–71.

Azzi, Mohamed Farid. "Maghrebi Youth: Between Alienation and Integration." In Yahia H. Zoubir (ed.). *North Africa in Transition: State, Society, and Economic Transformation in the 1990s*. Gainesville: University Press of Florida, 1999, pp. 109–26.

Baram, Amatzia. Ba'thi Iraq and Hashemite Jordan: From Hostility to Alignment." *Middle East Journal*, Vol. 45, No. 1 (Winter 1991), pp. 51–70.

—— "The Effect of Iraqi Sanctions: Statistical Pitfalls and Responsibility." *Middle East Journal*, Vol. 54, No. 2 (Spring 2000), pp. 194–223.

Beaujot, Roderic. "Attitudes Among Tunisians Toward Family Planning." *International Family Planning Perspectives*, Vol. 14, No. 2 (June 1988), pp. 54–60.

El-Beblawi, Hayam and Azza Mohamed Abedo. "Some Aspects of Child Labor in Egypt." CDC Working Paper, No. 41. 1999.

Beblawi, Hazem. "The Rentier State in the Arab World." In Giacomo Luciani (ed.). *The Arab State*. London: Routledge, 1990, pp. 85–98.

Binder, Leonard. "Gamal 'Abd al-Nasser: Iconology, Ideology and Demonology." In Elie Podeh and Onn Winckler (eds.). *Rethinking Nasserism: Revolution and Historical Memory in Modern Egypt*. Gainesville: University Press of Florida, 2004, pp. 45–71.

Birks, J. S. "The Demographic Challenge in the Arab Gulf." In B. R. Pridham (ed.). *The Arab Gulf and the Arab World*. London: Croom Helm, 1988, pp. 131–52.

——, I. Seragelding, C. A. Sinclair, and J. A. Socknat. "Who is Migrating Where? An Overview of International Labor Migration in the Arab World." In Alan Richards and Philip L. Martin (eds.). *Migration, Mechanization, and Agricultural Labor Markets in Egypt*. Boulder: Westview Press, 1983, pp. 103–16.

——, C. A. Sinclair, and J. A. Socknat. "The Demand for Egyptian Labor Abroad." In Alan Richards and Philip L. Martin (eds.). *Migration, Mechanization, and Agricultural Labor Markets in Egypt*. Boulder: Westview Press, 1983, pp. 117–34.

Bonine, Michael E. "Population Growth, the Labor Market and the Gulf Security." In David E. Long and Christian Koch (eds.). *Gulf Security in the Twenty-First Century*. Abu-Dhabi: The Emirates Center for Strategic Studies and Research, 1997, pp. 226–64.

Brand, Laurie A. "Economic and Political Liberalization in a Rentier Economy: The Case of the Hashemite Kingdom of Jordan." In Iliya Harik and Denis J. Sullivan (eds.). *Privatization and Liberalization in the Middle East*. Bloomington, IN: Indiana University Press, 1992, pp. 167–88.

Brown, K. L. "The Campaign to Encourage Family Planning in Tunisia and Some Responses at the Village Level." *Middle Eastern Studies*, Vol. 17, No. 1 (January 1981), pp. 64–83.

Bruton, Henry J. "Egypt's Development in the Seventies." *Economic Development and Cultural Change*, Vol. 33, No. 4 (July 1983), pp. 675–704.

Burguière, André. "Demography." In Jacques Le Goff and Pierre Nora (eds.). *Constructing the Past: Essays in Historical Methodology*. Cambridge: Cambridge University Press, 1985, pp. 99–122.

Cassandra. "The Impending Crisis in Egypt." *Middle East Journal*, Vol. 49, No. 1 (1995), p. 9–27.

Chamie, Joseph. "Trends, Variations, and Contradictions in National Policies to Influence Fertility." In Jason L. Finkle and C. Alison McIntosh (eds.). *The New Politics of Population: Conflict and Consensus in Family Planning*. Supplement to Vol. 20 of *Population and Development Review*. New York: The Population Council, 1994, pp. 37–50.

Chatty, Dawn. "Women Working in Oman: Individual Choice and Cultural Constrains." *IJMES*, Vol. 32, No. 2 (May 2000), pp. 241–54.

Choucri, Nazli. "The Hidden Economy: A New View of Remittances in the Arab World." *World Development*, Vol. 14, No. 6 (1986), pp. 697–712.

—— "Asians in the Arab World: Labor Migration and Public Policy." *Middle Eastern Studies*, Vol. 22, No. 2 (1986), pp. 252–73.

—— "Migration in the Middle East: Old Economics Or New Politics?" *Journal of Arab Affairs*, Vol. 7, No. 1 (Spring 1988), pp. 1–15.

Cleland, John. "Marital Fertility Decline in Developing Countries: Theories and the Evidence." In John Cleland and John Hobcraft (eds.). *Reproductive Change in Developing Countries*. Oxford: Oxford University Press, 1985, pp. 223–52.

Cochrane, Susan H. and David K. Guilkey. "The Effects of Fertility Intensions and Access to Services on Contraceptive Use in Tunisia." *Economic Development and Cultural Change*, Vol. 43, No. 4 (1995), pp. 779–804.

Colton, Nora Ann. "The Maghrebi Economies as Emerging Markets?" In Yahia H. Zoubir (ed.). *North Africa in Transition: State, Society, and Economic Transformation in the 1990s*. Gainesville: University Press of Florida, 1999, pp. 159–76.

Courbage, Youssef. "Issues in Fertility Transition in the Middle East and North Africa." *Economic Research Forum*, Working Paper 9903. Cairo, 1999.

Demeny, Paul. "Population Policy Dilemmas in Europe at the Dawn of the Twenty-First Century." *Population and Development Review*, Vol. 29, No. 1 (March 2003), pp. 1–28.

Dibbs, Mohamed Chafic. "The Relationship Between Censuses and Civil Registration in the Syrian Arab Republic." *Population Bulletin of ECWA*, No. 18 (June 1980), pp. 81–101.

Donaldson, Peter J. and Amy Ong Tsui. "The International Family Planning Movement." *Population Bulletin*, Vol. 45, No. 3 (November 1990), pp. 1–44.

Durand, John. "Historical Estimates of World Population: An Evaluation." *Population and Development Review*, Vol. 3, No. 3 (September 1977), pp.253–96.

"L'Explosion Démographique en Syrie." *Syrie & Monde Arabe*, Vol. 12, No. 253 (Fevrier 1975), pp. 4–11.

Faour, Muhammad. "Fertility Policy and Family Planning in the Arab Countries." *Studies in Family Planning*, Vol. 20, No. 5 (September/October 1989), pp. 254–63.

Farag, Mahmoud. "Differences in Age at Marriage in Syria." In S. H. Huzayyin and G. T. Acsadi (eds.). *Family and Marriage in some African and Asiatic Countries.* Research Monograph Series, No. 6. Cairo: CDC, 1976, pp. 493–504.

Fargues, Philippe. "Demographic Explosion or Social Upheaval?" In Ghassan Salamé (ed.). *Democracy without Democrats? The Renewal of Politics in the Muslim World.* London and New York: I. B. Tauris, 1994, pp. 156–79.

—— "State Policies and the Birth Rate in Egypt: From Socialism to Liberalism." *Population and Development Review*, Vol. 23, No. 1 (1997), pp. 115–38.

—— "Protracted National Conflict and Fertility Change: Palestinians and Israelis in the Twentieth Century." *Population and Development Review*, Vol. 26, No. 3 (September 2000), pp. 441–82.

Farid, Samir. "Fertility Patterns in the Arab Region." *International Family Planning Perspectives*, Vol. 10, No. 4 (December 1984), pp. 119–24.

Feiler, Gil. "The Number of Egyptian Workers in the Arab Oil Countries, 1974–1983: A Critical Discussion." *Occasional Papers*. The Moshe Dayan Center for Middle Eastern and African Studies, Tel Aviv University, October 1986.

—— "Migration and Recession: Arab Labor Mobility in the Middle East, 1982–1989." *Population and Development Review*, Vol. 17, No. 1 (March 1991), pp. 134–55.

Freedman, Ronald. "Family Planning Programs in the Third World." *The Annals of the American Academy*, No. 510 (July 1990), pp. 33–43.

—— and Bernard Berelson. "The Record of Family Planning Programs." *Studies in Family Planning*, Vol. 7, No. 1 (1976), pp. 1–40.

Findlay, Allan M. "Return to Yemen: The End of the Old Migration Order in the Arab World." In W. T. S. Gould and A. M. Findlay (eds.). *Population Migration and the Changing World Order*. Chichester: John Wiley & Sons, 1994, pp. 205–23.

Finkle, Jason L. and Barbara B. Crane. "Ideology and Politics at Mexico City: The United States at the 1984 International Conference on Population." *Population and Development Review*, Vol. 11, No. 1 (1985), pp. 1–28.

—— and C. Alison McIntosh. "The New Politics of Population." In Jason L. Finkle and C. Alison McIntosh (eds.). *The New Politics of Population: Conflict and Consensus in Family Planning*. Supplement to Vol. 20 of *Population and Development Review*. New York: The Population Council, 1994, pp. 3–34.

Fisher, W. B. "Jordan: A Demographic Shatter-Belt." In J. I. Clarke and W. B. Fisher (eds.). *Populations of the Middle East and North Africa: A Geographical Approach*. London: University of London Press, 1972, pp. 202–19.

Gebriel, Adil Osman. "Overview of Major Issues in the Development of National Human Resources in the Gulf." In Abbas Abdelkarim (ed.). *Change and Development in the Gulf*. London: Macmillan Press, and New York: St. Martin's Press, 1999, pp. 151–63.

Gallagher, Charles F. "Population and Development in Egypt, Part I: Birth and Death on the Nile." *American University Field Stuff Report*, No. 31 (1981).

Gerber, Haim. "The Population of Syria and Palestine in the Nineteenth Century." *Asian and African Studies*, Vol. 13, No. 1 (1979), pp. 58–80.

Ghita, Naguib. "A Seminar on the Preliminary Results of the 1996 Census on Population, Housing and Establishments in the Light of the National Population Strategy." *Population Studies*, Vol. 16, No. 81 (January-March 1998), pp. 99–109.

El-Ghonemy, M. Riad. "An Assessment of Egypt's Development Strategy, 1952–1970." In Elie Podeh and Onn Winckler (eds.). *Rethinking Nasserism: Revolution and Historical Memory in Modern Egypt*. Gainesville: University Press of Florida, 2004, pp. 253–63.

Gilbar, Gad G. "Family Planning Under Mubarak." In his *Population Dilemmas in the Middle East*. London and Portland: Frank Cass, 1997, pp. 113–36.

—— "Jordan's Road to Family Planning Policy." In his *Population Dilemmas in the Middle East*. London and Portland: Frank Cass, 1997, pp. 67–79.

—— "Nasser Soft Revolution." In his *Population Dilemmas in the Middle East*. London and Portland: Frank Cass, 1997, pp. 80–96.

—— and Onn Winckler. "Nasser's Family Planning Policy in Perspective." In Elie Podeh and Onn Winckler (eds.). *Rethinking Nasserism: Revolution and Historical Memory in Modern Egypt*. Gainesville: University Press of Florida, 2004, pp. 282–304.

Goujon, Anne Valia. "Population and Education Prospects in the Arab Region." In Ismail Sirageldin (ed.). *Human Capital: Population Economics in the Middle East*. Cairo: The American University in Cairo Press, 2002, pp. 116–40.

Grosse, Scott D. "The Politics of Family Planning in the Maghrib." *Studies in Comparative International Development*, Vol. 17, No. 1 (1982), pp. 22–48.

Hamed, Osama. "Egypt's Open Door Economic Policy: An Attempt at Economic Integration in the Middle East." *IJMES*, Vol. 13, No. 2 (May 1981), pp. 1–9.

Harik, Iliya. "Privatization: The Issue, the Prospects, and the Fears." In Iliya Harik and Denis J. Sullivan (eds.). *Privatization and Liberalization in the Middle East*. Bloomington, IN: Indiana University Press, 1992, pp. 1–23.

Hassanin, Mahasen Mostafa, Amany Mousa Mohamed, and Galaa Helmy Selem. "Estimating Family Planning Target Population of Egypt in 1997." In *CDC 24th Annual Seminar on Population Issues and the Challenges of the 21st Century in the Middle East, Africa, and Asia*. Research Monograph Series, No. 24. Cairo, 1995, pp. 440–55.

Heydemann, Steven. "Taxation without Representation: Authoritarianism and Economic Liberalization in Syria." In Ellis Goldberg, Reşat Kasaba, and Joel Migdal (eds.). *Rules and Rights in the Middle East: Democracy, Law, and Society*. Seattle and London: University of Washington Press, 1993, pp. 69–101.

Hill, Allan G. "The Gulf States: Petroleum and Population Growth." In J. I. Clarke and W. B. Fiecher (eds.). *Populations of the Middle East and North Africa: A Geographical Approach*. London: University of London Press, 1972, pp. 242–73.

—— "The Demography of the Kuwaiti Population of Kuwait." *Demography*, Vol. 12, No. 3 (August 1975), pp. 537–48.

—— "Population Growth in the Middle East and North Africa: Selected Policy Issues." In A. L. Udovich (ed.). *The Middle East: Oil, Conflict and Hope*. Lexington: Lexington Books, 1976, pp. 7–57.

—— "Population Growth in the Middle East since 1945 with Special Reference to the Arab Countries of West Asia." In John I. Clarke and Howard Bowen-Jones (eds.). *Change and Development in the Middle East*. London and New York: Methuen, 1981, pp. 130–53.

Hinnebusch, Raymond A. "Syria." In Tim Niblock and Emma Merphy (eds.). *Economic and Political Liberalization in the Middle East*. London and New York: British Academic Press, 1993, pp. 177–202.

Hoodfar, Homa and Samad Assadpour. "The Politics of Population Policy in the Islamic Republic of Iran." *Studies in Family Planning*, Vol. 31, No. 1 (March 2000), pp. 19–34.

Ibrahim, Saad Eddin. "Oil, Migration and the New Arab Social Order." In Malcolm H. Kerr and El Sayed Yassin (eds.). *Rich and Poor States in the Middle East: Egypt and the New Arab Order*. Boulder: Westview Press and Cairo: The American University in Cairo Press, 1982, pp. 17–70.

—— "State, Women, and Civil Society: An Evaluation of Egypt's Population Policy." In Carla Makhlouf Obermeyer (ed.). *Family, Gender, and Population in the Middle East*. Cairo: The American University in Cairo Press, 1995, pp. 57–79.

Al-Imadi, Mohammed. "The Economic and Investment Policies in Syria." In Hans Hopfinger and Raslan Khadour (eds.). *Economic Development and Investment Policies in Syria*. Neustadt an der Aisch: Verlagsdruckerei Schmidt, 1998, pp. 3–33.

International Planned Parenthood Federation-Middle East and North Africa Region. "Family Planning and Population Policies in the Middle East and North Africa." In James Allman (ed.). *Women's Status and Fertility in the Muslim World*. New York and London: Praeger, 1978, pp. 33–53.

Ismael, Jacqueline and Tareq Y. Ismael. "Social Policy in the Arab World." *Cairo Papers in Social Science*, Vol. 18, Monograph 1 (Spring 1995).

Kamel, Marwan Mohamed. "Population Strategy, 1992/2007." *Population Studies*, Vol. 14, No. 75 (July-September 1992), pp. 113–15.

Kanovsky, Eliyahu. "What's Behind Syria's Current Economic Problems?" *Occasional Papers*. The Moshe Dayan Center for Middle Eastern and African Studies, Tel Aviv University, May 1985.

—— "Jordan's Economy: From Prosperity to Crisis." *Occasional Papers*, No. 106. The Moshe Dayan Center for Middle Eastern and African Studies, Tel Aviv University, May 1989.

Karpat, Kemal H. "Ottoman Population Records and the Census of 1881/82–1893." *IJMES*, Vol. 9 (1978), pp. 237–74.

Kashef, A.S.M. "Egypt." In John Dixon (ed.). *Social Welfare in the Middle East*. London: Croom Helm, 1987, pp. 1–31.

Kay, Shirley. "Social Change in Modern Saudi Arabia." In Tim Niblock (ed.). *State, Society and Economy in Saudi Arabia*. London: Croom Helm, 1982, pp. 171–85.

Khalaf, Abdulhadi. "What the Gulf Ruling Families Do when They Rule." *Orient*, Vol. 44, No. 4 (2003), pp. 537–54.

Khalifa, Mona A. "Family Planning and Sustainable Development in Egypt." *CDC Series on Population and Development*, No. 5. 1994.

Khawaja, Marwan. "The Recent Rise in Palestinian Fertility: Permanent or Transient?" *Population Studies*, Vo. 54 (2000), pp. 331–46.

Khoury, Nabeel A. "The Politics of Intra-Regional Migration in the Arab World." *Journal of South Asian and Middle Eastern Studies*, Vol. 11, No. 2 (Winter 1982), pp. 3–20.

Kohli, K. L. and Musa'ad al-Omaim. "Mortality Levels, Trends and Differentials in Kuwait, 1957-1983." *Population Bulletin of ESCWA*, No. 28 (June 1986), pp. 91–123.

Kupferschmidt, Uri M. "A Note on the Muslim Religions Hierarchy Towards the End of the Ottoman Period." In David Kushner (ed.). *Palestine in the Late Ottoman Period*. Jerusalem: Yad Yzhak Ben-Zvi Press, 1986, pp. 123–29.

—— "Nasserist and Post-Nasserist Elites in an Official Biographical Lexicon." In Elie Podeh and Onn Winckler (eds.). *Rethinking Nasserism: Revolution and Historical Memory in Modern Egypt*. Gainesville: University Press of Florida, 2004, pp. 163–76.

Lapham, Robert J. "Population Policies in the Middle East and North Africa." *Middle East Studies Association Bulletin*, Vol. 11, No. 2 (May 1, 1977), pp. 1–30.

—— and W. Parker Mauldin. "Family Planning Program Effort and Birthrate Decline in Developing Countries." *International Family Planning Perspectives*, Vol. 10, No. 4 (December 1984), pp. 109–18.

Lee, Kelley and Gill Walt. "Linking National and Global Population Agendas: Case Studies From Eight Developing Countries." *Third World Quarterly*, Vol. 16, No. 2 (1995), pp. 257–72.

Lesch, David W. "History and Political Culture in Syria: Obstacles to Integration in the Global Economy After the Gulf War." In Moshe Ma'oz, Joseph Ginat, and Onn Winckler (eds.). *Modern Syria: From Ottoman Rule to Pivotal Role in the Middle East.* Brighton and Portland: Sussex Academic Press, 1999, pp. 57–78.

Looney, Robert E. "Patterns of Remittances and Labor Migration in the Arab World." *International Migration*, Vol. 24, No. 4 (1989), pp. 563–80.

Lutz, Wolfgang. "The Future of World Population." *Population Bulletin*, Vol. 49, No. 1 (June 1994).

Maddy-Weitzman, Bruce. "The Berber Question in Alggeria: Nationalism in the Making?" In Ofra Bengio and Gabriel Ben-Dor (eds.). *Minorities and the State in the Arab World.* Boulder: Lynne Rienner Publishers, 1999, pp. 31–52.

McCarthy, Justin. "The Population of Ottoman Syria and Iraq, 1878–1914." *Asian and African Studies*, Vol. 15 (1981), pp. 3–44.

Mazur, Laurie Ann. "Beyond the Numbers: An Introduction and Overview." In Laurie Ann Mazur (ed.). *Beyond the Numbers: A Reader on Population, Consumption, and Environment.* Washington, D.C.: Island Press, 1994, pp. 1–20.

McIntosh, Alison and Jason L. Finkle. "The Cairo Conference on Population and Development: A New Paradigm?" *Population and Development Review*, Vol. 21, No. 2 (1995), pp. 223–60.

Nagi, Mustafa. "Labor Immigration and Development in the Middle East: Patterns, Problems, and Policies." *International Review of Modern Sociology*, Vol. 12, No. 2 (1982), pp. 185–240.

Al-Najjar, Baquer Salman. "Population Policies in the Countries of the Gulf Co-operation Council: Politics and Society." *Immigrants & Minorities*, Vol. 12, No. 2 (July 1993), pp. 200–18.

Nonneman, Gred. "Rentiers and Autocrats, Monarchs and Democrats, State and Society: The Middle East Between Globalization, Human 'Agency,' and Europe." *International Affairs*, Vol. 77, No. 1 (2001), pp. 141–62.

Nosseir, Nazek. "Egypt: Population, Urbanization, and Development." In Dan Tschirgi (ed.). *Development in the Age of Liberalization: Egypt and Mexico.* Cairo: The American University in Cairo Press, 1996, pp. 187–197.

Notestein, Frank W. "Population – The Long View." In Theodore W. Schultz (ed.). *Food for the World.* Chicago: University of Chicago Press, 1945, pp. 36–57.

Obermeyer, Carla Makhlouf. "Islam, Women and Politics: The Demography of Arab Countries." *Population and Development Review*, Vol. 18, No. 1 (1992), pp. 33–60.

Omran, Abdel Rahim and Farzaneh Roudi. "The Middle East Population Puzzle." *Population Bulletin*, Vol. 48 (July 1993).

Oweiss, Ibrahim M. "Migration of Egyptian." *L'Egypte Contemporaine*, No. 381 (July 1980), pp. 5–16.

Palen, John J. "Population Policy: Singapore." In Godfrey Roberts (ed.). *Population Policy: Contemporary Issues.* New York: Praeger, 1990, pp. 167–78.

Perthes, Volker. "The Syrian Economy in the 1980s." *Middle East Journal*, Vol. 46, No. 1 (Winter 1992), pp. 37–58.

Podeh, Elie and Onn Winckler. "The Boycott that Never Was: Egypt and the Arab System, 1979–1989." *Durham Middle East Papers*, No. 72 (December 2002).

—— "Introduction: Nasserism as a Form of Populism." In Elie Podeh and Onn Winckler (eds.). *Rethinking Nasserism: Revolution and Historical Memory in Modern Egypt.* Gainesville: University Press of Florida, 2004, pp. 1–42.

Pritchett, Lant H. "Desired Fertility and the Impact of Population Policies." *Population and Development Review*, Vol. 20, No. 1 (1994), pp. 1–55.

Rabi, Uzi. "Majlis al-Shura and Majlis al-Dawla: Weaving Old Practices and New Realities in the Process of State Formation in Oman." *Middle Eastern Studies*, Vol. 38, No. 4 (October 2002), pp. 41–50.

—— and Joseph Kostiner. "The Shi'is in Bahrain: Class and Religious Protest." In Ofra Bengio and Gabriel Ben-Dor (eds.). *Minorities and the State in the Arab World.* Boulder: Lynne Rienner Publishers, 1999, pp. 171–88.

Rashad, Hoda and Zeinab Khadr. "The Demography of the Arab Region: New Challenges and Opportunities." In Ismail Sirageldin (ed.). *Human Capital: Population Economics in the Middle East.* Cairo: The American University in Cairo Press, 2002, pp. 37–61.

Richards, Alan. "Oil Wealth in the Arab World: Whence, to Whom, and Whither?" In Dan Tschirgi (ed.). *The Arab World Today.* Boulder and London: Lynne Rienner Publishers, 1994, pp. 67–76.

Rizk, Hanna. "Population Policies: Scope, Goals, Means and Problems." *Population Bulletin of ECWA*, No. 7 (July 1974), pp. 132–55.

—— "Trends in Fertility and Family Planning in Jordan." *Studies in Family Planning*, Vol. 8, No. 4 (1977), pp. 91–99.

Roberts, Godfrey. "Population Policy Issues in Selected Asian Countries." In Godfrey Roberts (ed.). *Population Policy: Contemporary Issues.* New York: Praeger, 1990, pp. 85–97.

Roy, Delwin A. "The Hidden Economy in Egypt." *Middle Eastern Studies*, Vol. 28, No. 4 (October 1992), pp. 689–711.

Russell, Sharon Stanton. "Remittances from International Migration: A Review in Perspective." *World Development*, Vol. 14, No. 6 (1986), pp. 677–96.

Rivlin, Paul. "The Syrian Economy in the 1990s." *Data and Analysis.* The Moshe Dayan Center for Middle Eastern and African Studies, Tel Aviv University, June 1999.

—— "Nasser's Egypt and Park's Korea: A Comparison of their Economic Achievements." In Elie Podeh and Onn Winckler (eds.). *Rethinking Nasserism: Revolution and Historical Memory in Modern Egypt.* Gainesville: University Press of Florida, 2004, pp. 264–81.

Sabagh, Georges. "The Demography of the Middle East." *Middle East Studies Association Bulletin*, Vol. 4, No. 2 (May 15, 1970), pp. 1–19.

Al-Sayegh, Fatma. "Domestic Politics in the United Arab Emirates: Social and Economic Policies, 1990–2000." In Joseph A. Kechichian (ed). *Iran, Iraq, and the Arab Gulf States* (New York: Palgrave, 2001), pp. 161–75.

Sayed, Hussein Abdel-Aziz. "The Population Family Planning Program in Egypt: Structure and Performance." *Population Studies*, Vol. 11, No. 70 (July-September 1984), pp. 3–38.

Seccombe, Ian J. "Immigrants Workers in an Emigrant Economy: An Examination of Replacement Migration in the Middle East." *International Migration*, Vol. 24, No. 2 (June 1986), pp. 377–96.

—— "Labour Emigration Policies and Economic Development in Jordan: From Unemployment to Labour Shortage." In Bichara Khader and Adnan Badran (eds.). *The Economic Development of Jordan.* London: Croom Helm, 1987, pp. 118–32.

—— and R. I. Lawless. "State Intervention and the International Labour Market: A Review of Labour Emigration Policies in the Arab World." In Reginald Appleyard (ed.). *The Impact of International Migration on Developing Countries.* Paris: Development Centre of the Organization for Economic Co-Operation and Development, 1989, pp. 69–89.

Seikaly, May. "Women and Social Change in Bahrain." *IJMES*, Vol. 26 (1994), pp. 415–26.

Sell, Ralph R. "Egyptian International Labor Migration and Social Processes: Toward Regional Integration." *International Migration Review*, Vol. 22, No. 3 (March 1988), pp. 87–108.

Shaban, Radwan A., Ragui Assaad, and Sulayman S. al-Qudsi. "The Challenge of Unemployment in the Arab Region." *International Labour Review*, Vol. 134, No. 1 (1995), pp. 65–81.

Shaker, Mohamed Hesham. "Main Features of Unemployment in Egypt (1990–1995)." In *CDC 28th Annual Seminar on Population Issues in the Middle East, Africa and Asia.* Research Monograph Series, No. 28. Cairo 1999, pp. 515–33.

Al-Shalkani, Mustafa. "A System for Collecting Vital Statistics in Gulf Cooperation Council Countries." *Population Bulletin of ESCWA*, Nos. 35–37 (1989–1990), pp. 43–97.

Share, M.A.J. "The Use of Jordanian Workers' Remittances." In Bichara Khader and Adnan Badran (eds.). *The Economic Development of Jordan*. London: Croom Helm, 1987, pp. 32–44.

Shaw, Stanford J. "The Ottoman Census System and Population, 1831–1914." *IJMES*, Vol. 9 (1978), pp. 325–38.

Shawky, Gihan A. "Detecting Changes in Fertility in Algeria, Egypt and Yemen." *CDC Working Paper*, No. 42. 1999.

Sheykhi, Mohammad Taghi. "The Socio-Psychological Factors of Family Planning with Special Reference to Iran: A Theoretical Appraisal." *International Sociology*, Vol. 10, No. 1 (March 1995), pp. 71–82.

Short, Susan E. and Fengying Zhai. "Looking Locally at China's One-child Policy." *Studies in Family Planning*, Vol. 29, No. 4 (December 1998), pp. 373–85.

Sirageldin, Ismail. "Population Dynamics, Environment, and Conflict." In Ismail Sirageldin and Eqbal al-Rahmani (eds.). *Population and Development Transformations in the Arab World*, Research in Human Capital and Development. Greenwich, Connecticut and London: JAI Press INC., 1996, pp. 185–217.

Soffer, Arnon. "Lebanon-Where Demography is the Core of Politics and Life." *Middle Eastern Studies*, Vol. 22, No. 2 (1986), pp. 197–205.

Al-Sulayti, Hamad. "Education and Training in GCC Countries: Some Issues of Concern." In The Emirates Center for Strategic Studies and Research. *Education and the Arab World: Challenges of the Next Millennium*. Abu Dhabi, 1999, pp. 271–78.

Tabbarah, Riad. "Challenges in Arab Demography." *Population Bulletin of ESCWA*, No. 33 (December 1988), pp. 3–16.

Teitelbaum, Michael S. "Relevance of Demographic Transition Theory for Developing Countries." *Science*, Vol. 188 (2 May 1975), pp. 420–25.

Thomas, John W. and Merilee S. Grindle. "Political Leadership and Policy Characteristics in Population Policy Reform." In Jason L. Finkle and C. Alison McIntosh (eds.). *The New Politics of Population: Conflict and Consensus in Family Planning*. Supplement to Vol. 20 of *Population and Development Review*. New York: The Population Council, 1994, pp. 51–70.

Thompson, Warren S. "Population." *The American Journal of Sociology*, Vol. 34, No. 6 (May 1929), pp. 959–75.

Tschirgi, Dan. "Egyptian Labor Migration: Social, Political and Economic Effects." In Mohammad Shtayyeh (ed.). *Labor Migration: Palestine, Jordan, Egypt and Israel*. Jerusalem: Palestine Center for Regional Studies, 1998, pp. 45–77.

Van Hear, Nicholas. "The Socio-Economic Impact of the Involuntary Mass Return to Yemen in 1990." *Journal of Refugee Studies*, Vo. 7, No. 1 (March 1994), pp. 18–38.

Warren, Charles W. et. al. "Fertility and Family Planning in Jordan: Results from the 1985 Jordan Husbands' Fertility Survey." *Studies in Family Planning*, Vol. 21, No. 1 (1990), pp. 33–39.

Waterbury, John. "The 'Soft State' and the Open Door: Egypt Experience with Economic Liberalization, 1974–1984." *Comparative Politics*, Vol. 18 (October 1985), pp. 65–83.

Weeks, John R. "The Demography of Islamic Nations." *Population Bulletin*, Vol. 43, No. 4 (December 1988).

Widmer, Robert. "Population." In Said B. Himadeh (ed.). *Economic Organization of Syria*. Beirut: The American University of Beirut Press, 1936, pp. 3–26.

Williamson, Jeffrey G. and Tarik M. Yousef. "Demographic Transitions and Economic Performance in the Middle East and North Africa." In Ismail Sirageldin (ed.). *Human Capital: Population Economics in the Middle East*. Cairo: The American University in Cairo Press, 2002, pp. 16–36.

Winckler, Edwin A. "Chinese Reproductive Policy at the Turn of the Millennium: Dynamic Stability." *Population and Development Review*, Vol. 28, No. 3 (2001), pp. 379–418.

Winckler, Onn. "Demographic Developments and Population Policies in Kuwait." *Data and*

Analysis. Tel Aviv University, The Moshe Dayan Center for Middle Eastern and African Studies, August 1998.

—— "The Economic Factor of the Middle East Peace Process: The Jordanian Case." In Joseph Ginat and Onn Winckler (eds.). *The Jordanian–Palestinian–Israeli Triangle: Smoothing the Path to Peace*. Brighton and Portland: Sussex Academic Press, 1998, pp. 156–77.

—— "Gulf Monarchies as Rentier States: The Nationalization Policies of the Labor Force." In Joseph Kostiner (ed.). *Middle East Monarchies: The Challenge of Modernity*. Boulder: Lynne Rienner Publishers, 2000, pp. 237–56.

—— "The Challenge of Foreign Workers in the Persian/Arabian Gulf: The Case of Oman." *Immigrants & Minorities*, Vol. 18, No. 2 (July 2000), pp. 23–52.

—— "Hafiz al-Asad's Socio-Economic Legacy: The Balance of Achievements and Failures." *Orient*, Vol. 42, No. 3 (September 2001), pp. 449–67.

—— "The Demographic Dilemma of the Arab World: The Employment Aspect." *Journal of Contemporary History*, Vol. 37, No. 4 (October 2002), pp. 617–36.

—— "Fertility Transition in the Middle East: The Case of the Israeli-Arabs." *Israel Affairs*, Vol. 9, Nos. 1&2 (Autumn/Winter 2003), pp. 39–67.

Wisensale, Steven K. and Amany A. Khodair, "The Two-child Family: The Egyptian Model of Family Planning." *Journal of Comparative Family Studies*, Vol. 29, No. 3 (Autumn 1998), pp. 503–16.

Yousif, Hassan M. and Ahmad A. Hammouda. "Alternative Population Projection Scenarios by Education Attainment for Egypt, the Sudan and Tunisia." *Population Bulletin of ESCWA*, No. 43 (1995), pp. 55–98.

Zohry, Ayman Gaafar and Lee L. Been. "Infant Mortality and Health Care in the Arabian Gulf Region." In *CDC 24th Annual Seminar on Population Issues and the Challenges of the 21st Century in the Middle East, Africa, and Asia*. Research Monograph Series, No. 24. Cairo, 1995, pp. 487–507.

Daily Newspapers

Arabic and Hebrew

Al-Ahram (Cairo, Arabic).
Al-Dustur (Amman, Arabic).
Ha'aretz (Tel Aviv, Hebrew).
Al-Hayat (London, Arabic).
Al-Khalij (Sharja, Arabic).
Ma'ariv (Tel-Aviv, Hebrew).
Al-Ra'y (Amman, Arabic).
Al-Sharq al-Awsat (London, Arabic).
Al-Thawra (Damascus, Arabic)
Tishrin (Damascus, Arabic).

English

The Egyptian Gazette (Cairo).
Financial Times (London).
Gulf News (Dubai).
Jordan Times (Amman).
The New York Times (New York).

Weeklies and Monthlies

Arabic

Al-Ahram al-Iqtisadi (Weekly, Cairo).
Al-Mussawar (Weekly, Cairo).

English

Africa Monitor (Monthly, London).
Al-Ahram Weekly (Weekly, Cairo).
The Arab Economist (Monthly, London).
Gulf States Newsletter (bi-weekly, West Sussex).
MEED (Middle East Economic Digest, Weekly, London).
The Middle East (Monthly, London).
Middle East International (Weekly, London).
Population Today (Monthly, New York).
Saudi Economic Survey (Riyadh, Weekly).

Quarterlies and Annuals

EIU (Economist intelligence Unit). *Country Report and Profile* of Algeria, Bahrain, Egypt, Jordan, Kuwait, Morocco, Oman, Qatar, Saudi Arabia, Syria, Tunisia, UAE (quarterly and annual profile, London).
Middle East Contemporary Survey (MECS). (Annual, The Moshe Dayan Center for Middle Eastern and African Studies, Tel Aviv University).

Internet Websites and Academic Databases

1 The U.S. Department of Commerce, U.S. Census Bureau [http:/www.census.gov].
2 The U.S. Ministry of Energy, EIA (Energy Information Administration) [http://www.eia.doe.gov].
3 The U.S. Department of State. *International Religious Freedom Report–2002* [http://www.state.gov].
4 U.S. Department of Labor, Bureau of Labor Statistics [http://www.bls.gov].
5 CIA (Central Intelligence Agency). *The World Factbook–2003* [http://www.cia.gov/publications/factbook].
6 The European Union (EU) Official Website [http://europa.eu.int].
7 The Hashemite Kingdom of Jordan, Department of Statistics [http://www.dos.gov.jo].
8 Population Reference Bureau (New York). *Population Reference Bureau Data Finder* [http://www.prb.worldpop.org/datafinder.htm].
9 UNRWA website [http://www.un.org/unrwa].
10 ECA (UN Economic Commission for Africa) Website [http://www.uneca.org].
11 WHO (World Health Organization). *Estimates for Health Personnel* [http:// www3.who.int/whosis/health_personnel/health_personnel.cfm].
12 ILO (International Labour Organization). *Press Release* [http://www.ilo.org].
13 The World Bank Group [http://www.worldbank.org/data].
14 Insight Guides [http://www.insightguides.com].
15 Library of Congress, *Country Studies* [http://lcweb2loc.gov].
16 IPR Strategic Business Information Database. *LEXIS-NEXIS Academic Universe.* [http://www.infroprod.co.il].

Index